INDIA
A Critical Bibliography

INDIA

A Critical Bibliography

by

J. Michael Mahar

THE UNIVERSITY OF ARIZONA PRESS

TUCSON   ARIZONA

To David H. French — Master Filer

FOREWORD

India: A Critical Bibliography is one result of a continuing effort by the Oriental Studies staff of the University of Arizona, largely financed by the Carnegie Corporation of New York, to produce a series of reference guides that might facilitate the study of Asia in American colleges. Two guides in this series have already appeared, Charles O. Hucker's *China,* and Bernard S. Silberman's *Japan and Korea;* a fourth guide covering Southeast Asia is in preparation.

The present work follows the general pattern of earlier guides in this series; it is a selected, graded, annotated list of works, mainly in English, that contribute to the academic study of traditional and modern India. Unlike the earlier guides, most of the entries cited in this work are books rather than articles. The criterion of availability entered into the selection of these items with works published after 1940 receiving higher priority. However, authoritative books of an earlier date are cited in many instances.

Entries are arranged in topical groupings, so that the user, by consulting the Table of Contents, can readily pin-point those works pertaining to any particular subject. The major sections are divided among sub-sections — in some cases, several orders of sub-sections — that have been suggested by the subject matter. The sequence of sub-sections reflects a combination of chronological and topical analyses. In most instances, entries appear in an order that begins with works of general scope and proceeds to those of narrow scope. Works of value in more than one area have duplicate listings in an attempt to make each sub-section a complete unit in itself.

For help of various kinds in the preparation of this bibliography I am greatly indebted to Charles O. Hucker, Bernard S. Silberman, Martha Grier, Deanna Bowman, Herbert Lennhoff, Margaret Vincent, and especially Elizabeth Shaw of the University of Arizona Press, whose patience knows no bounds.

J. Michael Mahar

The University of Arizona
Tucson, Arizona   1964

CONTENTS

CONTENTS

CONTENTS

CONTENTS

CONTENTS

INDIA

India as a cultural or historical entity eludes ready characterization. Though commonly equated with the region set off from the rest of Asia by the Himalayas and the sea, India has no precise geographical boundary, nor has it sustained a tradition of political unity such as is found in China. India is best conceived as a civilization comparable to Europe in size, antiquity, and ethnic diversity reinforced by differences in languages. The most distinctive feature of Indian civilization as seen from the West is the religious and philosophical tradition that gave rise to Buddhism and Hinduism. Despite centuries of political dominance by rulers of other faiths, and the adherence to other religions by a substantial part of the population, it is the yogi and the sacred cow that come to mind when India is mentioned in the West. This association is often used to thread together a wide variety of historical and cultural developments; and for good reason, since many unique aspects of the indigenous art and literature are derived from such beliefs as the transmigration of souls. Religious beliefs and practices are also reflected in a social order based on caste, while many distinctive features of the traditional institutions of government and politics are intimately bound to this religious tradition.

In the following work, however, the term Indian is used in a more inclusive sense, one that draws a sweeping circle around the historical and cultural developments of the subcontinent of South Asia prior to 1947 when India experienced the division into Pakistan and the Republic of India. Care has been taken in the following pages, therefore, to make it clear when the term "India" or "Indian" is used solely in reference to the Republic of India and its citizens. Works treating major events of the post-independence period are presented in separate sections for the two nations. All of the materials relating to Pakistan appear at the end of the history section. Similar materials relating to the Republic of India's economy and political life are presented under appropriate topic headings.

INTRODUCTORY WORKS

1

Brown, W. Norman (ed.). *India, Pakistan, Ceylon.* Ithaca: Cornell University Press, 1951. A collection of articles, originally prepared for the *Encyclopedia Americana,* providing an authoritative survey of the geography, history, and major cultural features of South Asia.

2

DeBary, William T., et al. *Sources of Indian Tradition.* New York: Columbia University Press, 1958. Paper ed., 1964. This work consists mainly of translations selected to convey an understanding of the intellectual and spiritual traditions of India, including political, economic, and social thought, from ancient to modern times. Background information is provided for the general reader.

3

Basham, Arthur Llewellyn. *The Wonder That Was India.* London: Hawthorn Books, rev. ed., 1963. New York: Grove Press, paperbound ed., 1959. A comprehensive and scholarly survey of traditional Indian civilization. Although primarily concerned with ancient India, the presentation of such topics as caste and Hinduism provides an excellent introduction to many facets of contemporary Hindu culture.

4

Nehru, Jawaharlal. *The Discovery of India.* New York: John Day, 1946. New York: Doubleday, paperbound, abridged ed., R. I. Crane (ed.), 1959. A subjective view of India's past by a man destined to play a major role in the shaping of India's future.

5

Spear, Percival. *India; A Modern History.* Ann Arbor: University of Michigan Press, 1961. A survey of South Asian history from earliest times to the present, stressing those aspects of the past most relevant to understanding the present.

6

Rawlinson, Hugh G. *India; A Short Cultural History.* New York: F. A. Praeger, rev. ed., 1952. Intended for the general reader, this scholarly survey is primarily concerned with India's aesthetic and intellectual achievements, and their historical context. Little attention is given to the modern period.

7

Garratt, Geoffrey T. (ed.). *The Legacy of India.* London: Oxford University Press reprint, 1962. A collection of articles by fifteen distinguished scholars on major aspects of traditional Indian civilization, including science as well as religion, philosophy, and the arts. First published in 1937.

8

Bhattacharyya, Haridas (ed.). *The Cultural Heritage of India,* 4 vols. Calcutta: Ramakrishna Mission, Institute of Culture, rev. ed., 1953–61. A collection of essays on such subjects as religion, philosophy, art, language, and history. Although much of this work does not meet the standards of Western scholarship, it provides interesting examples of the orthodox Hindu view of Indian culture.

9

Biardeau, Madeleine. *India.* Trans. from the French by F. Carter. New York: Viking Press, paperbound, 1960. This useful introduction artfully combines history, custom, and splendid illustrations with the impressions of a sensitive and well-informed observer to convey much of the flavor and feeling of modern India.

10

Singer, Milton (ed.). *Introducing India in Liberal Education.* Chicago: University of Chicago Press, 1957. The proceedings of a conference held in 1957 to discuss what has been and might be done in the field of South Asian studies. This is a very useful guide for teachers planning courses on South Asia, and for librarians interested in establishing a South Asia collection.

BIBLIOGRAPHIES—SELECT

11

Wilson, Patrick. *South Asia; a Selected Bibliography on India, Pakistan, Ceylon.* New York: American Institute of Pacific Relations, rev. ed., 1957. Addressed to the general reader, this annotated bibliography provides the nonspecialist with an excellent well-balanced reading list. Prices are noted for many of the items cited.

12

Patterson, Maureen L. P. & R. B. Inden. *South Asia: An Introductory Bibliography.* Chicago: University of Chicago Press, Syllabus Division, 1962. A comprehensive survey of books, monographs, dissertations, and articles on the history and culture of South Asia with an emphasis on works relating to the social sciences and humanities; most of the more than four thousand items cited are in English.

13

Mandelbaum, David G. "A Guide to Books on India," *The American Political Science Review*, XLVI, 4, (1952), 1154–1166. This bibliographic essay provides the non-specialist with expert guidance to an understanding of the principal aspects of Indian life, past and present.

14

Talbot, Phillips (ed.). *Select Bibliography: Asia, Africa, Eastern Europe, Latin America*. New York: American Universities Field Staff, 1960, 110–148. Religion and philosophy, history, and the modern period are the principal subjects covered in this annotated bibliography. An evaluation of entries is provided for those seeking to choose between books on the same subject. Prices are noted in many instances; most entries include Library of Congress catalog card numbers.

15

Bacon, Elizabeth E., Morris E. Opler, and Edward E. Le-Clair, Jr. *Selected and Annotated Bibliography of the Sociology of India*. New Haven: Human Relations Area Files, 1957. Despite its title, this is a fairly comprehensive survey including sections on art, history, and religion.

16

Crane, Robert I. *The History of India, Its Study and Interpretation*. Washington, D. C.: Service Center for Teachers of History, Publication No. 17, 1958. A brief bibliography, mainly concerned with historical materials, accompanies this discussion of some of the major problems of Indian historiography.

17

Renou, Louis. *Bibliographie Védique*. Paris: Adrien-Maisonneuve, 1931. Religion, history, and literature are the principal subjects included in this list of about 6500 works in various European languages. (See next entry for a continuation of this survey.)

18

Dandekar, R. N. *Vedic Bibliography*. Bombay: Karnatak Publishing House, 1946. A continuation of Renou's work (see preceding entry), it contains about 3500 items, including publications on the Indus Valley civilization.

19

Dandekar, R. N. *Vedic Bibliography*. Vol. 2. Poona: University of Poona, 1961. A continuation of the work cited in the previous entry; this volume covers the period since 1946. The content of important reviews is provided for more entries than before.

BIBLIOGRAPHIES—GENERAL

20

Wilson, Patrick. "A Survey of Bibliographies on Southern Asia," *The Journal of Asian Studies*, XVIII, 3, (1959), 365–376. (Reprinted by the Institute of International Studies, University of California, Berkeley, Reprint No. 12, 1959.) A scholarly survey of the basic reference works on Southern Asia, including works in European languages other than English.

21

Linton, Howard P. (ed.). "Bibliography of Asian Studies 1956–," *Journal of Asian Studies*. This bibliography, prior to 1956 the *Far Eastern Bibliography* (see following entry), is published annually as the September issue of the *Journal of Asian Studies*. An attempt is made to list all scholarly books and articles written on South Asia during the preceding year. Listings are by subject and are not annotated.

22

Linton, Howard P. (ed.). "Far Eastern Bibliography 1954–55," *Far Eastern Quarterly*. Appeared as the August issue of the *Far Eastern Quarterly*, precedessor of the above entry. Listings for South Asia were introduced in 1955.

23

Kesavan, B. S. (ed.). *Indian National Bibliography*. Calcutta: Indian National Library, Central Reference Library, 1957–. This represents an attempt by the Republic of India to maintain a complete record of Indian publications, including works in the fourteen major Indian languages, and official government publications. Issued quarterly; entries are classified, with subject, author, and title indexes.

24

India (Republic). National Library. *A Bibliography of Indology, Enumerating Basic Publications on All Aspects of Indian Culture*. Calcutta: Indian National Library, 1960–. An ongoing series of select bibliographies, partially annotated, that includes the following: Volume I, Indian Anthropology; Volume II, Indian Botany; Volume III, Bengali Language and Literature (Early Period).

25

India. Imperial Library. *Author Catalogue of Printed Books in European Languages*. 5 vols. Calcutta: Manager, Government of India Press, 1941–53. The library and its bibliographic services are now part of the National Library of the Republic of India (see preceding entry).

26

India. Imperial Library. *Catalogue*. 7 vols. Calcutta: Superintendent of Government Printing, 1904–29. This catalogue, arranged by author, lists books in European languages held by the Imperial library. A subject index is provided.

27

Royal Asiatic Society. *Catalogue*. A catalogue of printed books published before 1932 in the library of the Royal Asiatic Society. London: Royal Asiatic Society, 1940. Mainly works on history and Indology. Appendices contain information on gazetteers and periodicals.

28

Lewin, Evans. *Subject Catalogue of the Library of the Royal Empire Society*. 4 vols. London: Royal Empire Society, 1930–37. South Asia is treated in volume IV. Contains references to books, documents, articles, and the contents of such large sets as the Indian district gazetteers.

29

Sutton, S. C. *A Guide to the Indian Office Library*. London: H. M. Stationery Office, 1952. This is a description of the India Office Library's catalogues and its collections of books and manuscripts.

30

Library of Congress. Orientalia Division. *Southern Asia Accessions List*. Monthly. Washington: Library of Congress, Orientalia Division, 1952–60. Published through Vol. 5 (1956) as a quarterly under the title: *Southern Asia publications in Western languages, a quarterly accessions list*. Includes references to books, articles, and documents in European and Asian languages, as well as in English. Discontinued in December, 1960.

31

Office of the High Commission of India. *List of Publications Received*. London: Office of the High Commission of India, India House, Aldwych, London, W. C. 2. Issued monthly; about half of this list contains official publications by the central and state governments of the Republic of India. Non-official publications include periodicals and pamphlets as well as books.

32

Quarterly Check-List of Oriental Studies. Darien, Conn.: American Bibliographic Service, 1963. A listing of recently published works on all of Asia; cannot be relied upon for completeness.

33

India (Republic). *Catalogue of Civil Publications*. New Delhi: Manager of Publications, 1948–. This list of the central government's official publications is kept up-to-date by monthly and annual supplements. A guide to these materials is cited in the following entry. Official publications of the state governments are usually published as sections of state gazettes.

34

Shukla, C. P. "A Study on the Publications of the Government of India with Special Reference to Serial Publications." Ann Arbor: University Microfilms, 1953. Unpublished Ph.D. dissertation in library science prepared for the University of Michigan. A useful guide for those seeking a way through the maze of Indian government publications.

35

Stucki, Curtis W. *American Doctoral Dissertations on Asia, 1933–1962.* Ithaca: Southeast Asia Program, Department of Far Eastern Studies, Cornell University, 1963. A guide to otherwise almost inaccessible material, available on microfilm through University Microfilms, Ann Arbor, Michigan.

36

Impex Reference Catalog of Indian Books. New Delhi: Indian Book Export and Import Co., 1960. A list of books on India written in English and currently in print; the addresses of major Indian publishing firms are also provided.

37

Indian Library Institute and Bibliographical Centre. *Catalogue Cards.* New Delhi: 5C/67 Rohtak Road. The institute provides catalogue cards, similar to those used by the Library of Congress, for recently published books on India. It also plans to prepare and publish a retrospective, comprehensive, Indian national bibliography, and a world union catalogue of India.

JOURNALS

38

Journal of Asian Studies. Ann Arbor: Association for Asian Studies, 1956–. Known as the *Far Eastern Quarterly* prior to 1956. Since 1956, many of its articles and reviews have been concerned with South Asia. The range of subjects and periods is wide, and represents some of the best efforts of scholars concerned with South Asia.

39

Journal of the American Oriental Society. 1843–. Published quarterly; regularly contains technical articles on traditional India emphasizing subjects of humanistic rather than social science interest; also authoritative book reviews.

40

Journal of the Royal Asiatic Society of Great Britain and Ireland. 1834–. Published quarterly in London; regularly carries scholarly articles on South Asia. Indexes to this journal were prepared by Frederick E. Pargiter and published by the Society in 1923.

41

Bulletin of the School of Oriental and African Studies. London University, 1917–. Regularly carries scholarly articles on South Asia.

42

Pacific Affairs. Richmond, Va.: Institute of Pacific Relations, 1928–. Since 1943, this quarterly has frequently published articles on contemporary South Asia.

43

Asian Survey. Berkeley: Institute of International Studies, University of California, 1961–. A fortnightly review of contemporary Asian affairs. Successor to the *Far Eastern Survey* published from 1932–1961 by the Institute of Pacific Relations. South Asian political and economic developments are frequently treated in this publication.

44

The Modern Review. 1907–. Published quarterly in Calcutta; many of the political and social changes of the past fifty years are reflected in this journal of opinion and current events.

45

The Economic Weekly. 1949–. Published in Bombay; a journal of current economic and political affairs.

46

Seminar. 1959–. Published monthly in New Delhi; each issue is devoted to a single problem of social, political, or economic significance in modern India.

47

Quest. Bombay: Indian Committee for Cultural Freedom. 1957–. Published bimonthly; a journal of opinion and criticism, containing articles and reviews on contemporary Indian literature, society, and politics.

48

Indian Affairs Record. New Delhi: Diwan Chand Information Centre, 1955–. A monthly review of major political events based on extensive quotation from the press, political parties, and government; references are provided for important articles and documents, with an occasional reprinting of major documents in full.

49

Asian Recorder. New Delhi: The Times of India Press. 1955–. A weekly digest of the Asian press, including a trimonthly and annual index arranged by country, subject, and proper name.

50

The Indo-Asian Culture. New Delhi: Indian Council for Cultural Relations. 1952–. Addressed to the general reader this quarterly contains semischolarly articles about traditional India and contemporary developments in art and literature.

Specialized journals, such as the following, also upon occasion carry articles pertaining to South Asia; *Journal Asiatique, Asiatische Studien, Comparative Studies in Society and History, Economic Development and Culture Change, Journal of the Economic and Social History of the Orient, Foreign Affairs, Indo-Iranian Journal, Philosophy East and West,* and *Royal Central Asian Journal.*

LAND AND PEOPLE

TOPOGRAPHY, CLIMATE, RESOURCES

India, geographically defined as the subcontinent South Asia, comprises a broad array of natural phenomena ranging from the Himalayas to the tropical shore of Malabar. A major physiographic division is the Indo-Gangetic alluvial plain stretching from the Arabian Sea to the Bay of Bengal. Peninsular India lies to the south, its fertile coastal plains bordering the gross triangle formed by the semiarid Deccan plateau. The Vindhya mountains divide the Deccan from the great northern plain. Though modest in size, the Vindhyas appear in legend and history as a major landmark between the markedly different traditions of North and South India. The annual monsoon (rainy season) is a crucial factor in farming, the principal occupation of India. A succession of droughts has led to famine in the past and continues to be a major threat to the economy. With the exception of coal reserves, South Asia's resources are modest compared to other areas of the world, and insufficient for the future needs of a rapidly expanding population.

General Works

51

Spate, Oscar H. K. *India and Pakistan: A General and Regional Geography*. With a chapter on Ceylon by B. H. Farmer. New York: E. P. Dutton, 1954. A comprehensive work covering physical, economic, and cultural geography, including information on social structure and demography.

52

Ginsburg, Norton (ed.) *The Pattern of Asia*. Englewood Cliffs, N. J.: Prentice-Hall, 1958. Pages 458–697 contain a concise description of the physical, economic, and political geography of South Asia.

53

Spencer, Joseph E. *Asia, East by South: A Cultural Geography*. New York: John Wiley, 1954. South Asian materials appear throughout the book in addition to two chapters devoted solely to the region.

54

Stamp, Lawrence D. *Asia: A Regional and Economic Geography*. London: Methuen, rev. ed., 1959. The South Asia section of this book has been published as a separate work (see following entry).

55

Stamp, Lawrence D. *India, Pakistan, Ceylon, and Burma*. London: Methuen, 1957. An introductory geography emphasizing the topography and resources of South Asia. This is a slightly revised reprint of Stamp's *Asia* (see previous entry).

56

Cressey, George B. *Asia's Lands and Peoples*. New York: McGraw-Hill, 3rd ed., 1963. Provides a brief introduction to the geography of South Asia; includes a description of the principal regions.

57

East, William O. and Spate, O. H. K. (eds.). *The Changing Map of Asia: A Political Geography*. New York: E. P. Dutton, rev. ed., 1953. Pages 121–180. Contains a brief account by Spate of the modern geographical, political, and demographic situation in South Asia.

58

Oxford Economic Atlas for India and Ceylon. Oxford: Oxford University Press, 1953. Comparative materials pertaining to other areas of the world accompany this collection of maps and statistics on South Asia's climate, population, physical features, economic resources and activities.

59

India (Republic). *National Atlas of India*. 1/5:000:000. Dehra Dun: Ministry of Education and Scientific Research, 1957. Full use of this atlas is limited to those with a command of Hindi, as most of the legends appear in that language. An English edition is in preparation.

Maps

A wide variety of excellent maps are prepared and published by the Survey of India and other organizations of the Republic of India. Although large-scale maps are sometimes restricted for military reasons, many Survey of India maps may be purchased from:

Officer in Charge
Map Record and Issue Officer
Survey of India
Hathibarkala, Dehra Dun
India

Maps published by the Republic of India may also be obtained from the English map distributor: Edward Stanford, Ltd., 12—14 Long Acre, London, WC 2.

Another source of useful maps is the United States Corps of Engineers. Many of their maps may be purchased from the U. S. Army Map Service, 6500 Brooks Lane, Washington 25, D. C.

60

Survey of India. Republic of India. *India and Adjacent Countries*. 70″ x 65″. Scale: 1:2,534,400. 40 miles per inch. 3rd ed., 1959. An excellent map showing political boundaries, roads, cities, and resources.

61

U. S. Corps of Engineers. U. S. Army. Army Map Service. *India*. Index Series No. U50.2. Scale: 1:250,000.

62

John Bartholomew Son, Ltd. (U. S. Distributor, W. Pitkin Co., 270 Park Ave., New York 17, New York) *India, Pakistan, Burma and Ceylon*. Scale: 1:4,000,000. 1952. An excellent single-sheet map showing relief features by layer tints.

63

Gemini Publications. (Distributed by Denoyer-Geppert Map Co.). *India, Political and Commercial*. 86″ x 70″. 26 miles per inch. Catalogue No. D16p. The largest map of India ever published.

64

Survey of India. Republic of India. *Political Map of India*. Scale: 1:4,435,000. 70 miles per inch. 4th ed., 1958.

65

U. S. Government Printing Office. *India and Pakistan: Internal Administration*. 22″ x 31½″. Scale: 1:6,000,000. 1953. Especially useful for the location of districts.

66

U.S. Corps of Engineers. U. S. Army. Army Map Service. *India Road Map, 1961*. Index Series No. 5206. 32″ x 44″. Scale: 1:3,168,000.

67

U.S. Corps of Engineers. U. S. Army. Army Map Service. *India*. Plastic Relief Series 1301p. Scale: 1:1,000,000. This series is an authoritative relief map of the world done in plastic. All topographical features are accurately reproduced to scale. The sections covering India are as follows: NB 43–44, NC 43–44, 47; ND 43–44, 46–47; NE 43–47; NF 42–47; NG 42–47; NH 42–47; NI 42–44; NJ 44. All sections are not yet available, but will be shortly. They may be purchased from the Army Map Service for $4.00 a section.

68

Geological Survey. Republic of India. *Geological Map of India*. Scale: 1:6,000,000. 1957.

69

Denoyer-Geppert Map Co. *India*. 64″ x 50″. 50 miles per inch. Catalogue No. RS16. This is a blank slated outline map of South Asia, for use with chalk.

70

McKinley Publishing Co. *India*. 9″ x 13″. No. 148a. An outline map of South Asia, including Pakistan and Ceylon, showing the major rivers.

71

Denoyer-Geppert Map Co. *India, Pakistan, Ceylon*. An outline map, 11″ x 8½″ or 16″ x 11″. Catalogue No. 8016.

RACE

South Asia's population, greater in number than the combined populations of Africa and South America, includes elements of most of the major races. Since no skeletal remains of early man have been found in India, theories on the racial composition of the region are based largely on extrapolations from the present population and knowledge of historic times. Some authorities believe that centuries of invasion and migration have sufficiently intermixed the population to warrant distinguishing a "typical" Indian racial type, characterized by tawny brown skin, black eyes, a long head, and straight-to-slightly-wavy hair. Departures from this norm are many; regional, class, and tribal gene clusters provide several subtypes. In the northwest, blue eyes and fair complexions may be encountered, while Mongoloid features prevail in some areas of the northeast. Caste restrictions affecting marriage often contribute to the preservation of genetic characteristics distinguishing one caste group from another residing in the same area. A frequently noted contrast is that of skin pigmentation; there is a higher incidence of dark skins in the south than in the north. This difference, coupled with widespread prejudice against dark complexions, has been a divisive factor of considerable social and political importance.

72

Cohn, Bernard S. "India as a Racial, Cultural and Linguistic Area," in *Introducing India in Liberal Education* (Milton Singer, ed.; Chicago: University of Chicago Press, 1957), 51–68. A concise, authoritative review and evaluation of scholarly opinion on the subject.

73

Guha, B. S. *Racial Elements in the Population.* Oxford: Oxford University Press, 1944. Oxford Pamphlets on Indian Affairs, No. 22. A non-technical presentation of the most widely accepted classification of South Asia's races based on physical measurements.

74

Chatterjee, S. K. "Race-Movements and Prehistoric Culture" in *The Vedic Age* (R. C. Majumdar, ed.; London: George Allen & Unwin, 1951), 319–32. Relates Guha's racial classification (see preceding entry) to South Asian linguistic classifications.

75

Boyd, William C. "Blood Groups in Pakistan," in *American Journal of Physical Anthropology*, 12, 3 (1954), 393–405. Includes a brief summary of blood groups and races in South Asia.

76

Risley, Sir Herbert. *The People of India.* Calcutta: Thacker, Spink, 1915. A summary of data and analysis drawn from the 1901 census; one of the first studies to employ physical measurements for the classification of India's races.

77

Hooton, Ernest G. *Up From the Ape.* New York: Macmillan, rev. ed., 1946. Contains a standard classification of South Asia's races based on physical measurement; presented in the context of a world-wide racial classification.

78

Majumdar, Dhirendra Nath. *Races and Cultures of India.* New York: Asia Publishing House, rev. ed., 1961. Contains a summary of the principal racial classifications for South Asia.

LANGUAGE

Although more than 200 distinct languages and numerous dialects exist in South Asia, most of the people speak one of fourteen major languages. The languages of South Asia, its Tibeto-Burman border excluded, may be grouped into three main families: Indo-Aryan, Dravidian, and Munda or Kolarian. Munda, least used of the three, is confined to tribal peoples and is related to languages of Southeast Asia. Dravidian languages predominate in South India and are unknown elsewhere in the world. Most of the North Indian languages are Indo-Aryan, forming part of the great Indo-European family found in the Middle East and Europe. Sanskrit, a classical literary form of Indo-Aryan, has been used to convey a common set of religious and philosophical ideas throughout South Asia. This provides a distinct "Indic" stamp on the regional traditions supported by linguistic diversity. Another language, transcending linguistic boundaries, was developed during Mughal times from a synthesis of Arabic, Persian, and western Hindi. Its spoken form is known as Hindustani and has long served as the lingua franca of North India. When written in the Devanagari script, used for Sanskrit, it is known as Hindi, and today serves as an official language of the Republic of India. Written in modified Persian script it is known as Urdu, and is an official language of Pakistan. English, a legacy of the British period, is widely spoken by the educated classes and continues to play an important role in higher education, business, and government.

General Works

79

Grierson, Sir George A. (ed.). *Linguistic Survey of India.* 11 vols. Calcutta: Gentral Publication Branch, Government of India. 1903–1928. This work remains the most complete factual account of South Asian languages. A summary is contained in Vol. I, part 1, published in 1927. A good summary may also be found in S. K. Chatterji's *Languages and the Linguistic Problem,* (see following entry).

80

Chatterji, Suniti Kumar. *Languages and the Linguistic Problem.* London: Oxford University Press, 3rd ed., 1945. Oxford pamphlets on Indian Affairs, No. 11. Contains a good summary of the *Linguistic Survey of India,* edited by Grierson, (see preceding entry).

81

India (Republic). *Census of India Paper No. 1.* Delhi: Manager of Publications, 1954. Describes the languages recorded in the 1951 census.

82

Emeneau, Murray B. "India as a Linguistic Area" in *Language* (Journal of the Linguistic Society of America, Vol. 32, No. 1, 1956), pp. 3–16. A scholarly article, by an eminent authority on South Asian languages, concerning linguistic traits shared by South Asian languages.

83

Ferguson, Charles A. and John J. Gumperz, (eds.). "Linguistic Diversity in South Asia; Studies in Regional, Social and Functional Variation," in *International Journal of American Linguistics,* Vol. 26, No. 3, (1960). A pioneering venture in the study of dialect diversity within the major languages of South Asia.

84

Ginsburg, Norton (ed.). *The Pattern of Asia.* Englewood Cliffs, N. J.: Prentice-Hall, 1958. An excellent map of the major South Asian languages appears on p. 466.

85

Brown, W. Norman (ed.). *Resources for South Asian Language Studies in the United States.* Philadelphia: University of Philadelphia Press, 1960. This is the report of a conference attended by American scholars engaged in the preparation of teaching materials for South Asian languages. Pp. 17–21 contain an assessment of what is available or under preparation in the way of grammars, dictionaries, reading materials, and teaching aids for all the major South Asian languages.

Grammars and Dictionaries

SANSKRIT AND PALI

86

Perry, Edward D. *Sanskrit Primer.* New York: Columbia University Press, 1936.

87

Whitney, William D. *Sanskrit Grammar.* Cambridge: Harvard University Press, 1950.

88

Macdonell, Arthur A. *A Vedic Grammar For Students.* London: Oxford University Press, 1962.

89

Burrow, T. *The Sanskrit Language.* London: Faber and Faber, 1955.

90

Apte, Vaman S. *The Practical Sanskrit-English Dictionary.* 3 vols. Poona: Prasad Prakashan, 1957–1959.

91

Macdonell, Arthur A. *A Practical Sanskrit Dictionary.* London: Oxford University Press, 1958.

92

Monier-Williams, Sir Monier. *A Sanskrit-English Dictionary.* Oxford: Clarendon Press, rev. ed., 1960.

93

Monier-Williams, Sir Monier. *A Dictionary, English-Sanskrit.* Lucknow: Akhila Bharatiya Sanskrit Parishad, 1957.

94

Edgerton, Franklin. *Buddhist Hybrid Sanskrit Grammar and Dictionary.* 2 vols. New Haven: American Oriental Society, 1953.

95

David, T. W. Rhys and W. Stede (eds.). *Pali-English Dictionary.* Chipstead, Surrey: The Pāli Text Society, 1949.

96

Widurupola, Piyatissa M. N. T. The *English-Pali Dictionary.* Colombo: Colombo Apothecaries' Co., 1949.

97

Malalasekera, George P. *Dictionary of Pali Proper Names.* 2 vols. London: Luzac, 1960.

MODERN LANGUAGES

98

Lambert, Hester M. *Introduction to the Devanagri Script.* London: Oxford University Press, 1953. This script is used in the writing of Hindu, Marathi, and Sanskrit.

99

Anderson, James D. *A Manual of the Bengali Language.* Cambridge: Cambridge University Press, 1962.

100

Chatterji, Suniti K. *Bengali Self-Taught by the Natural Method.* London: E. Marlborough, 1927.

101

Page, Walter. *An Introduction to Colloquial Bengali.* Cambridge: W. Heffer, 1934. A set of phonograph records issued by the Linguaphone Institute were prepared to accompany the text.

102

Dev, Ashu Tosh. *Concise Dictionary, Bengali to English.* Calcutta: S. C. Mazumder, 4th ed., rev., 1957.

103

Dev, Ashu Tosh. *Students' Favourite Dictionary, English to Bengali.* Calcutta: S. C. Mazumder, 17th ed., 1960.

104

Dabbs, Jack A. *A Short Bengali-English, English-Bengali Dictionary.* College Station, Texas: A.M. College of Texas, 1962. A collection of words and phrases used for everyday activities; entries are presented initially in phonetic transcription followed by Bengali script.

105

Tisdall, W. St. Clair Towers. *A Simplified Grammar of the Gujarati Language.* New York: F. Ungar, 1961.

106

Belsare, Malhar B. *An Entymological Gujarati-English Dictionary.* Ahmedabad: C. M. Shah, 3rd ed., rev., 1940.

107

Oza, Shantilal S. *Taraporevala's Up-to-Date Gujarati-English Dictionary.* Bombay: Taraporevala, 1938.

108

Mehta, Bhanusukhram N. *The Modern Gujarati-English Dictionary.* 2 vols. Baroda: M. C. Kothari, 1925.

109

Harter, J. Martin, N. K. Choudry, and V. Budhraj. *Hindi Basic Course.* Units 1–18. Washington, D. C.: Center for Applied Linguistics of the Modern Language Association of America, 1960. Prepared originally for use in the U. S. Foreign Service Institute; principles of grammar are presented with extensive drills and guides to pronunciation; vocabulary appears in Romanized form.

110

Harter, J. Martin, J. Joshi, and N. K. Choudry. *Hindi Basic Reader.* Washington, D. C.: Center for Applied Linguistics of the Modern Language Association of America, 1960. This reader, printed in Devanagri script, was designed to accompany the preceding entry.

111

Hoenigswald, Heinrich M. F. *Spoken Hindustani.* 2 vols. New York: Henry Holt, 1946. A reprint of materials prepared for the U. S. Armed Forces Institute. This text is concerned solely with the spoken language; a set of phonograph records matching the text may be obtained from the publisher.

112

Fairbanks, Gordon, J. J. Gumperz, and others. *Hindi Exercises.* Ithaca: Cornell University Press, 1955. A useful set of variation drills in Romanized script.

113

Gumperz, John J. *Hindi Reader.* Berkeley: University of California Press, 1960. This text contains an introduction to the Hindi writing system with graded readings and exercises in Devanagari script.

114

Sharma A. *A Basic Grammar of Modern Hindi.* Delhi: Ministry of Education and Scientific Research, 1958. The most recent official grammar published by the Republic of India.

115

Pathak, R. C. *Bhargava's Standard Illustrated Dictionary, Anglo-Hindi.* Banaras: Shree Ganga Pustakalaya, 11th ed., rev., 1959.

116

Pathak, R. C. *Bhargava's Standard Illustrated Dictionary, Hindi-English.* Banaras: Shree Ganga Pustakalaya, rev. ed., 1959.

117

Lambert, Hester M. *Marathi Language Course.* London: Oxford University Press, 1943.

118

Vaze, Shridhar G. *The Aryabhushan School Dictionary; Marathi-English.* Poona: Aryabhushan Press, 1960.

119

Virkar, Krishnaji B. *The Student's Concise Modern Dictionary, English into English and Marathi.* Bombay: K. B. Dhawale, 1944.

120

Ranade, Nilkanth B. *The Twentieth Century English-Marathi Dictionary.* 2 vols. Bombay: Nirnaya-Saga Press, 1916.

121

Tisdall, W. St. Clair Towers. *A Simplified Grammar and Reading Book of the Panjabi Language.* New York: F. Ungar, 1961. First published in 1889.

122

Newton, E. P. and T. G. Bailey. *Panjabi Manual and Grammar.* Patiala: Patiala University, 1961. A reprint of an 1896 work by Newton, and a section of a 1925 publication by Bailey and T. F. Cummings.

123

Singh, Teja. *The Standard English-Panjabi Dictionary.* Chandigarh: Punjab University, 1953.

124

Hares, Walter P. *An English-Punjabi Dictionary.* London: Kegan Paul, 1929.

125

Singh, Maya. *The Punjabi Dictionary.* Patiala: Patiala University, 1961. A reprint of an 1895 edition published by Munshi Gulab Singh of Lahore.

126

Geiger, Wilheim. *A Grammar of the Sinhalese Language.* Colombo: Royal Asiatic Society, Ceylon Branch, 1938.

127

Jayatilaka, Sir D. B. *A Dictionary of the Sinhalese Language.* Colombo: Royal Asiatic Society, Ceylon Branch, 1935.

128

Ratnasuriya, M. Dharmasiri, and P. B. F. Wijeratne. *The Shorter Sinhalese-English Dictionary.* Colombo; University of Ceylon Press Board, 1949.

129

Bailey, Frederick G. (ed. by J. R. Firth and A. H. Harley). *Teach Yourself Urdu.* London: English Universities Press, 1960.

130

Platts, John T. *A Grammar of the Hindustani or Urdu Language.* London: Oxford University Press, 1920.

131

Bright, William, and Saeed A. Khan. *The Urdu Writing System.* New York: American Council of Learned Societies, 1958.

132

Gumperz, John J. and C. M. Naim. *Urdu Reader.* Berkeley: Center for South Asia Studies, University of California, 1960.

133

Platts, John T. *Dictionary of Urdu, Classical Hindi and English,* 2 vols. London: Oxford University Press, 1960.

134

Majid, 'Abdul. *A New Urdu Dictionary.* 4 vols. Lahore: Jami' ul-Lugat Press, 1935.

135

Ferozsons Board of Editors. *English-Urdu Dictionary.* Karachi: Ferozsons, 4th ed., 1961.

DRAVIDIAN

136

Bloch, Jules. Trans. from the French by R. G. Harshe. *The Grammatical Structure of Dravidian Languages.* Poona: Deccan College Postgraduate and Research Institute, 1954.

137

Burrow, Thomas and M. B. Emeneau. *A Dravidian Etymological Dictionary.* Oxford: Clarendon Press, 1961.

138

Pellai, R. P. Sethu, N. V. Rao, S. K. Nayar, and M. H. Bhat. *Dravidian Comparative Vocabulary.* Madras: University of Madras, 1959.

139

Bright, William. *An Outline of Colloquial Kannada.* Poona: Deccan College Postgraduate and Research Institute, 1958.

140

Bright, William, S. Rau, and M. Narvekar. *Spoken Kannada.* Berkeley: Center for South Asia Studies, University of California, 1960. A beginning course in Kannada, also called Kanarese, with the Kannada material presented in transcription.

141

Spencer, Harold. *A Kanarese Grammar.* Mysore: Wesleyan Mission Press, 1914.

142

Ziegler, Friedrich. *A Practical Key to the Kanarese Language.* Mangalore: Basel Mission Book and Tract Depository, 5th ed., 1935.

143

Venkatanaranappa, R. B. and M. R. Sreenivasamurty (eds.). *The Mysore University English-Kannada Dictionary.* Mysore: Mysore University, 1947.

144

Ziegler, Friedrich. *English-Kanarese School Dictionary.* London: Kegan Paul, 6th ed., rev., 1929.

145

Bucher, J. and C. Watsa. *A Kannada-English School Dictionary.* Mangalore: Basel Mission Book and Tract Depository, 2nd ed., 1923.

146

Frohnmeyer, L. J. *A Progressive Grammar of the Malayalam Language for Europeans.* Mangalore: Basel Mission Book and Tract Depository, 2nd ed., rev., 1913.

147

Raman Menon, K. *The V. V. English Malayalam Dictionary.* Quilon, South India: S. T. Reddiar, V. V. Press, 6th ed., 1960.

148

Zacharias, Tobias. Revised by Oliver F. E. Zacharias. *Anglo-Malayalam Dictionary.* Mangalore: Basel Mission Book and Tract Depository, 2nd ed., 1933.

149

Zacharias, Tobias. *A Malayalam-English School Dictionary.* Mangalore: Kanarese Mission Book and Tract Depository, 2nd ed., rev., 1921.

150

Arden, Albert H. Revised by A. C. Clayton. *A Progressive Grammar of Common Tamil.* Madras: Christian Literature Society for India, 5th ed., 1942.

151

University of Madras. *Tamil Lexicon.* 6 vols. London: Luzac, 1926–37. Supplement, 1938–39.

152

Thangavel, C. D. *Money's New Model Students' Standard Dictionary (English-English-Tamil).* Madras: A. S. Money, 1951.

153

Muthu Iyengar, Vidwan S. *Srivilli's English-Tamil Dictionary.* Madras: Srivilli, 2nd ed., rev., 1949.

154

Master, Alfred. *Introduction to Telugu Grammar.* London: Luzac, 1947.

155

Lisker, Leigh. *Introduction to Spoken Telugu.* New York: American Council of Learned Societies, 1963. This work may be purchased from the Columbia University Press of New York.

156

Sankaranarayana, Paluri. *An English-Telugu Dictionary.* Madras: V. R. Sastrulu, 7th ed., rev., 1951.

157

Sankaranarayana, Paluri. *A Telugu-English and English-Telugu Dictionary.* 2 vols. Madras: V. R. Sastrulu, 1927–28.

158

Galletti, di. Cadillac, A. *Galletti's Telugu Dictionary.* London: Oxford University Press, 1935.

HISTORY

Myths and bardic lays served as the principal indigenous repositories of Indian history until Muslim invaders introduced court chronicles in the thirteenth century. Travelers' accounts, coins, and inscriptions provide the few substantiated dates for early times, beginning with Alexander the Great's invasion of India in 326 B.C. Due to the paucity of historical documents, historians have relied heavily on religious and literary works for information about life in the past and for tracing the principal lines of India's historical development. Consequently, it is not uncommon to find the date of an event or person given in terms of decades or even centuries. Recurrent invasions and migrations have been a major factor in the shaping of India's destiny. Until the eighteenth century, invaders usually entered India from the northwest, moved across the Punjab, and settled in the middle reaches of the Gangetic plain. There in the region of modern Patna, old cultural elements mixed with new to produce a unique and virile tradition characterized by Hinduism, caste, and a distinct mode of aesthetic expression. This tradition spread throughout most of South Asia, borne in part by military conquests, but more effectively through the offices of Brahmin priests and the widespread acceptance of Sanskrit language and literature by the upper classes. Despite the unifying effect of the Sanskrit tradition, a marked division has prevailed from earliest times between the regions of north and south India grossly demarcated by the Vindhya mountains. This division appears in the historical distribution of political power, as well as in matters of custom and language. Due to the preponderance of source material for North India, and the North India origin of Sanskrit, general histories of India often have little to say about South India. Two major non-Hindu traditions, Islamic and European, were brought to South Asia by force of arms. Although Muslim rulers reigned over much of India from the thirteenth to the eighteenth century, followed by their British successors until 1947, these two traditions were never completely assimilated. However, when the British withdrew, the existence of these traditions contributed to the partition of South Asia into the separate Islamic state of Pakistan, and the creation of the secular Republic of India.

REFERENCE AIDS

159

Davies, Cuthbert C. *An Historical Atlas of the Indian Peninsula.* London: Oxford University Press, 1957. This atlas graphically portrays, with excellent accompanying text, the areal distribution of the principal political entities in India from the 6th century B.C. to modern times. Maps showing topography, climate, population, language, and economic products are also included.

160

Imperial Gazetteer of India. 26 vols. Oxford: Clarendon Press, rev. ed., 1907–09. This monumental work, initiated in 1869, is based on a statistical survey of the topography, ethnology, agriculture, industry and administration of the 240 districts under the British, and similar information gathered by diverse means for the native states. Individual gazetteers were prepared for many of the districts; a list of these works may be found in the Royal Empire Society Library catalog (see entry 28). Census and historical materials are also incorporated in the gazetteers. Although uneven in quality, these works have served as a major source for much that has been written on India.

161

Imperial Gazetteer of India. Provincial Series. 25 vols. Calcutta: Superintendent of Government Printing, 1908–09. This series contains the same information presented in the preceding entry, arranged according to the fifteen provinces of British India.

162

India. Census Commissioner. *Census of India.* Delhi: Manager of Publications, Government of India Press. The first systematic enumeration of India's population was undertaken between 1867 and 1872. A synchronous census was completed in 1881 and has been repeated every ten years to the present. After 1947, census work was continued separately by Pakistan and the Republic of India for the years 1951 and 1961. Numerous publications have emanated from the vast store of information collected during census surveys. A summary of these findings is issued by the Census Commissioner of the Central Government in volumes called Parts. Reports for each province and major state are prepared in two parts, one for description, the other for tables. District handbooks, published by state governments, are also issued. Other publications issued by the Census Commissioner include special papers, ethnographic appendices, and in recent years, village monographs.

163

Buckland, Charles E. *Dictionary of Indian Biography.* London: Swan Sonnenschein, 1906. Contains 2600 biographies from mid-18th to late 19th century.

164

Dowson, John. *A Classical Dictionary of Hindu Mythology and Religion, Geography, History and Literature.* London: Routledge & Kegan Paul, 10th ed., 1961. This work is mainly a dictionary of names and terms from Hindu mythology and religion; includes short descriptions of Sanskrit works frequently mentioned by European writers.

165

Philips, Cyril H. (ed.). *Handbook of Oriental History.* London: Royal Historical Society, 1951. Pages 47–95 contain useful information on the transliteration of Indian words, the basis for personal and place names, a glossary of common terms, a list of Hindu and Muslim dynasties, and British Governor-Generals.

166

Brown, C. J. *The Coins of India.* London: Oxford University Press, 1922. An excellent introduction to the principal series of Indian coins and their historical context from earliest times to 1857.

167

Singhal, C. R. *Bibliography of Indian Coins.* 2 vols. London: Arthur Probsthain, 1950–52. A fairly exhaustive list of all the technical articles on Indian coins published in various periodicals.

168

South Asia Microform Newsletter. Vol. 1, No. 1, February, 1964. A quarterly published by the Inter-University Committee on South Asia Scholarly Resources. The first issue of this mimeographed newsletter provides a list of South Asia microfilm holdings in the University of Chicago library. Similar listings from other universities and archival repositories will appear in future issues. Information concerning this publication may be obtained from the editor, Mrs. Lois Zanow, Department of Indian Studies, University of Wisconsin, 905 University Avenue, Madison 15, Wisconsin.

SERIALS

Scores of learned societies have flourished in India, many of them publishing journals in English about one or another aspect of Indian history. Some of the most frequently cited journals are listed below.

170

Journal of the Asiatic Society. 1832–. Calcutta: The Society. Formerly the *Journal of the Asiatic Society of Bengal;* since 1935 this journal has been published in three parts: Letters, Science, and Yearbook.

171

Journal of Indian History. 1921–. Allahabad: Allahabad University.

172

Indian Historical Quarterly. 1925–. Calcutta: Oriental Book Agency.

173

Indian Antiquary. 1872–1933. Published in Bombay by various organizations including the Education Society's Press, the British India Press, and from 1925–33 the Royal Anthropological Institute.

174

New Indian Antiquary. 1938–. Bombay: Karnatak Publishing House.

175

Annals of the Bhandarkar Oriental Research Institute. 1918–. Poona: Bhandarkar Oriental Research Institute.

176

Indian Culture. 1934–. Calcutta: Indian Research Institute.

177

Journal of the Bihar Research Society. 1915–. Patna: The Society. Issued from 1915 to 1943 under the title: *Journal of the Bihar and Orissa Research Society.*

178

Journal of the Andhra Historical Research Society. 1926–. Rajamundry: The Society.

179

Karnataka Historical Review. 1931–. Dharwar: Karnataka Historical Research Society.

180

Medieval India Quarterly. 1950–. Aligarh: Aligarh Muslim University.

181

Journal of the Numismatic Society of India. 1938–. Calcutta: The Society.

GENERAL WORKS

182

Dodwell, Henry H. (ed.). *The Cambridge History of India.* Cambridge: Cambridge University Press, 1922–53. Only five of the planned six volumes have been published. Professor A. L. Basham of London is preparing the missing work, volume II, covering the first thousand years of the Christian era. A supplementary volume on the Indus Civilization was published in 1953 and revised in 1959. A revised edition of volume VI, published in 1958, brings the historical coverage up to 1947. Volumes V and VI appear as volumes IV and V of the *Cambridge History of the British Empire.* Although somewhat outdated, volume I remains a basic work on ancient India. Volumes III and IV are essentially chronicles of the Muslim period; volumes V and VI consist mainly of essays on the political and administrative activities of the British. Comprehensive bibliographies are to be found in each volume.

183

Majumdar, Ramesh C. (ed.). *The History and Culture of the Indian People.* 10 vols. Bombay: Bharatiya Vidya Bhavan, 1951–1960. (Also published by George Allen & Unwin of London). Nine of the proposed 11 volumes have been published. These are: *The Vedic Age* (1951), *The Age of Imperial Unity* (1951), *The Classical Age* (1954), *The Age of Imperial Kanauj* (1955), *The Struggle for Empire* (1957), and *The Delhi Sultanate* (1960). The work of modern Indian historians, this series will remain a basic reference for many years. Individual chapters vary greatly in quality. Extensive bibliographies appear at the end of each volume.

184

Nilakanta Sastri, K. A. (ed.). *A Comprehensive History of India.* 12 vols. Bombay: Orient Longmans, 1957–. London: Longmans, Green, 1959–. A projected twelve-volume series under the combined auspices of the Indian History Congress and the Bhāratīya Itihās Parishad. Only volume II, *The Mauryas and the Satavahanas,* has been published.

185

The New History of the Indian People. Lahore: Motilal Banarsidass, 1946. This projected twenty-volume series was initiated in 1937 by a group of Indian historians known as the Bhāratīya Itihās Parishad. Only one volume, VI, *The Vakataka-Gupta Age,* was published as part of this series; another product of this group, *The Age of the Nandas and Mauryas,* was published as an independent work. In 1948, this project was amalgamated with the twelve-volume series *A Comprehensive History of India* (see preceding entry).

186

Smith, Vincent A. (ed.). *The Oxford History of India.* Oxford: Clarendon Press, rev. ed., 1958. This is a fundamental revision of earlier editions; part I revised by J. B. Harrison; part III rewritten by Percival Spear, who also edited this edition. This book represents a "Western view" of Indian history as seen by four of Britain's most eminent historians. It will probably remain one of the best single-volume texts for many years.

187

Majumdar, Ramesh C., H. C. Raychaudhuri, and K. K. Datta. *An Advanced History of India.* London: Macmillan, 1948. A standard work prepared for readers with an elementary knowledge of the subject. This is one of the better single volume surveys of the entire span of Indian history, it discusses cultural as well as political developments; written by three of India's leading historians whose views sometimes provide an interesting contrast with those expressed in such works as the *Oxford History of India* (see preceding entry).

188

Allan, John, T. W. Haig, H. H. Dodwell, and R. R. Sethi. *The Cambridge Shorter History of India.* Delhi: S.

Chand, 1958. A basic reference for the political history of India from earliest times to 1947.

189

Spear, Percival. *India: A Modern History*. Ann Arbor: University of Michigan Press, 1961. A survey of South Asian history from earliest times to the present. Spear's interpretations provide the reader with an awareness of historical trends and major issues that more detailed histories often fail to convey.

190

Nehru, Jawaharlal. *The Discovery of India*. New York: John Day, 1946. New York: Doubleday, paperbound, abridged ed., R. I. Crane (ed.), 1959. A panoramic, frankly subjective view of Indian history, written in prison during 1944 by the man who became India's first Prime Minister.

191

Moreland, William H., and A. C. Chatterjee. *A Short History of India*. London: Longmans, Green, 4th ed., 1957. A useful introduction, especially to the social and economic history of India; somewhat partisan in its treatment of the British, who are presented as beneficent agents of progress.

192

Rawlinson, Hugh G. *India; A Short Cultural History*. New York: F. A. Praeger, rev. ed., 1952. The aesthetic and intellectual achievements of the Hindu and Muslim periods provide the principal referents for this scholarly survey.

193

Panikkar, Kavalam, M. *A Survey of Indian History*. Bombay: Asia Publishing House, 4th ed. rev., 1962. A provocative overview of Indian history by a noted Indian historian, useful for comparison with the work of British historians. The author presumes knowledge of many names and events of Indian history.

194

Nilakanta Sastri, K. A. *History of India*. 3 vols. Madras: S. Viswanathan, 1950–52. A general review of Indian history up to 1947 by one of India's leading historians; organized around political events.

195

Kosambi, Damodar D. *An Introduction to the Study of Indian History*. Bombay: Popular Book Depot, 1956. An attempt to use Marxist theories about property relations and economic production to account for dynastic changes and religious movements; many assumptions are poorly documented.

196

Sarkar, Sir Jadunath. *Military History of India*. Calcutta: M. C. Sarkar, 1960. A brief survey of the art of war as practiced in India from the time of Alexander the Great to the latter part of the 18th century; tactics, equipment, and major battles are described for each major period.

HISTORIOGRAPHY

197

Philips, Cyril H. (ed.). *Historians of India, Pakistan and Ceylon*. London: Oxford University Press, 1961. A collection of essays on South Asian historiography prepared by leading authorities from Asia and the West for a conference held at the University of London. This pioneering work provides a valuable assessment of assumptions and points of view used in the writing of South Asian history from earliest times to the present.

198

Majumdar, Ramesh C. (ed.). *History and Culture of the Indian People*. London: Allen & Unwin, 1951. Vol. 1, pp. 47–64. The first two chapters of Volume I contain a discussion of the nature, sources, and methods of Indian history and the sources for historical study.

199

Nilakanta Sastri, Kallidaikurichi A. A., and H. S. Ramanna. *Historical Method in Relation to Indian History*. Madras: S. Viswanathan, 1956. A revised and amplified version of Nilakanta Sastri's *Historical Method in Relation to Problems of South Indian History* published in 1941; contains an excellent discussion of the sources for Indian history, and brief sketches of the background and contributions of several leading scholars in this field.

200

Crane, Robert I. *The History of India, Its Study and Interpretation*. Washington, D. C.: Service Center for Teachers of History, Publication No. 17, 1958. In part a bibliographic essay about the study of Indian history from ancient to modern times. Problems of interpretation, periodization, and the use of source materials are also discussed.

201

Ghoshal, Upendra Nath. *Studies in Indian History and Culture*. Bombay: Orient Longmans, rev. ed., 1957. A revision of *The Beginnings of Indian Historiography* published in 1944. A collection of critical essays concerned mainly with problems of ancient Indian history; by one of India's leading historians.

202

Thorner, Daniel. "Feudalism in India," in *Feudalism in History* (R. Coulborn, ed.; Princeton: Princeton University Press, 1956), pp. 133–150. A review and assessment of the concept of feudalism as applied to periods of Rajput rule in western India, and the Muslim regimes of northern India.

203

Panikkar, Kavalam M. *Geographical Factors in Indian History*. Bombay: Bharatiya Vidya Bhavan, 2nd ed. rev., 1959. A consideration of geographical determinants of India's historical development, especially the concentration of political power and cultural development in the Gangetic plain.

204

Panikkar, Kavalam M. *India and the Indian Ocean*. London: G. Allen & Unwin, 3rd ed., 1962. A brief insightful essay on the influence of sea power on Indian history.

205

Gokhale, B. G. *The Indian View of History*. Bombay: Asia Publishing House, 1961. A survey of various approaches to Indian history used by such Indian authors as Gandhi, Aurobindo, Nehru, D. P. Mukherji, and D. D. Kosambi. Gokhale concludes that the dominant Indian view of history is essentially spiritual and based on the concepts of Hindu philosophy.

206

Pargiter, Frederick E. *Ancient Historical Tradition*. London: Oxford University Press, 1922. An examination of the historical value of dynastic lists and related materials contained in the Puranas and Epics; a pioneering work now in general disrepute due to Pargiter's uncritical acceptance of his sources.

207

Kalhana. *Rajatarangini*. Trans. from the Sanskrit by R. S. Pandit. London: A. Probsthain, 1935. A history of Kashmir written in the 12th century; the only extant historical text in all of Sanskrit literature. Kalhana's critical approach to his sources and mode of analysis compares favorably with the standards of modern Western historians.

PRE-HISTORY AND ARCHAEOLOGY

Little is known of South Asian prehistory for want of research and of satisfactory means of dating and correlating archaeological finds, such as glacial movements have provided in Europe. Although no skeletal remains of early man have been found in

India, stone implements indicate human activity in the area about 400,000 years ago. The best known aspect of India's prehistory is the Indus Valley or Harappan Civilization, tentatively dated from 2500 to 1500 B.C.; it is noted for well-planned cities and uniformity of material culture throughout its existence. Brought to an end for reasons still under debate, the Harappan Civilization may have been the cradle of historic Indian culture. However, there is little evidence to link Harappa with its Aryan successors that are known from literary sources. Paradoxically, few material remains of the Aryans have been recovered, while the vast quantities of Harappan finds are without literary or epigraphic support, since the Harappan script has not yet been deciphered.

Until recent years archaeological efforts in India were largely directed to the reconstruction and preservation of temples and monuments under the auspices of the government-supported Archaeological Survey, whose numerous reports and memoirs are mainly of interest to the specialist. Where systematic excavations of ancient settlements were undertaken, as in the Indus valley, the failure in many instances to use established stratigraphic techniques seriously limit the usefulness of the data obtained. During the past decade Indian archaeology has markedly increased in quantity and quality with university and private research groups as well as government agencies participating in the task. Greater collaboration between historian and archaeologist has also developed with the realization that the answer to many unsolved problems of historic times must be sought with the shovel.

References and Serials

208

COWA Survey. 1960–. *Southern Asia.* Cambridge, Mass.: Council for Old World Archaeology, Area 16, No. II. This is the first of a series of periodic surveys designed to review and assess current archaeological research in Ceylon, India, and Pakistan. This survey provides an excellent introduction to the principal problems of South Asian archaeology. Publications appearing in the years 1957, 1958, and 1959 are discussed in this initial issue. (see following entry for a bibliography of these publications).

209

COWA Bibliography. 1960–. *Southern Asia.* Cambridge, Mass.: Council for Old World Archaeology, Area 16, No. II. An annotated bibliography of the principal publications on South Asian archaeology to appear in 1957, 1958, and 1959: prepared to accompany *COWA Survey* (see preceding entry).

210

Kern Institute. *Annual Bibliography of Indian Archaeology.* 1926–. Leyden: E. J. Brill. The latest volume published in 1962 covers the period from 1954–57. Introductory surveys as well as annotated bibliographies appear in this series. Information is included on history, art, geography, and other fields related to archaeology.

211

Ancient India. 1946–. New Delhi: Director General of Archaeology in India. Intended as a semiannual publication, this journal has appeared irregularly; contains schol-larly articles on history, prehistory, and accounts of the restoration of temples and monuments.

212

Indian Archaeology. 1955–. New Delhi: Ministry of Scientific Research and Cultural Affairs. An annual review of archaeological research and related activities conducted under the auspices of the director general of archaeology; edited by A. Ghosh.

213

M. S. University of Baroda Archaeology Series. 1953–. Baroda: Maharaja Sayajiro University of Baroda, Department of Archaeology. This monograph series consists of site reports and technical studies based on current research by one of the most active research groups in India today.

General Works

214

Wheeler, Sir Mortimer. *Early India and Pakistan.* New York: Frederick A. Praeger, 1959. The author, former director general of archaeology in India, provides an excellent overview of South Asian prehistory to the third century B.C., with an authoritative appraisal of the principal unsolved problems.

215

Piggott, Stuart. *Prehistoric India.* Harmondsworth, Middlesex: Penguin Books, reprint, 1961. An inexpensive, readily available introduction; surveys the prehistory of South Asia up to 1000 B.C.

216

Subbarao, Bendapudi. *The Personality of India.* Baroda: M. S. University of Baroda Archaeology Series, No. 3, 2nd ed., rev., 1958. Despite the title, this is one of the most complete surveys of the present state of knowledge about South Asian archaeology; primarily of use to the specialist.

217

Gordon, D. H. *The Pre-Historic Background of Indian Culture.* Bombay: Bhulabhai Memorial Institute, 1958. A review of the standard interpretations of Indian archaeology from the early stone age to the coming of the Iron Age; somewhat technical, but of use to the general reader.

218

Childe, V. Gordon. *New Light on the Most Ancient East.* New York: F. A. Praeger, 1954. (Paperbound edition, New York: Evergreen Press, No. E-72, 1952.) A discussion of the Indus valley civilization in relation to the ancient civilizations of Egypt and Mesopotamia.

219

India, Republic of. *Archaeology in India.* Delhi: Manager of Publications, Bureau of Education, Publication No. 66, 1950. Addressed to the general reader, this work by members of the department of archaeology provides an excellent survey of archaeological activities in South Asia, including a history of the Archaeological Survey, and a review of the principal archaeological finds in the prehistoric and historic periods.

220

Cumming, Sir John (ed.). *Revealing India's Past.* London: India Society, 1939. A review and assessment of archaeological research in South Asia by men intimately engaged in the task; contains a fairly comprehensive bibliography of archaeological publications on South Asia up to 1939.

221

Sankalia, H. D. *Indian Archaeology Today.* New York: Asia Publishing House, 1962. A brief survey of the development of archaeology in India with a summary of recent work in numismatics, epigraphy, architecture, and sculpture and the relation of these works to major problems awaiting further research.

Special Studies

222

Movius, Hallam L., Jr. "The Lower Palaeolithic Cultures of Southern and Eastern Asia," in *Transactions of the*

American Philosophical Society, new series, 38:4:329–420 (1949). A technical article in which a leading authority presents his views on the chronology of Stone Age India.

223

Fairservis, Walter A., Jr. "The Harappan Civilization — New Evidence and More Theory," in *American Museum Novitates* (New York: American Museum of Natural History), Number 2055, 17 November, 1961. A provocative appraisal of current interpretations of the Harappan civilization.

224

Raikes, Robert and R. Dyson, Jr. "The Prehistoric Climate of Baluchistan and the Indus Valley," in *The American Anthropologist,* 63: 2: 265–281, 1961. A critique of assumptions employed in most current interpretations of the rise and fall of the Indus Valley Civilization.

225

Hrozny, Bedrich. *Ancient History of Western Asia, India and Crete.* New York: Philosophical Library, 1953. Chapter XVI provides an interesting example of the more bizarre interpretations of the Indus valley script.

Major Site Reports

226

Vats, M. S. *Excavations at Harappa.* 2 vols. New Delhi: Archaeological Survey of India, 1940. The most comprehensive report on this major site of the Indus Valley Civilization.

227

Wheeler, Sir Mortimer. "Harappa," *Ancient India,* 3, 58–130, (1947). An account of excavations made after the publication of Vats' report (see preceding entry).

228

Marshall, Sir John H. *Mohenjo-Daro and the Indus Civilization.* 3 vols. London: A. Probsthain, 1931. An official account of the archaeological excavation of Mohenjo-Daro carried out by the Government of India between 1922 and 1927.

229

Mackay, Ernest J. H. *Further Excavations at Mohenjo-Daro.* 2 vols. Delhi: Manager of Publications, Government of India, 1938. A report of research conducted after the work described by Marshall in the preceding entry.

230

Mackay, Ernest J. H. *Chanhu-Daro Excavations.* New Haven: American Oriental Society, 1943. A report of investigations conducted during 1935–36 at one of the major sites of the Indus Valley Civilization.

231

Marshall, Sir John. *Taxila.* 3 vols. Cambridge University Press, 1951. A well-illustrated report of twenty-two years of archaeological research on the ancient site of Taxila in northwestern India, a region occupied by successive waves of invaders from 500 B.C. to A.D. 500.

232

Marshall, Sir John. *A Guide to Taxila.* Cambridge: Cambridge University Press, 4th ed., rev., 1961. A popular account of the findings reported in detail in the preceding entry. Taxila was for many centuries a major center of trade between India and Central and Western Asia.

233

Lal, B. B. "Excavations at Hastinapura and Other Explorations in the Upper Ganga and Sutlej Basins, 1950–52," in *Ancient India* Nos. 10 and 11, pp. 1–151, (1954–55). Although a technical account, this has interest for the general reader as an example of recent finds that may serve to fill the archaeological gap between the post-Harappan and Mauryan periods.

ANCIENT INDIA
c.1500 B.C.-A.D. 1000

The term "Ancient India" is commonly used for all or part of the period from 1500 B.C. to the eleventh century A.D. During this time the distinctive features of "Traditional Indian Culture" or "Hindu Civilization" emerged as a synthesis of diverse traditions. The best known of these traditions is that of Aryan speaking invaders who obtained dominance of the Gangetic plain by the 6th century B.C.; their religious literature, the Vedas, provide most of our knowledge of the period up to this time. For this reason, the period from 1500 to 500 B.C. is often called the "Vedic" or "Aryan" age. Intellectual and social ferment in the sixth century gave rise to the "Buddhist" age; what is known of the succeeding two centuries is largely derived from Buddhist sources. In the 4th century the first major dynasty of India, the "Mauryan Empire," was founded on the Gangetic plain reaching its greatest heights under Asoka; after his death about 232 B.C. the dynasty declined. An "Age of Invasions" came after the fall of the Mauryans with the establishment of Greek kingdoms in the northwest and the movement of Saka and Kushan tribal groups into North India from Central Asia. The political ascendance of the Gupta dynasty in the 4th century A.D. was accompanied by great literary and artistic activity, India's "Classic Age." After the decline of the Guptas in the sixth century and the brief reign of Harsha, a nebulous period characterized by numerous kingdoms persisted until A.D. 1206, when Muslim invaders established their capital in Delhi. Historical development outside the Gangetic plain followed a different course described below.

Since much of what is known about ancient India is derived from religious and literary sources, a description and full citation of these materials appears under *Intellectual and Aesthetic Patterns* and *Religion and Philosophy.* Other primary sources for the period, the accounts of pilgrims, emissaries, and invaders appear below under *Indian-Foreign Relations to A.D. 1000.* The reader is also directed to the section on *Archaeology* for works relating to ancient India.

General Works

234

Basham, Arthur L. *The Wonder That Was India.* London: Sidgwick Jackson, 1954. New York: Grove Press, paperbound ed., 1959. The best single volume work on ancient India; organized topically with extensive treatment of religion, government, politics, literature, and the social order.

235

Rapson, Edward J. (ed.). *Ancient India.* Vol. 1. *The Cambridge History of India.* New York: Macmillan, 1922. Although somewhat outdated, this substantial work of high quality remains a basic reference for Indian history from earliest times to the middle of the first century, A.D.

236

Raychaudhuri, Hemchandra. *Political History of Ancient India.* Calcutta: University of Calcutta, 6th ed., rev., 1953. A classic work; reconstructs the dynastic history of northern India from Vedic times to the fall of the Gupta Empire.

237

Renou, Louis. *The Civilization of Ancient India*. Trans. from the French by P. Spratt. Calcutta: Susil Gupta, 1959. A brief, comprehensive survey of historic India up to the middle of the 7th century, by a leading Indologist.

238

Masson-Oursel, Paul, Wilman-Grabowska, and P. Stern. *Ancient India and Indian Civilization*. London: Kegan Paul, Trench, Trübner, 1934. A concise survey of the aesthetic, intellectual, and social aspects of ancient India.

239

Filliozat, Jean. *Political History of India*. Trans. from the French by P. Spratt. Calcutta: Susil Gupta, 1957. A compact and lucid survey of political events and personages from earliest times to the 7th century A.D.; includes a review and assessment of the principal sources for the period.

240

Smith, Vincent A. *The Early History of India*. Revised by S. M. Edwards. Oxford: Clarendon Press, 4th ed., 1958. For many years a standard text on India's political history from 600 B.C. to the Muslim conquest; although somewhat out-dated, it provides some useful examples of the "Imperial" British view of Indian history.

241

Majumdar, Ramesh C. *Ancient India*. Delhi: Motilal Banarsidass, rev. ed., 1960. A semi-popular survey by one of India's leading historians, includes an account of dynastic developments in areas outside the Gangetic heartland of Indian history. A revision of Majumdar's *Outline of Ancient History and Civilization*, first published in 1927.

242

Sen, Gertrude (Emerson). *The Pageant of India's History*. New York: Longmans Green, 1948. A popular account of the pre-Muslim period.

Special Studies

243

Smith, R. Morton. "On the Ancient Chronology of India," in *Journal of the American Oriental Society*, 77(1957): 2: 116–129; 77: 4: 226–280; 78 (1958): 3: 174–192. A detailed technical study based on literary sources and epigraphic evidence of the dates, reigns, and succession of ancient Indian rulers.

244

Altekar, Anant Sadashiv. *State and Government in Ancient India*. Banaras: Motilal Banarsidass, 3rd ed., rev., 1958. One of the best introductory surveys of Hindu political theory and practice from Vedic times to about A.D. 1000.

245

Sharma, Ram Sharan. *Aspects of Political Ideas and Institutions in Ancient India*. Delhi: Motilal Banarsidass, 1959. A study of the influence of social, religious, and economic factors on political development in early India; includes a review of previous work on the subject.

246

Ghoshal, Upendra Nath. *Studies in Indian History and Culture*. Bombay: Orient Longmans, rev. ed., 1957. Many of the essays in this collection of scholarly articles concern governmental and political institutions of ancient India, including theories of kingship, fiscal practices, and revenue systems.

247

Altekar, Anant Sadashiv. *Village Communities in Western India*. Oxford: Oxford University Press, 1929. One of the few accounts of village organization prior to modern times, mainly concerned with the Gupta period.

248

Dikshitar, V. R. Ramachandra. *War in Ancient India*. Madras: Macmillan, 2nd ed., 1948. A useful source of information on the subject; weak in interpretation.

249

Majumdar, Bimal Kanti. *The Military System in Ancient India*. Calcutta: Firma K. L. Mukhopadhyay, 2nd ed., 1960. A survey of military organization in North India from Vedic times to the 12th century A.D.

250

Jain, Jagdish Chandra. *Life in Ancient India as Depicted in the Jain Canons*. Bombay: New Book Co., 1947. One of the few attempts to explore a potentially fruitful source of information on social and economic conditions in ancient India.

251

Mookerji, Radha Kumud. *Indian Shipping: A History of the Sea-Bourne Trade and Maritime Activity of the Indians from the Earliest Times*. Calcutta: Orient Longmans, rev. ed., 1957. First published in 1912. A well-documented and relatively objective exposition of the thesis that India's command of the seas in ancient times was comparable in level of technology and enterprise to that of other peoples.

252

Bandyopadhyaya, Narayan C. (sometimes cited as N. C. Banerji or Banerjee). *Economic Life and Progress in Ancient India*. Calcutta: University of Calcutta, 2nd ed., 1945. An account based on literary sources of economic organization and activities from earliest times to the rise of the Mauryan Empire.

253

Aiyangar, K. V. Rangaswami. *Aspects of Ancient Indian Economic Thought*. Benares: Hindu University, 1934. A classic work which provides a critical appraisal of sources.

254

Pran Nath. *A study in the Economic Condition of Ancient India*. London: Royal Asiatic Society, Monograph XX, 1929. A reconstruction of economic institutions, practices, including wages and prices, and related political features of pre-Muslim India.

255

Bose, Atindranath. *Social and Rural Economy of Northern India*. 2 vols. Calcutta: K. L. Mukhopadhyay, 2nd ed., 1961. First published by the University of Calcutta, 1942–45. A descriptive account of North India's rural economy during the five centuries preceding the Christian era; based on the Buddhist *Jataka* sources, archaeological evidence, and the Hindu *smriti* literature.

256

Bhargava, Brijkishore. *Indigenous Banking in Ancient and Medieval India*. Bombay: D. B. Taraporevala, 1943. A study of the banking system developed to facilitate commerce in India prior to the introduction of Western financial institutions.

257

Majumdar, Ramesh C. *Corporate Life in Ancient India*. Calcutta: Calcutta University, 2nd ed., 1922. A useful account of guilds and trade organizations in anciant India and early developments in the caste system.

258

Saran, K. M. *Labour in Ancient India*. Bombay: Vora, 1957. A brief study of wages and the conditions of labor as described in such ancient works as Kautilya's *Arthaśastra*.

259

Chanana, Dev Raj. *Slavery in Ancient India*. New Delhi: People's Publishing House, 1960. A useful account of a seldom studied subject; based on the Hindu Epics and Buddhist canonical texts. The period covered is mainly from the 6th century B.C. to the beginning of the Christian era.

260

Ghoshal, Upendra Nath. *The Agrarian System in Ancient India*. Calcutta: University of Calcutta, 1930. Treats the North Indian revenue system from 300 B.C. to A.D. 1200.

261

Dutt, B. B. *Town Planning in Ancient India*. Calcutta: Thacker, Spink, 1925. A useful, though sometimes speculative, treatment of the subject.

262

Sircar, Dines Chandra. *Studies in the Geography of Ancient and Medieval India*. Delhi: Motilal Banarsidass, 1960. A scholarly discussion of some of the principal problems in the field, by one of India's eminent historians.

263

Dey, Nundolal. *The Geographical Dictionary of Ancient and Medieval India.* London: Luzac and Co., 2nd ed., rev., 1927. A useful reference for place names frequently encountered in Indian history.

264

Cunningham, Sir Alexander (ed. by S. N. Majumdar). *The Ancient Geography of India.* Calcutta: Chuckervertty, Chatterjee, 2nd ed., 1924. First published in 1871; based on information from the accounts of Alexander's campaign, and the records left by Hsüan-tsang.

265

Chaudhuri, Sashi, Bhusan. *Ethnic Settlement in Ancient India.* Calcutta: General Printers and Publishers, 1955. A study of the distribution and movement of tribal groups in ancient India, based on literary and epigraphic evidence.

266

Law, Bimala C. *Tribes in Ancient India.* Poona: Bhandarkar Oriental Research Institute, 1943. A standard work concerned mainly with the identification and location of tribes in Vedic India.

267

Law, Bimala C. *Historical Geography of Ancient India.* Paris: Societé Asiatique de Paris, 1954. A useful reference for those seeking the modern location of ancient place names.

268

Shafer, Robert. *Ethnography of Ancient India.* Weisbaden: Otto Harrassowitz, 1954. A bold attempt at identifying the tribal composition and regions of Vedic India; based on linguistic evidence from the *Mahabharata.*

269

Mookerji, Radha Kumud. *Ancient Indian Education.* London: Macmillan, 2nd ed. 1951. Brahmanical and Buddhist educational theories and practices from Vedic times to about A.D. 1000 are authoritatively described in this work.

270

Das, Santosh Kumar. *The Education System of the Ancient Hindus.* Calcutta: S. K. Das, 1930. One of the most complete studies of the subject.

271

Altekar, Anant Sadashiv. *Education in Ancient India.* Benares: Nand Kishore, 4th ed., 1951. An excellent introduction to the subject, less technical than the initial edition; written in part for those interested in comparative studies.

272

Mookerji, Radha Kumud. *Men and Thought in Ancient India.* Bombay: Hind Kitabs, 2nd ed., 1957. Five brief biographical sketches of Yajnavalkya, Buddha, Asoka, Samudragupta, and Harsha, presented as representing the major facets of Indian culture; a popular account.

273

Meyer, Johann J. *Sexual Life in Ancient India.* New York: Barnes and Noble, 1953. A reprint of an earlier two-volume edition published in London in 1930. Despite the title, this work is mainly concerned with the role and status of women as described in the *Mahabharata and Ramayana*: a scholarly study.

274

Indra, Professor. *The Status of Women in Ancient India.* Banaras: Motilal Banarsidass, 2nd ed., rev., 1955. A popular account of the political, social, and legal status of women in pre-Muslim India as described in Hindu, Buddhist, and Jain literature.

275

Prakash, Om. *Food and Drinks in Ancient India.* Delhi: Munshi Ram Manohar Lal, 1961. A brief survey of the subject covering the period from earliest times to the 13th century.

276

Piggott, Stuart. *Some Ancient Cities of India.* London: Oxford University Press, 1945. Prepared for travelers; contains brief historical and descriptive sketches of eleven city-sites characteristic of northern and western India from Harappan to Mughal times.

277

Majumdar, Ramesh Chandra. *Ancient Indian Colonization in South-East Asia.* Baroda: M. S. University of Baroda, 1955. A study of the expansion of India, primarily for purposes of overseas trade, from Gupta times to about A.D. 1000.

Indian-Foreign Relations to A.D. 1000

278

Rawlinson, Hugh G. *Intercourse Between India and the Western World.* Cambridge: Cambridge University, 1926. A succinct account of the intercourse between India and the Greco-Roman world from earliest times to the fall of Rome; based on the accounts of classical writers.

279

Wheeler, Sir Mortimer. *Rome Beyond the Imperial Frontiers.* New York: Philosophical Library, 1955. (Penguin, paperbound ed., 1955). Archaeological evidence and the work of classical authors are the two sources for this account of Roman contact with Europe, Africa, and Asia; 56 pages of this book pertain to South Asia.

280

Majumdar, Ramesh C. (ed.). *The Classical Accounts of India.* Calcutta: Firma K. L. Mukhopadhyay, 1960. A compilation of translations from the accounts of ancient India left by Megasthenes, Arrian, Strabo, and other classical authors. Earlier publications of these translations, by such scholars as J. W. McCrindle, are now difficult to acquire.

281

McCrindle, John W. *Ancient India as Described by Megasthenes and Arrian.* London: Trübner, 1877. A translation of fragments from the first foreign accounts of India, preserved by ancient historians. Megasthenes was a Greek ambassador to the court of Chandragupta Maurya from 302 B.C. to 298 B.C. Arrian's account is the main historical source for Alexander the Great's invasion of India in 326 B.C.

282

McCrindle, John W. *The Invasion of India by Alexander the Great.* Westminister: A. Constable, 2nd ed., 1896. This account of Alexander's military exploits in India contains an excellent introduction, and extensive translations from Arrian and other classical authors.

283

Arrianus, Flavius (E. Iliff Robson, Trans.) *Arrian, History of Alexander and India.* 2 vols. Cambridge: Harvard University Press, 1949. A translation, without supplementary material, of Arrian's account of Alexander the Great's military exploits including his invasion of India. Written in the second century of the Christian era by a Greek historian who drew on the work of earlier classical authors.

284

Schoff, Wilfred H. (trans.). *The Periplus of the Erythraen Sea.* New York: Longmans, 1912. An account, translated from the Greek, by a merchant of the first century of the Christian era who engaged in travel and trade on the Indian Ocean.

285

McCrindle, John W. *Ancient India as Described by Ptolemy.* Ed. by S. N. Majumdar. Calcutta: Chuckervertty, Chatterjee, rev. ed., 1927. A translation, with introduction and commentary, of those portions of Ptolemy's classic work which describe India, Central, and Eastern Asia; written about 150 A.D.

286

Saletore, Bhasker A. *India's Diplomatic Relations with the East.* Bombay: Popular Book Depot, 1960. A study of diplomatic missions exchanged between India and other Asian countries, mainly China, from about A.D. 300 to 1300.

287

Giles, Herbert A. *The Travels of Fa-Hsien*. London: Routledge Kegan Paul, 1956. This is a new translation by Giles of his earlier translation published in 1923. An account of Fa-hsien's observations on fifth century India; he was a Chinese Buddhist pilgrim-scholar, residing in northern India from A.D. 405–411.

288

Beal, Samuel (trans.). *Travels of Fah-Hian and Sung Yun*. London: Trübner, 1869. A translation from the Chinese of travel accounts by two Buddhist pilgrim-scholars. Fah-Hian (Fa-hsien) visited India in the early fifth century; Sung Yun visited India in the early sixth century.

289

Watters, Thomas (trans.). *On Yüan Chwang's Travels in India*. 2 vols. London: Royal Asiatic Society, 1904–05. An account of seventh-century India by the most famous of the Chinese Buddhist pilgrim-scholars. Yüan Chwang (also transliterated as: Hsüan-tsang, Hiuen Tsiang, Hiouen Thsang) resided in India from 629 to 645 A.D. Watters' translation is held to be most authoritative, and it corrects many of the errors in Beal's earlier translation (see following entry).

290

Beal, Samuel (trans.). *Chinese Accounts of India*. Translated from the Chinese of Hiuen Tsiang. Calcutta: Susil Gupta, 1957–58. This is a reprint of four volumes of Beal's *Si-Yu-Ki; Buddhist Records of the Western World* published by Trübner in 1884.

291

Saint-Hilaire, J. Barthelemy. *Hiouen-Thsang in India*. Trans. from the French by Laura Enser. Calcutta: Susil Gupta, paperbound, 1952. A popular account of Hiouen-Thsang's travels in India during the 7th century; based on translations from the Chinese by Stanislas Julien.

292

Cosmas "Indicopleustes." *Topographia Christiana*. Trans. from the Greek and edited by J. W. McCrindle. London: Hakluyt Society, first Series, *Vol. 98*, 1897. An account by an Egyptian merchant who visited the Malabar coast in the sixth century.

293

Takakusu, J. (trans.). *A Record of the Buddhist Religion as Practiced in India and the Malay Archipelago*. Oxford: Clarendon Press, 1896. An account by the Chinese pilgrim I Tsing who traveled in the area from A.D. 671–695.

294

Petech, Luciano. *Northern India According to the Shui-Ching-Chu*. Rome: Instituto Italiano Per Medio Ed Estremo Oriente, 1950. A scholarly translation of a Chinese text, probably written during the third century, prepared by a Chinese geographer from the accounts of Buddhist pilgrims to India.

Vedic Period   c.1500-500 B.C.

295

Majumdar, Ramesh C. (ed.). *The Vedic Age*. Vol. I, *The History and Culture of the Indian People*. London: George Allen and Unwin, 1951. A detailed survey by Indian historians; some sections are marred by nationalist sentiments extolling the glory and antiquity of Vedic India.

296

Childe, V. Gordon. *The Aryans*. New York: Alfred A. Knopf, 1926. A study of the little known origin of the Aryan people and their movement into Europe, the Middle East, and India.

297

Raychaudhuri, Hemchandra. *Political History of Ancient India*. Calcutta: University of Calcutta, 6th ed., rev., 1953. This work contains the most authoritative chronology for the Vedic period.

298

Kaegi, Adolf. *Life in Ancient India*. Trans. from the German by R. Arrowsmith. Calcutta: Susil Gupta, paperbound, 1950. A reprint of a 19th century work concerning the earliest phase of the Vedic age; based on a study of the Rig Vedic hymns; emphasis on religious ideas and practices.

299

Basu, Prophullachandra. *Indo-Aryan Polity*. London: P. S. King & Son, Ltd., 1925. A scholarly account of early developments in Indian polity.

300

Bhargava, Purushottam L. *India in the Vedic Age*. Lucknow: Upper India Publishing House, 1956. A reconstruction of the Aryan expansion into India based on Vedic and Puranic sources.

Early Buddhism and the Mauryan Empire c.563-183 B.C.

301

Rapson, E. J. (ed.). *Ancient India*. Vol. I, *Cambridge History of India*. New York: Macmillan, 1922. An authoritative survey of the Buddhist and Mauryan period is contained in this history of India to the beginning of the Christian era.

302

Majumdar, Ramesh C. (ed.) *The Age of Imperial Unity*. Vol. II, *The History and Culture of the Indian People*. Bombay: Bharatiya Vidya Bhavan, 1953. The first six chapters, by R. K. Mookerji and B. C. Law, provide a useful introduction to the Mauryan period.

303

Nilakanta Sastri, K. A. (ed.). *Age of the Nandas and Mauryas*. Banaras: Motilal Banarsidass, 1952. Religion, literature, and art, as well as political events receive due consideration in this history of North India from about 400 to 185 B. C. Originally conceived as part of a 20-volume series, this work was issued independently by the Bharatiya Itihas Parishad due to the amalgamation of that group's efforts with the Indian History Congress.

304

Nilakanta Sastri, K. A. (ed.). *The Mauryas and the Satavahanas, 325 B.C.–A.D. 300*. London: Longmans, Green, 1959. Volume II of the projected 12-volume *Comprehensive History of India*. This volume covers the rise of Buddhism, the establishment of the Mauryan empire, and the intrusion of Greek, Saka, and other peoples into northern India.

305

Davids, Thomas W. Rhys. *Buddhist India*. Calcutta: Susil Gupta, 6th ed., 1957. First published in 1903, this classic work remains a useful brief introduction to the society, religion, and literature of the period.

306

Agrawala, Vasudeva S. *India as Known to Panini*. Lucknow: Varansi: Prithvi Prakashan, 2nd ed. rev., 1963. A useful study of the geographical, historical, and cultural materials contained in Panini's grammar, the *Ashtadhyayi*, probably written in the 5th Century B.C.

307

Mookerji, Radha Kumud. *Chandragupta Maurya and His Times*. Delhi: Motilal Banarsidass, 3rd ed., 1960. An excellent account of the founder of the Mauryan Empire, who ruled much of northern India from about 322 to 298 B.C.; information is also included on the social and economic conditions of the time and Chandragupta's system of administration.

308

Mookerji, Radha Kumud. *Asoka*. London: Macmillan, 2nd ed., rev., 1955. A good introduction to the life and times of Asoka whose forty-year reign, from about 269 to 232 B.C., is one of the high points of Indian history.

309

Smith, Vincent A. *Asoka, the Buddhist Emperor of India.*
Delhi: S. Chand., rev. ed., 1957. First published in
1901, this is a standard account of the great Mauryan
ruler and his times; contains translations of the Asokan
edicts.

310

Thapar, Romila. *Asoka and the Decline of the Mauryas.*
London: Oxford University Press, 1961. An excellent
review and assessment of what is known about Asoka
and his times.

311

Sen, Amulyachandra (Trans.). *Asoka's Edicts.* Calcutta:
Institute of Indology, 1956. A translation with commentary of the proclamations and exhortations of Asoka
that were inscribed on rocks, pillars, and caves; background information is provided for the general reader.

312

Eggermont, Pierre H. L. *The Chronology of the Reign of
Asoka Moriya.* Leiden: E. J. Brill, 1956. A technical
study comparing the chronology of the Asokan inscriptions with that of tradition preserved in such texts as
the *Dīpavamsa.*

313

Kautilya. *Arthaśastra.* Trans. by R. Shamasastry. Mysore:
Sri Raghuveer Printing Press, 5th ed., 1956. A primary
source of information about the Mauryan administrative
system; much of what has been written about traditional
Indian political theory and practice is based on this
text.

314

Dikshitar, V. R. Ramachandra. *Mauryan Polity.* Madras:
University of Madras, reprint, 1953. First published in
1932. A reconstruction of the political and religious institutions of the Mauryan Empire (ca. fourth to second
centuries B.C.), based mainly on the *Arthaśastra* and the
Edicts of Asoka. The author views Mauryan rule as: "A
benevolent form of monarchy with democratic institutions, almost modern in character."

315

Law, Bimala C. *India as Described in Early Texts of
Buddhism and Jainism.* London: Luzac, 1941. A scholarly account of the period based on non-Brahmanical
sources.

316

Fick, Richard. *The Social Organization of Northeast India
in Buddha's Time.* Trans. from the German by S. K.
Maitra. Calcutta: University of Calcutta, 1920. A scholarly work based on Pāli texts; concerned mainly with
the upper classes, contains information and interpretations about the origin of the caste system.

Age of Invasions   c.190 B.C.–c.A.D. 320

317

Chattopadhyaya, Sudhaker. *Early History of North India.*
Calcutta: Progressive Publishers, 1958. A political history of North India from the fall of the Mauryas to
the death of Harsha, c. 200 B.C.–A.D. 650.

318

Jayaswal, K. P. *History of India,* A.D. *150–350.* Lahore:
Motilal Banarsidass, 1933. A bold attempt to reconstruct the history of one of the more obscure periods
in India's past.

319

Nilakanta Sastri, K. A. (ed.). *The Mauryas and the Sata-
vahanas.* London: Longmans, Green, 1959. Chapters
VII–IX provide a useful introduction to the period when
Greek, Saka, and other invaders entered North India.

320

Majumdar, Ramesh C. (ed.). *The Age of Imperial Unity.*
Vol. II, *The History and Culture of the Indian People.*
Bombay: Bharatiya Vidya Bhavan, 1953. A substantial part of this work is concerned with the various
invaders who entered India after the fall of the Mauryan empire.

321

Tarn, William W. *The Greeks in Bactria and India.* Cambridge: Cambridge University Press, rev. ed., 1951. A
reconstruction of the history of Greek kingdoms in
India from 206 B. C. to the first half of the second
century B.C., with background material on the Middle
East; Tarn's interpretations should be read in conjunc-
tion with those of Narain (see next entry).

322

Narain, A. K. *The Indo-Greeks.* Oxford: Clarendon Press,
1957. A technical study of the political history of the
Greek kingdoms in India; numismatic evidence is extensively used to advance earlier accounts by Tarn (see
preceding entry) and others.

323

Chattopadhyaya, Sudhaker. *The Sakas in India.* Santiniketan: Visva-Bharati Studies, No. 21, 1955. A brief
sketch of the early history and subsequent assimilation
of a Central Asian tribe that invaded North India in
the early centuries of the Christian era.

324

Leeuw, Von Lohuizen de. *The Scythian Period.* Leiden:
E. J. Brill, 1949. Especially useful for its treatment of
the chronology of the period.

325

McGovern, William M. *The Early Empires of Central
Asia.* Chapel Hill: University of North Carolina Press,
1939. One of the few accounts of developments in
Central Asia that contributed to the movement of the
Scythians and Huns into India.

326

Puri, Baij Nath. *India in the Time of Patanjali.* Bombay:
Bhartiya Vidya Bhavan, 1957. An account of those
aspects of Indian life of the second century B.C. referred to in Patanjali's grammatical treatise, the *Ma-
habhasya.*

327

Pandey, Raj Bali. *Vikramaditya of Ujjayini.* Banaras:
Shatadala Prakashana, 1951. A review and assessment
of historical materials relating to a major figure in
Indian legend; Vikramaditya is believed to have lived
in the first century B.C.

328

Chaladar, Haran C. *Social Life in Ancient India.* Calcutta:
Susil Gupta, 2nd ed., rev., 1954. A study of Indian
society in the early centuries of the Christian era, based
on Vatsyayana's *Kamasutra;* somewhat biased by orthodox views on caste.

Gupta Empire and the Reign of Harsha   320-647

329

Majumdar, Ramesh C. (ed.). *The Classical Age.* Vol. III,
The History and Culture of the Indian People. Bombay:
Bharatiya Vidya Bhavan, 1954. The best single volume
account of the Gupta Empire, known as the "Classical
Age" due to the great achievements in art and literature
that accompanied this period of political stability and
integration.

330

Majumdar, Ramesh C. and A. S. Altekar. *The Vakataka-
Gupta Age.* Lahore: Motilal Banarsidass, 1946. A history of North India from about A. D. 200 to 550; contains a complete list of the Gupta inscriptions, a
primary source for the period.

331

Mookerji, Radha Kumud. *The Gupta Empire.* Bombay:
Hind Kitabs, 3rd ed., rev., 1959. A valuable account of
the period by one of India's leading historians.

332

Basak, Radhgovinda. *The History of Northeastern India.*
London: Kegan Paul, Trench, Trübner, 1934. A scholarly account of the founding of the Gupta Empire and
the post-Gupta kingdoms of Bengal, Orissa, and Nepal;
from about A.D. 320 to 760.

333

Dikshitar, V. R. Ramachandra. *Gupta Polity*. Madras: University of Madras, 1952. A study of the governmental structure of the Gupta dynasty which ruled much of northern India from c. 320 A.D. to 540.

334

Saletore, Rajaram N. *Life in the Gupta Age*. Bombay: The Popular Book Depot, 1943. A standard work on Indian society of the period.

335

Maity, Sachindra K. *Economic Life of Northern India in the Gupta Period*. Calcutta: World Press, 1957. An excellent survey of the land and revenue systems, industry, trade, and agriculture of North India from about A.D. 300 to 550.

336

Pires, Edward A. *The Maukharis*. Madras: B. G. Paul, 1934. The history of a short-lived dynasty that ruled much of modern Bihar after the fall of the Guptas in the 6th century.

337

Tripathi, Rama Shankar. *History of Kanauj*. Banaras: Indian Book Shop, 1937. Contains one of the best accounts of Harsha's reign in the 7th century.

338

Mookerji, Radha Kumud. *Harsha*. New York: Oxford University Press, 1925. Delhi: M. Banarsidass, 2nd ed., 1959. A standard account of the life and times of Harsha whose reign in the 7th century is often described as a brief renaissance of the Gupta "Golden Age."

NORTHERN INDIA AFTER HARSHA 647-1300

Following the fall of the Guptas and the brief renaissance under Harsha, political authority in North India was dispersed among many kingdoms until the Muslim conquests of the twelfth and thirteenth centuries. No single work surveys this obscure period in Indian history; what is known must be sought in the accounts of particular dynasties or regions. Although some view this area as the Dark Ages of Indian history, patronage provided in many Hindu courts served to perpetuate learning and the arts; the temples of Khajuraho being one example of architectural achievements during the period. This was also the time when many of the vernacular literary traditions were established. Although political integration on the order of the Mauryans or Guptas was not achieved during this time, the assimilation of diverse peoples and traditions occurred on a grand scale. Hindu caste categories were accommodated to changes in political fortune, as exemplified by the appelation Rajput or Kshatriya for rulers of tribal origin. The Hindu social and cultural synthesis emerging from this period persists to a considerable extent down to the present.

339

Majumdar, Ramesh C. (ed.). *The Age of Imperial Kanauj*. Vol. IV, *History and Culture of the Indian People*. Bombay: Bharatiya Vidya Bhavan, 1955. The best single-volume treatment of north Indian history from the time of the Guptas to the invasion of the Muslims.

340

Ray, H. C. *The Dynastic History of Northern India*. 2 vols. Calcutta: Calcutta University Press, 1931–36.

A major work among historical studies of the Hindu states that arose after the fall of Harsha's empire.

341

Vaidya, C. V. *History of Mediaeval Hindu India*. 3 vols. Poona: Oriental Book Agency, 1921–26. An account of the political history of the period from the fall of the Guptas to the invasion of the Muslims.

342

Mazumdar, Bhakat Prasad. *Socio-Economic History of Northern India*. Calcutta: K. L. Mukhopadhyay, 1960. A useful account of Northern India during the period 1000–1200 A.D.; includes a discussion of the rise of "feudalism," public finance, land, labor, and daily life.

343

Tripathi, Rama Shankar. *History of Kanauj*. Banaras: Indian Book Shop, 1937. A standard work on North Indian history up to the Muslim conquest.

344

Sinha, B. P. *The Decline of the Kingdom of Magadha*. Patna: Motilal Banarsidass, 1954. A competent, if somewhat arid, study of the dynastic history of Magadha from the middle of the 5th century to A.D. 1000.

345

Niyogi, Roma. *The History of the Gahadavala Dynasty*. Calcutta: Calcutta Oriental Book Agency, 1959. A political history of a dynasty that ruled in the region of modern Banaras from the late 11th to the end of the 12th century.

346

Mitra, Sisir Kumar. *The Early Rulers of Khajuraho*. Calcutta: Firma K. L. Muhopadhyay, 1958. A general account of the Candellas of Bundelkhand, a prominent Hindu dynasty that controlled much of the area between the Jumna river and the Vindhya mountains prior to the Muslim conquest.

347

Bose, Nemai Sadhan. *History of the Candellas of Jejakabhukti*. Calcutta: Firma K. L. Mukhopadhyay, 1956. A study of the political history of the Candellas from about A.D. 950 to 1300.

348

Sharma, Dasharatha. *Early Chauhan Dynasties*. Delhi: S. Chand, 1959. A study of the history and political institutions of one of the foremost Rajput clans who controlled much of modern Rajasthan from the 9th to the 14th centuries.

349

Tod, James. *Annals and Antiquities of Rajasthan*. 2 vols., London: Routledge, Kegan Paul, rev. ed., 1957–60. First published in 1829; Tod's use of bardic lays and other sources of traditional history make this a valuable source as well as one of the few accounts of the central and western Rajput states during "medieval" times. The following entry contains a critique of this work.

350

Thorner, Daniel. "Feudalism in India," in *Feudalism in History* (R. Coulborn, ed.; Princeton: Princeton University Press, 1956), pp. 133–150. Much of this essay is a critique of Tod's use of the concept of feudalism in *Annals and Antiquities of Rajasthan* (see preceding entry).

351

Qanungo, Kalika Ranjan. *Studies in Rajput History*. Delhi: S. Chand, 1960. A brief sketch of a little-known aspect of Indian history by one of India's leading historians. Rajasthan was a bastion of Hinduism during the period of Muslim rule.

352

Ganguly, Dhirendra Chandra. *History of the Paramara Dynasty*. Dacca: Dacca University, 1943. The Paramaras were a contender for power in North India of the 11th century, they controlled Malwa, an area to the north of the Vindhya mountains.

353

Puri, Baij Nath. *The History of the Gurjara-Pratiharas.* Bombay: Hind Kitabs, 1957. This dynasty ruled much of northern India in the 9th century, reaching the height of its power under Bhoja I, who is celebrated in legend as one of the great Hindu kings.

354

Majumdar, Ramesh C. (ed.). *History of Bengal,* Vol. I. Dacca: Dacca University, 1943. A detailed account of Bengal prior to the Muslim invasion; occasionally marred by unwarranted claims for the past glory and power of the region; especially useful for the 9th and 10th centuries when the Palas of Bengal fought for control of northern India with the Rashtrakutas of the Deccan and the Gurjara-Pratiharas of the north.

355

Sarkar, Sir Jadunath (ed.). *The History of Bengal.* Vol. II. Calcutta: Calcutta University, 1948. A continuation of the work cited in the preceding entry.

356

Basak, Radha Govinda. *The History of North-Eastern India.* London: Kegan Paul, Trench, Trübner, 1934. An account of the region approximating modern Bengal, from the early 4th to the mid-8th century.

357

Ray, Sunil Chandra. *Early History and Culture of Kashmir.* New Delhi: Munshi Ram Manohar Lal (distributor), 1957. A survey of the social, economic, cultural, and political aspects of Kashmir from the earliest times to the Muslim conquest of 1338 A.D.

THE DECCAN TO THE 14TH CENTURY

The term "Deccan" is rather nebulous despite frequent usage and considerable antiquity; most commonly it refers to the northern half of the Deccan plateau and the adjacent coastal areas. Situated midway between the Gangetic plain and the far south, the Deccan has shared in the cultural development and political history of both areas. Although cultural and historical forces originating in the north and south may be seen as the major determinant of the Deccan's destiny, a sufficient number of distinct regional traditions of considerable antiquity and dynasties of major importance have originated within the area to warrant treating the Deccan as a separate entity. However, relatively few scholarly attempts have been made to synthesize what is known of Deccan history in comparison to the number of such syntheses of North or South Indian history. This is due in part to the paucity of historical materials prior to the Muslim conquest of the area in the fourteenth century, and the reluctance of scholars to venture beyond the compilation of dynastic chronologies based on the interpretation of coins and inscriptions.

General Works

358

Yazdani, Ghulam, (ed.). *The Early History of the Deccan.* 2 vols. London: Oxford University Press, 1960. This is the most recent attempt to bring order into the complex history of the Deccan from 200 B.C. to the 14th century. Although some of India's best modern historians contributed to this work, their primary concern with details of chronology provide little assistance for those seeking broad interpretations or historical syntheses.

359

Bhandarkar, Sir Ramakrishna G. *Early History of the Deccan.* Calcutta: Susil Gupta, rev. ed., 1957. A classic work first published in 1884 concerned mainly with the Western Deccan prior to the Muslim conquest. The original text is reprinted in this edition with changes added as separate notes; an index and list of recent publications on the subject have also been added.

360

Rao, M. Rama. *Glimpses of Dakkan History.* Calcutta: Orient Longmans, 1951. A brief popular survey of Deccan political history from the 1st to the 18th century.

Dynastic and Regional Studies

361

Nilakanata Sastri, K. A. (ed.). *The Mauryas and Satavahanas.* Vol. II, *A Comprehensive History of India.* Calcutta: Orient Longmans, 1957. Chapter X contains a review of the problems of Satavahana chronology; this dynasty emerged as a major power during the decline of the Mauryan empire, founded the earliest empire in the Deccan and maintained the longest dynasty in India's history, one that finally fell in the middle of the 4th century A.D.

362

Sircar, Dines Chandra. *Successors of the Satavahanas.* Calcutta: University of Calcutta, 1939. A scholarly and detailed account of the early dynasties in the Deccan.

363

Altekar, Anant Sadashiv. *The Rashtrakutas and Their Times.* Poona: Oriental Book Agency, 1934. An account of the Western Deccan in the 9th century; the Rashtrakutas were a major power controlling most of central India at this time.

364

Majumdar, Manjulal R. (ed.). *The Historical and Cultural Chronology of Gujarat.* Baroda: M. S. University of Baroda, 1960. A scholarly attempt to clarify the chronology of the region from earliest times to A.D. 942.

365

Majumdar, Asoke Kumar. *The Chaulukyas of Gujarat.* Bombay: Bharatiya Vidya Bhavan, 1956. An account of the Western Chaulukyas who ruled the region of modern Gujarat from the middle of the 10th to the end of the 13th century; includes information on art, religion, social life, and political administration.

366

Venkataramanayya, N. *The Eastern Chalukyas of Vengi.* Madras: University of Madras, 1950. This history concerns a dynasty that ruled the coastal region between the mouths of the Godavari and Krishna rivers from the middle of the 7th century to the latter part of the 10th century.

367

Banerji, Rakhal Das. *History of Orissa.* 2 vols. Calcutta: R. Chatterjee, 1930–31. A detailed survey of Orissan history from earliest times to the British period.

368

Sahu, N. K. (ed.). *A History of Orissa.* 2 vols. Calcutta: Susil Gupta, 1956. This work consists of selections from the writing of three 19th-century historians, W. W. Hunter, A. Stirling, and J. Beams, and supplementary material by the editor bringing the historical coverage up to 1947.

369

Mahtab, Harekrushna. *The History of Orissa.* Lucknow: Lucknow University, 1957. A useful summary and reworking of material contained in earlier more detailed accounts now difficult to acquire.

SOUTH INDIA TO THE
17TH CENTURY

The southern part of the Indian peninsula, consisting of the modern states of Madras, Andhra, Mysore, and Kerala, has pursued a course of historical development independent in many ways from that of the North. This area shares a common linguistic bond in the Dravidian derived languages that predominate in the region. Although the Brahmanical tradition of the Gangetic plain entered South India around the fourth century A.D., gradually gaining cultural dominance, people of the South still point with pride to their own literary tradition reaching back to the beginning of the Christian era. Political independence also fostered feelings of regional identity that today offset demands based on pan-Indian nationalism. Maritime commerce contributed to this sense of independence, providing an economic base for military power that thwarted all but a few brief intrusions from the north. The extension of Indian influence to Southeast Asia was mediated in large part by South Indian merchants and priests. After the Muslim conquest of North and Central India, the South remained a bastion of Hinduism preserving many features of the Brahmanical tradition destroyed elsewhere.

General Works

370

Nilakanta Sastri, K. A. *A History of South India*. London: Oxford University Press, 2nd ed., rev., 1958. The only general history of South India; a reliable survey from prehistoric times to the 17th century.

371

Dikshitar, V. R. Ramachandra. *Pre-Historic South India*. Madras: University of Madras, 1951. Addressed to the general reader; this partisan account stresses the cultural independence and achievements of South India. Information on South Indian geography, history, ethnology, and linguistics is provided in addition to a survey of South Indian archaeology.

Dynastic and Regional Studies

372

Kanakasabhai, V. *The Tamils Eighteen Hundred Years Ago*. Tirunelveli, Madras: South India Saiva Siddhanta Works Publishing Society, 2nd ed., rev., 1956. First published in 1904; this account of life and literature during the Sangam period from A.D. 50 to 150 is often cited to justify South India's claim to its own "Golden Age."

373

Iyengar, P. T. Srinivasa. *History of the Tamils*. Madras: C. Commeraswamy Naidu & Sons, 1929. A survey of South Indian history from earliest times to A.D. 600; much of this account concerns the period corresponding to Gupta times in the north.

374

Gopalan, R. *History of the Pallavas of Kanchi*. Madras: University of Madras, 1928. An excellent account of a major dynasty in South Indian history; the Pallavas were the paramount power in South India from the 5th to the 9th century when political prominence passed to the Cholas.

375

Minakshi, Cadambi. *Administration and Social Life Under the Pallavas*. Madras: University of Madras, 1938. A classic work on the subject.

376

Nilakanta Sastri, K. A. *The Colas*. 2 vols. Madras: University of Madras, rev. ed., 1955. An excellent history of a dynasty that played a major role in South Indian history from mid-9th to late 13th centuries, the Colas controlled South India and Ceylon at the height of their power in the 11th century.

377

Karmarkar, A. P. *A Cultural History of Karnataka*. Dharwar: Karnataka Vidyanardhaka Sangha, 1947. An account of the region approximating modern Mysore state; traces early development in literature and language.

378

Hukkerikar, R. S. (ed.). *Karnataka Darshana*. Bombay: R. S. Hukkerikar, 1955. Distributed by the Popular Book Depot, Bombay; a collection of fifty-five essays on the pre-history, history, and cultural achievements of the Kannada people including religion, drama, langauge, and Kanarese literature.

379

Derrett, J. Duncan M. *The Hoysalas, a Medieval Indian Royal Family*. London: Oxford University Press, 1957. A study of the institution of kingship as exemplified by a South Indian dynasty that ruled in the region of modern Mysore from about 940 to 1346.

380

Venkataraman, K. R. *Hoysalas in the Tamil Country*. Annamalainagar: Annamalai University, 1950. An account of the Hoysala dynasty from the 12th to the 14th centuries.

381

Nilakanta Sastri, K. A. *The Pandyan Kingdom*. London: Luzac, 1929. This work supersedes previous accounts of the Pandyan dynasty that controlled the Tamil region around Madura in southern India from the early 13th to the middle of the 14th centuries.

382

Mahalingam, T. V. *Administration and Social Life Under Vijayanagar*. Madras: Madras University Press, 1940. An account of a revenue system and mode of governmental organization that differed in many ways from that of North India; the Vijayanagar Empire was the last of the great Hindu powers, reigning over South India from A.D. 1336 to 1565 when Muslim invaders undermined the empire.

383

Saletore, Bhasker Anand. *Social and Political Life in the Vijayanagara Empire*. 2 vols. Madras: B. G. Paul, 1934. A scholarly account of the last great Hindu power organized along traditiional lines; Vijayanagara was a stronghold of Hinduism from mid-14th to mid-17th centuries.

384

Appadorai, Angadipuram. *Economic Conditions in Southern India, 1000–1500 A.D.* 2 vols. Madras: Madras University, 1936. An economic history of South India prior to the disruptions caused by Muslim, Maratha, and European intruders; based in the main on epigraphic evidence and travelers' accounts. A complementary account extending the period covered through the 16th century is cited in the following entry.

385

Venkata Ramanayya, N. *Studies in the History of the Third Dynasty of Vijayanagara*. Madras: University of Madras, 1935. A narration of the principal events that occurred in the Vijayanagar Empire between 1529 and 1543; includes a description of the administrative system, religion, and social conditions of the times.

386

Mahalingam, T. V. *Economic Life in the Vijayanagar*. Madras: University of Madras, 1951. A useful study based in part on European accounts of the great wealth and splendour of the nobility and the economic oppression of the common people.

387

Arokiaswami, M. *The Kongu Country*. Madras: University of Madras, 1956. A history of an area in modern Madras state during the 16th century, when Vijayanagar rulers dominated the region.

388

Sewell, Robert. *A Forgotten Empire*. London: S. Sonnenschein, 1924. First published in 1900; this classic work on the Vijayanagar Empire continues to be of value.

389

Panikkar, Kavalam M. *A History of Kerala*. Annamalainagar: Annamalai University, 1960. An account of the coastal region of southwestern India noted for its maritime trade; one of the earliest areas of contact between India and Europe.

390

Swaminathan, K. D. *The Nayakas of Ikkeri*. Madras: P. Varadachary, 1957. A study of a petty Hindu kingdom located south and east of Goa arising after the fall of the Vijayanagar Empire and maintaining its independence until 1763.

391

Raja, P. K. S. *Mediaeval Kerala*. Annamalainagar: Annamalai University, 1953. A survey of the political and institutional history of Kerala from the ninth to the eighteenth century with special attention to administration and social life.

MUSLIM PERIOD 1206-1707

Although Arab Muslims conquered the lower Indus valley region of Sind in 712, the forces of Islam did not penetrate the Hindu heartland until the 12th century. During the intervening centuries the banner of Islam passed to such Turkish rulers as Mahmud of Ghazni, who ruled in the region known today as Afghanistan. Mahmud led many raids into northern India during the 11th century leaving his heirs with tenuous control of the Punjab. The Ghaznavide dynasty was succeeded by another Turk, Muhammad of Ghor, who captured Delhi in 1193 and appointed a viceroy to govern the Indian portion of his domain. In 1206, Delhi became an independent power known as the Sultanate of Delhi; it was the first Muslim power based in India. Consequently, the year 1206 is often used to designate the beginning of the Muslim period in India. A succession of militant and resourceful leaders extended the Sultanate's control over much of northern India. During the 13th century Delhi became a refuge for Muslims fleeing the ravages of Chinghiz Khan's Mongols in Persia and adjacent lands. Persian savants and men of letters were welcome in Delhi where their talents and Persian culture set the tone of court life. Numerous dynasties of ethnically diverse origin ruled during the Delhi Sultanate, including the Lodis of Afghan descent whose defeat by Babur in 1526 led to the founding of the Mughal Empire. The Mughals reigned as the paramount power in India until the early 18th century when the waning of Mughal authority gave rise to an extended struggle among native and foreign aspirants for political supremacy, a contest ultimately decided in favor of the British. Although the term Muslim is often used to describe the period of Indian history sketched above, it should be noted that Muslim cultural and religious influences did not affect all classes and regions to the same degree. The majority of the people were Hindus, and many Hindu rulers remained independent or exercised considerable autonomy during this period. The Hindu kingdom of Vijayanagar ruled much of South India from 1336 to 1565 and the Rajput chieftains of Rajasthan were never completely subdued. Although Muslims predominated in the upper classes of many regions, schisms within this military aristocracy were common, leading to the formation of such independent powers as the Bahmani dynasty that ruled central India from 1347 to 1526. Due to the ethnic diversity of the Muslims their cultural contributions to the Indian scene were often a consequence of their Arab, Turk, Afghan, or Persian heritage rather than of their religion. Islam itself underwent a major transformation in India, notably the acceptance of caste practices within the Muslim community that ran counter to the basic tenets of Islam. A discussion of Islam in India, with appropriate references, appears below under *Religion* and *Philosophy*.

General Works

392

Smith, Vincent (ed.). *The Oxford History of India*. Oxford: Clarendon Press, rev. ed., 1958. Chapters on the Muslim period provide a ready reference to the principal events and personages of the time.

393

Sharma, Sri Ram. *The Crescent in India*. Bombay: Hind Kitabs, 2nd ed., rev., 1954. A useful survey of Muslim rule in India from the eighth to the eighteenth century, principally concerned with political history; in part an abridgement of the author's *Mughal Empire in India*.

394

Spear, Percival. *India*. Ann Arbor: University of Michigan Press, 1961. Spear's chapters on the Muslim period provide a lucid and perceptive overview seldom found in more detailed histories where the enumeration of events tends to obscure the distinctive features of the period.

395

Prasad, Ishwari. *History of Mediaeval India*. Allahabad: Indian Press, 3rd ed., 1933. A standard work which surveys events from 647 to the early sixteenth century. Based almost entirely on Muslim chronicles of kings and court life. Political developments are viewed as mainly due to Hindu-Muslim conflict, with some bias in favor of the Hindus.

396

Panikkar, Kavalam Madhava. *A Survey of Indian History*. New York: Asia Publishing House, rev. ed., 1962. Panikkar's discussion of the Muslim period contains many provocative interpretations, especially his account of the Hindu resistance to Muslim conquest.

397

Lane-Poole, Stanley. *Mediaeval India Under Mohammedan Rule*. 2 vols. Calcutta: Susil Gupta, paperbound, 1951. First published in 1903; though somewhat out-dated and prejudiced, this work provides a useful introductory history centered about Muslim courts and kings from 712 to 1764.

398

Roolvink, R. and others. *Historical Atlas of the Muslim People*. Cambridge: Harvard University Press, 1958. A useful reference in which Islam in India may be seen as part of a broader historical phenomenon.

Special Studies

399

Moreland, William H. *The Agrarian System of Moslem India*. Cambridge: W. Heffer, 1929. An authoritative account of the Muslim land revenue system from the 12th to the 18th century; provides an interesting analysis of economic factors affecting the decline of Muslim power in India.

400

Ahmad, Muhammad Basheer. *The Administration of Justice in Mediaeval India*. Aligarh: Aligarh University Historical Research Institute, 1941. A study of the Muslim judicial system based mainly upon records of court cases tried between 1206 and 1750.

401

Husain, Wahid. *Administration of Justice During the Muslim Rule in India*. Calcutta: University of Calcutta, 1934. An account of the Muslim judiciary in India and its relation to earlier Islamic legal institutions.

402

Jaffar, S. M. *Education in Muslim India*. Peshawar: S. M. Sadiq Khan, 1936. A standard work on Muslim educational institutions and practices in India to the 19th century.

403

Husain, Yusaf. *Glimpses of Medieval Indian Culture*. Bombay: Asia Publishing House, 1957. A useful though brief examination of Islamic influence on such aspects of Indian life and thought as mysticism, bhakti cults, education, language, and social and economic conditions.

404

Qureshi, Ishtiaq H. *The Muslim Community of the Indo-Pakistan Subcontinent*. New York: Columbia University, Near and Middle East Institute, 1960. A survey of the origin and development from 610 to 1947 of major values shared by Muslims in India.

405

Nizami, Khaliq Ahman. *Studies in Medieval Indian History*. Vol. I. Aligarh: Cosmopolitan Publishers, 1956. The first in a projected series of monographs, edited by Nizami, concerning all aspects of medieval Indian history; this volume, a collection of brief essays on the Sultanate period, is of little use to the general reader.

406

Sherwani, Haroon Khan. *Studies in Muslim Political Thought and Administration*. Lahore: Sh. Muhammad Ashraf, 3rd ed., rev., 1959. A collection of scholarly essays on the Muslim period by an authority on the subject.

Regional Studies

407

Commissariat, M. Sorabshah. *A History of Gujarat*. 3 vols. Bombay: Orient Longmans, 1938–57. One of the best regional histories for the Muslim period. Volume I survey events in Gujarat from 1297 to 1573, volume II continues the narrative to 1758 with emphasis on Mughal influence, volume III reviews the period covered in volume II with special attention given to the role of European trading companies and the Marathas in Gujarat affairs.

408

Misra, Satish Chandra. *The Rise of Muslim Power in Gujarat*. New York: Asia Publishing House, 1963. A historical study of the Muslim penetration of an important area of trade and commerce in western India during the years 1298 to 1442.

409

Qanungo, Kalika Ranjan. *Studies in Rajput History*. Delhi: S. Chand, 1960. A brief sketch of a little-known aspect of Indian history by one of India's leading historians. Rajasthan was a bastion of Hinduism during the period of Muslim rule.

410

Tod, James. *Annals and Antiquities of Rajasthan*. 2 vols. London: Routledge, Kegan Paul, 1957–60. Tod's account, based mainly on oral tradition and native history, provides a Rajput view of Muslim policy far different from what appears in the Muslim court chronicles.

411

Sherwani, Harun Khan. *The Bahmanis of the Deccan*. London: Luzac, 1953. An excellent history of a Muslim dynasty that ruled as an independent power in central India from 1347 to 1526.

412

Husaini, Abdul Qadir. *Bahman Shah*. Calcutta: K. L. Mukhopadhyay, 1959. A useful account of the founder of the Bahmani kingdom in the area of central India known as the Deccan.

413

Akbar, Muhammad. *The Punjab Under the Mughals*. Lahore: Ripon Press, 1948. A political history of the Punjab from 1555 to 1707 with some information on social and economic conditions; this region gave rise to the Sikhs, who fought vigorously against Muslim rule.

414

Sarkar, Jadunath (ed.) *History of Bengal*. Volume II. Dacca: Dacca University Press, 1948. This second volume in the two volume *History of Bengal* provides an excellent account of Bengal during Muslim times.

415

Karim, Abdul. *Social History of the Muslims in Bengal*. Dacca: Asiatic Society of Pakistan, 1959. An account of the customs, kinship practices, and related characteristics of the Muslim community in the eastern part of India prior to the Mughal empire.

416

Krishnaswami Aiyangar, Sakottai. *South India and Her Muhammadan Invaders*. London: Oxford University Press, 1921. A classic work, though somewhat out-dated, of the expansion of Islamic influence and political control into the far reaches of peninsular India.

417

Sathianathaier, R. *Tamilaham in the 17th Century*. Madras: University of Madras, 1956. An account of political events following the battle of Talikota in 1565 when the Muslims undermined Vijayanagar power; European missionary activities in South India during the 17th century are also described.

418

Roolvink, R. and others. *Historical Atlas of the Muslim Peoples*. Cambridge: Harvard University Press, 1958. This excellent reference provides a pictorial overview of the variegated and frequently shifting pattern of Muslim power in India and the relation of this pattern to general historical developments in the Muslim world.

Translations of Chronicles and Other Muslim Works

In contrast to Ancient India, the Muslim period abounds with source material in such forms as court chronicles, biographies, and travel accounts. Much of this literature was written in highly ornate Persian, the language of court life and the upper classes, replete with religious idiom. The reliability of these accounts varies greatly; some were written to please a patron, often a king desiring the perpetuation of ancestral glory or his own achievements. Other "histories" sought to convey a moral message with events from the past serving primarily to illustrate religious truth.

The fortunes of kings and events of court life receive the most attention in accounts of this period. This interest reflects a view of history in which kings are seen as the major determinants of change. Social and economic conditions receive scant attention and descriptions of the common man are rare.

The translations cited below are ordered according to date of composition, however, many of them contain a survey of earlier times often based on an uncritical acceptance of prior works.

419

Taraporevala, V. D. B. and D. N. Marshall. *Mughal Bibliography*. Bombay: New Book Co., 1962. An annotated bibliography of selected Persian manuscripts relating to Mughal India; information is provided concerning the location of manuscripts and the availability of published texts and translations.

420

Lane-Poole, Stanley (ed.). *Medieval India from Contemporary Sources*. Bombay: K. & J. Cooper, 2nd ed., 1920. A well-selected collection of brief extracts from Arabic and Persian chronicles and European travellers' accounts from 1000 to 1764.

421

Al-Idrisi. *India and the Neighbouring Territories*. Leiden: E. I. Brill, 1960. A translation of excerpts from the *Nuzhat-ul-Mushtak*, a geography of the early 12th century written by an Arab residing in Sicily, based on earlier works and travellers' accounts.

422

Al Biruni. *Alberuni's India*, 2 vols. Trans. by E. C. Sachau. London: Trübner, 1910. A translation of the *Tarikh-ul-Hind*, a primary source for North India of the early 11th century. The author, a famous savant of his day, was a native of Khwarizm; he resided in India for several years in the service of Mahmud of Ghazni. This account is especially valuable for the information it provides on Hindu science, literature, and religion. Excerpts appear in volume 5 of entry 440.

423

Siraj, Minhaj-us. *Tabaqat-i-Nasiri*. Trans. by H. G. Raverty. Calcutta: Royal Asiatic Society of Bengal, 1881. A general history of the Muslim world completed in 1260 by an eye witness to Muhammad of Ghor's conquest of North India. The author held a high office in the Delhi Sultanate and his account is a major source for the early history of this dynasty. Volume 16 of entry 440 contains selections from this work.

424

Khusrau, Hazrat Amir. *The Campaigns of Alauddin Khilji*. Trans. by M. Habib. Madras: University of Madras, 1931. A translation of the *Khazain-ul-Futuh*, the only extant source for Alauddin's reign from 1296 to 1316. The author was court poet from 1290 to 1325, a post that enabled him to witness many of the events in his account. Khusrau's florid style reflects his primary interest in literary effect and the pleasing of his patron, rather than a dispassionate recording of history. Volume 22 of entry 440 contains excerpts from this work.

425

Habib, Muhammad and A. U. S. Khan. *The Political Theory of the Delhi Sultanate*. Allahabad: Kitab Mahal, 1961. Contains the first translation into English of Zia-ud-din Barani's *Fatawah-i-Jahandari*, a treatise of the early 14th century in which the author presents an ideal political code for Muslim rulers to follow in matters sacred and secular; a biography of Barani is also included.

426

Ibn Batuta. *Ibn Batuta's Travels*. 3 vols. Trans. by H. A. R. Gibb. London: Hakylut Society, 1929–62. Two of the proposed three volumes have been published. This is an abridged translation of the *Kitab-ur-Rahlah*, a valuable description of 14th century India. The author, a learned scholar of Morocco, reached India in 1333 and returned to his home in North Africa in 1353. Ibn Batuta was appointed Qazi of Delhi by Muhammad-bin-Tughlaq and held this judicial post for eight years. A substantial selection from the India portion of Batuta's account appears in volume 30 of entry 440.

427

Sirhindi, Yahiya A. *The Tarikh-i-Mubarakshahi*. Trans. by K. K. Basu. Baroda: Gaekwad's Oriental Series, No. LXIII, 1932. The only extant contemporary account of the early 15th century Sayyid Dynasty of Delhi; this work ends in 1434, the dynasty continued to 1451. Excerpts from this work appear in volume 29 of entry 440.

428

Babur. *Memoirs of Babur*. 2 vols. Trans. by Annette S. Beveridge. London: Luzac, 1922. A translation of the *Babur Nama* based on the Turki manuscript preserved in Hyderabad. A revealing account of the personality and achievements of the 16th century founder of the Mughal empire; Babur emerges from this account a cultivated and observant poet as well as a roistering soldier of fortune. This translation is generally held to be superior to the Leyden and Erskine translation cited in the following entry. Excerpts from Babur's memoirs appear in volume 12 of entry 440.

429

Babur. *Memoirs of Babar*. Trans. by J. Leyden and W. Erskine, edited by L. King. London: Oxford University Press, rev. ed., 1921. First published in 1826, this translation is based on a Persian version prepared in 1589 by Abdur Rahim, instructed by Akbar to translate the memoirs from the original Turki into Persian. An abridged version of the 1826 edition was edited by F. G. Talbot and published in London by A. L. Humphreys in 1909.

430

Gulbadan Begam. *Life and Memoirs of Gulbadan Begam*. Trans. by Annette S. Beveridge. London: Royal Asiatic Society, 1902. Also known as *Humayun Namah* or *Gulbadan Namah*; one of the few accounts of Mughal times by a woman. The author, a daughter of Babur, lived from about 1523 to 1603. Most of her memoir concerns the trials and tribulations of her brother Humayun. While political events find a place in this narrative, its primary value lies in the description of court life and social customs as experienced by a woman of noble birth.

431

Abul Fazl. *Akbar Namah*. 3 vols. Trans. by Henry Beveridge. Calcutta: Royal Asiatic Society of Bengal, 1897–1921. An official chronicle commissioned by Akbar, it traces Mughal history from Timur to the author's assassination in 1602. The reigns of Akbar and his father, Humayun, are treated in greatest detail. Although the author's adulation of Akbar is reflected in matters of opinion and interpretation, this work is a valuable source for dates and other factual information. A less complete translation is cited as volume 9 of entry 440.

432

Abul Fazl. *Ani-i-Akbari*. 3 vols. Trans. by H. F. Blockman and H. S. Jarrett. Calcutta: Royal Asiatic Society of Bengal, 1873–96. Volume I was revised by D. C. Phillott in 1939, volumes II and III were revised by J. Sarkar in 1948–49; these revisions were published by the Society. This work, submitted to Akbar in 1593, was prepared as an appendix to the *Akbar Namah*. It provides a detailed statistical account of Akbar's administration and is one of the main sources of information on Mughal government in the 16th century. The author actively participated in developing many of the institutions that he describes. Information on contemporary Hinduism and Islam is also included.

433

Badauni, Abdul Qadir. *Muntakhab-ut-Tawarikh.* 3 vols. Trans. by G. S. A. Ranking, W. H. Lowe, and T. W. Haig. Calcutta: Royal Asiatic Society of Bengal, 1884–1925. This work, also known as *Tarikh-i-Badauni,* was completed in 1596 by a member of Akbar's court who disliked Akbar's unorthodox religious ideas. Badauni's critical view of Akbar provides a useful corrective and supplement to Abul Fazl's eulogistic account in the *Akbar Namah.* Badauni also provides biographical sketches of contemporary Muslim scholars and theologians. Volume 10 of entry 440 contains selections from this work.

434

Bakhshi, Nizamuddin Ahmad. *Tabaqat-i-Akbari.* 3 vols. Trans. by B. De. Calcutta: Royal Asiatic Society of Bengal, 1927–1939. Also known as *Tarikh-i-Nizami;* an arid non-official history of Islamic rule in India to the thirty-ninth year of Akbar's reign. Written in the latter part of the 16th century by Akbar's military secretary, whose orthodox views apparently prompted him to omit any reference to Akbar's unorthodox religious activities. A less complete translation appears as volumes 6 and 7 of entry 440.

435

Firishta, Muhammad Kasim. *History of the Rise of Muhammadan Power in India.* Trans. by J. Briggs. Calcutta: Susil Gupta, 1958. This is part of a proposed eight-volume reprint of the four-volume edition published by R. Cambray of Calcutta in 1908–10. Firishta's history, known as the *Tarikh-i-Firishta* or *Gulshan-i-Ibrahimi,* was completed in the early 17th century. Most of this work consists of an uncritical selection of materials from earlier chronicles with some information concerning Deccan affairs based on personal experience. A translation of Firishta's introduction to this work appears in volume 11 of entry 440.

436

Jahangir. *Memoirs of Jahangir.* 2 vols. Trans. by A. Rogers, edited by H. Beveridge. London: Royal Asiatic Society, 1909–1914. Commonly known as the *Tuzuk-i-Jahangiri.* A candid account of Jahangir's personal life, including his vices as well as his virtues, and the important events that occurred during the early years of his reign that began in 1605 and ended in 1627. Excerpts may be found in volume 8 of entry 440.

437

Khan, Saqui Mustad. *Maasir-i-Alamgiri.* Trans. by J. Sarkar. Calcutta: Royal Asiatic Society of Bengal, 1947. A highly condensed history of Aurangzeb's reign written by a member of Aurangzeb's court who witnessed many of the events described. The author relies heavily on Muhammad Kasim's *Alamgir Namah* for the first ten years of the reign.

438

Aurangzeb. *Letters of Aurangzebe* (Rukaat-i-Alamgiri). Trans. by J. H. Bilimoria. London: Luzac, 1908. A collection of letters written by Aurangzeb to his officers and sons while engaged in military campaigns in the Deccan from 1683 to 1707. Most of the letters concern personal affairs with an occasional reference to minor historical events.

439

Sarkar, Jadunath. *Anecdotes of Aurangzeb.* Calcutta: M. C. Sarkar, 2nd ed., 1925. A translation, with commentary, of contemporary accounts revealing much of the personality of the last great Mughal.

440

Elliot, Henry M. (ed.). *A History of India as Told by Its Own Historians.* 8 vols. Edited and continued by John Dowson. London: Trübner, 1867–77. Calcutta: Susil Gupta, paperbound, 31 vols., 1952–59. The 31-volume edition by S. Gupta appears to be a fairly complete reprint of the earlier edition, although the sequence of articles has been changed and some editorial comments deleted. This monumental compilation of translations by various hands provides ready access to a vast amount of source material from the 9th to the 19th century, culled from court chronicles, travel accounts, biographies, and similar works written mainly in Persian and Arabic. Although the translations vary greatly in quality and completeness, and the general reader will find few guidelines through the maze of names and events, no other collection of this scope has been published. A detailed critique of this compilation is cited in entry 441. The notations presented below refer to the S. Gupta edition.

Vol. 1. *Aurangzeb* by Khafi Khan, Muhammad Hashim. This contemporary account of Aurangzeb's reign is taken from the *Muntakham-ut-Lubab,* a history of Mughal rule from 1519 to 1733. It is one of the few histories of the period as Aurangzeb prohibited the preparation of official court chronicles. The author, a Mughal official, enlivens his account with personal observations and information obtained from participants in the events he describes. This work, written between 1717 and 1733, includes an account of Khafi Khan's experience as an envoy from the Muslim Viceroy of Gujarat to the English at Bombay. Volume 3, cited below, is a continuation of this translation.

Vol. 2. *Autobiography of Timur* and *Zafar Nama* of Sharaf-ud-din. These excerpts from Timur's memoirs, *Malfuzat-i-Timuri* or *Tuzak-i-Timuri,* and Sharaf-ud-din's biography of Timur, describe the battles and related military activities of Timur during his invasion of India in 1398.

Vol. 3. *Later Moghuls* by Khafi Khan, Muhammad Hashim. A continuation of the account begun in volume 1 cited above. This volume covers the period from the accession in 1707 of Shah Alam Badhshah (Bahadur Shah) to the 14th regnal year (1733) of Muhammad Shah. Events arising from court intrigues are the major concern of this volume. Elliot's preface is an interesting example of the view of Muslim rule held by many English historians.

Vol. 4 *Sher Shah* by Abbas Khan Sharwani. An extensive translation of the *Tarikh-i-Sher Shahi,* a biography completed about 1579 at Akbar's behest. The author, a distant relative of Sher Shah, appears to have interviewed officials who served Sher Shah during his brief period of power from 1540 to 1545. Sharwani tends to discount earlier accounts praising Sher Shah's accomplishments and character. See entry 488 for a different view of Sher Shah.

Vol. 5. *Subuktigin* by Abdul Fazl Al Baihaki. More than half of this volume is a translation of the *Tarikh-us-Subuktigin,* an account written in the 10th century about the founder of the Yamini dynasty in Ghazni. Subuktigin's son, Mahmud, led the first major thrust of Muslim power into the Hindu heartland. Another selection, the *Kitab-ul-Yamini* of Al Utbi, is a literary rather than historical account of Mahmud's forays into India down to 1020. A brief excerpt from Al Beruni's *Tarikh-ul-Hind,* concerning the pre-Muslim kings of Kabul is also included. See entry 422 for a more complete translation of Al Beruni's work.

Volumes 6 and 7. *Akbar* by Nizam-ud-din Ahmad. Excerpts from the *Tabakat-i-Akbari,* a chronicle of political events from the early Sultans of Delhi to the 38th year of Akbar's reign, written in 1592–93 by a member of Akbar's court. This work is generally considered to be one of the most reliable histories of Akbar's reign. A more complete translation is cited in entry 434.

Vol. 8. *Memoirs of Jahangir.* Excerpts from various versions of the memoirs of a Mughal emperor who ruled from 1605 to 1627. An appendix contains some of Jahangir's proclamations on commercial taxes and related matters with excerpts from European merchants' accounts that indicate the Mughal regulation of commerce differed markedly from what is implied in Jahangir's statements. Entry 436 cites a more complete translation of Jahangir's memoirs.

Vol. 9. *Akbar-Nama* by Abul Fazl. Excerpts from a eulogistic account of Akbar's reign, 1556 to 1605, when the Mughal empire reached its greatest heights. Additional information on this official chronicle appears under entry 431.

Vol. 10. *Akbar* by Badauni. A partial translation of the *Tarikh-i-Badauni,* a general history of Muslim rule from the 12th century to the 40th year of Akbar's reign; brief excerpts from other contemporary accounts of Akbar's reign are also included. Entry 433 cites a more complete translation of Badauni's work.

Vol. 11. *Studies in Indian History,* Part I. This volume contains a full translation of the introduction to the *Tarikh-i-Firishta,* completed in 1606. Also included are two essays by Elliot on the "Early Use of Gunpowder in India," and an analysis of Amir Khusrau's poems; Khusrau was court poet from 1290–1325. Entry 435 cites a more complete translation of Firishta's work.

Vol. 12. *Babar and Humayun.* Entries 428 and 430 cite more complete translations of material concerning Babar, founder of the Mughal empire, and his son Humayun.

Vol. 13. *Shahjahan.* Excerpts from eight biographies of the Mughal who ruled from 1628 to 1658. Several of these accounts were read and amended by Shahjahan, so they provide some of the advantages as well as the disadvantage of an autobiography.

Vol. 14. *The Later Kings of Delhi.* Excerpts from Zia-uddin Barani's *Tarikh-i-Firuz Shahi,* an unmethodical and careless history of the Delhi Sultans written primarily to illustrate religious truths; completed in 1357. The highly interpretative nature of Barani's work sets it apart from the writings of other early Indian historians. Several relatives of Barani held important posts under the Delhi Sultans.

Vol. 15. *Firoz Shah* by Shams-i-Siraj Afif. Fragments from the *Tarikh-i-Firoz Shahi,* an account of the reign of Firoz Tughluq, who ruled from 1351–88, by a courtier who wrote this work after Timur's sack of Delhi in 1398. Afif wrote in a vein usually reserved for the pious biographies of Muslim holy men.

Vol. 16. *Ghazanivide, Ghor and Slave Dynasties.* A translation of part of the *Tabqat-i-Nasiri* by Minhaj-us-Siraj, a high official in the early Delhi Sultanate. Completed in 1260, this work contains first-hand information on the Muslim conquests in North India. Volume 18 cited below contains notes on this work by the editors. Entry 423 cites a more complete translation.

Vol. 17. *Ghazanivide, Ghor and Slave Dynasties.* Translations of several contemporary accounts appear here including the *Tajul-Maasir* by Hasan Nizami who entered India during Muhammad Ghor's conquest of Delhi. Nizami's work relates events that occurred between 1192 and 1228. Muhammad Ghor's military exploits are also treated in the *Kamil-ut-Tawarikh* by Abdul Hasan, also known as Ibuul Asir, a Mesopotamian in the service of Muhammad Ghor. This account was completed in 1230. Excerpts are also included from the *Jami-ul-Hikayat* by Muhammad Ufi and the *Tarikh-i-Jahan Kusha* which describes forays into Ghazni by the Mongols of Chingiz Khan.

Vol. 18. *History of Ghazni.* Part I. This volume contains the editors' discussion of materials translated in volumes 16 and 17, with additional translations for the period; material relating to the Ghazanivides also appears in volume 22.

Vol. 19. *Studies in Indian History.* This volume consists in the main of excerpts from contemporary accounts of the 18th century when invasions from Persia, and internal rebellion undermined the Mughal Empire.

Vol. 20. *Studies in Indian History.* Part III. Translations from contemporary accounts of the 18th century; includes information on the Hindu Marathas who controlled much of the old Mughal domain at this time.

Vol. 21. *Studies in Indian History.* Part IV. Excerpts from numerous 18th-century accounts of various kingdoms that arose with the disintegration of Mughal rule; the British also appear in these accounts.

Vol. 22. *History of Ghazni.* Part. II. This volume consists in part of materials from the Ghazanivide period, but much of it concerns the early years of the Delhi Sultans, including excerpts from Amir Khusrau's *Khazain-ul-Futuh.* Entry 424 cites a more complete translation of Khusrau's work.

Vol. 23. *Afghan Dynasties.* A translation of the *Tarikh-i-Salatin-i-Afaghana* by Ahmad Yadgar who relates the dynastic fortunes of the Lodis and Surs, Afghan Sultans of Delhi in the 15th century. This work was written a century later during Akbar's reign. Part of the *Tarikh-i-Khan-Jahan Lodi* by Niamatullah also describing events of the Lodi dynasty appears here. It was written in the 17th-century reign of Jahangir. Other materials concerning the Afghan period appear in volume 28.

Vol. 24. *Early Arab Geographers.* Excerpts, mainly relating to Sind, are here translated from the work of nine Arab geographers of the 9th and 10th centuries. Entry 421 cites a more complete translation of one of these accounts, that of al-Idrisi.

Vol. 25. *Historians of Sind.* Part I. The *Chach-Nama,* a contemporary account of the eighth-century Arab conquest of Sind, is represented here as well as excerpts from the *Tarikh-i-Sindh* by Mir Muhammad Masum. The latter work, written about 1600, relates the history of Sind from the Arab invasion to Akbar's time.

Vol. 26. *Historians of Sind.* Part II. This volume contains translations from various histories of Sind after the Arab conquest in the 8th century; Sind remained relatively independent of the political powers based in Delhi until Akbar's reign in the 16th century. A discussion by the editors of place names mentioned by the early Arab geographers also appears here.

Vol. 27. *Historians of Sind.* Part III. This volume comprises the historial, ethnological and miscellaneous portion of the editor's discussion of translations relating to Sind presented in volumes 24–26.

Vol. 28. *Studies in Indian History.* Part V. The translations comprising this volume concern the 15th century Afghan dynasty of the Delhi Sultanate.

Vol. 29. *Studies in Indian History.* Part VI. Materials translated in this volume range from the 15th century Afghan Sultans of Delhi to the declining years of the Mughal empire in the 18th century; included are excerpts from the *Tarikh-i-Mubarak Shahi* by Yahia bin Ahmed Sirhindi, the only contemporary source on the Sayyid dynasty that ruled in Delhi during the first half of the 15th century. A more complete translation of Sirhindi's work is cited under entry 427.

Vol. 30. *Studies in Indian History.* Part VII. This is a companion to volumes 1, 3, & 13; it contains excerpts from contemporary accounts of the last phase of Mughal power in the 18th century. Also included is a substantial selection from the 14th century travel account of Ibn Batuta. Entry 426 cites a more complete translation of Batuta's work.

Vol. 31. *Studies in Indian History.* Part VIII.

441

Hodivala, Shahpurshah H. *Studies in Indo-Muslim History.* 2 vols. Bombay: Popular Book Depot, 1939–57. A systematic critique of the contents of Elliot and Dowson's *History of India;* Hodivala rectifies errors of transliteration and interpretation, clarifies questions of chronology, and corrects the names of persons and places.

Sultanate of Delhi   1206-1526

When Delhi broke free of the kingdom of Ghor in 1206, the Delhi viceroy was of slave origin due to the Turkish custom of training captured children of noble birth for government positions. Consequently, the first Sultans of Delhi are often referred to as the "Slave dynasty" though they came from the Turkish ruling class. They laid the foundation of Muslim power, kept out the Mongols, and destroyed the last vestiges of Buddhism in India. The brief reign of the Khilji dynasty, 1296 to 1320, saw Muslim armies penetrate South India and Rajasthan. Their successors, the Tughluqs, achieved military supremacy over much of India in the second quarter of the 14th century, but schisms and revolts soon fragmented their empire. In 1398 the Mongols under Timur sacked Delhi leaving the Sultanate a shattered power rent by factions during the following century. Babur, a descendant of Timur, entered India and defeated the Afghan Sultans of Delhi in 1526. However, Babur's son, Humayun, was driven from India by the Afghan Sher Shah who revived the sultanate for a brief period. In 1555 Babur's son re-established a base in North India upon which his son, Akbar, was to erect the Mughal empire.

GENERAL WORKS

442

Majumdar, Ramesh C. (ed.). *The Struggle for Empire.* Volume V of *The History and Culture of the Indian People.* Bombay: Bharatiya Vidya Bhavan, 1957. A history of the period from about 1000 to 1300; a time of political turmoil and instability brought about by the invasions of Muslim Turks and the decline of Hindu kingdoms in North India. An account is also given of the independent kingdoms of South and Central India. Separate chapters are provided for the literature, art, and social conditions of the period.

443

Haig, Sir Wolseley (ed.). *Turks and Afghans.* Vol. III of *The Cambridge History of India.* New York: Macmillan, 1928. A standard detailed account of the 8th to the early 16th century period of Muslim rule in India. Although most of this work concerns the Sultanate of Delhi, several chapters describe the Hindu kingdoms of South India and other rulers beyond the Sultanate's control including those in Burma and Ceylon. Apart from a chapter on monuments of the period, most attention is given to political history.

444

Srivastava, Ashirbadi Lal. *The Sultanate of Delhi.* Agra: Shiv Lal Agarwala, 2nd ed. rev., 1953. A survey of Muslim power in India from 711 to 1526 in which Muslim rule and influence are viewed as detrimental to the cultural traditions and national interests of the Hindus. Much of the analysis attempts to explain how the Muslims conquered India and why Hinduism was unable to absorb Islam.

445

Habibullah, A. B. M. *The Foundation of Muslim Rule in India.* Allahabad: Central Book Depot, 2nd ed., rev., 1961. A standard history of the Sultanate of Delhi in the 13th century.

446

Haq, Syed Moinul. *A Short History of the Sultanate of Delhi.* Karachi: H. M. Said, 3rd ed., 1956. A sketchy survey, pro-Muslim in orientation, of political events

from the Arab conquest of Sind in the eighth century to the early 16th century; prepared for university students.

SPECIAL STUDIES

447

Hardy, Peter. *Historians of Medieval India.* London: Luzac, 1960. A novel departure from the narration of political events common to most historical writings on medieval India. Hardy examines the underlying assumptions and world-view of five Muslim historians whose works, written from about 1350 to 1550, are major sources for the Sultanate period.

448

Nazim, Muhammad. *Sultan Mahmud of Ghazna.* Cambridge University Press, 1931. A chronicle of events in the life of a twelfth-century Muslim invader whose campaigns in India are portrayed as part of a deliberate plan of political expansion rather than as looting expeditions or attempts at religious conversion.

449

Ahmad, Muhammad Aziz. *The Early Turkish Empire of Delhi.* Lahore: Muhammad Ashraf, 1949. A detailed account of the political history and institutions of the Delhi Sultans in the 13th century; Muslim rule is here viewed as a boon to the peasantry.

450

Lal, S. K. *History of the Khalijis.* Allahabad: Indian Press, 1950. A useful account of a Turkish dynasty that extended the Sultanate of Delhi into Rajasthan and South India from 1290 to 1320.

451

Husain, Agha Mahdi. *The Rise and Fall of Muhammad-bin-Tughluq.* London: Luzac, 1938. An excellent account of the reign, from 1325 to 1351, of one of the most eccentric and militant of the Turkish sultans of Delhi, who carried Islam and his rule deep into South India; the major chronicles for the Turkish period are cited in this work.

452

Haq, Syed Moinul. *Barani's History of the Tughluqs.* Karachi: Pakistan Historical Society, 1959. A concise and lucid critique of those parts of the *Tarikh-i-Firuz-Shahi* by Barani concerning the Tughluq dynasty that fell in the 14th century. Factors affecting Barani's interpretations of events, many of which he witnessed, are the main subject of this study.

453

Pandey, Awadh Bihari. *The First Afghan Empire in India (1451–1526 A.D.).* Calcutta: Bookland, 1956. An account of the Lodi dynasty that maintained tenuous control over a loose confederacy of Afghan chieftains ranging from Bengal to the Punjab.

454

Rahim, Muhammad A. *History of the Afghans in India; 1541–1631.* Karachi: Pakistan Publishing House, 1961. A study of the Afghans after their brief period of ascendancy in North India, with particular attention given to their relations with the Mughals.

455

Qureshi, Ishtiaq Husain. *The Administration of the Sultanate of Delhi.* Karachi: Pakistan Historical Society, 4th ed., rev., 1958. First published in 1942; a standard work covering the period from 1206 to 1555. Qureshi views Muslim rule as tolerant and beneficial for most of the Hindu subjects.

456

Tripathi, Ram Prasad. *Some Aspects of Muslim Administration.* Allahabad: Central Book Depot, 1956. First published in 1936. A scholarly work with coverage down to Akbar's reign, with most attention given to the Sultanate period; contains a useful discussion of the Turko-Mughal theory of kingship.

457

Day, U. N. *Administrative System of Delhi Sultanate.* Allahabad: Kitab Mahal, 1959. A relatively brief survey of the Sultanate's administrative system from 1206 to 1413; prepared for use as an undergraduate text; pro-Muslim in its view of the period.

458

Karim, Abdul. *Social History of the Muslims in Bengal.* Dacca: Asiatic Society of Pakistan, 1959. An account of the customs, kinship practices, and related characteristics of the Muslim community in the eastern part of India prior to the Mughal empire.

459

Mirza, Mohammad Wahid. *The Life and Works of Amir Khusrau.* Calcutta: University of Calcutta, 1935. Amir Khusrau, 1253–1325, was a courtier in the Delhi Sultanate whose literary works in prose and poetry contain some information of historical value.

Mughal Empire   1526-1707

Babur, a descendant of Timur, the Mongol who sacked Delhi in 1398, was the founder of India's greatest Muslim dynasty. Though ethnically of Turkish derivation, Babur and his forces were called Mughals (Mongols) due to Babur's descent from Timur and the 16th Century Indian practice of identifying any invader from Central Asia by this name. Babur was a king in search of a kingdom and conditions in North India provided ample opportunity for his strong and forceful personality. Though opposed by Muslim and Hindu rulers, and often outnumbered in battle, dissension among the native rulers and Babur's well disciplined army enabled him to gain military supremacy in North India by 1526. However, Babur died before consolidating his power and his son Humayun was forced to flee India in 1543. In 1555, Humayun regained a foothold in Delhi from which his son Akbar was to stride forth across most of northern and central India. Akbar's forty-nine-year reign is noted not only for his conquests, but also for his administrative system that bound much of India under a central government. Akbar's success is often attributed to religious tolerance reflected in his appointment of Hindus to high positions and in his attempt to promote an eclectic religion that he hoped would reduce religious conflict among his subjects. Akbar's reign is also the period when Europe began to develop sustained contacts with India. The century following Akbar's death in 1605 was one of relative stability and prosperity. The empire reached its greatest extent under Aurangzeb, whose orthodox Muslim policies contributed to the disruption of empire that followed his death in 1707. Although the Mughal line continued for more than a century, invasions from Persia and Afghanistan coupled with internal revolt by Hindu Marathas, Muslim governors, and others, reduced the Emperor to a figurehead. After a century of political turmoil in which native and foreign powers sought to attain supremacy, the British emerged as the heirs to the Mughal throne.

GENERAL WORKS

460

Sharma, Sri Ram. *A Bibliography of Mughal India.* (1526–1707 A.D.). Bombay: Karnatak Publishing House, 1942. A valuable reference compiled by an outstanding student of the period.

461

Taraporevala, Vicaji D. B. and D. N. Marshall. *Mughal Bibliography.* Bombay: New Book Co., 1962. A select annotated bibliography of Persian sources for the Mughal period; organized by author with information on the date of composition, location of manuscripts, and translations available in English.

462

Burn, Sir Richard (ed.) *The Mughal Period.* Volume IV of *The Cambridge History of India.* New York: Macmillan, 1937. A detailed and authoritative enumeration of political events from Babur's founding of the Mughal empire in 1526 to the early 19th century. This work reflects to an unfortunate degree the court oriented view of history contained in the Persian chronicles upon which it is based.

463

Edwardes, Stephen M. and H. L. O. Garrett. *Mughal Rule in India.* Delhi: S. Chand, 1956. Reprint of a 1930 edidition by the Oxford Uinversity Press. A concise and authoritative survey addressed to the general reader; about half of this book consists of biographical sketches of the emperors. The remainder describes the administration, economy, society, art, and architecture of the entire period with a final chapter on reasons for the Mughal decline.

464

Srivastava, Ashirbadi Lal. *The Mughul Empire.* Agra: S. L. Agarwala, 2nd ed., rev., 1957. A useful survey of the principal features of the Mughal Empire from 1526–1803; prepared as a college text.

465

Tripathi, Ram Prasad. *Rise and Fall of the Mughal Empire.* Allahabad: Central Book Depot, 1956. 2nd ed. 1960. The first of three projected volumes on the subject; this work surveys the major political events from the time of Babur to Aurangzeb. Little attention is given to the part played by Europeans in this period.

466

Jaffar, S. M. *The Mughal Empire from Babur to Aurangzeb.* Peshawar: S. M. Sadiq Khan, 1936. A partisan view of Mughal rule as characterized by tolerance and progress greater than that of many European rulers of the time.

SPECIAL STUDIES

467

Sharma, Sri Ram. *Mughal Government and Administration.* Bombay: Hind Kitabs, 1951. One of the more successful attempts at a comprehensive survey of Mughal government practices from 1526 to 1707.

468

Sarkar, Jadunath. *Mughal Administration.* Calcutta: M. C. Sarkar, 4th ed., rev., 1952. A concise study of various branches of Mughal government including the role of the emperor and his court, with a review and appraisal of factors contributing to the downfall of the empire. The following entry contains a critique of Sarkar's interpretations.

469

Saran, Parmatma. *The Provincial Government of the Mughals.* Allahabad: Kitabistan, 1941. A study of provincial administration from 1526 to 1658. Saran characterizes J. Sarkar's work, cited in the previous entry, as an undeservedly dismal picture of Mughal administration in its effects on the people.

470

Ibn Hasan. *The Central Structure of the Mughal Empire.* London: Oxford University Press, 1936. An outline of the administrative system developed by Akbar. This is an enumeration of office holders' duties rather than an analytical study of Mughal government.

471

Irvine, William. *The Army of the Indian Moghuls.* New Delhi Eurasia Publishing House, reprint, 1962. First published in 1903 by Luzac, London. A classic work on the organization and administration of the Mughal army; describes tactics, equipment, ranks and pay, with brief accounts of some major battles. Much of this account concerns the reign of Aurangzeb and his successors.

472

Aziz, Abdul. *The Mansabdari System and the Mughal Army.* London: A. Probsthain, 1946. A description of organizational methods employed by the Mughals to raise and maintain troops. This is one of several works by Aziz on the Mughal court and its institutions.

473

Aziz, Abdul. *Arms and Jewellery of the Indian Mughals.* London: A. Probsthain, 1947. A description of arms and ornaments worn by emperors, nobles, and their harems; based on literary accounts of presents given at the Mughal court.

474

Raychaudhuri, Tapankumar. *Bengal Under Akbar and Jahangir; An Introductory Study in Social History.* Calcutta: A. Mukherjee, 1953. One of the few studies of social and economic conditions in Bengal during the late sixteenth century, with particular attention to the role of the "middle class."

475

Akbar, Muhammed. *The Punjab Under the Mughals.* Lahore: Ripon Printing Press, 1948. A description of social and economic life in northwestern India during the sixteenth and seventeenth centuries; based on Abul Fazl's *Ain-i-Akbari* and local chronicles.

476

Chopra, Pran Nath. *Some Aspects of Society and Culture During the Mughal Age.* Agra: S. L. Agarwala, 1955. A useful description of such rarely studied features of the period as food, dress, recreation, education, festivals, and the position of women; mainly based on the accounts of contemporary foreign travellers.

477

Yasin, Mohammad. *A Social History of Islamic India.* Lucknow; Upper India Publishing House, 1958. A sketchy account of the ethnic composition, religious customs, and economic life of the North Indian Muslim community from 1605 to 1748; mainly of interest as an expression of intellectual anguish by an Indian Muslim seeking to reconcile his religious heritage with demands of the twentieth century.

478

Roy Choudhury, Makhanlal. *The State and Religion in Mughal India.* Calcutta: Indian Publishing Society, 1951. A description of the religious background of the Mughal state with an evaluation of the influence on Mughal government of Islamic movements, in and outside India. Primacy is attributed to political and administrative considerations, rather than religious forces, in the shaping of Mughal policy.

479

Roy Choudhury, Makhanlal. *The Din-i-Ilahi.* Calcutta: University of Calcutta, 1941. An account of the eclectic religion developed during the 16th century under the auspices of the emperor Akbar in an attempt to reduce religious discord among his subjects. The religion died with Akbar.

480

Moreland, William H. *India at the Death of Akbar.* London: Macmillan, 1920. A classic study of economic conditions under the Mughals in the early 17th century; although much of this work is an apology for British policy, which is claimed to have created social and economic conditions superior to those during Mughal

times, Moreland's grasp of the subject has yet to be equaled.

481

Moreland, William H. *From Akbar to Aurangzeb.* London: Macmillan, 1923. A description of economic conditions in early 17th century India, based mainly on accounts of European merchants and travelers, especially Dutch records seldom used by historians prior to Moreland's efforts.

482

Habib, Irfan. *The Agrarian System of Mughal India, 1556–1707.* New York: Asia Publishing House, 1963. A readily available economic history, this does not supersede the work of W. H. Moreland cited above.

483

Sarkar, Jadunath. *The India of Aurangzib.* Calcutta: Bose Brothers, 1901. A comparison of the reigns of Aurangzib and Akbar, based on descriptions and statistics from Persian sources. Includes a partial translation of the *Chahar Gulshan.*

MODERN BIOGRAPHIES OF MUSLIM RULERS

484

Grenard, Fernand. *Baber, First of the Moguls.* Trans. and adapted by H. White and R. Glaenzer. New York: R. M. McBride, 1930. A popular account of the bold and resourceful founder of the Mughal empire; based on Babur's memoirs.

485

Williams, L. F. Rushbrook. *An Empire Builder of the 16th Century.* Delhi: S. Chand, reprint, 1962. This account of Babur, based mainly on his memoirs, remains one of the best introductions to the life and times of the founder of the Mughal Empire.

486

Lane-Poole, Stanley. *Babar.* Delhi: S. Chand, 1957. Reprint of an 1899 work in the Rulers of India series published by Oxford University Press; an account of Babur's life based mainly on Babur's memoirs, addressed to the general reader.

487

Edwardes, Stephen M. *Babur, Diarist and Despot.* London: A. M. Philpot, 1926. A brief popular sketch of Babur's character and experiences, mainly based on A. S. Beveridge's translation of Babur's *Memoirs.*

488

Zulfiqar Ali Khan. *Sher Shah Suri.* Lahore: Civil & Military Gazette, 1925. A popular account of an Afghan who controlled much of North India from 1540 to 1545, a period when succession to the Mughal throne was in dispute. Sher Shah, noted for his administrative reforms, is here portrayed as a benefactor of the people.

489

Prasad, Ishwari. *The Life and Times of Humayun.* Bombay: Orient Longmans, rev. ed., 1956. One of the best works on the subject; contains an excellent description and appraisal of primary and secondary sources for the first half of the 16th century.

490

Banerjee, S. K. *Humayun Badshah.* 2 vols. London: Oxford Press, 1938. An excellent account of the life and times of Humayun (1507–1556), whose troubled career was spent attempting to secure the empire left by his father, Babur; a struggle not resolved until the 20th year of the reign of Akbar, Humayun's son.

491

Smith, Vincent A. *Akbar, the Great Mogul.* Delhi: S. Chand & Co., 1958. A reprint of the 2nd rev. ed. published by Oxford University Press in 1919. Although marred by prejudice, this work remains the most comprehensive account of Akbar's life and times; covers the period from 1542 to 1604.

492

Shelat, Jayendra M. *Akbar.* Bombay: Bharatiya Vidya Bhavan, 1959. An account of Akbar's life and times by an Indian historian whose views provide an interesting contrast to those advanced by Smith in the preceding entry.

493

Binyon, Lawrence. *Akbar*. London: Nelson Press, 1939. A brief character sketch that presents Akbar in a more sympathetic light than V. Smith's more detailed work.

494

Kohli, P. *A Short History of Akbar*. Delhi: S. Chand, 1949. Primarily a compilation of extracts from more scholarly works organized to show variations in interpretation of Akbar's personality and administration.

495

Srivastava, Ashirbadi Lal. *A Short History of Akbar*. Agra: Shiva Lal Agarwala, 1957. A brief summary of the author's views on the subject, presented as a prelude to a more detailed three-volume work.

496

Prasad, Beni. *History of Jahangir*. London: Oxford University Press, 2nd ed., 1930. A critical study of the Mughal who ruled from 1605 to 1627; based on extensive use of original sources cited in a detailed bibliography.

497

Saksena, Banarsi Prasad. *History of Shah Jahan of Delhi*. Allahabad: Central Book Depot, reprint, 1962. An able account of the 17th century Mughal ruler whose reign is noted for such cultural achievements as the Taj Mahal; contains an excellent bibliography for the period.

498

Qanungo, Kalika Ranja. *Dara Shukoh*. Calcutta: S. C. Sarkar, 2nd ed., 1952. A scholarly account of the life and times of Shah Jahan's eldest son, who is noted for his philosophical interests and religious tolerance. Dara was executed in 1659 after losing a bitter struggle with his brother Aurangzeb for succession to the Mughal throne.

499

Sarkar, Jadunath. *History of Aurangzib*. 5 vols. Calcutta: M. C. Sarkar, 1912–25. All five volumes have passed through at least two editions including a revision of volume four in 1930. This is a monumental work based on original sources; the first two volumes concern the reign of Aurangzeb's father, Shah Jahan, the third volume describes Aurangzeb's political activities in North India from 1658 to 1681, volume four recounts his efforts to control South India from 1645 to 1689, and the final volume treats the last phase of Aurangzeb's life from 1698 to 1707.

500

Sarkar, Jadunath. *A Short History of Aurangzeb*. Calcutta: M. C. Sarkar, 3rd ed., rev., 1962. An abridged version of Sarkar's five volume work cited above; covers the period from 1618 to 1707.

501

Faruki, Zahir-un-din. *Aurangzeb and His Times*. Bombay: Taraporevala, 1935. A pro-Muslim interpretation in which Aurangzeb's repression of the Hindus is attributed to political rather than religious motives. This work attempts to counter the interpretations in J. Sarkar's books on Aurangzeb.

502

Lane-Poole, Stanley. *Aurangzib*. Delhi: S. Chand, 1957. A reprint of an 1896 publication in the *Rulers of India* series; this work remains one of the better introductions to Aurangzeb (1618–1707) and the decline of the Mughal empire.

EUROPEAN TRAVELLERS ACCOUNTS

Many European accounts of India have been published through the efforts of the Hakluyt Society, organized in 1846 for the purpose of printing and distributing rare volumes on voyages and travels. One hundred volumes, forming Series I, were issued from 1847 to 1898. Series II reached 115 volumes by 1961 and continues to grow. Volumes in print may be obtained from the Cambridge University Press.

Individual Accounts

503

Polo, Marco. *Marco Polo: The Description of the World*. 2 vols. Trans. by A. C. Moule and P. Pelliot. London: Routledge, 1938. A small portion of this famous travel account concerns Marco Polo's brief visit to a few ports of western India in 1294. A third volume containing notes and addenda may be published later.

504

Gama, Vasco da. *Journal of the First Voyage*. Trans. by E. G. Ravenstein. London: Hakluyt Society, Series I, vol. 99, 1898. An anonymous journal of Vasco da Gama's historic voyage to India in 1497. Part of the journal describes Calicut, a port on the southwest coast of India, and the reception tendered the Portuguese upon their arrival.

505

Albuquerque, Alfonso de. *The Commentaries of Albuquerque*. 4 vols. Ed. & trans. by W. Birch. London: Hakluyt Society, 1875–84. Valuable information on South India in the early 16th century is contained in this account by the bold and vigorous founder of Portuguese power in Asia.

506

Varthema, Ludovico di. *Travels*. Trans. by J. W. Jones. London: Hakluyt Society, Series I, vol. 32, 1863. A description of life on the southwest coast of India as observed by an Italian, who visited there from 1503 to 1508.

507

Barbosa, Duarte. *The Book of Duarte Barbosa*. 2 vols. Trans. by M. L. Dames. London: Hakluyt Society, 1918–21. Though the author's identity is uncertain, he is thought to be a Portuguese merchant who lived in South India from about 1500 to 1516. His description of the land and people, including an account of the Hindu kingdom of Vijayanagar, is held to be generally trustworthy.

508

Nuniz, Fernao. "Chronicle." Trans. by R. Sewell in *A Forgotten Empire*. London: S. Sonnenschein, 1900. An account by a Portuguese horse trader who resided in the kingdom of Vijayanagar from 1535–37. His chronicle of the Vijayanagar rulers is a major primary source for the history of this kingdom.

509

Linschoten, John Huyghen van. *Voyage*. 2 vols. London: Hakluyt Society, Series I, vols. 70, 71, 1885. Linschoten, a Dutchman, resided in Goa from 1583–1589 as a secretary to the Archbishop of Goa. Though his travels were limited to Goa, his account contains an extensive survey of the Portuguese commercial empire in Asia with a keen appraisal of the vulnerability of this empire that encouraged other European nations to venture into the area.

510

Monserrate, Antonio. *The Commentary of Father Monserrate*. Trans. & ed. by J. S. Hoyland and S. N. Banerji. London: Oxford University Press, 1922. An account of the first Jesuit mission from Goa to Akbar's court, written in 1582.

511

Roe, Sir Thomas. *The Embassy of Sir Thomas Roe to India*. Ed. by W. Foster. London: Oxford University Press, rev. ed., 1926. Roe, an experienced English diplomat, was sent by King James to negotiate a treaty with Jahangir to further the interests of English merchants seeking to participate in the India trade. Roe arrived in India in 1615 and remained at Jahangir's court for three years. The journal is mainly of value for his description of Mughal court life and appraisal of the political conditions of the day.

512

Moreland, William H. (ed.). *Relations of Golconda in the Early 17th Century*. London: Hakluyt Society, Series II, vol. 66, 1931. This book consists of three accounts or "relations" by Europeans engaged in trade on the east coast of India in present-day Andhra state. The first and principal account was written by William Methwold, an employee of the English East India Co. He describes the social and economic conditions of the independent Muslim kingdom of Golconda and the port of Masulipatam where he resided from 1618 to 1622. The other two accounts are by Dutch merchants who lived in the same area a decade earlier.

513

Valle, Pierto della. *The Travels of Pietro della Valle in India.* 2 vols. Ed. by E. Grey. London: Hakluyt Society, 1892. This highly educated and intelligent Italian visited India in 1623–24 in search of knowledge rather than riches. His descriptions of Portuguese coastal settlements and adjacent native territories, most of them outside Mughal control, are held to be very accurate and complete.

514

Pelsaert, Francisco. *Jahangir's India, The Remonstrantie of F. Pelsaert.* Trans. by W. H. Moreland and P. Geyl. Cambridge: W. Heffer, 1925. A Dutch merchant whose account includes a description of places that he visited from 1620 to 1627, including Agra, Lahore, and Kashmir. He also reports on contemporary Muslim and Hindu religious practices, and other aspects of everyday life. He mentions the existence of district courts of justice and regulations prohibiting cow slaughter.

515

Manrique, Sebastian. *The Travels of Sebastian Manrique.* 2 vols. Trans. & ed. by C. E. Luard & H. Hosten, London: Hakluyt Society, Series II, vols. 59 & 61, 1926–27. A Portuguese missionary who travelled over much of North India including Bengal and Lahore in the early 17th century. Although his report of political events is often inaccurate, he provides interesting glimpses of social life and the condition of the common people with considerable detail on the more horrendous aspects of popular Hinduism.

516

Mundy, Peter. *The Travels of Peter Mundy.* 5 vols. Ed. by R. C. Temple. London: Hakluyt Society, 1907–36. Mundy, an employee of the English East India Co. travelled in northern India from 1628 to 1634. His descriptions are held to be quite accurate of people, places, and conditions under the reign of Shah Jahan, including the severe famine of 1630 and the destruction of Hindu temples in Benares. However, his account of the Mughal system of government contains many errors.

517

Tavernier, Jean B. *Travels in India.* 2 vols. Trans. by V. Ball, ed. by W. Crooke. London: Oxford University Press, 2nd ed., 1925. Tavernier, a French jeweller, made six prosperous trips to India between 1641 and 1666, residing there about ten years. He visited many ports on the east and west coasts and obtained an audience with Aurangzeb in 1665. His description of cities, and of the social and economic conditions that he observed are considered to be trustworthy, though his account of political events is often inaccurate.

518

Fryer, Dr. John. *A New Account of East India and Persia.* 3 vols. Ed. by W. Crooke. London: Hakluyt Society, Series II, vols. 19, 20, 39, 1909–1915. Dr. Fryer visited India and Persia between 1672 and 1681. His travels in India were mainly along the south and west coasts with a brief trip inland near Goa. His account of the kingdom of Bijapur and its precarious position between the Mughals and the rising Maratha power under Sivaji is especially valuable.

519

Sen, S. N. (ed.). *Indian Travels of Careri and Thevenot.* Delhi: National Archives of India, 1949. Jean Thevenot, a French student of geography and ethnology, arrived on the West coast of India in 1666, traveled inland to Ahmedabad and departed from Surat in 1667. Much of his account concerns the history of Gujarat and a description of the chief towns of northwest India based on information from others. Dr. John F. Gemelli-Careri, a Neapolitan noble trained in law, is noted for his descriptions of such towns as Goa and his visit to Aurangzeb's camp where he observed the demoralized state of the Mughal army in 1695 during the Deccan campaign. He relies on hearsay for most of his account of history and civil administration.

520

Bernier, François. *Travels in the Moghul Empire.* Trans. by A. Constable, ed. by V. A. Smith. London: Oxford University Press, rev. ed., 1934. Bernier, a French physician, arrived in India in 1658 and resided in the court of Aurangzeb for twelve years. He obtained first-hand knowledge of much of North India and life at the Mughal court. The accuracy of his descriptions and his analysis of the strength and weakness of Mughal rule make this a primary source of major importance.

521

Manucci, Niccolo. *Storia Do Mogor; or Mogul India.* 4 vols. Trans. by W. Irvine. London: John Murray, 1906–08. Manucci, a Venetian, came to India as a youth in 1653 and managed to survive more than fifty years of colorful adventures throughout the land. Although the veracity of his account is generally discounted, the details that accompany his bits of court gossip and embroidered tales convey the atmosphere of life at the Mughal court.

522

Manucci, Niccolo. *A Pepys of Moghul India.* Ed. by M. L. Irvine. New York: E. P. Dutton, 1913. An abridged edition of the translation cited in the preceding entry.

523

Manucci, Niccolo. *Memoirs of the Mogul Court.* Ed. by M. Edwardes. London: Folio Society, 1957. Selections from the W. Irvine translation cited above; these excerpts relate Manucci's experience at the Mughal Court and in the Deccan.

Collections

524

Pinkerton, John. (Compiler). *A General Collection of the Best and most Interesting Voyages and Travels in all Parts of the World.* 17 vols. London: Longman, Hurst, Rees, & Orme, 1808–14. Volume 8 contains several important accounts by European travellers to India including those of Sir Thomas Roe (1615–19) and François Bernier (1656–1668).

525

Hakluyt, Richard. (Compiler). *The Principal Navigations, Voyages, Traffiques & Discoveries of the English Nation.* 10 vols. New York: Dutton, 1927–28. First published in the late 16th century, this collection of several hundred original narratives by travellers to distant lands, including India, conveys some of the fascination that Asia held for Europeans of the day.

526

Locke, John C. (ed.). *The First Englishmen in India.* London: G. Routledge, 1930. A selection from texts published in the Hakluyt collection cited above, with a brief and informative introduction. Letters written by Queen Elizabeth to Akbar are reproduced as well as the adventurous tale of Ralph Fitch, the first Englishman to reach Akbar's court.

527

Purchas, Samuel. (Compiler). *Hakluytus Posthumus, or Purchas His Pilgrimes.* 20 vols. Glasgow: J. MacLehose, 1905–07. A reprint of the 1625 edition of Purchas' collection of original narratives of voyages and travels. Many of the accounts were written by European travellers in India, notably those of William Hawkins, an English merchant who stayed at the Mughal court in Agra from 1609 to 1611 in an attempt to negotiate a commercial agreement with Jahangir. The journal of a later representative of England, Sir Thomas Roe, relates his experience in 1615 to 1619 while attempting to obtain a similar treaty on behalf of King James.

528

Rawlinson, Hugh G. (ed.). *Narratives from Purchas, his Pilgrimes.* Cambridge: Cambridge University Press, 1931. Two of these narratives are directly concerned with India; one describes a battle between British and Portugese merchant ships, the other is an abridged version of Sir Thomas Roe's embassy to the court of Jahangir.

529

Major, Richard H. (ed.). *India in the Fifteenth Century.* London: Hakluyt Society, Series I, Vol. 22, 1857. A useful collection of European travel accounts prefaced with an extensive introduction. A particularly valuable account of South India is that of Nicolo Conti, a Venetian merchant who visited the kingdom of Vijayanagar about 1420.

530

Foster, William (ed.). *Early Travels in India.* London: Oxford University Press, 1921. Accounts ranging from 1583 to 1619 are represented here including those of the English merchants, Ralph Fitch, William Hawkins, and John Mildenhall, who sought to negotiate commercial agreements with the Mughal Court.

Studies

531

Oaten, Edward F. *European Travellers in India during the 15th, 16th, & 17th Centuries.* London: Kegan Paul, Trench, Trubner, 1909. An authoritative appraisal of the information reported by European travellers concerning social institutions and the role of government during the Muslim Period.

532

Du Jarric, Father Pierre. *Akbar and the Jesuits.* Trans. by C. H. Payne. New York: Harper, 1926. A part of du Jarric's *Histoire* based on letters written by Jesuits at Akbar's court in the latter part of the 16th century.

533

Maclagan, Sir Edward D. *The Jesuits and the Great Mogul.* London: Burns, Oates & Washbourne, 1932. A critical study of the Jesuit missionaries and other Europeans at the court of Jahangir in the early 17th century; contains an excellent guide to the literature on the subject.

534

Camps, Arnulf. *Jerome Xavier, S. J., and the Muslims of the Mogul Empire.* Schöneck-Beckenried, Switzerland: Nouvelle Revue de Science Missionaire, 1957. A scholarly study, based on archival material not available to Maclagan (see previous entry), of the Jesuit mission to the Mughal court from 1594 to 1614; most attention is given to the methods used by the missionaries.

535

Correia-Afonso, John. *Jesuit Letters and Indian History.* Bombay: St. Xavier's College, 1955. An evaluation of the historic value of correspondence written by Jesuit missionaries residing in India from 1542 to 1773.

536

Wheeler, James T. and M. Macmillan. *European Travellers in India.* Calcutta: Susil Gupta, 1956. A set of brief sketches relating the experiences and observations reported by twelve Europeans who traveled in 17th century India.

EUROPEAN TRADING COMPANIES

Portuguese

537

Jayne, K. G. *Vasco da Gama and His Successors.* London: Methuen, 1910. A general history of Portuguese efforts to establish a commercial empire in Asia between 1460 and 1580.

538

Danvers, Frederick C. *The Portuguese in India,* 2 vols. London: W. H. Allen, 1894. A detailed study of the rise and decline of Portugal's commercial empire, based in large part on the work of Portuguese historians of the 16th and early 17th century.

539

Whiteway, Richard S. *The Rise of Portuguese Power in India.* Westminster: A. Constable, 1899. A history of the first fifty years of Portuguese activities in India.

540

Sanceau, Elaine. *Indies Adventure.* London: Blackie, 1936. An excellent account of Alfonso de Albuquerque's efforts to build a Portuguese commercial empire in Asia during the early years of the 16th century.

541

Sanceau, Elaine. *Knight of the Renaissance.* London: Hutchinson, 1949. An account of Dom Joao de Castro, Portuguese viceroy of India in mid-16th century, who maintained the unstable commercial empire developed by Albuquerque.

Dutch

542

Glamann, Kristof. *Dutch-Asiatic Trade.* Copenhagen: Danish Science Press, 1958. A scholarly study of the economic aspects of the Dutch East India Company during the years 1620–1740. Dutch commercial activities in India are described and analyzed in relation to European and Asian markets.

543

Goonewardena, K. W. *The Foundation of Dutch Power in Ceylon.* Amsterdam: Netherlands Institute for International Cultural Relation, 1958. An account of the Dutch displacement of the Portuguese as the dominant European power in Ceylon during the middle of the 17th century, prefaced with a succinct survey of the Dutch in South Asia.

544

Raychaudhuri, Rapan. *Jan Company in Coromandel, 1605–1690.* The Hague: M. Nijhoff, 1962. A history of the Dutch East India Company on the southeastern coast of India during a period of Dutch dominance in the area's external trade; problems of trade, politics, and Dutch policy are considered.

545

Poonen, T. I. *A Survey of the Rise of the Dutch Power in Malabar.* Trichinopoly: University of Travancore Press, 1948. A study of the successful Dutch effort to wrest from Portugal control of the profitable spice trade on the southwest coast of India during the years 1603 to 1678.

546

Panikkar, Kavalam M. *Malabar and the Dutch.* Bombay: D. B. Taraporevala, 1931. An examination of Dutch influence, especially upon local forms of government, in the coastal region of southwest India during the years 1663 to 1795.

547

Lohuizen, Jan van. *The Dutch East India Company and Mysore.* The Hague: N. Nijhoff, 1961. A study of Dutch activities in southern India during the 18th century, including their struggle with the British and the native rulers of Mysore.

548

Datta, Kalinkinkar. *The Dutch in Bengal and Bihar.* Patna: University of Patna, 1948. An account of Dutch mercantile activities in northeastern India from 1740 to 1825.

British

549

Hunter, William W. *History of British India.* 2 vols. London: Longmans, Green, 1899–1900. Volume I of this work remains one of the best accounts of the British East India Company during the years when commerce was its primary concern.

550

Foster, William. *England's Quest of Eastern Trade.* London: A. & C. Black, 1933. A narrative of England's effort to establish trade with Asian lands, including India, in the late 16th and early 17th centuries.

551

Krishna, Bal. *Commercial Relations Between India and England.* London: Routledge, 1924. A useful study of the organization and administration of the British East India Company and the nature of its trade with India from 1601 to 1757.

552

Wilbur, Marguerite K. *The East India Company and the British Empire in the Far East*. New York: R. R. Smith, 1945. A survey in which England's role in India is presented within a broader context of political, military, and mercantile developments from the 16th century to modern times.

553

Khan, Shafaat Ahmad. *The East India Trade in the 17th Century in Its Political and Economic Aspects*. London: Oxford University Press, 1923. An important study, based on extensive use of original sources.

554

Foster, William (ed.). *English Factories in India*, 1618–1669. 13 vols. Oxford: Clarendon Press, 1906–1927. A monumental collection of letters, reports, and other documents written by the company's servants in India. The editor provides the general setting and inter-relations for this material which is primarily concerned with local events and issues.

555

Fawcett, Charles (ed.). *The English Factories in India*, 1670–1684. 4 vols. Oxford: Clarendon Press, 1936–1955. A continuation of the work cited in the previous entry.

556

India, National Archives of. *Fort William-India House Correspondence*. Delhi: Manager of Publications, Government of India, 1949–. Only a few volumes have appeared in this proposed 21-volume series on the correspondence exchanged between the East India Company representatives at Fort William in Calcutta and the Court of Directors in London. These letters are important source material for the history of the Company's affairs in the 18th and early 19th century.

557

Sainsbury, Ethel B. (ed.). *Court Minutes of the East India Company, 1635–79*. 11 vols. Oxford: Clarendon, 1907–38. Minutes of the company's directors' meetings and correspondence relating to company affairs are reproduced in this valuable source on the home administration of the East India Company.

558

Strachey, Rachel (Costelloe). *Keigwin's Rebellion*. Oxford: Clarendon Press, 1916. A sprightly account of Bombay in 1683, when a reduction in funds for the garrison prompted the commandant, Richard Keigwin, to take over the settlement's government for a year.

559

Das, Harihar. *The Norris Embassy to Aurangzib*. Calcutta: K. L. Mukhopadhyay, 1959. A study based on diaries maintained by Sir William Norris from 1699 to 1702 while attempting to negotiate trade agreements for the English with Aurangzib; it provides a view of Mughal court life and institutions shortly before their decline and conveys the conception of Mughal power held by Europeans at this time.

560

Burnell, John. *Bombay in the Days of Queen Anne*. London: Hakluyt Society, 1933. A description of Bombay and environs by an English soldier stationed there in the early 18th century; includes some information on native customs.

561

Bhattacharya, Sukumar. *The East India Company and the Economy of Bengal*. London: Luzac, 1954. A brief but useful survey of economic conditions and the mode of trade in Bengal from 1704 to 1740; centered about the activities of European trading companies.

French

562

Sen, Siba Pada. *The French in India, First Establishment and Struggle*. Calcutta: University of Calcutta, 1947. A major work on the French trading company's activities in India from its relatively late arrival in mid-17th century to mid-18th century, when only the British surpassed them in volume of trade with India.

563

Sen, Siba Pada. *The French in India*. Calcutta: K. L. Mukhopadhyay, 1958. A study of France's participation in the struggle for power in India from 1763 to 1816; a continuation of the work cited in the previous entry.

564

Malleson, George B. *History of the French in India*. London: W. H. Allen, 2nd ed., 1893. First published in 1867; the author, an Englishman, credits the French with the conception of policies and methods for the conquest of India ultimately put into effect by the British.

565

Dodwell, Henry H. *Dupleix and Clive*. London: Methuen, 1920. An authoritative study of the roles played by two of the major figures in the struggle between France and England for dominance in India. Dupleix led the French between 1742 and 1754, his political policies and methods were later used by Clive and other Englishmen in their conquest of India.

566

Dupleix, Joseph F. *Dupleix and His Letters*. Ed. by V. M. Thompson. New York: O. Ballou, 1933. This correspondence, written between 1742 and 1754 while Dupleix was in charge of the French trading company in India, conveys the qualities of imagination and boldness underlying Dupleix's often brilliant policies.

567

Anandaranga Pillai. *Private Diary of Ananda Ranga Pillai*. 12 vols. Trans. & ed. by J. F. Price & H. H. Dodwell. Madras: Superintendent, Government Press, 1904–28. Pillai recorded much of value about the struggle for power in South India during the decisive middle years of the 18th century. His post as secretary to the French Governor General, Dupleix, provided Pillai with intimate knowledge of important persons and matters of state.

568

Srinivasachari, Chidambaram S. (ed.). *Ananda Ranga Pillai, the "Pepys" of French India*. Madras: P. Varadachary, 1940. A one-volume abridged edition of the diary described in the preceding entry.

569

Martineau, Alfred A. *Bussy in the Deccan*. Trans. by Cammaide. Pondicherry: Bibliothèque Publique, 1941. Extracts from a French work published in Paris in 1935. Bussy was the first European to engage in the political guidance of a native state; acting as Dupleix's political agent, Bussy spent seven years in residence at the Nizam of Hyderabad's court during the middle of the 18th century.

570

Hatalkar, V. G. *Relations Between the French and the Marathas, 1668–1851*. Bombay: University of Bombay, 1958. A study of the French and a major native power with which they had to contend.

THE 18TH CENTURY CONTEST FOR POWER

Following the death of Aurangzeb, last of the "Great" Mughal emperors, in 1707, political fragmentation occurred throughout India. The lines of division were in most instances drawn during the previous century, when Mughal control was maintained in many areas solely through force of arms. Militant opposition to Mughal authority in western India was organized by Sivaji (1630–1680), who rallied the martial Marathas with an appeal to their common Hindu heritage. During the 18th century,

Maratha armies reached Delhi in the north and the Bay of Bengal in the east, overthrowing Hindu and Muslim rulers in their wake. However, effective Maratha government was confined to western India with Poona serving as the headquarters for a loose Maratha confederacy that succumbed to British dominance in 1818. Anti-Muslim zeal also served to rally the Sikhs, a religious sect established in the 15th century, whose military organization controlled the Punjab region of northern India throughout most of the 18th century and successfully thwarted British efforts in the area until the 1840's. In southwestern India, a Muslim adventurer named Haidar Ali gained control of the Hindu state of Mysore in 1761 and, under his reign and that of his son, Tipu Sultan, withstood Maratha and European forces until conquered by the British in 1799. Muslim governors in eastern, southern, and central India established virtually independent kingdoms early in the 18th century, although many of them maintained nominal allegiance to the Mughal emperor. Among the most powerful of these Muslim rulers were the Nawabs of Bengal, whose submission to British authority in 1757 is often cited as the first major step taken in the British conquest of India. After several decades of struggle, waged in India and elsewhere, France renounced her political aspiration in India in the Treaty of Paris of 1763, leaving Britain's role in India unrivalled by other European powers. During the latter part of the 18th century, the British consolidated their position in Bengal, Madras, and Bombay while continuing to extend their influence into the hinterlands through diplomacy and force of arms. Major transformations also occurred at this time in the nature and organization of the East India Company. The Company's assumption of revenue-collecting rights in 1765, in Bengal, Bihar, and Orissa, was soon followed by its further involvement in governmental affairs. In 1773, British Parliament passed the first of many Regulating Acts that curbed the Company's powers and formally acknowledged Britain's governmental responsibilities in India. Although British rule was maintained in the name of the Company until 1858, and commercial activities in India were continued by the Company until their termination by the Charter Act of 1833, the Company was well on its way to becoming an instrument of the British government early in the 19th century.

Decline of the Mughals

571

Spear, T. G. Percival. *Twilight of the Mughuls.* Cambridge: Cambridge University Press, 1951. A scholarly study of Delhi and adjacent territory from 1761 to 1857; provides an excellent summary of political forces in North India at the time and a description of village conditions and forms of local government seldom studied.

572

Sarkar, Jadunath. *Fall of the Mughal Empire.* 4 vols. Calcutta: M. C. Sarkar, 1932–1950. Volumes I through III

have appeared in a second edition: a detailed and scholarly study of the factors contributing to the decline of the Mughals, by a leading authority on the subject. Periods covered are: Vol. I, 1739–1754; Vol II, 1754–1771; Vol. III, 1771–1788; Vol. IV, 1789–1803.

573

Owen, Sidney J. *The Fall of the Mogul Empire.* Varanasi: Chowkhamba Sanskrit Series, 2nd ed., 1960. First published in 1912: a useful survey of factors affecting the decline of the Mughals during the period 1657 to 1761. Owen attributes the Mughal's downfall to Aurangzeb's religious bigotry and lack of political insight.

574

Chandra, Satish. *Parties and Politics at the Mughal Court.* Aligarh: Department of History, Muslim University, 1959. A description of the organization, ethnic composition, and power struggles of the Mughal nobility during the decline of their empire from 1707 to 1740.

575

Irvine, William. *Later Mughals.* 2 vols. Edited by Jadunath Sarkar. Calcutta: M. C. Sarkar, 1921–22. A classic study of Mughal political history from 1707 to 1739, with copious references to original sources; a useful supplement to this work is cited in the next entry.

576

Polier, Antoine L. *Shah Alam II and His Court.* Ed. by P. C. Gupta. Calcutta: S. C. Sarkar, 1947. A brief but informative narrative of men and events in the Mughal court of Delhi by a Swiss engineer in residence there from 1771 to 1779 as an employee of the East India Company.

577

Sarkar, Jadunath. *Bihar and Orissa During the Fall of the Mughal Empire.* Patna: Patna University, 1932. A brief account of political developments in Bihar, Orissa, and Bengal during the middle of the 18th century; much of this study concerns the effects of Maratha forays into the area.

578

Gadgil, Dhananjaya R. *Origins of the Modern Indian Business Class.* New York: Institute of Pacific Relation, 1959. A brief sketch of the main features of the Indian economy in the middle of the eighteenth century; presented as an "interim report" of a more extended study that will cover the subject to the present day.

The Marathas

579

Sardesai, Govind S. *A New History of the Marathas.* 3 vols. Bombay: Phoenix Publications, rev. ed., 1948–56. A detailed survey of Maratha history from 1600 to 1848. The Marathas, a militant and resourceful people of western India, successfully defied the Mughals in the latter part of the 17th century, dominated much of western India during the 18th century, and were among the last of the native powers to succumb to British dominance in the early 19th century.

580

Duff, James G. *History of the Mahrattas.* 2 vols. Ed. by S. M. Edwards. London: Oxford University Press, rev. ed., 1921. A classic work first published in 1826; in many instances this is a primary source due to the author's use of materials no longer in existence, and his utilization of personal observations made while serving as a British political agent in Maratha territory during the early 19th century.

581

Kincaid, Charles A. and R. B. Parasnis. *A History of the Maratha People.* 3 vols. London: Oxford University Press, 2nd ed., 1931. A standard work; though a product of modern historical writing, it lacks the feeling for the Maratha people conveyed in Duff's history cited above.

582

Sardesai, Govind S. *Main Currents of Maratha History.* Bombay: Phoenix Publications, rev. ed., 1959. An examination of some of the more important and controversial views of Maratha history by a pioneer in the use of Maratha sources.

583

Sharma, Shripad R. *Maratha History Re-examined.* Bombay: Karnatak Publishing House, 1944. A noted Indian historian here reviews Maratha history from 1295 to 1707 in the light of Maratha sources that provide a different view from earlier work based mainly on British and Muslim material.

584

Sarkar, Jadunath (ed.). *The Persian Sources of Maratha History.* Bombay: Bombay Government, 1953. These selections from texts written in Persian reveal how the Mughals viewed the militant Marathas, who challenged Muslim control of western India in the 17th century.

585

Sen, Surendra Nath. *Administrative System of the Marathas.* Calcutta: University of Calcutta, rev. ed., 1925. Though written several decades ago, this work has yet to be displaced as the principal study of the system used by the Marathas to administer their delicately balanced confederation.

586

Gune, Vithal T. *The Judicial System of the Marathas.* Poona: Deccan College, 1953. A study of the village-based judicial system developed by the Marathas during the 17th and 18th centuries when they governed much of western India.

587

Sen, Surendra Nath. *Military System of the Marathas.* Bombay: Orient Longmans, new ed., 1958. An excellent study of the military organization and tactics employed by the Marathas in the 18th century contest for power in which they figured as a major native contestant.

588

Sarkar, Jadunath. *Shivaji and His Times.* Calcutta: M. C. Sarkar, 6th ed., rev., 1961. Shivaji, a militant Hindu leader of the 17th century, led the Marathas of western India in a protracted struggle with the Mughals. Shivaji's relations with minor Muslim powers and European traders are also described.

589

Sarkar, Jadunath. *House of Shivaji.* Calcutta: M. C. Sarkar, 3rd ed., rev., 1955. A collection of documents and Sarkar's essays on the royal period of Maratha rule from 1626 to 1700.

590

Balakrishna, R. *Shivaji the Great.* New York: Asia Publishing House, 1962. A popular biography of the 17th century founder of Maratha power in the Deccan; Shivaji became a symbol of militant Hindu nationalism.

591

Srinivasan, C. K. *Baji Rao I — The Great Peshwa.* New York: Asia Publishing House, 1962. Following Shivaji's death in 1680 his family's authority waned and in 1714 Shivaji's grandson relinquished active leadership to his prime minister, or Peshwa. This office was inherited by Baji Rao in 1720.

592

Srinivasan, C. K. *Maratha Rule in the Carnatic.* Annamalainagar: Annamalai University, 1944. A useful account of Maratha efforts to control the eastern reaches of the Deccan during the 18th century.

593

Ray, Bhabani C. *Orissa Under the Marathas.* Allahabad: Kitab Mahal, 1960. This work treats the period of Maratha control in the Orissa region of eastern India from 1751 to 1803.

594

Varma, Shanti P. *A study in Maratha Diplomacy.* Agaraw: Shiva Lal Agrawala, 1956. Primarily a study of Maratha diplomatic and military efforts directed against the British during the crucial years 1772 to 1783.

595

Choksey, Rustom D. *A History of British Diplomacy at the Court of the Peshwas,* 1786–1818. Poona: R. D. Choksey, 1951. Based in the main on correspondence by British agents at Maratha headquarters; it conveys the atmosphere of strife, intrigue, and corruption that stifled Maratha resistance to British conquest.

596

Broughton, Thomas D. *Letters Written in a Mahratta Camp.* London: A. Constable, rev. ed., 1892. A vivid description of native customs and manners by a British official residing in the camp of the Maratha leader Sindia during 1809.

597

Ballhatchet, Kenneth. *Social Policy and Social Change in Western India.* London: Oxford University Press, 1957. One of the best works in the field of Indian history. Ballhatchet analyzes the effect of British administration and social reform in Maratha territory during the years 1817 to 1830. Information is presented on the system of government developed by the Marathas during the previous century.

The Sikhs

598

Cunningham, Joseph D. *A History of the Sikhs.* Ed. by H. L. O. Garrett & R. R. Sethi. Delhi: S. Chand, 1955. A classic work first published in the 19th century; traces Sikh history from its origin as a religious sect in the 16th century to the middle of the 19th century when the Sikhs fought the British for control of the Punjab.

599

Singh, Khushwant. *The Sikhs.* London: Allen & Unwin, 1953. A brief survey of Sikh history from the 16th century to modern times with a discussion of Sikh religion.

600

Singh, Khushwant. *History of the Sikhs. 1469–1839.* Princeton: Princeton University Press, 1963. The first of two proposed volumes surveying the history of the Sikhs from the birth of the sect's founder, Guru Nanak, to the present; an appendix provides selections from the Sikh's sacred writings.

601

Gupta, Hari Ram. *History of the Sikhs.* 3 vols. Lahore: Minerva Book Shop, 1939–44. A detailed account of the ascendance of Sikh power in the Punjab during the 18th century.

602

Sinha, Narendra K. *Rise of the Sikh Power.* Calcutta: University of Calcutta, 2nd ed., 1946. A scholarly survey of the political fortunes of the Sikhs from mid-18th to mid-19th century.

603

Sinha, Narendra K. *Ranjit Singh.* Calcutta: University of Calcutta, 1933. A detailed biography of the leader who united the Sikh community, developed a powerful army organized on European lines, and maintained control of the Punjab until his death in 1839.

604

Singh, Khushwant. *Ranjit Singh, Maharajah of the Punjab.* London: G. Allen & Unwin, 1962. A popular account of the famous Sikh leader.

605

Griffin, Sir Lepel. *Ranjit Singh.* Oxford: Clarendon Press, 1911. A useful biographical sketch; part of the "Rulers of India" series. Reprinted in 1957 by S. Chand of Delhi.

606

Singh, Ganda. *The Punjab in 1839–40.* Patiala: New Age Press, 1952. A collection of records relating to a decisive period in the political fortunes of the Sikhs; published for the Sikh History Society.

607

Gupta, Hari Ram (ed.). *The Punjab on the Eve of the First Sikh War.* Hoshiarpur: Punjab University, 1956.

An annotated edition of daily intelligence reports on political, economic, and social conditions in the Punjab, prepared by British officials stationed there during a ten-month period ending October, 1844; includes a detailed bibliography of records, travel accounts, and secondary sources concerning the Punjab in the 18th and 19th centuries.

Nawabs of Bengal

608

Datta, Kalikinkar. *Alivardi and His Times*. Calcutta: University of Calcutta, 1939. An account of the Muslim governor of Bengal whose peaceful and prosperous regime from 1740 to 1756 was only nominally subordinate to Mughal authority.

609

Ali, Yusuf. *Nawabs of Bengal*. Trans. by J. Sarkar. Calcutta: Asiatic Society of Bengal, 1952. A translation of the *Waqa-i-Mahabat Jang* which relates the martial exploits of Ali Vardi Khan in the early 18th century.

610

Gopal, Ram. *How the British Occupied Bengal*. New York: Asia Publishing House, 1962. An examination of political conditions in Bengal during the years 1756–65; corruption within the native government is held to have left the area vulnerable to British conquest.

611

Gupta, Brijen K. *Sirajuddaullah and the East India Company, 1756–1757*. Leiden: E. J. Brill, 1962. A study of the economic and political background of the conflict between the British company and the Muslim ruler of Bengal whose defeat in the battle of Plassey is often cited as the first major step towards the British conquest of India.

612

Roy, Atul Chandra. *Career of Mir Jafar Khan. 1757–65*. Calcutta: Das Gupta, 1955. A study of the Muslim noble whose nominal rule of Bengal, begun in 1757, was based on British support for which a high price was levied.

613

Chatterji, Nandalal. *Mir Qasim, Nawab of Bengal, 1760–1763*. Allahabad: Indian Press, 1935. Mir Qasim, an able and ambitious man, succeeded his pliant father-in-law, Mir Jafar, as the ruler of Bengal; Mir Qasim sought to wrest free of British control, but was defeated in the battle of Baksar in 1764.

Other Native Powers

614

Sinha, Narendra K. *Haidar Ali*. Calcutta: A. Mukherjee, 3rd ed., 1959. Haidar Ali, a Muslim military adventurer, gained control of the Hindu state of Mysore in 1761 and frustrated European and Maratha attempts to dominate this area of South India.

615

Khan, Mohibbul Hasan. *History of Tipu Sultan*. Calcutta: Bibliophile, 1951. An excellent account of the reign of Haidar Ali's son, Tipu Sultan, from 1782 to 1799. Battles and political events are the main subject of this work, accompanied by a succinct description of Tipu's government, army, and religious policy; a useful bibliography is included.

616

Kirmani, Husain Ali Khan. *History of Tipu Sultan*. Trans. by W. Miles. Calcutta: Susil Gupta, 2nd ed., 1958. A translation of the *Nishan-i-Haidari*, the only extant contemporary history of the reigns of Haidar Ali and his son Tipu Sultan, written by a courtier in their service; dates and sequence of events are often incorrect.

617

Hayavadana Rao, Conjeeveram. *History of Mysore, 1399–1799*. 3 vols. Bangalore: Superintendent of the Government Press, 1943–46. A comprehensive and scholarly history of a region that has played an active role in the political history of South India; coverage ends with the British conquest of the area.

618

Wilks, Mark. *Historical Sketches of the South of India*. 2 vols. Mysore: Government Branch Press, 1930-32. One of the earliest histories of the Mysore region, coverage extends from ancient times to the 19th century; written shortly after the British overthrew and killed Tipu Sultan in 1799. Though often inaccurate, its prejudicial views of Tipu and his father provide valuable material on British attitudes at this time.

619

Khan, Yusuf Husain. *The First Nizam*. New York: Asia Publishing House, 1962. First published in 1936. An account of Asaf Jah and his times; he resigned as Mughal prime minister in 1723 and founded the independent Nizam dynasty that ruled much of central India in the 18th century.

620

Srivastava, Ashirbadi L. *The First Two Nawabs of Oudh*. Agra: S. L. Agarwala, 2nd ed., rev., 1954. An account of political events during the first half of the 18th century in a kingdom located in the Ganges plain.

621

Banerjee, Anil C. *The Rajput States and the East India Company*. Calcutta: A. Mukherjee, 1951. A history of the major principalities of Rajputana during the expansion of British control in north central India from 1790 to 1818; including a brief survey of the traditional Rajput system of government and its relation to feudalism.

622

Chablani, S. P. *Economic Conditions in Sind, 1752–1843*. Calcutta: Orient Longmans, 1951. An economic history of the lower Indus valley prior to the British conquest of the area; particularly useful for its account of efforts at irrigation.

British Transition from Commerce to Conquest

GENERAL WORKS AND SOURCES

623

Roberts, Paul Ernest. *History of British India*. Completed by T. G. P. Spear. London: Oxford University Press, 3rd ed., 1952. An excellent summary of the East India Company's transformation from a commercial enterprise to a governing power appears in this judicious history.

624

Hunter, William W. *A History of British India*. 2 vols. London: Longmans, Green, 1899–1900. A scholarly survey based on a wide variety of original sources, particularly useful for its interpretation of the factors affecting the transformation of the East India Company.

625

Mills, James. *History of British India*. 10 vols. Ed. by H. Wilson. London: J. Madden, 5th ed., 1858. First published in 1817, later editions extend the period covered from 1805 to 1834. One of the most influential of the early British histories of India; it includes considerable material on the pre-British period. Mills' interpretations, based on principles derived from utilitarian philosophy, helped shape British opinion concerning the nature of Indian civilization and how India should be governed.

626

Lyall, Alfred C. *The Rise and Expansion of the British Dominion in India*. London: John Murray, 5th ed., 1910. One of the most candid and competent statements of the imperialist view of the British conquest of India.

627

India, National Archives of. *Fort William-India House Correspondence*. Delhi: Manager of Publications, Government of India, 1949–. Only a few volumes have appeared in this proposed 21-volume series on the correspondence exchanged between the East India Company representatives at Fort William in Calcutta and the Court of Directors in London. These letters are important source material for the history of the Company's affairs in the 18th and early 19th century.

628

Srinivasachari, Chidambaram S. (ed.). *Selections from the Orme Manuscripts*. Annamalainagar: Annamalai University, 1952. A useful selection from Robert Orme's collection of original source material concerning the British conquest of Bengal.

SPECIAL STUDIES

629

Sheppard, Eric W. *Coote Bahadur*. London: W. Laurie, 1956. A biography of Lt.-General Sir Eyre Coote, one of the most effective professional soldiers in the East India Company's service. Coote's forces decisively defeated the French in 1761 and he led the British campaign against Haidar Ali of Mysore two decades later.

630

Richmond, Herbert W. *The Navy in India, 1763-1783*. London: E. Benn, 1931. A study of British naval power in Indian waters during a period when superiority at sea was an important factor in the struggle for power in India.

631

Banerjee, Debendra Nath. *Early Administrative System of the East India Company*. London: Longmans, Green, 1943. A detailed description of the English development of the means of governing Bengal between 1765 and 1774; contemporary sources are profusely quoted.

632

Chatterji, Nandalal. *Bengal Under the Diwani Administration, 1765-1772*. Allahabad: Indian Press, 1956. A study of the period between the regimes of Clive and Warren Hastings, noted for the famine of 1770 and for the appointment of Englishmen to supervise the collection of land revenue.

633

Ramsbotham, Richard B. *Studies in the Land Revenue History of Bengal, 1769-1787*. London: Oxford University Press, 1926. A scholarly study of early attempts by the British to comprehend and adapt the administrative system used by their predecessors.

634

Majumdar, Niharkana. *Justice and Police in Bengal, 1765-1793*. Calcutta: K. L. Mukhopadhyay, 1960. A scholarly monograph on the dire consequences of the dual system of government initiated by Clive, modified by Hastings, and revoked by Cornwallis in 1793 when the British assumed responsibility for law and order.

635

Patra, Atul Chandra. *The Administration of Justice Under The East India Company in Bengal, Bihar and Orissa*. New York: Asia Publishing House, 1963. A critique of he legal system developed by the East India Company when it undertook to govern its conquests.

636

Misra, Bankey B. *The Administration of the East India Company*. New York: Barnes & Noble, 1960. A structural analysis of the constitutional and administrative instruments of government forged by the English in India during the years 1773-1834, when the demands of empire building transformed the aims and organization of the Company.

637

Sinha, Narendra K. *The Economic History of Bengal from Plassey to the Permanent Settlement*. 2 vols. Calcutta: K. L. Mukhopadhyay, 1961-62. A survey of economic conditions in Bengal during the last half of the 18th century; mainly concerned with commercial activities involving European trading companies.

638

Tripathi, Amales. *Trade and Finance in the Bengal Presidency, 1793-1833*. Bombay: Orient Longmans, 1956. A study of the economic policies and practices of the East India Company during the last phase of its existence as a commercial organization; some of the positive consequences of the company's activities for the Indian economy are touched upon. Much of the data is presented in undigested form and prior knowledge of the historical setting of the study is presumed.

639

Furber, Holden. *John Company at Work*. Cambridge: Harvard University Press, 1948. An excellent study of the commercial and financial condition of the English East India Company between 1783-1793; statistics are artfully woven into an analysis that conveys the adventure of commerce while advancing a scholarly appraisal of economic forces behind European expansion in India. Other trading companies, including the Danish, appear in this account; contains an extensive bibliography.

640

Philips, Cyril H. *The East India Company, 1784-1834*. Manchester: Manchester University Press, 2nd ed., 1961. A scholarly study of the conflicts that arose in London between various interest groups during the Company's transformation from a commercial enterprise to a governing power. Consideration is given to the influence of these conflicts on matters of policy and administration.

641

Sutherland, Lucy S. *The East India Company in 18th Century Politics*. Oxford: Clarendon Press, 1952. The London setting of corruption and intrigue within the Company and in the Company's relations with Parliament is delineated with skill in this study.

BRITISH GOVERNOR-GENERALS

642

Davies, Alfred M. *Clive of Plassey*. New York: C. Scribner's 1939. The most objective biography of the man commonly associated with the emergence of the British as a major power in mid-18th century India. The controversies that raged between Clive's earlier biographers are reviewed and assessed.

643

Forrest, George. *The Life of Lord Clive*. 2 vols. London: Cassell, 1918. A detailed though poorly organized biography of Clive; less biased than earlier works.

644

Chatterji, Nandalal. *Clive as an Administrator*. Allahabad: Indian Press, 1955. An account of Clive's efforts to restore order in Bengal after his return to India in 1765; his vigorous policies left a strong imprint on the initial organization of British rule in India.

645

Macaulay, Thomas B. *Essay on Lord Clive and Warren Hastings*. New York: C. E. Merrill, 1910. A trenchant appraisal of politics and practices employed in the early years of empire building in India; written in the early 19th century, these sketches reveal some of the differences within British opinion concerning the proper role of British rule in India.

646

Moon, Penderal. *Warren Hastings and British India*. New York: Collier, paperbound ed., 1962. A highly readable and well-balanced biography of the first governor-general of India; Moon's account of Hastings' administration from 1772 to 1785 provides an excellent introduction to a decisive period in the establishment of British power in India.

647

Feiling, Keith G. *Warren Hastings*. London: Macmillan, 1954. A detailed biography; Hastings' private life, as well as his thirty-year career in India is given due consideration.

648

Jones, M. E. Monckton. *Warren Hastings in Bengal, 1772-1774*. Oxford: Clarendon Press, 1918. Especially useful for the reproduction of documents that illustrate crucial changes in policy that led to the British assumption of governmental responsibility in India.

649

Davies, Cuthbert C. *Warren Hastings and Oudh.* London: Oxford University Press, 1939. A scholarly study of relations in the late 18th century between the East India Company and the kingdom that served as a buffer state between British-held Bengal and the Marathas.

650

Sen, S. N. *Anglo-Maratha Relations, 1772–1785.* Calcutta: K. L. Mukhopadhyay, 1961. A detailed study of the policy pursued by Hastings in his efforts to cope with the Marathas; based on English, Marathi, and Persian sources.

651

Furber, Holden. *Indian Governor Generalship.* Cambridge: Harvard University Press, 1953. A valuable study of British policy in India at the end of the 18th century, based on the private record of Sir John Shore whose relatively peaceful administration from 1793 to 1798 is noted for adherence to a policy of non-intervention in conflicts between the native powers.

652

Aspinall, Arthur. *Cornwallis in Bengal.* Manchester: Manchester University Press, 1931. An account of Lord Cornwallis' regime as governor-general from 1786–93; a period of consolidation of prior gains and a re-ordering of the company's goals from commerce to politics and government.

653

Roberts, Paul E. *India Under Wellesley.* London: G. Bell, 1929. One of the best accounts of a governor-general; Wellesley's energetic and militant regime from 1798 to 1805 coincided with a shift in British opinion towards a "forward policy" that envisaged British rule over all of India.

654

Wellington, Arthur Wellesley. *A Selection From the Despatches, Memoranda, and Other Papers of the Marquess Wellesley Relating to India.* Ed. by S. J. Owen. Oxford: Clarendon Press, 1877. A valuable collection of primary source material for the turn of the 19th century when Britain set upon a course of conquest in India directed at complete domain.

BRITISH RULE c.1800-1947

British conquest of India was a gradual process of almost a century's duration, culminating in the British government's assumption of direct rule in 1858. Prior to that time British authority in India was represented by the East India Company, a private corporation granted the monopoly of British trade in India, early in the 17th century. Through diplomacy and force of arms, the company had become the major political power in India by the end of the 18th century. The administrative head of this commercial empire was the company's Court of Directors located in London. The company maintained three regional divisions in India. These were the "presidencies" of Bengal, Madras, and Bombay, with a relatively autonomous governor for each area. Abuse of company power and an increasing involvement of British national interest in company affairs led to a series of "Regulating Acts" by which Parliament asserted its supervisory rights over the company. The first of these acts, passed in 1773, made Bengal the chief presidency and its chief executive

the over-all governor-general, a title later supplemented with that of viceroy when India came under direct crown rule. The "India Act" of 1784 created a Board of Control, appointed by the crown, vested with the power to recall any British official from India. Further restrictions of the company's authority continued until 1858, when the crown assumed the direct administration of India through the cabinet post of secretary of state for India.

The effect of British rule, and the extent of Western influence on India during British times, cannot be fully assessed as yet. However it is already evident that Indian life in many spheres underwent considerable change. Perhaps the best reflection of these changes may be seen in the emergence of India in the 20th century as a modern nation-state. The basis of this state was the British-created colonial administration, which provided a national unity never before realized in Indian history. The structure of national unity was further enhanced by technological developments in transport and communication, which incorporated India as an economic unit into the world market. The development also of a common body of law, other than the law affecting family and religious matters, did much to further nationwide patterns of government and commerce. In addition to law, British policies often resulted in profound and far-reaching changes, notably, the introduction of new revenue systems that radically altered rights to land, local authority, and village organization.

Influence of a more subtle order may also be seen emanating from the system of Western education introduced by the British, and from the use of English as the language of government. Such changes opened avenues of inter-cultural contact and shaped the thinking of the Indian elite that arose in the 20th century to challenge and ultimately overthrow British rule in India.

Reference Works and Sources

655

Dodwell, Henry H. (ed.) *The Cambridge History of India.* Volumes V and VI. Cambridge: Cambridge University Press, 1929 (V) and 1958 (rev. ed., VI). Volume V covers the period 1497–1858, volume VI to 1947. Extensive bibliographies, including references to the voluminous source material for this period, appear in both volumes.

656

Datta, Kali Kinkar. *A Survey of Recent Studies on Modern Indian History.* Patna: Patna University, 1957. A rambling discourse on some aspects of Indian history during the British era interspersed with brief descriptions of books, articles, and dissertations on the subject; of some value as a measure of current efforts by Indian historians.

657

Cohn, Bernard S. *The Development and Impact of British Administration in India.* New Delhi: Indian Institute of Public Administration, 1961. A useful bibliographical essay.

658

Matthews, William. *British Autobiographies.* Berkeley: University of California Press, 1955. Many accounts by British officials and travellers in India are cited in this annotated bibliography of British autobiographies published or written before 1951; indexed by subject and place.

659

Buckland, Charles E. *Dictionary of Indian Biography*. London: Swan Sonnenschein, 1906. Contains 2600 biographical sketches of men prominent in Indian affairs from mid-18th to late 19th century.

660

Mersey, Clive B. *Viceroys and Governor Generals of India, 1757–1947*. London: J. Murray, 1949. A collection of thirty-three brief eulogistic biographical sketches of the British rulers of India.

661

Philips, Cyril H. (ed.) *The Evolution of India and Pakistan, 1858–1947*. London: Oxford University Press, 1962. This is Volume IV in a proposed four-volume series. *Select Documents on the History of India and Pakistan*, under the general editorship of C. H. Philips. This volume will undoubtedly become a major source for future work on modern Indian history. Economic and social developments are well represented in contrast to prior works of this kind in which government and politics tend to be of sole concern.

662

India, National Archives of. *Fort William-India House Correspondence*. Delhi: Manager of Publications, Government of India, 1949–. Only a few volumes have appeared in this proposed 21-volume series on the correspondence exchanged between the East India Company representatives at Fort William in Calcutta and the Court of Directors in London. These letters are important source material for the history of the Company's affairs in the 18th and early 19th century.

663

Imperial Gazetteer of India. Provincial Series. 25 vols. Calcutta: Superintendent of Government Printing, 1908–09. A monumental collection of information on the topography, ethnology, economy, administration, and history of the fifteen provinces of British India.

General Works

664

Roberts, Paul E. *History of British India*. London: Oxford University Press, 3rd ed., rev., 1952. Coverage extended to 1947 by Percival Spear. A succinct and authoritative narrative of British rule in India from its inception to India's independence. Political events and institutional developments are presented in terms of major political personages, particularly British viceroys, with a judicious balancing of interpretations.

665

Dodwell, Henry H. (ed.). *The Cambridge History of India*. 6 vols. Cambridge: Cambridge University Press, 1922–32. The British period is treated in volumes V and VI of this major work; historical developments to 1947 are presented in a revised edition of volume VI, published in 1958. Although volume VI is generally excellent for administrative history, it provides very little on the social and cultural developments of the time.

666

Thompson, Edward and G. T. Garratt. *Rise and Fulfilment of British Rule in India*. Allahabad: Central Book Depot, reprint, 1958. A provocative view of British rule in India; first published in 1934, when Britain's future role in India was a topic of lively debate. The Indian nationalist movement is sympathetically treated and many British policies severely criticized. Economic and cultural developments are given more attention than in most other histories of the period.

667

Smith, Vincent A. (ed.). *The Oxford History of India*. Oxford: Clarendon Press, rev. ed., 1958. More than half of this standard work concerns the British period; Percival Spear has rewritten this section and extended its coverage to 1947.

668

Majumdar, Ramesh C., H. C. Raychaudhuri, and K. K. Datta. *An Advanced History of India*. London: Macmillan, 1960. Part III provides a survey of the British period of Indian history as viewed by Indian scholars whose interpretations differ at many points with views expressed by British historians.

669

Spear, Percival. *India: a Modern History*. Ann Arbor: University of Michigan Press, 1961. Contains a readable and well-balanced survey of the British and modern periods; written to elucidate the transformation of India into a modern nation state.

670

Wallbank, Thomas W. *A Short History of India and Pakistan*. New York: Mentor, paperbound ed., 1958. An abridged, revised version of the author's *India in the New Era*. All but a few pages are devoted to the period of British rule and modern times; a readable introductory survey.

671

Philips, Cyril H. *India*. New York: Hutchinson's University Library, 1949. A lucid summary of political and economic developments during the British period occupies most of this brief survey.

672

Woodruff, Philip. (Pseud. of Philip Mason). *The Men Who Ruled India*. 2 vols. New York: St. Martin's Press, 1954. A eulogistic account of the British in India from 1600 to 1947; organized around biographical sketches of Englishmen who played a decisive role in Indian affairs.

673

Reynolds, Reginald. *White Sahibs in India*. New York: John Day, 1937. An extensively documented polemic review of the negative aspects of British rule written in support of the nationalist movement; contains information not readily available elsewhere.

674

Griffiths, Percival J. *The British Impact on India*. London: Macdonald, 1952. An evaluation of British rule by an ex-member of the Indian Civil Service. Though pro-British, this appraisal gives some consideration to the claims of Indian nationalists. Administrative and economic aspects of British rule, as well as political, are evaluated through comparison with India before the British conquest.

675

Rawlinson, Hugh G. *The British Achievement in India*. London: W. Hodge, 1948. A comparison of British rule with earlier Hindu and Muslim rule, in which British political and economic innovations are viewed as positive contributions to Indian life.

676

Nehru, Jawaharlal. *The Discovery of India*. New York: Doubleday, paperbound ed., 1959. Abridged and edited by R. I. Crane. Contains a trenchant critique of British rule in India by a leader of the nationalist movement who attributes many of India's contemporary problems to British policy.

677

Lewis, Martin D. (ed.). *The British in India, Imperialism or Trusteeship?* Boston: D. C. Heath, 1962. A judicious selection of opposing interpretations of questions often raised about the nature and consequence of British rule in India; intended for use in college courses.

678

Gopal, Ram. *British Rule in India; An Assessment*. New York: Asia Publishing House, 1963. A relatively successful attempt to provide an objective review and assessment of British rule in India; written by a historian with access to sources only recently available.

679

Wint, Guy. *The British in Asia.* New York: Institute of Pacific Relations, rev. ed., 1954. British rule in India is analyzed in comparison with Russian efforts in Asia.

Special Studies

CONSTITUTIONAL HISTORY

680

Keith, Arthur B. *A Constitutional History of India, 1600–1935.* London: Methuen, 1936. A classic in the field; an authoritative and lucid description and evaluation of the legal and administrative aspects of British rule in India.

681

Coupland, Reginald. *The India Problem.* New York: Oxford University Press, 1944. Published originally in England in three volumes, 1942–43. A detailed and well-documented study of constitutional developments in India, mainly between 1909–42, in which changes in the forms of government are related to major political events of the day. Information acquired by personal interviews with political leaders in 1941, as well as public documents and newspaper reports, are used to assess the problem of deciding upon India's future form of government.

682

Coupland, Reginald. *India: A Re-statement.* New York: Oxford University Press, 1945. A summary of the author's *The Indian Problem;* a scholarly and sophisticated defense of British rule in India in which constitutional developments leading to India's independence are lucidly surveyed. The problem of introducing Western political institutions into India is discussed in relation to the past and the future.

683

Singh, Gurmukh Nihal. *Landmarks in Indian Constitutional and National Development.* Delhi: Atma Ram, 4th ed., 1959. A detailed and well-documented survey ranging from 1600 to 1919 with special attention given to developments after 1858; presented from a nationalist's point of view.

684

Ilbert, Courtenay P. *The Government of India.* Oxford: Clarendon Press, 1922. A digest of statute law relating to constitutional developments during British rule in India.

685

Curzon, George N. *British Government in India.* 2 vols. London: Cassell, 1925. An account by one of the most effective viceroys of India; contains valuable information not readily available elsewhere.

686

Gledhill, Alan. *The Republic of India.* London: Stevens & Sons, 2nd ed., 1954. A historical account of the development under British rule of formal governmental institutions, including central and provincial legislatures and the administrative and legal systems. Similar aspects of the Republic of India are then described with special attention given to the new Indian Constitution and the problems of federalism in India.

687

Palande, Manohar R. *Introduction to the Indian Constitution.* New York: Oxford University Press, 6th ed., 1956. Previously published under the title: *Introduction to Indian Administration.* A historical survey of the growth of governmental institutions in India, particularly useful for developments in the Dyarchy Period that followed the 1919 reforms.

688

Sethi, R. R. and V. D. Mahajan. *Constitutional History of India.* Delhi: S. Chand, 3rd ed., rev., 1956. A useful reference prepared as a college textbook; surveys the organization of India's government from the days of the East India Co. through the early years of the Republic of India.

689

Philips, Cyril H. (ed.). *The Evolution of India and Pakistan, 1858–1947.* London: Oxford University Press, 1962. A judicious selection of documents including many relevant to constitutional history.

690

Keith, Arthur B. *Speeches and Documents on Indian Policy, 1750–1921.* 2 vols. London: Oxford University Press, 1922. Many of the major pronouncements on Britain's policy in India are reproduced in this excellent account.

691

Gwyer, Maurice L. and A. Appadorai (eds.). *Speeches and Documents on the Indian Constitution, 1921–47.* 2 vols. London: Oxford University Press, 1957. Intended as a sequel to Keith's work cited in preceding entry. This collection of 380 items contains statutes, committee reports, party announcements, letters, and biographical notes on major political figures of the day.

692

Banerjee, Anil C. (ed.). *Indian Constitutional Documents.* 3 vols. Calcutta: A. Mukherjee, 3rd ed., rev., 1961. A useful collection of documents from the period 1757 to 1947. The writings of journalists, scholars, and nationalist leaders are included as well as statutes and official statements.

693

Stokes, Eric. *The English Utilitarians and India.* Oxford: Clarendon Press, 1959. An exploration of the impact of Utilitarian ideas on British policy in India, especially in regard to law, administrative organization, taxation, and land tenure systems. Consideration is also given to the late 19th-century conflict between those Indian nationalists who favored a continuation of the utilitarian-inspired authoritarian bureaucracy and those favoring representative government.

694

Mendis, G. C. (ed.). *The Colebrooke-Cameron Papers.* 2 vols. New York: Oxford University Press, 1957. A collection of documents on British colonial policy in Ceylon between the years 1796–1833, mainly the reports of a parliamentary commission that investigated civil, military, and judicial affairs in Ceylon in 1829–31. The recommendations of this commission reflect many of the utilitarian and humanitarian ideas that influenced the development of colonial government in South Asia.

695

Char, S. V. Desika. *Centralised Legislation.* New York: Asia Publishing House, 1963. A study of 27 years of Indian legislative history, beginning with Macaulay's appointment to the governor-general's council in 1834.

696

Macaulay, Thomas B. *Lord Macaulay's Legislative Minutes.* Ed. by C. D. Dharkar. London: Oxford University Press, 1946. Macaulay's minutes on education, press laws, and the penal system were very influential in the spirited debate that accompanied the development of British government in India during the second quarter of the 19th century.

697

Saran, Pramatha. *The Imperial Legislative Council of India, 1861–1920.* Delhi: S. Chand, 1961. A study of the council from its inception as a body of advisors to the central government, through its development in power and Indian membership until its replacement by the legislative assembly.

698

Masaldan, P. N. *Evolution of Provincial Autonomy in India, 1858–1950.* Bombay: Hind Kitabs, 1953. A lucid account of a complex and important aspect of India's constitutional development during the past century.

699

Jain, Mahabir P. *Outline of Indian Legal History.* Delhi: Dhanwantra Medical & Law Book House, 1952. A detailed historical survey of the Indian judiciary from the late 18th century to the years immediately after India's independence.

NATIVE STATES

700

Panikkar, Kavalam M. *Indian States and the Government of India.* London: M. Hopkinson, 2nd ed., 1932. A succinct study of the complex and varied relations between the native states and the paramount power of India; the terms feudal and federal are shown to be inappropriate characterizations of this unique system.

701

Thompson, Edward J. *The Making of the Indian Princes.* London: Oxford University Press, 1944. A detailed study of the incorporation of princely states into a subordinate position within the political system developed by the British during the first two decades of the 19th century. Many of these states were created by the British.

702

Lee-Warner, William. *The Native States of India.* London: Macmillan, 1910. A description of the relationship between Indian native rulers and Britain; written by a British official with many years of experience in this sphere of colonial relations.

703

Forster, Edward M. *The Hill of Devi.* New York: Harcourt, Brace, 1953. An intimate view of life in the court of an Indian prince based on letters written by the author in 1912–13 and 1921 while residing in the Indian state of Dewas Senior.

704

Menon, Vapal P. *The Story of the Integration of the Indian States.* New York: Macmillan, 1956. The end of the Indian states as separate political entities after India's independence in 1947 is authoritatively described by one who played an important role in this event.

705

India (Republic). Ministry of States. *White Paper on Indian States.* Delhi: Manager of Publications, Government of India, rev. ed., 1950. First published in 1948. A detailed official report on the past and present status of the princely states.

706

Wilcox, Wayne A. *Pakistan. The Consolidation of a Nation.* New York: Columbia University Press, 1963. A provocative, often unsubstantiated, account of political developments prior to Independence and shortly thereafter in the ten princely states that became part of Pakistan.

BRITISH ADMINISTRATION

707

Dodwell, Henry H. (ed.). *The Indian Empire.* Vol. VI of *The Cambridge History of India.* New York: Macmillan, 1932. Most of this volume concerns the development of Britain's administrative system in India during the 19th century.

708

Blunt, Edward A. H. *The I. C. S.; The Indian Civil Service.* London: Faber & Faber, 1937. A historical survey by an ex-member of the I.C.S. with a description of the organization whose legacy continues to influence Indian public life.

709

O'Malley, Lewis S. S. *The Indian Civil Service, 1601–1930.* London: J. Murray, 1931. One of the few systematic descriptions and analyses of the British bureaucracy in India.

710

Roy, Naresh Chandra. *The Civil Service in India.* Calcutta: K. L. Mukhopadhyay, 2nd ed., 1960. A useful survey of the administrative system developed by the British and its modification after India's independence, with special attention given to the recruitment and training of administrators.

711

Ghosal, Akshoy Kumar. *Civil Service in India Under the East India Company.* Calcutta: University of Calcutta, 1944. A scholarly study of the bureaucracy developed by the British to implement British rule of India, from the beginning to mid-19th century.

712

Strachey, John. *India; Its Administration and Progress.* London: Macmillan, 4th ed., 1911. This work by a high-ranking British official contains valuable material and a lucid presentation of the basic assumptions underlying British administrative policy, here viewed as mainly beneficial to the Indian people.

713

Ruthnaswamy, Mariadas. *Some Influences That Made the British Administrative System in India.* London: Luzac, 1939. A poorly organized collection of prosaic generalizations about British administrators and policies; of some value for descriptive details and copious references to other works.

714

Blunt, Edward A. H. (ed.). *Social Service in India.* London: H. M. Stationery Office, 2nd ed., 1946. An interesting example of materials used to instruct probationers for the Indian Civil Service; this text describes social conditions and the problems confronted by social welfare agencies.

715

Rao, V. Venkata. *A Hundred Years of Local Self-Government and Administration in the Andhra and Madras States, 1850 to 1950.* Bombay: C. D. Barfivala, 1960. An extensive compilation of information from district records and other difficult-to-obtain sources; lacking in interpretation and analysis.

716

Douie, Sir James McCrone. *Punjab Settlement Manual.* Chandigarh: Controller of Printing and Stationery, 4th ed., 1960. A reprint of a guide first published in 1899 for use by government official engaged in "settling" the amount of land revenue due the government; many other features of village political and economic life were also treated in the reports based on such manuals.

ECONOMIC HISTORY

717

Morris, Morris D. and Burton Stein. *"The Economic History of India,"* in *Journal of Economic History,* XXI, (June, 1961), pp. 179–207. A bibliographic essay in which the current state of the field is astutely and authoritatively appraised.

718

Dutt, Romesh C. *The Economic History of India Under Early British Rule.* Delhi: Ministry of Information and Broadcasting, Govt. of India, 1960. First published in 1901, this study and its companion volume concerning the Victorian Age considerably influenced early nationalists' views of British rule and continue to be cited by those who attribute India's poverty to British policy.

719

Dutt, Romesh C. *The Economic History of India in the Victorian Age.* London: Routledge & Kegan Paul, 7th ed., 1956. Though this work and its companion cited above are much out of date and rely solely on government records for information, they are the closest approach to a comprehensive economic history of British India prior to 1900.

720

Baden-Powell, B. H. *Land Systems of British India.* 3 vols. Oxford: Clarendon Press, 1892. A one-volume summary was published in 1894. A classic account of the many different forms of land tenure in India; based on official sources no longer readily available.

721

Gadgil, Dhananjaya R. *The Industrial Evolution of India in Recent Times.* London: Oxford University Press, rev.

ed., 1944. A valuable study of the changes wrought by industrial development during British times. Though less comprehensive than Dutt's work cited above, this study is probably the best survey of the Indian economy from mid-19th century to World War II.

722

Thorner, Daniel. *Investment in Empire: British Railway and Steam Shipping Enterprise in India, 1825–1849.* Philadelphia: University of Pennsylvania Press, 1950. An informative study of the factors that attracted private British capital to India during the years 1825–1849.

723

Buchanan, Daniel H. *The Development of Capitalist Enterprise in India.* New York: Macmillan, 1934. A valuable descriptive study that has yet to be superseded. Plantation agriculture as well as industrial activity is treated here.

724

Gupta, Om Prakash. *Central Banking in India, 1777–1934.* New Delhi: Hindustan Times Press, 1953. A historical account of the development of a modern banking system in India.

725

Mehta, S. D. *The Cotton Mills of India, 1854 to 1954.* Bombay: Textile Association of India, 1954. One of the few historical studies of an Indian industry. Textile manufacturing was among the first areas of the Indian economy to be affected by Western technology.

726

Bernstein, Henry T. *Steamboats on the Ganges.* Bombay: Orient Longmans, 1960. A study of the part played by science and technology in the modernization of India.

727

Sinha, N. C. *Studies in Indo-British Economy A Hundred Years Ago.* Calcutta: A. Mukherjee, 1946. A historical study of the Indian economy in mid-19th century; thin, but provocative.

728

Anstey, Vera. *The Economic Development of India.* London: Longmans, Green, 4th ed., 1952. A compilation of information concerning the Indian economy between 1900 and World War II, with a brief appraisal of factors likely to impede or promote economic development.

729

Arokiaswami, M. and T. M. Royappa. *The Modern Economic History of India.* Madras: S. Devotta, 4th ed., 1955. A brief survey of the main features of the Indian economy in the 20th century, with some information on its historic background.

730

Ganguli, Birendranath. *India's Economic Relations with the Far Eastern and Pacific Countries in the Present Century.* Calcutta: Orient Longman's, 1956. A useful summary by an economist of the main trends in trade between India and its Asian neighbors from the early 20th century to shortly after World War II; it provides statistical information not readily available elsewhere on economic aspects of the colonial system in Asia.

731

Rao, A. V. Raman. *Economic Development of Andhra Pradesh, 1766–1957.* Bombay: Popular Book Depot, 1958. One of the few attempts at regional economic history; though a monumental compilation of data from sources not readily available, it offers little in the way of interpretation or analysis.

732

Choksey, Rustom D. *Economic History of the Bombay Deccan.* Bombay: Asia Publishing House, 1955. Description and analysis of the changes wrought by the introduction of Western technology and the influence of the world market on a region of western India from 1818 to 1939. Many of the interpretations lack substantiation.

733

Raju, A. Sarada. *Economic Conditions in the Madras Presidency.* Madras: Madras University Press, 1941. One of the few economic histories of South India, confined in time to the first half of the 19th century.

734

Mukherjee, Nilmani. *The Ryotwari System in Madras, 1792–1827.* Calcutta: K. L. Mukhopadhyay, 1962. The first of a proposed two-volume study covering the subject to 1855. A study of the social, economic, and administrative consequences of a system of land revenue in which the government made direct settlements with the cultivator. This volume traces the development of the system from its beginning to the death of its most noted advocate, Thomas Munro.

735

Neale, Walter. *Economic Changes in Rural India.* New Haven: Yale University Press, 1962. A study of the land tenure system in the state of Uttar Pradesh between 1880 and 1955, with an assessment of the policies of reform attempted by the British and post-Independence governments.

736

Trevaskis, Hugh K. *The Land of the Five Rivers.* London: Oxford University Press, 1928. Although the author makes uncritical use of several antiquated theories of history, he provides valuable information on the economic history of the Punjab in the 19th century, based in part on his experience as director of land records.

737

Hamilton, C. J. *Trade Relations Between England and India, 1600–1896.* Calcutta: Thacker, Spink, 1919. A standard work on the subject in which, like most studies of this kind, only those aspects of the Indian economy relevant to foreign trade are given much consideration.

738

Naoroji, Dadabhai. *Poverty and Un-British Rule in India.* London: Swan Sonneschein, 1901. A detailed and well-ordered study by a leader in the early years of the nationalist movement. The author argues that India's poverty is due to British policy.

739

Lajpat Rai, Lala. *England's Debt to India.* New York: B. W. Huebsch. 1917. A forceful critique of Britain's fiscal policy in India by an early spokesman for the Indian nationalist movement.

740

Kumarappa, Joseph C. *Public Finance and Our Poverty.* Ahmedabad: Navajivan, 3rd ed., 1948. A brief review of economic conditions in India from 1918 to 1945 by a Gandhian economist, who attributes India's economic plight to British policy.

741

Bhatia, B. M. *Famines in India.* New York: Asia Publishing House, 1963. A study of the causes of famines and scarcities in India from 1860 to 1945 and their effect on government policy.

742

Desai, Rajanikant. *Standard of Living in India and Pakistan, 1931–32 to 1940–41.* Bombay: Popular Book Depot, 1953. One of the more judicious discussions of a subject about which little is known for want of adequate statistics.

743

India (Government of). Famine Enquiry Commission. *Final Report of the Famine Enquiry Commission.* New Delhi: Manager of Publications, Government of India, 1945. A thorough survey of agrarian relations and economic conditions in rural India during the final years of British rule.

744

Harris, Frank R. *Jamsetji Nusserwaniji Tata.* Bombay: Blackie & Sons, 2nd ed., 1958. First published in 1925 by Milford of London. An adulatory biography of an Indian pioneer in the field of heavy industry.

745

Moraes, Francis R. *Sir Purshotamdas Thakurdas.* Bombay: Asia Publishing House, 1957. A popular biography of a prominent member of the Indian business community. Very few accounts have been written about this important segment of Indian society.

WESTERN REACTIONS TO INDIA

746

Bearce, George D. *British Attitudes Towards India,* 1784–1858. London: Oxford University Press, 1961. A study of the intellectual basis and ideological atmosphere which supported and shaped British policy in India prior to the Mutiny of 1857.

747

Busteed, Henry E. *Echoes From Old Calcutta.* London: Thacker, 4th ed., 1908. A vivid description of the European community in Calcutta during the latter part of the 18th century; based on letters, newspapers, and other contemporary materials.

748

Das Gupta, Anil Chandra (ed.). *The Days of John Company.* Calcutta: Superintendent of Government Printing, West Bengal, 1959. A selection of articles, editorials, and advertisements published in the *Calcutta Gazette* from 1824–32; provides material on East India Company administration and policy, social life and customs of the day, and the concern with social reform that existed in Bengal during this period.

749

Spear, Percival. *The Nabobs.* London: Oxford University Press, paperbound ed., 1963. A study of the social and cultural aspects of Anglo-Indian relations from the period of initial contact through the 18th century; Spear considers these relations to be relatively free of the prejudice and arrogance manifested by many Englishmen in later times.

750

Dodwell, Henry H. *The Nabobs of Madras.* London: Williams & Norgate, 1926. A description of English social life in the Madras area during the 18th century.

751

Kincaid, Dennis C. *British Social Life in India,* 1608–1937. London: Routledge, 1939. An often satirical view of the society within a society created by the British in India in contrast to earlier conquerors whose social and cultural life was a more intimate part of the Indian scene.

752

Brown, Hilton. *The Sahibs.* London: W. Hodge, 1948. An often amusing selection from personal accounts by British residents in India reflecting some of the attitudes and activities of minor officials and their wives.

753

Forster, E. M. *A Passage to India.* New York: Harcourt, Brace, 1924. A novel of the first order in which the personal dimensions of social and cultural interchange between India and the West are subtly portrayed.

754

Mayo, Katherine. *Mother India.* New York: Harcourt, Brace, 1927. A classic example of one type of Western response to India; "shocking" customs are described in a distorted manner to justify a militant variety of missionary "reform."

755

Lajpat Rai, Lala. *Unhappy India.* Calcutta: Banna, 1928. A scathing critique of *Mother India* by a leading spokesman for the Indian nationalist movement.

756

Isaacs, Harold. *Scratches on Our Minds.* New York: John Day, 1958. Reprinted in paperbound form as *Images of Asia* by G. P. Putnam of New York. A study of the source and effect of mental images of India, China and Japan held by 181 "informed" Americans; based on interviews.

757

Subba Rao, G. *Indian Words in English.* Oxford: Clarendon Press, 1954. A brief informative study of an interesting aspect of Indo-British cultural and linguistic relations.

TRANSFORMATION OF SOCIAL AND INTELLECTUAL TRADITION

758

O'Malley, Lewis, S. S. (ed.). *Modern India and the West.* London: Oxford University Press, 1941. A useful collection of essays that survey Western influence on various aspects of Indian life including education, the arts, and Hindu society. British bias is manifest in many instances where evaluations of this process are attempted.

759

De Bary, William T., et al. (compilers). *Sources of Indian Tradition.* New York: Columbia University Press, 1958. More than 300 pages of this collection of original source material concern the response of Indian leaders to Western influence and the political, social, and economic problems of modern India.

760

Ingham, Kenneth. *Reformers in India,* 1793–1833. Cambridge: Cambridge University Press, 1956. A well-documented monograph on European, primarily missionary, efforts at social reform during a period of experimentation with deliberate changes in indigenous customs.

761

Ballhatchet, Kenneth. *Social Policy and Social Change in Western India.* London: Oxford University Press, 1957. An excellent study of British policy, mainly that of Mountstuart Elphinstone, in the western Deccan between 1817 and 1830. The effect of this policy on native institutions, especially the weakening of traditional modes of social organization, is ably demonstrated.

762

Natarajan, Swaminath. *A Century of Social Reform in India.* Bombay: Asia Publishing House, 2nd ed., 1963. A historical survey of Indian leaders and programs of social reform in the 19th century; a movement particularly active in the field of education.

763

Farquhar, John Nicol. *Modern Religious Movements in India.* New York: Macmillan, 1915. One of the few studies of the numerous religious groups that developed during the 19th century as part of the "Indian renaissance" stimulated by the impact of the West.

764

Bose, N. S. *The Indian Awakening and Bengal.* Calcutta: K. L. Mukhopadhyay, 1960. A judicious survey of the literature in Bengali and English on the part played by Bengal in the 19th-century Indian renaissance, including the work of such social reformers as Ram Mohan Roy, and Bengal's contribution to the nationalist movement.

765

Rammohun Roy, Raja. *The English Works of Raja Rammohun Roy.* 3 vols. Ed. by K. Nag and D. Burman. Calcutta: Sadharan Brahmo Samaj, 1945–51. Rammohun Roy was one of the first and most effective Indians to attempt a synthesis of Indian and Western ideas. He helped found the first institution of Western higher education in India and pioneered in social and religious reforms in early 19th-century Bengal.

766

Singh, Iqbal. *Rammohun Roy.* New York: Asia Publishing House, 1958. A biographical study of the famous Bengali reformer of the early 19th century.

767

Karve, D. D. (ed. and trans.). *The New Brahmans: Five Maharashtrian Families.* Berkeley: University of California Press, 1963. A translation of five life histories, originally written in Marathi, of five Brahman men who actively participated in the social and political changes of twentieth century India. Among the five men are two artists, a college professor, a poet, and a historian.

768

McCully, Bruce T. *English Education and the Origins of Indian Nationalism.* New York: Columbia University Press, 1940. A history of education in 19th-century India; contains many insights concerning Western influence on Indian society, especially on ideas of political freedom. Includes a detailed bibliography.

769

Nurullah, Syed and J. P. Naik. *A History of Education in India During the British Period.* Bombay: Macmillan, rev. ed., 1951. A detailed survey of the development of education in modern India and the type of education available under British rule.

770

Misra, Bankey Bihari. *The Indian Middle Classes: Their Growth in Modern Times.* London: Oxford University Press, 1961. A pro-British pioneering study of the social consequences of Western influence introduced in India during British times.

771

Shils, Edward. *The Intellectual Between Tradition and Modernity; the Indian Situation.* The Hague: Mouton, 1960. Issued as Supplement No. 1 to the journal, *Comparative Studies in Society and History.* A brief insightful analysis of the contemporary plight of India's intellectuals, caught in a position of alienation from the common man, but with few opportunities of an uncommon kind.

19th Century

Historical accounts of India in the 19th century are written mainly in relation to the careers of British administrators, notably governor-generals. Prior to the development of rapid transport, the Suez canal, and the introduction of the telegraph, these men possessed great authority and considerable latitude in framing policies that bore the mark of their personal views and motives. The voluminous accounts of administrative policies and their implementation have few counterparts in the economic and social developments of the time.

The first half of the 19th century is a tale of British conquest, annexation, and diplomatic neutralization of isolated segments of native power. It was also a period in which the basic framework of government was built from a combination of indigenous and European institutions and inventions of British administrators coping with problems of particular regions. A lull subsequent to the completion of this process was followed by the 1857 military revolt of the Bengal army, one of the three company armies in India. Though short-lived and confined to northern India, this unplanned mutiny received the support of various native princes and left a legacy of fear and suspicion on both sides. The mutiny also precipitated the India Act of 1858, which transferred all the East India Company's authority to the crown and established the cabinet post of secretary of state for India directly to administer India.

The character of the British administration also changed after the mutiny. Career-oriented men, recruited through competitive examinations rather than the earlier system of patronage, came out to India with their wives and children for a "tour of duty," rather than for high adventure and the rapid amassing of riches. These bureaucrats created a separate social world of their own, from which even British-educated Indians were excluded. By 1885, India had become a modern colony, ruled by an aloof elite whose identity and loyalty were intimately bound to a remote foreign power, more alien, and in many ways more pervasive, than any other invader of India.

CONSOLIDATION OF POWER c.1800-1857

772

Chaudhuri, Sashi B. *Civil Disturbances During the British Rule in India, 1765–1857.* Calcutta: World Press, 1955. A useful though partisan survey of local uprisings and disturbances directed against British authority; one of the few studies concerned with social and political forces outside the mainstream of events that occupy most general histories.

773

Embree, Ainslie T. *Charles Grant and British Rule in India.* New York: Columbia University Press, 1962. A study of the career of an East India Company official noted for his advocacy of Christian reforms in India during the early 19th century.

774

Low, Ursula. *Fifty Years with John Company.* London: J. Murray, 1936. An account of Sir John Low's career as soldier-administrator in India from 1805–58; based on Low's letters to his family. This correspondence provides information on British attitudes towards India and indicates the existence of strong bonds of kinship and friendship among high-ranking company officials.

775

Bradshaw, John. *Sir Thomas Munro and the British of the Madras Presidency.* Oxford: Clarendon Press, 1894. A study of Thomas Munro, Governor of Madras in the early 19th century, who implemented an administrative system in South India that differed markedly from that developed in Bengal.

776

Dubois, Jean A. *Hindu Manners, Customs and Ceremonies.* Trans. & ed. by H. K. Beauchamp. Oxford: Clarendon Press, 3rd ed., 1928. A classic account of South India in the early 19th century by a Catholic missionary who resided there for thirty years; Dubois' descriptions are strongly colored by his personal biases and those common to other Europeans of the day.

777

Banerjee, Anil Chandra. *The Eastern Frontier of British India, 1784–1826.* Calcutta: A. Mukherjee, 2nd ed., 1946. A detailed study of British activities leading to annexation of the predominantly tribal area of Assam in 1824.

778

Lahiri, Mohan R. *The Annexation of Assam.* Calcutta: General Printers, 1955. A history of British expansion into northeastern India between 1824 and 1854.

779

Bhanu, Dharma. *History of Administration of the North-Western Provinces, 1803–1858.* Agra: Shiva Lal Agarwala, 1957. History of a region, known as the United Provinces in later times and Uttar Pradesh today, that has always been a major prize in contests for political supremacy in India.

780

Edwardes, Michael. *The Orchid House; Splendours and Miseries of the King of Oudh, 1827–1857.* London: Cassell, 1960. An account of the political fortunes of a strategically located kingdom in the central Gangetic plain during a period of external threat and inner turmoil, ultimately resolved by British annexation of the area in 1857.

781

Thompson, Edward J. *Life of Charles, Lord Metcalfe.* London: Faber & Faber, 1937. Metcalf reached India in 1800 and resided there as a British official for more than thirty years. He gained fame for diplomatic skill in negotiations with native rulers and served as acting governor-general in 1835. He was most active in Rajputana and northern India.

782

Sleeman, William H. *Rambles and Recollections of an Indian Official.* Ed. by V. A. Smith. London: Oxford University Press, rev. ed., 1915. First published in 1844; a varied collection of essays on the land and people of north and central India in the early 19th century by an Englishman with thirty-five years' experience in India including special duty suppressing *thuggee.*

783

Taylor, Philip Meadows. *Confessions of a Thug.* Ed. by C. W. Stewart. London: Oxford University Press, 1933. First published in 1839; a semi-fictional account of a society of murderers, who strangled and robbed travellers in India as an act of worshipping the goddess Kali as well as for personal gain. The author participated in the British campaign to suppress *thuggee* and based this work on several "confessions" by *thug* informers.

784

Malcolm, John. *A Memoir of Central India.* 2 vols. London: Parbury, Allen, 3rd ed., 1832. A classic account of political conditions in central India during the early 19th century by the British officer in charge of the area from 1818 to 1822.

785

Boulger, Demetrius C. *Lord William Bentinck.* Oxford: Clarendon Press, 1897. One of the few accounts of a Governor-General, 1828–35, whose policies were strongly influenced by Utilitarian ideas; Bentinck initiated major reforms in the judicial and revenue systems, abolished such customs as *suttee,* and promoted Western education.

786

Imlah, Albert H. *Lord Ellenborough.* London: Oxford University Press, 1939. A biography of one of the least effective governor-generals, 1842–44, whose indecisive policies contributed to British losses in an abortive effort to control Afghanistan in the 1840's.

787

Kaye, John W. *History of the War in Afghanistan.* 3 vols. London: W. H. Allen, 4th ed., 1890. The standard work on the least successful phase of British expansion in the 1840's; military efforts in this area were prompted by unfounded fears of Russian penetration in the northwest frontier.

788

Huttenback, Robert A. *British Relations with Sind, 1799–1843; An Anatomy of Imperialism.* Berkeley: University of California Press, 1962. The British annexation of the lower Indus valley in 1843 is here shown to be part of a deliberate policy of expansion; Charles Napier's role in this affair occupies about half of the book.

789

Lambrick, Hugh T. *Sir Charles Napier and Sind.* Oxford: Clarendon Press, 1952. An authoritative account of the British conquest of Sind in 1843 by the impetuous and swashbuckling General Napier whose conduct in the affair is often censured.

790

Lambrick, Hugh T. *John Jacob of Jacobabad.* London: Cassell, 1960. An account of a man whose talents as soldier, administrator, and engineer were vigorously applied to the settlement of Sind where he served as deputy commissioner in mid-19th century; Jacob exemplified the qualities of character often attributed in fiction to officials in the lower echelon of the British administration.

791

Lee-Warner, William. *Life of the Marquis of Dalhousie.* 2 vols. London: Macmillan, 1904. A biography of a governor-general, 1848–56, whose forceful personality and commitment to "progress" led to rapid and far-reaching changes in education, commerce and industry, as well as government. Dalhousie's promotion of public works and modern transportation did much to thrust Western technology into Indian life.

792

Hunter, William W. *The Marquess of Dalhousie.* London: Oxford University Press, 1905. A brief, authoritative biography of an important governor-general: part of the Rulers of India series.

793

Das, Manindra N. *Studies in the Economic and Social Development of Modern India, 1848–56.* Calcutta: K. L. Mukhopadhyay, 1959. A study of the effects of Dalhousie's policy of furthering Western technology and ideas in India.

794

Arnold, Edwin. *The Marquess of Dalhousie's Administration of British India.* 2 vols. London: Saunders, Otley, 1862–65. A detailed review of Dalhousie's regime from 1848–1856 when the last stronghold of native power was subdued with the annexation of the Punjab, and major changes were made in the organization of the government.

795

Edwardes, Michael. *The Necessary Hell.* London: Cassell, 1958. A study of the paternalistic school of administration developed in the Punjab in the middle of the 19th century by John and Henry Lawrence whose diaries are the main source. The Lawrence brothers served under Dalhousie and shared his belief in the superiority of Western culture and the need for economic reforms. John's policies as governor-general are discussed in entry 807.

796

Morison, John Lyle. *Lawrence of Lucknow. 1806–1857 the Life of Sir Henry Lawrence.* London: George Bell, 1934. A biography of the soldier-administrator whose efforts at social and economic reform, and disregard for bureaucratic convention, contributed to the development of a distinct tradition of administration in the Punjab and other areas of North India.

MUTINY OF 1857

797

Kaye, John W. and G. B. Malleson. *History of the Indian Mutiny.* 6 vols. London: Longmans, new ed., 1897–98. The most comprehensive general history of the mutiny; presented from the British point of view. This publication consists of two works published separately in several editions before and after this combined version which has the added advantage of an index.

798

Sen, Surendra, Nath. *Eighteen Fifty-Seven.* New Delhi: Ministry of Information & Broadcasting, Government of India, 1957. A remarkably objective review of the causes, character, and consequences of the mutiny of 1857; contains an extensive bibliography.

799

Chaudhuri, Sashi Bhusan. *Civil Rebellion in the Indian Mutiny.* Calcutta: World Press, 1957. An able presentation of a partisan view in which the events of 1857–59 are seen as part of a national revolutionary movement.

800

Majumdar, Ramesh Chandra. *The Sepoy Mutiny and the Revolt of 1857.* Calcutta: K. L. Mukhopadhyay, 1957. An Indian historian here argues against interpretations that attribute the events of 1857 to an independence movement based on nationalism. He considers the uprising to be an attempt by some native rulers to regain lost power by capitalizing on the mutiny of disgruntled troops in the Bengal Army.

801

Marx, Karl. *The First Indian War of Independence, 1857–1859.* Moscow: Foreign Languages Publishing House, 1960. A collection of articles written by the famous revolutionary for the *New York Daily Tribune* at the time of the uprisings; Marx discusses these events within a general analysis of the Western impact on India.

802

Embree, Ainslie T. *1857 in India; Mutiny or War of Independence?* Boston: D. C. Heath, 1963. A collection of interpretive writings in which conflicting views of the events of 1857 are ably presented for use in college courses; contemporary accounts are included as well as retrospective appraisals.

803

Leasor, James. *The Red Fort.* New York: Harcourt Brace, 1957. A popular account of the seige of Delhi in 1857 based on diaries and other contemporary sources that convey personal reactions to the Mutiny.

IMPERIAL PERIOD c.1858-1905

804

Philips, Cyril H. (ed.). *The Evolution of India and Pakistan, 1858 to 1947.* London: Oxford University Press, 1962. Part One of this judicious selection of documents from public and private papers treats political developments in India between 1858 and 1917. Part three contains material on economic, social, military, administrative, and diplomatic subjects for the period 1858–1947.

805

Dodwell, Henry H. *A Sketch of the History of India, 1858–1918.* London: Longmans, 1925. A survey of political developments during this period by a leading authority.

806

Prasad, Bisheshwar. *The Foundations of India's Foreign Policy, 1860–1882.* Bombay: Orient Longmans, 1955. Volume I of a projected four-volume history; this study is well documented, readable, and occasionally moves beyond description to a consideration of the motives that entered into the formulation of policy.

807

Pal, Dharma. *Administration of Sir John Lawrence in India, 1864–1869.* Simla: Minerva Book Shop, 1952. A study of the vigorous policy of public works and land reform initiated by Lawrence when he was Governor-General of India.

808

Kisch, Hermann M. *A Young Victorian in India.* London: J. Cape, 1957. This collection of "letters home," written by the future Director-General of the Indian post office, conveys the duty-oriented outlook of British officials in the late 19th century.

809

Roberts, Frederick S. *Forty-One Years in India.* New York: Longmans, Green, 1914. The autobiography of a British officer, ultimately Commander-in-Chief of the Indian Army, whose classic march from Kabul to Kandahar in 1880 contributed to the tradition that inspired Kipling's accounts of warfare on the Afghan frontier.

810

Balfour, Elizabeth. *History of Lord Lytton's Indian Administration, 1876–1880.* London: Longmans, 1899. A readable account of an eventful period noted for Lytton's frontier policy which sought to bring pressure on Russia through Afghanistan. Lytton's domestic policies, including restrictions on the vernacular press, increased tension between the British and politically sensitive Indians.

811

Gopal, Sarvepalli. *The Vice-Royalty of Lord Ripon, 1880–1884.* London: Oxford University Press, 1953. A scholarly study based on sources only recently available. Ripon was sent to India to implement policies that favored the introduction of representative institutions in India. He initiated self-government at the local level and lifted restrictions on the press.

812

Singh, Hira Lal. *Problems and Policies of the British in India, 1885–1898.* New York: Asia Publishing House, 1963. A study of the British response to demands for greater participation in government by the rising Indian middle class.

813

Ronaldshay, Earl of. *The Life of Lord Curzon.* 3 vols. London: E. Benn, 1928. Volume II is one of the best accounts of Curzon's career as Viceroy of India from 1898 to 1905. Curzon's skilled and vigorous administrative measures contributed to India's development into a modern nation state and unwittingly gave impetus to the independence movement.

20th Century

The dominant theme of 20th Century Indian history is the emergence of a successful nationalist movement. Opposition to British rule appeared in the early 1900's in a movement that sought to change the traditional order of Indian society in addition to obtaining Indian participation in government. The roots of this movement may be traced back to Indian efforts at social and religious reform early in the 19th century. The early reformers, and later nationalist leaders, were mainly Western-educated members of an urban middle class committed to modernization and Western institutions of government. The main organizational instrument of this movement was the Indian National Congress, founded in 1885 with the modest goal of greater participation in government by the urban middle class, and a reliance on moderate methods, consisting mainly of petitioning the British for constitutional reform.

Leaders of a more radical persuasion entered the Congress in the early 1900's with demands that were not satisfied by the Morley-Minto reform of 1909, giving Indians a majority of the seats in provincial legislatures, but little actual power. The introduction of parliamentary forms of government also contributed to the development of communal differences that centered about the rights of religious and other special interest groups to a proportionate share of legislative seats, due to fear of dominance by the Hindu majority. The formation of the All-India Muslim League in 1906 was one expression of this concern that ultimately led to the creation of Pakistan.

Another attempt to satisfy nationalist demands appears in the Montagu-Chemsford reform of 1919, which created a system of dual government, known as dyarchy, at the provincial level. Under this system, Indian ministers were given responsibility for agriculture, health, sanitation, and education, but few funds were provided for the implementation of their programs. Control of the budget and police, and the power to veto legislation were retained by the British governor.

The emergence of Mohandas K. Gandhi as a major leader of Congress in 1920 led to the development of a mass base for the nationalist movement. "Mahatma" Gandhi's use of traditional symbols, and his genius for presenting issues in a political idiom comprehensible to the peasant, generated popular support for the Congress. Gandhi's use of non-violent techniques of political agitation, though often leading to disorder and bloodshed, captured the sympathy of many Westerners and proved quite effective in conflicts with the British.

The Government of India Act of 1935 extended the principle of dyarchy to the national government. This act provided for a completely Indian cabinet at the provincial level and a federal union of British provinces and native states. Although never fully implemented, due to fear on the part of the princely powers of nationalist radicalism and other factors, the Act of 1935 provided the initial framework of government at the time of India's independence in 1947. The transfer of power was accomplished with relatively little ill feeling towards the British. However, a legacy of fear and hatred was created at the same time due to the bloodshed and destruction that accompanied the partition of British India into Pakistan and the Republic of India. This legacy, most clearly manifest in the continuing dispute over Kashmir, remains one of the major problems of South Asia.

REFERENCES, SOURCES, AND GENERAL WORKS

814
Wilson, Patrick. *Government and Politics of India and Pakistan, 1885–1955*. Berkeley: South Asia Studies, Institute of East Asiatic Studies, University of California, 1956. A 356-page bibliography of works in Western languages.

815
Majumdar, J. K. (ed.). *Indian Speeches and Documents on British Rule, 1821–1918*. Calcutta: Longmans, Green, 1937. A collection of speeches and writings by Indian leaders in political thought and action.

816
Phillips, Cyril H. (ed.). *The Evolution of India and Pakistan, 1858 to 1947*. London: Oxford University Press, 1962. Part Two of this valuable collection of documents contains material relating to developments in government and politics between 1917 and 1947 including India's attainment of independence and subsequent partition into India and Pakistan.

817
Mitra, H. N. (ed.). *Indian Annual Register*. 29 vols. Calcutta: The Annual Register Office, 1919–47. This digest provides about one thousand pages of documents annually on the major events in India from 1919 to 1947. Information on a plan to microfilm the entire series may be obtained from the Inter-University Committee on South Asian Scholarly Resources of the Association of Asian Studies.

818
Indian Affairs Record. New Delhi: Diwan Chand Information Centre, 1955–. A monthly review of major political events based on extensive quotation from the press, political parties, and government; references are provided for important articles and documents, with an occasional reprinting of major documents in full.

819
Bombwall, K. R. *Indian Politics and Government Since 1885*. Delhi: Atma Ram, 1951. A survey of the Indian nationalist movement and constitutional developments to 1950; prepared for use as a college text in India.

820
Parkin, George R. *India Today*. New York: John Day, 1946. A revised edition of *India Today* by W. E. Duffett, published in 1942. A useful reference guide to major events in Indian history and politics between 1919 and 1945.

821
Brown, W. Norman. *The United States and India and Pakistan*. Cambridge: Harvard University Press, rev. ed., 1963. Written to acquaint the American public with these newly emergent nations, this work provides a succinct and readable overview of the British period and the development of Indian nationalism.

822
Chirol, Sir Valentine. *India*. London: E. Beam, 1926. A useful introduction, pro-British oriented, to early 20th-century Indian politics and the historical and cultural setting. Contains an account of the influence of Western education, the non-cooperation of the nationalists, and the early years of the Indian legislatures.

823
Cumming, John (ed.). *Political India, 1832–1932*. London: Oxford University Press, 1932. A collection of essays on political forces in modern India, mainly those affecting the growth of nationalism in the early 20th century. The twenty contributors include an ex-viceroy and other high-ranking British officials whose views are of special value as a reflection of British attitude towards India in the early 1930's.

824
Beauchamp, Joan. *British Imperialism in India*. London: M. Lawrence, 1934. A critique of British policy in India by the British Labour Party; India's independence was attained when this party came to power after World War II.

825
Panikkar, Kavalam M. *The Foundations of New India*. London: G. Allen & Unwin, 1963. A review and assessment of Britain's legacy to independent India, especially the institutions of government, by one of India's most provocative historians; most attention is given to the period 1930–47.

826
Dutt, Rajani P. *India, Today and Tomorrow*. Delhi: People's Publishing House, 1955. A revised and abridged edition of Dutt's *India Today*. A Marxist analysis of the nationalist movement and conditions in modern India that may affect future political developments.

MEN AND EVENTS   c.1900-1947

827
Chaudhuri, Nirad C. *Autobiography of an Unknown Indian*. New York: Macmillan, 1951. A portrayal with considerable insight of an educated Indian's response to the ideological and social forces of the late 19th and early 20th centuries; contains a critical appraisal of nationalist sentiment.

828
Reed, Stanley. *The India I Knew, 1897–1947*. London: Odhams, 1952. A wide-ranging and informed overview of the period by the editor of an influential English newspaper in India.

829
Besant, Annie. *Annie Besant; An Autobiography*. London: Unwin, 2nd ed., 1908. Annie Besant was a leader in the Theosophist movement that served to promote equal relations between Indians and Westerners; she also helped found the Benares Hindu University in 1910 and played an active part in the early years of the Indian struggle for independence.

830
Minto, Mary C. *India, Minto and Morley, 1905–1910*. London: Macmillan, 1934. A valuable collection of papers compiled from correspondence between Viceroy Minto and Morley, Secretary of State for India, supplemented with information from Countess Minto's diary.

831

Waley, David. *Edwin Montagu*. New York: Asia Publishing House, 1964. An account of the personal and public life of a man who led two British Cabinet missions to India in the early 20th century; contains previously unpublished excerpts from Montagu's diary kept during his 1912–13 mission to India.

832

Montagu, Edwin S. *An Indian Diary*. Ed. by V. Montagu. London: W. Heinemann, 1930. An intimate view of high policy-making during the turbulent years 1917–1922, When Montagu served as secretary of state for India.

833

Prasad, Rajendra. *Satyagraha in Champaran*. Ahmedabad: Navajivan, 2nd ed., rev., 1949. An account of the Nationalists' use of non-violent techniques in a 1917 campaign to aid oppressed peasants in Champaran; written by a participant destined to be the first president of India.

834

Gopal, Sarvepalli. *The Vice-Royalty of Lord Irwin, 1926–31*. Oxford: Clarendon Press, 1957. A lucid study, based on previously restricted sources, of a turbulent period and a steadfast man, who sought to reconcile nationalist demands and British interests.

835

Irwin, Edward F. L. W. *Indian Problems*. London: G. Allen, 1932. A collection of speeches made by Lord Irwin in India while serving as viceroy from 1926–31; provides a record of major events of the day and official statements of policy.

836

Andrews, Charles F. *India and the Simon Report*. New York: Macmillan, 1930. A critique, by an Englishman sympathetic to the nationalist movement, of a parliamentary commission that investigated political conditions in India during 1928–29.

837

Moon, Penderel. *Strangers in India*. New York: Reynal & Hitchcock, 1945. An entertaining and informative attempt to convey some of the major problems of India in the 1930's through the presentation of illustrative incidents in dialogue form; the author was a British official in the Punjab.

838

Brailsford, Henry N. *Subject India*. New York: John Day, 1943. A journalist's critique of Britain's response to the Indian nationalist movement; includes observations made by the author while in India during the 1930's.

839

Anand, Mulk Raj. *Letters on India*. London: G. Routledge, 1942. A polemic assessment of British rule in India, in the form of letters exchanged with a British factory worker; useful as an example of Indian nationalist propaganda.

840

Coupland, Reginald. *The Indian Problem*. New York: Oxford University Press, 3 vols. in 1, 1944. Volume II contains information not readily available elsewhere: an excellent detailed account of the workings of provincial legislature and related efforts at representative government in India between 1936 and 1942; the following entry by the first president of India provides a nationalist's view of the same period.

841

Prasad, Rajendra. *India Divided*. Bombay: Hind Kitabs, 1946. A well-argued critique of schemes for India's partition into Muslim and Hindu states; contains useful statistical information and a history of Muslim-Hindu relations. Prasad's criticism of Britain's role in this conflict complements Coupland's work cited in the previous entry.

842

Bhagat, K. P. *A Decade of Indo-British Relations, 1937–47*. Bombay: Popular Book Depot, 1959. A rambling narrative of political events containing extensive quotes from individuals and organizations engaged in forging the final form of India's independence.

843

Chatterji, A. C. *India's Struggle for Freedom*. Calcutta: Chuckervertty, Chatterjee, 1947. A history of the Indian National Army from 1942–45 by an officer of the army organized in South-East Asia by militant nationalists allied with Japanese forces.

844

Amery, Leopold C. M. S. *India and Freedom*. London: Oxford University Press, 1942. A brief selection of speeches by the secretary of state for India during the early years of World War II; it provides an excellent summary of official British policy regarding Indian demands for independence and the Conservative party point of view.

845

Alexander, Horace G. *India Since Cripps*. Harmondsworth: Penguin, 1944. A succinct appraisal of the stalemate in negotiations that developed in 1942–43 between Britain and leaders of the nationalist movement.

846

Gandhi, Mohandas K. *Gandhiji's Correspondence with the Government, 1944–47*. Ahmedabad: Navajivan Publishing House, 1959. A collection of useful source material for the final years of the independence movement when Gandhi's role as India's chief spokesman in negotiations with the British was rapidly diminishing.

Indian Leaders—Biographies and Autobiographies

847

Tandon, P. D. *Leaders of Modern India*. Bombay: Vora, 1955. Contains brief biographical sketches of prominent Indian leaders of the 20th century, mainly those active in the nationalist movement.

848

Dhanapala, D. B. *Eminent Indians*. Bombay: Nalanda, 1947. A collection of biographical sketches of modern Indian leaders of thought and action, including Krishnamurti, Sarojini Naidu, and Gandhi.

849

Meherally, Yusuf. *Leaders of India*. 2 vols. Bombay: Padma, 1942–46. A thin collection of biographical sketches of prominent Indian nationalists active in the early 1940's.

850

Brown D. Mackenzie (ed.). *The Nationalist Movement: Indian Political Thought from Ranade to Bhave*. Berkeley: University of California, paperbound, 1961. A selection from the writings of nine eminent Indian leaders of the 20th century, accompanied by an excellent brief historical and personal background.

851

Keer, Dhananjay. *Dr. Ambedkar; Life and Mission*. Bombay: A. V. Keer, 1954. A sympathetic account of an Untouchable who rose to national prominence as a political leader often opposed to Congress policy; Ambedkar played a major role in the writing of the Indian Constitution adopted in 1951.

852

Azad, Maulana Abul Kalam. (1888–1958). *India Wins Freedom*. New York: 1960. A personal account of 20th century political events, including trenchant views on Partition, by an eminent Muslim leader who served as President of the Indian National Congress and held a cabinet post in the Republic of India.

853

Banerjea, Surendranath. *A Nation in the Making; Being the Reminiscences of Fifty Years of Public Life*. London: Oxford University Press, 1925. A classic account by one of the first nationalists to attempt an awakening of Indian political unity. Especially useful for political developments in 19th-century Bengal and the response of a "moderate" to the non-cooperation movement.

854

Bose, Subhas Chandra. *Netaji's Life and Writings*. 2 vols. Calcutta: Thacker, Spink, 1948. Volume I contains an autobiographical sketch of Bose's early years, 1897–1920. Volume II is a reprint of *The Indian Struggle, 1920–34*, a collection of Bose's writings on the national movement first published in London in 1935.

855

Bose, Subhas Chandra. *The Indian Struggle, 1935–42*. Calcutta: Chuckervertty, Chatterjee, 1952. A continuation of Bose's writings contained in the preceding entry. During this period Bose broke with Congress and left India to lead the Japanese-supported Indian National Army in Southeast Asia.

856

Bose, Subhas Chandra. *Crossroads; 1938–40*. New York: Asia Publishing House. A useful collection of Bose's writings during a period when his advocacy of force as the means of ridding India of the British caused considerable controversy within the Congress.

857

Ayer, Subbier A. *The Lone Sentinel*. Bombay: Popular Book Depot, 1960. An uncritical sketch of the political career of Morarji Desai, a leader of the "Conservative" wing of the Congress Party, former Finance Minister of the Union government, and a possible candidate for Prime Minister.

858

Sharma, Jagdish Saran. *Mahatma Gandhi; A Descriptive Bibliography*. Delhi: S. Chand, 1955. A valuable guide to the vast literature by and about Gandhi; contains 3,671 entries, most of them annotated, in ten major languages, with English accounting for about 90 per cent of the total.

859

Deshpande, Pandurang G. *Gandhiana; A Bibliography of Gandhian Literature*. Ahmedabad: Navajivan, 1948. Contains almost 3,000 references to the writings of Gandhi and his followers: about half in English, the others in various Indian languages.

860

Gandhi, Mohandas K. (1869–1948). *The Collected Works of Mahatma Gandhi*. Delhi: Publications Division, Government of India, 1958–. An awesome undertaking numbering five volumes to 1961, when volume V, covering the years 1905–06, was published.

861

Gandhi, Mohandas K. *An Autobiography, or the Story of My Experiments with Truth*. Trans. by M. Desai. New York: Beacon Press, paperbound ed., 1957. A candid and intimate account by the most eminent Indian of the 20th century. A supplementary work is cited in the following entry.

862

Gandhi, Mohandas K. *Satyagraha in South Africa*. Trans. by V. G. Desai. Ahmedabad: Navajivan, 2nd ed., rev., 1950. Gandhi's life and career in South Africa during the latter part of the 19th century are described in this supplement to his autobiography, cited in the preceding entry.

863

Gandhi, Mohandas K. *Mahatma Gandhi: His Own Story*. Ed. by C. F. Andrews. New York: Macmillan, 1930. An abridgement of the two preceding entries.

864

Gandhi, Mohandas K. *Hind Swaraj, or Indian Home Rule*. Ahmedabad: Navajivan, rev. ed., 1946. First published in 1909; this brief statement, written upon Gandhi's return to India from South Africa, provides an interesting foreshadowing of the career that Gandhi was to pursue during the following three decades as a leader of the national movement.

865

Gandhi, Mohandas K. *The Gandhi Reader*. Ed. by H. A. Jack. Bloomington: Indiana University Press, 1956. New York: Grove Press, paperbound ed., 1961. A well-organized reference and introduction to Gandhi's life and main ideas, based on Gandhi's writings with supplementary material from his associates. The editor provides background information and an excellent select bibliography.

866

Fischer, Louis. *The Life of Mahatma Gandhi*. New York: Harper, 1950. An abridged paperbound edition was published in 1954 by Signet of New York. Though marred by a few factual errors, this is the most readable account of Gandhi's life.

867

Nanda, Bal Ram. *Mahatma Gandhi; A Biography*. Boston: Beacon, 1959. A well-organized narrative, mainly concerned with Gandhi's public life and principal ideas; contains an excellent bibliography.

868

Tendulkar, Dinanath G. *Mahatma: Life of Mohandas Karamchand Gandhi*. 8 vols. Delhi: Publications Division, Government of India, rev. ed., 1960–63. A detailed though poorly-organized account of Gandhi's life; contains valuable information not readily available elsewhere.

869

Guha, Charuchandra. *Seven Months with Mahatma Gandhi*. Ed. by R. B. Gregg. Ahmedabad: Navajivan, abridged ed., 1951. An intimate account of Gandhi based on a diary kept by the author while accompanying Gandhi in Assam during 1921–22.

870

Nair, Pyarelal. *Mahatma Gandhi — the Last Phase*. 2 vols. Ahmedabad: Navajivan, 1956–58. A detailed and interpretive biography of Gandhi during the years 1944–48 by his private secretary.

871

Birla, Ghanshyam D. *In the Shadow of the Mahatma*. Bombay: Orient Longmans, 1953. A collection of letters, with commentary, exchanged between Gandhi and a leading Indian industrialist; provides valuable information about the national movement and Gandhi.

872

Shahani, Ranjee. *Mr. Gandhi*. New York: Macmillan, 1961. A popular biography mainly concerned with Gandhi's personal life. Though filled with dubious interpretations, it provides previously unpublished material obtained through interviews with Gandhi's family and associates.

873

Parvate, Tryambak V. *Gopal Krishna Gokhale*. (1866–1915). Ahmedabad: Navajivan, 1959. An account of the life and times of an early nationalist and reformer who was a leader in the moderate wing of the Congress in the early 20th century.

874

Wolpert, Stanley A. *Tilak and Gokhale. Revolution and Reform in the Making of Modern India*. Berkeley: University of California Press, 1962. An excellent comparative biographical study of two nationalist leaders from Maharashtra whose conflicting views reflect the division that developed within Congress in the early 20th century. Includes a useful guide to sources and secondary works.

875

Patwardhan, R. P. and D. V. Ambekar (eds.). *The Speeches and Writings of Gopal Krishna Gokhale*. Bombay: Asia Publishing House, 1962. The first of three proposed volumes of Gokhale's writings and speeches; this volume contains Gokhale's views on economic subjects presented to the Imperial and Bombay Legislative Councils during the years 1901–1912 and the Welby Commission of 1897.

876

Husain, Azim. *Fazl-i-Husain, A Political Biography*. London: Longmans, Green, 1946. One of the few accounts of provincial politics and non-Congress political activity during the first three decades of the 20th century.

Fazl-i-Husain founded the Unionist Party in the Punjab where he played a leading role in government and politics from 1905 to 1936.

877

Jayakar, M. R. *The Story of My Life.* Bombay: Asia Publishing House, 1958. Volume I of a proposed four-volume series of memoirs covers the period 1873–1922. This is an annotated political diary, supplemented with letters and other contemporary material, by a Maharashtrian nationalist. It provides information on lesser-known leaders and reveals regional variations within the national movement.

878

Bolitho, Hector. *Jinnah, Creator of Pakistan.* New York: Macmillan, 1954. An official biography, commissioned by the Pakistan Government, of the man who led the Muslim League during the fateful days that saw the emergence of Pakistan as an independent Islamic state.

879

Saiyid, Matlulbul Hasan. *Mohammad Ali Jinnah: A Political Study.* Lahore: Shaikh Muhammad Ashraf, 2nd ed., 1953. A detailed account of Jinnah's political life which spanned the first half of the 20th century.

880

Jinnah, Muhammad Ali. *Some Recent Speeches and Writings of Mr. Jinnah.* 2 vols. Lahore: Shaikh Muhammad Ashraf, 1942–47. A fifth edition of volume I was issued by the same publisher in 1952. A collection of speeches made by the leading spokesman for the Muslim League during a period when the creation of Pakistan was transformed from a nebulous idea into a political fact.

881

Chopra, Pran Nath. *Rafi Ahmad Kidwai; His Life and Work.* Agra: S. L. Agarwala, 1960. A political biography of a Muslim who was active in the Indian National Congress and held high office in the early years of the Republic of India.

882

Sastri, V. S. Srinivasa. *Life and Times of Sir Pherozeshah Mehta.* Madras: 1945. A biography of a 19th century nationalist (1845–1915) of the moderate school, who served as President of the sixth annual meeting of the Indian National Congress.

883

Madhok, Balraj. *Dr. Shyama Prasad Mookerjee: A Biography.* New Delhi: Deepak Prakashan, 1954. A biography of a Bengali educator and politician, who served as a major spokesman of Hindu communal groups within the Indian National Congress. He was also president of the only national Hindu political party, the *Bharatiya Jan Sangh,* founded in 1951; Mookerjee died in 1953.

884

Masani, Rustom Pestonji. *Dadabhai Naoroji.* London: G. Allen & Unwin, 1939. An account of the life (1825–1917) and times of one of the more militant 19th century Nationalists. Naoroji was the first Indian elected to the British Parliament.

885

Narain, Jaya Prakash. *Towards Struggle.* Ed. by Y. Meherally. Bombay: Padma, 1946. A selection from speeches and writings composed between 1935–46 by a leader of the Socialist wing of the Indian National Congress.

886

Sharma, Jagdish Saran. *Jawaharlal Nehru: A Descriptive Bibliography.* Delhi: S. Chand, 1955. Articles as well as books by and about Nehru are contained in this extensive reference.

887

Nehru, Jawaharlal. *Toward Freedom; the Autobiography of Jawaharlal Nehru.* London: Bodley Head, rev. ed., 1955. A paperbound edition was published in Boston by Beacon Press in 1958. An account of Nehru's life to his 55th year with most attention given to his experience in the nationalist movement.

888

Nanda, Bal Ram. *The Nehrus. Motilal and Jawaharlal.* New York: John Day, 1962. A study of the political careers and personal affairs of India's first prime minister, Jawaharlal Nehru, and his father, Motilal; based on previously unpublished letters and documents of the Nehru family.

889

Nehru, Jawaharlal. *The Unity of India; Collected Writings, 1937–1940.* Ed. by J. K. Krishna Menon. New York: John Day, 1948. A valuable source for Nehru's views on the independence movement and British rule, during a period when he served as a major spokesman for the Congress.

890

Nehru, Jawaharlal. *Independence and After; A Collection of Speeches, 1946–1949.* New York: John Day, 1950. Statements of policy, especially those concerning foreign affairs, occupy much of this collection of Nehru's speeches during his first years as Prime Minister of India. Reprinted as Volume One of the next entry.

891

Nehru, Jawaharlal. *Jawaharlal Nehru's Speeches.* 3 vols. Delhi: Publications Division, Government of India, 1954–58. Nehru's major speeches between 1946 and the middle of 1957 are reproduced in this collection.

892

Nehru, Jawaharlal. *A Bunch of Old Letters.* Bombay: Asia Publishing House, rev. ed., 1960. A useful selection from Nehru's correspondence: mainly letters exchanged with Gandhi and other Indian nationalists.

893

Brecher, Michael. *Nehru; A Political Biography.* London: Oxford University Press, 1959. The best biography of Nehru to date; this detailed account is an excellent introduction to the politics of modern India in that Nehru's ideas and actions are ably placed within a historical context.

894

Moraes, Francis R. *Jawaharlal Nehru; A Biography.* New York: Macmillan, 1956. A critical though sympathetic portrayal and assessment of Nehru's personality and policies by an Indian journalist; much attention is given to the political setting of Nehru's career.

895

Pal, Bipin Chandra. (1858–1932). *Memories of My Life and Times.* 2 vols. Calcutta: Modern Book Agency, 1932–51. An autobiography by a militant nationalist, who advocated complete independence for India early in the 20th century; Pal played an important role in early efforts to enlist mass support for the nationalist movement.

896

Mukherjee, Haridas. *Bipin Chandra Pal and India's Struggle for Swaraj.* Calcutta: K. L. Mukhopadhyay, 1958. A brief sketch of a militant nationalist from Bengal who was a major political figure in the early 20th century.

897

Shyam, Sunder. *Political Life of Pandit Govind Ballabh Pant.* Lucknow: Shailanil, 1960. The first in a proposed several volume biography of a major figure in the political life of Uttar Pradesh, Pant also served for several years as Home Minister of the Union government during the initial decade of India's independence; this volume covers the years 1887 to 1945, Pant died in 1961.

898

Parikh, Narahari D. *Sardar Vallabhbhai Patel.* 2 vols. Ahmedabad: Navajivan, 1953–56. A biography of the "strong man" of the Indian National Congress. Though little known outside India, Patel (1875–1950) was a member of the Congress top command.

899

Patel, Sardar Vallabhbhai. *On Indian Problems.* New Delhi: Indian Printing Works, 1949. A selection of Patel's speeches delivered when he was Deputy Prime Minister and one of the leading politicians of post-independence India.

900

Khan, Abdul Majid. *Life and Speeches of Sardar Patel*. New Delhi: Indian Printing Works, 1951. Patel's major speeches are included with this account of his career and character.

901

Prasad, Rajendra. *Autobiography*. Bombay: Asia Publishing House, 1957. A well-written and informative narration of personal and public events in the life of India's first president; provides an inside view of the nationalist movement.

902

Prasad, Rajendra. *At the Feet of Mahatma Gandhi*. New York: Asia Publishing House, 1961. An autobiographical account of more than three decades of close association between Gandhi and one of his staunchest supporters; illustrates Gandhi's ability to attract and hold a wide variety of followers.

903

Wasi, S. M. *President Prasad*. Calcutta: Thacker, Spink, 1962. A conventional biography of a courageous, dedicated, though somewhat prosaic, nationalist leader noted for his Hindu orthodoxy.

904

Perumal, Nilkan, *Rajaji*. Madras: Umadevan, 1953. A brief biography of C. Rajagopalachari (1908–   ), one of the leading politicians of South India and a major spokesman for the conservative point of view within Congress.

905

Felton, Monica. *I Meet Rajaji*. New York: St. Martin's Press, 1962. A brief collection of anecdotes and impressions obtained through interviews with Chakravarti Rajagopalachari (Rajaji or C. R.) and others; although little substantial information is provided about this elder statesman and major spokesman of India's political "right wing," some of his personal qualities and the nature of his political environment are conveyed.

906

Parvate, Tryambak V. *Mahadeo Govind Ranade*. New York: Asia Publishing House, 1963. A biography of the Maharashtrian scholar and social reformer whose intellectual influence and leadership left a strong imprint on the national movement.

907

Karve, Dattatraya G. *Ranade: The Prophet of Liberated India*. Poona: Aryabhushan Press, 1942. A study of M. G. Ranade (1842–1901), an early nationalist leader and reformer whose idea of Swadeshi and advocacy of welfare measures were later adopted by Congress leaders seeking mass support.

908

Rao, P. Kodanda. *The Right Honourable V. S. Srinivasa Sastri: A Political Biography*. Bombay: Asia Publishing House, 1963. Essentially a political history of the three decades preceding India's independence, centered about the political career of an Indian "liberal" often opposed to both Gandhi's views and British policy; written by a follower and personal friend of Sastri's.

909

Sampurnanand. *Memories and Reflections*. New York: Asia Publishing House, 1962. A personal account of the political life of a Congress leader of the "second rank," who played a prominent role in the politics of Uttar Pradesh in the post-independence period.

910

Karandikar, Shivram L. *Lokamanya Bal Gangadhar Tilak (1856–1920)*. Bombay: Siddhamohan Art Printery, 1957. A detailed sympathetic biography of a militant nationalist who led the "extremist" faction of Congress in the early 20th century.

911

Tahmankar, Dattatraya V. *Lokamanya Tilak; Father of Indian Unrest and Maker of Modern India*. London:

J. Murray, 1956. A partisan portrayal of Tilak's political career as one of the first advocates of force and mass agitation within the national movement.

912

Gopal, Ram. *Lokamanya Tilak*. Calcutta: Asia Publishing House, 1956. A well-rounded though sometimes uncritical biography of B. G. Tilak.

913

Wolpert, Stanley A. *Tilak and Gokhale*. Berkeley: University of California Press, 1962. A comparative biographical analysis of two early nationalist leaders from Maharashtra, whose conflicting views represent the major division within the Indian National Congress in the early 20th century; Tilak is treated more critically than in the biographies cited above.

Nationalist Movement

914

Sharma, Jagdish Saran. *Mahatma Gandhi; A Descriptive Bibliography*. Delhi: S. Chand, 1955. In addition to being a comprehensive survey of works relating to Gandhi, this annotated bibliography provides considerable guidance to the literature on the national movement in the 20th century.

915

Majumdar, J. K. (ed.). *Indian Speeches and Documents on British Rule, 1821–1918*. Calcutta: Longmans, Green, 1937. A collection of speeches and writings by Indian leaders that traces the development of nationalist sentiment from early requests for reform to clearly articulated demands for independence.

916

Smith, William R. *Nationalism and Reform in India*. New Haven: Yale University Press, 1938. A detailed survey of the growth to 1935 of Indian nationalism and related social and constitutional reforms. The political consequences of Hindu-Muslim relations are also examined.

917

Lajpat Rai, Lala. *Young India, an Interpretation and a History of the Nationalist Movement from Within*. New York: B. W. Huebsch, rev. ed., 1917. One of the most lucid and forceful statements of the nationalists' point of view by an eminent leader in the early years of the national movement.

918

Chirol, Sir Valentine. *Indian Unrest*. London: Macmillan, 1910. This remains one of the best accounts of 19th-century revolutionary and revivalist movements that gave rise to Indian nationalism and to the middle class that provided India's leaders.

919

Cotton, Henry J. S. *New India; or, India in Transition*. London: K. Paul Trench. 1907. An authoritative study of early developments in Indian nationalism with a critical appraisal of Britain's response.

920

Chand, Tara. *History of the Freedom Movement in India*. 3 vols. Delhi: Publications Division, Government of India, 1961–. To date only volume I, covering the period 1750–1857, has been published. This series, when completed, should serve as a major statement of the Indian view of British rule and the nationalist movement.

921

Aggarwala, Rama Nand. *National Movement and Constitutional Development*. Delhi: Metropolitan, 2nd ed., 1956. A review and appraisal of British rule by an Indian political scientist sympathetic to the nationalist cause.

922

Bombwall, K. R. *India Politics and Government Since 1885*. Delhi: Atma Ram, 1951. A survey of the Indian nationalist movement and constitutional developments to 1950; prepared for use as a college text in India.

923

McCully, Bruce T. *English Education and the Origins of Indian Nationalism.* New York: Columbia University Press, 1940. A perceptive and well-documented study of the influence of Western ideas of political freedom on Western-educated Indians of the 19th century.

924

Mukherjee, Haridas. *The Origins of the National Education Movement, 1905–1910.* Calcutta: Jadavpur University, 1957. This is volume I of a proposed four-volume study of the Swadeshi movement that sought mass support for complete independence from Britain. Development of an Indian-oriented system of higher education was an integral part of this program.

925

Mukherjee, Haridas and Uma. *Growth of Nationalism in India, 1905–1910.* Calcutta: Jadavpur University, 1957. A valuable account of the forces and leaders that shaped Indian nationalism in a period when moderate reforms were the main demands made of the British.

926

Bose, Nemai Sadhan. *The Indian Awakening and Bengal.* Calcutta: K. L. Mukhopadhyay, 1960. An account of the 19th-century background of the nationalist movement in a region that provided many of the ideas and leaders opposed to British rule.

927

Desai, Akshayakumar R. *Social Background of Indian Nationalism.* Bombay: Popular Book Depot, 3rd ed., rev., 1959. An attempt to use Marxian concepts in accounting for the development of Indian nationalism; superficial in many places as a result of the author's effort to span two centuries of history and to encompass a wide array of economic, social, and religious forces.

928

Desai, Akshayakumar R. *Recent Trends in Indian Nationalism.* Bombay: Popular Book Depot, 1960. A supplement to the author's *Social Background of Indian Nationalism* cited in the preceding entry.

929

Shukla, Bramha D. *History of the Indian Liberal Party.* Allahabad: Indian Press, 1960. An objective study, ranging from the early 19th century to 1948, of those Indian nationalists who favored qualified co-operation with the British. Consideration is given to the National Liberal Federation formed in 1918 by the "moderates" after they lost control of the Indian National Congress.

930

Chintamani, Chirravoori Y. *Indian Politics Since the Mutiny.* London: Allen & Unwin, 1940. A "liberal" nationalist's view of Indian nationalism; provides a useful survey of developments prior to the organization of the Congress, and a critique of Gandhi's methods by one who favored a moderate approach.

931

Bagal, Jogesh C. *History of the Indian Association, 1876–1951.* Calcutta: 1953. A useful account of an organization influential in the early years of the nationalist movement. Although later eclipsed by Congress, the leaders of this moderate party sometimes served as mediators between British and Congress leaders.

932

Sharma, Jagdish Saran. *Indian National Congress: A Descriptive Bibliography of India's Struggle for Freedom.* Delhi: S. Chand, 1959. A comprehensive work more than 800 pages in length.

933

Indian National Congress. *Congress Presidential Addresses.* 2 vols. Madras: Natesan, 1935. A collection of speeches delivered at the annual meetings of the Indian National Congress by presidents of that organization.

934

Pattabhi Sitaramayya, Bhogaraju. *History of the Indian National Congress.* 2 vols. Bombay: Padma, 1946–47.

The official history of Congress; volume I was first published in 1936 as a complete work covering the period 1885–1935, volume II carries the history to 1947. The drama inherent in many of the events is obscured by the language of formal proceedings from which this account is derived.

935

Ramana Rao, M. V. *A Short History of the Indian National Congress.* Delhi: S. Chand, 1959. A sympathetic overview of Congress history from the 1880's to 1947 with an account of major leaders and their policies.

936

Ghosh, Pansy Chaya. *The Development of the Indian National Congress, 1892–1909.* Calcutta: K. L. Mukhopadhyay, 1960. An able description of Congress' transformation from a moderate debating society to an organized political movement: concise and scholarly, with little interpretation.

937

Andrews, Charles F. and G. Mukerji. *Rise and Growth of the Congress in India.* London: Allen & Unwin, 1938. A sympathetic summary of Congress' development to 1920; an able presentation of the 19th-century cultural and social milieu that gave rise to the nationalist movement.

Muslim Organization

938

Gopal, Ram. *Indian Muslims; A Political History (1858–1947).* New York: Asia Publishing House, 1959. A review of Muslim efforts to participate in Indian politics during the past century, with particular attention to the conflicts that developed between the Muslim and Hindu communities.

939

Smith, Wilfred C. *Modern Islam in India.* London: Gollancz, rev. ed., 1946. A study of the ideas, leaders, and political movements that influenced Indian Muslims of the 20th century; includes an analysis of British policy concerning Muslims and an appraisal of Hindu-Muslim relations that underestimates the importance of religious differences that contributed to the creation of Pakistan in 1947.

940

Bahadur, Lal. *The Muslim League.* Agra: Agra Book Store, 1954. A history of an organization founded by upper-class Muslims in 1906 to protect and further the political interests of Muslims in India; the Muslim League became involved in the national movement and ultimately served as a means for organizing mass support for the creation of Pakistan.

941

Rajput, Allah Bakhsh. *The Muslim League, Yesterday and Today.* Lahore: Muhammad Ashraf, 1948. A study of the growth of the Muslim League prior to 1947 and the part it played in furthering the idea of a separate nation for the Muslims of India.

942

Faruqi, Ziya-ul-Hasan. *The Deoband School and the Demand for Pakistan.* New York: Asia Publishing House, 1963. A study of one segment of Indian Muslim opinion that opposed the creation of Pakistan.

943

Bolitho, Hector. *Jinnah, Creator of Pakistan.* New York: Macmillan, 1954. An official biography, commissioned by the Pakistan Government, of the man who led the Muslim League during the fateful days that saw the emergence of Pakistan as an independent Islamic state.

944

Saiyid, Matlulbul Hasan. *Mohammad Ali Jinnah: A Political Study.* Lahore: Shaikh Muhammad Ashraf, 2nd ed., 1953. A detailed account of Jinnah's political life which spanned the first half of the 20th century.

945

Jinnah, Muhammad Ali. *Some Recent Speeches and Writings of Mr. Jinnah.* 2 vols. Lahore: Shaikh Muhammad Ashraf, 1942–47. A fifth edition of volume I was issued by the same publisher in 1952. A collection of speeches made by the leading spokesman for the Muslim League during a period when the creation of Pakistan was transformed from a nebulous idea into a political fact.

946

Singh, Iqbal. *The Ardent Pilgrim.* London: Longmans, Green, 1951. A biographical sketch of the life and work of Mohammad Iqbal, poet and philosopher, who was among the first to articulate the idea of a separate nation for the Muslims of India.

Transfer of Power

947

Menon, Vapal, Pangunni. *The Transfer of Power in India.* Princeton: Princeton University Press, 1957. An authoritative account of events from 1942 to 1947 that led to India's independence and partition; written by an Indian official who participated in every major phase of the transfer of power.

948

Lumby, Esmond W. R. *The Transfer of Power in India, 1945–47.* New York: Praeger, 1954. A summary of events relating to the transfer of sovereignty from Britain to India and Pakistan.

949

Campbell-Johnson, Alan. *Mission With Mountbatten.* New York: Dutton, 1953. A detailed account of the decisions, events, and personalities involved in the final months of negotiation that preceded the transfer of power and partition; written by the Viceroy's press attaché.

950

Mountbatten, Lord. *Time Only to Look Forward.* London: N. Kaye, 1949. A selection of speeches delivered by the last Viceroy of India during the turbulent years 1947–48.

951

Menon, Vapal Pangunni. *The Story of the Integration of the Indian States.* New York: Macmillan, 1956. The withdrawal of British rule from India raised many questions about the future status of the Indian native states. Integration of these states into the Republic of India in 1947 is ably described here by one who played an important role in this event.

Partition and Kashmir Conflict

952

Ambedkar, Bhimrao R. *Pakistan, or the Partition of India.* Bombay: Thacker, 3rd ed., 1946. A well-documented presentation of the arguments for and against the creation of a separate nation for the Muslims of India; written prior to partition by a leader of the "Untouchables," who supported the idea of Pakistan.

953

Moon, Penderel. *Divide and Quit.* Berkeley: University of California Press, 1962. An analysis of the forces that created Pakistan, especially political events in the Punjab from 1937 to 1947; includes information on the seldom publicized "moderate" position on this issue, and an account of the author's experience as a public official in an Indian native state during the period of disorder that accompanied partition.

954

Tuker, Francis. I. S. *While Memory Serves.* London: Cassell, 1950. An account of the conflict and chaos that accompanied partition by the British general in charge of maintaining order in northern India during the last two years of British rule. Presents a patronizing view of Indian political leaders.

955

Jones, George E. *Tumult in India.* New York: Dodd, Mead, 1948. An overview of political events in India during the years 1946–47, by a correspondent for the *New York Times*.

956

Bourke-White, Margaret. *Half-Way to Freedom.* New York: Simon & Schuster, 1949. A moving account of the events that accompanied partition by a journalist whose photographs convey something of the suffering and hardships of the people uprooted by the division of India.

957

Lohia, Rammanohar. *Guilty Men of India's Partition.* Allahabad: Kitabistan, 1960. A critical appraisal of the men and issues that gave rise to the 1947 partition of India into Pakistan and the Republic of India: by a leading Indian Socialist.

958

Alexander, Horace G. *New Citizens of India.* London: Oxford University Press, 1951. An account of the evacuation and rehabilitation of Hindu and Sikh refugees who left Pakistan after partition.

959

Vakil, Chandulal N. and others. *Economic Consequences of Divided India.* Bombay: Vora, 1950. A survey of the economic effects of partition on India and Pakistan is provided in this description of economic conditions in both countries after their independence.

960

Birdwood, Lord. *Two Nations and Kashmir.* London: Robert Hale, 1956. A detailed review of the background and issues concerning the controversy between Pakistan and India over Kashmir with useful appendices containing basic documents on the conflict; in matters of interpretation and emphasis the author tends to favor Pakistan's position.

961

Brecher, Michael. *The Struggle for Kashmir.* New York: Oxford University Press, 1953. A survey of events from 1947 to 1953 concerning the Kashmir conflict with an analysis of this controversy's effect on the internal politics of India and Pakistan.

962

Korbel, Josef. *Danger in Kashmir.* Princeton: Princeton University Press, 1954. An account of the conflict over Kashmir and the United Nations role in this dispute by a member of the United Nations Commission appointed to help solve this problem.

INDEPENDENCE AND AFTER

Following the creation of Pakistan and the Republic of India in 1947, leaders of the nationalist movement sought to implement policies of reform and modernization which they advanced during the struggle for freedom as a major justification of their right to rule. The most notable articulation of these aspirations appears in the constitution adopted in 1950 by the Republic of India. This document calls for equality of opportunity in economic as well as political affairs, a secular social order based upon the rule of law, and a parliamentary form of democratic government. The assumptions and values underlying these goals are in many instances diametrically opposed to those of traditional India. Efforts to abolish discriminatory features of the caste system, land reform, the introduction of universal suffrage, and changes in laws affecting family relations, are among the many experiments initiated since independence — experiments whose final results remain to be seen.

Political and economic problems confronting India and Pakistan present a major challenge to the present forms of government of these countries. Threats to national unity, commonly expressed in demands for linguistic states, have beset these nations during the past decade. Towering over all other problems is the monumental task of reordering the economic structure to meet the basic needs of a rapidly expanding population bound to an inadequate agrarian base. The current rates of industrialization provide little hope for the solution of these problems in the near future.

Republic of India

MEN AND EVENTS

963

Poplai, Sunder L. (ed.). *India, 1947–50.* 2 vols. Bombay: Oxford University Press, 1959. A collection of documents on Indian affairs after independence, includes political pronouncements by the major parties and policy statements by the government.

964

Poplai, Sunder L. (ed.). *Select Documents on Indian Affairs.* New York: Asia Publishing House, 1961. Documents relating to the internal and external affairs of India in 1960 are contained in this collection that includes treaties, legislation, constitutional amendments, and statements of government policy.

965

Griffiths, Percival J. *Modern India.* London: Benn, 3rd ed., rev., 1962. A useful introductory survey of economic and political conditions in India since independence presented with historical background for the general reader.

966

Mellor, Andrew. *India Since Partition.* New York: F. A. Praeger, 1951, A brief description of the form of government and political developments in the early years of the Republic of India, with a summary of events during the decade preceding independence.

967

Moraes, Frank. *India Today.* New York: Macmillan, 1960. A critical review of developments in Indian government and politics during the years 1947–59, by the editor of a leading Indian newspaper.

968

Harrison, Selig S. *India: The Most Dangerous Decade.* Princeton: Princeton University Press, 1960. An appraisal of recent political trends in India viewed against their historic background; the author emphasizes the influence of divisive forces arising from caste and regional differences.

969

India (Republic). States Reorganization Commission. *Report of the States Reorganization Commission.* Delhi: Manager of Publications, Government of India, 1955. A report of the findings and recommendations of the commission appointed to investigate the problem of realigning state boundaries. A major political issue in the years following India's independence.

970

Talbot, Philips (ed.). *South Asia in the World Today.* Chicago: University of Chicago, 1950. A collection of papers that provide an introduction to the social, political, and economic conditions of modern India.

971

Hangen, Welles. *After Nehru, Who?* New York: Harcourt, Brace, 1963. An appraisal of contemporary Indian politics by an American journalist stationed in Delhi; pre-sented in the form of biographical sketches of prominent Indian leaders.

972

Wofford, Clare and Harris Jr., *India Afire.* New York: John Day, 1951. The awesome economic and political problems of independent India provide the catalyst for this emotional account by two young World Federalists from the United States who visited India for six months.

973

Lyon, Jean. *Just Half a World Away.* New York: Crowell, 1954. Probably the best "traveller's account" of India in the years immediately after independence; written by an observant and objective journalist whose contacts ranged throughout Indian society.

974

Zinkin, Taya. *India Changes.* London: Oxford University Press, 1958. A journalist with extensive personal experience in India provides a perceptive view of the forces at work in post-independence India, especially efforts at social reform.

975

Zinkin, Taya. *Reporting India.* London: Chatto & Windus, 1962. A journalist's account of major events and political developments in India during the past decade; includes an informative account of the Communist ministry in Kerala.

976

Lamb, Beatrice P. *Indian; A World in Transition.* New York: F. A. Praeger, paperbound, 1963. A popular survey of political issues and problems of economic development confronting India today with descriptive sketches of Indian society and history.

FOREIGN RELATIONS

977

Rajkumar, Nagoji V. (ed.). *The Background of India's Foreign Policy.* New Delhi: All-India Congress Committee, 1952. A brief compilation of resolutions on foreign policy adopted by the Indian National Congress from 1885 to 1952.

978

Kundra, Jagdish C. *Indian Foreign Policy, 1947–1954; A Study of Relations with the Western Bloc.* Bombay: Vora, 1955. A well-documented and relatively objective study of a few key foreign policy issues during the period surveyed; especially useful for its account of India's relationship to the Commonwealth.

979

Karunakaran, Kotta P. *India in World Affairs, August, 1947–January 1950.* Calcutta: Oxford University Press, 1952. A review of Indian foreign policy, especially in the United Nations, during India's initial years as an independent nation. This is the first in a series of volumes prepared under the auspices of the Indian Council of World Affairs.

980

Karunakaran, Kotta P. *India in World Affairs, 1950–53.* Calcutta: Oxford University Press, 1958. A continuation of the series described in the preceding entry.

981

Varma, S. N., S. Gupta, and B. V. Krishna Murti. *Aspects of India's Foreign Relations, 1954–57.* New York: Institute of Pacific Relations, 1958. A third volume in the series sponsored by the Indian Council of World Affairs.

982

India (Republic). Parliament. House of the People. *Foreign Policy of India: Texts of Documents, 1947–59.* New Delhi: Lok Sabha Secretariat, 2nd ed., 1959. A valuable collection of source material issued by the lower house of the Indian Parliament.

983

Levi, Werner. *Free India in Asia.* Minneapolis: University of Minnesota Press, 1952. A review of India's relations with other Asian nations during the years following independence, and India's initial response to communism.

984

Das Gupta, Jyoti Bhusan. *Indo-Pakistan Relations, 1947–55.* Amsterdam: Djamatan, 1958. A useful, though poorly organized and partisan, review of the many issues that arose between these two nations during the initial eight years following their partition.

985

Rosinger, Lawrence K. *India and the United States.* New York: Macmillan, 1950. A succinct account of political and economic relations between India and the United States.

986

Talbot, Phillips and S. L. Poplai. *India and America.* New York: Harper, 1958. A lucid appraisal of the positions held on major issues of foreign policy by India and the United States, prepared jointly by the Indian Council of World Affairs and the Council on Foreign Relations of New York.

987

Harrison, Selig S. (ed.). *India and the United States.* New York: Macmillan, 1961. Essentially an edited transcript of a conference held in Washington, D. C., to review the first decade of United States foreign aid to India. Some unusually frank and authoritative opinions are quoted from American and Indian politicians and civil servants actively engaged in this program.

988

Chakravarti, Prithwis C. *India's China Policy.* Bloomington: Indiana University Press, 1962. A survey of events, especially the border disputes, affecting Indo-Chinese relations between 1950–61; the interpretations of these events is uncritical due to a partisan view of India's claims and a poorly substantiated appraisal of Nehru's policies.

989

Jain, Girilal. *Panchsheela and After.* New York: Asia Publishing House, 1960. A journalist's critique of India's policies relating to China from 1949 to 1960; India's acceptance of China's claim to Tibet is seen as a dangerous departure from British frontier policies.

990

Fisher, Margaret W. and Joan V. Bondurant. *Indian Views of Sino-Indian Relations.* Berkeley: Institute of International Studies, University of California, 1956. Indian Press Digests, Monograph Series, No. 1. Opinions expressed in Indian newspapers regarding official relations between China and India during 1954 and 1955 form the basis of this account, with related government documents reproduced as appendices. Agreements over Tibet and the status of Nepal were of major concern during this period.

991

Sen, Chanakya. *Tibet Disappears.* New York: Asia Publishing House, 1960. A "documentary history" of communist China's activities in Tibet and its border dispute with India into 1959; the documents are almost entirely Indian.

992

India. Ministry of External Affairs. *White Paper: Notes, Memoranda and Letters Exchanged and Agreements Signed Between the Governments of India and China, 1954–1959.* New Delhi: Government of India, 1959. A basic source on Chinese activities in Tibet and the Sino-Indian border disputes; supplemented by *White Paper* No. II, covering the period September-November 1959 (New Delhi: 1959) and *White Paper* No. III, covering the period November, 1959 to March, 1960 (New Delhi: 1960).

993

India. Ministry of External Affairs. *Report of the Officials of the Governments of India and the People's Republic of China on the Boundary Question.* New Delhi: Government of India, 1961. A formal statement of the official positions held on this issue by these nations in 1961.

994

China, People's Republic of. *The Sino-Indian Boundary Question.* Peking: Foreign Languages Press, 1962. A collection of official policy statements released by the Chinese in 1959 and 1962; accompanied by detailed maps of the area in question.

995

Fisher, Margaret W., Leo E. Rose, and R. A. Huttenback. *Himalayan Battleground; Sino-Indian Rivalry in Ladakh.* New York: F. A. Praeger, 1963. A perceptive analysis of the Chinese-Indian border dispute; contemporary events and the points at issue are presented in relation to the history and geography of the region.

PAKISTAN

Pakistan entered the world of nations in 1947 with much the same legacy of government as that inherited from the British by the Republic of India. However, Pakistan's division into two units, located more than eight hundred miles apart, reflects the important role of religion in the creation of this largest of Islamic states. Despite marked differences in language and custom, these two areas became a common nation on the basis of high concentration of Muslims in their population. The initial years of Pakistan's existence were filled with turmoil and horrendous problems, including the assimilation of more than five million refugees and the reordering of an economy deprived of many key personnel due to the mass exodus of Hindus to the Republic of India. Previously integrated systems of transport, communication, and jute production were also disrupted and divided. The task of reorganizing Pakistan's economic, social, and political life was further complicated by the death of her major leaders. Although religious motives played an important part in the creation of Pakistan, there was little consensus as to the proper role of Islam in governmental affairs. The relative powers of the eastern and western wings of the nation, and their relation to the central government, were also subjects of heated debate and discord.

Conflict and tension delayed the framing of Pakistan's constitution until 1956, and though it survived until October, 1958, the constitution proved of little use in a government rent with factions. Martial law was declared by the President of Pakistan in October, 1958. The central and provincial legislatures were dismissed, political parties abolished, and the constitution abrogated. General Muhammad Ayub Khan was appointed chief martial law administrator, and shortly thereafter he assumed the presidency. His military regime introduced reforms, dismissed members of the bureaucracy, and forced the resignation of many politicians. In October, 1959, Ayub Khan introduced a new system of government based on "Basic Democracies," locality-based electoral units with limited governmental powers, that sought to enlist the support of "people of substance" in the rural areas. A new constitution, promulgated in March of 1962, established a federal form of government in which power was concentrated in the office of the president. The previous parliamentary system, with the executive responsible to the legislature, was rejected; and the prohibition of political parties remained in effect.

The task of nation building confronting Pakistan includes not only the search for an integrated and viable political system; Pakistan's economic problems are equally formidable. The pressure of population common to other areas of Asia, has offset most of the gains made to date in industrialization and increased agricultural production.

Men and Events

996

Abernethy, George L. *Pakistan: A Selected, Annotated Bibliography*. New York: American Institute of Pacific Relations, rev. ed., 1960. A useful selection of books and articles written in English on all aspects of Pakistan; addressed to the general reader.

997

Moreland, George B. and A. H. Siddiqui. *Publications of the Government of Pakistan, 1947–59*. Karachi: University of Karachi, 1958. A useful, though incomplete, bibliographic guide through the maze of government publications issued in Pakistan.

998

Pakistan Bibliographical Working Group. *A Guide to Pakistan Libraries, Learned and Scientific Societies and Educational Institutions*. Karachi: University of Karachi Library, rev. ed., 1960. Publication number three in a series of reference works.

999

Khan, Tahavar Ali (ed.). *Biographical Encyclopedia of Pakistan*. Lahore: Biographical Research Institute, 1961. A useful reference for those seeking information about leading personalities on the Pakistan scene.

1000

Kahin, George McT. (ed.). *Major Governments of Asia*. Ithaca: Cornell University Press, 2nd ed., rev., 1963. First published in 1958; includes a valuable introductory survey of the historical background and contemporary developments of Pakistan's government and politics.

1001

Callard, Keith B. *Pakistan: A Political Study*. New York: Macmillan, 1958. A political scientist's analysis of Pakistan's politics and government institutions during the years following independence. Considerable attention is given to the Constituent Assembly's efforts to reconcile Islamic doctrine with Western concepts of the state.

1002

Ahmad, Mushtaq. *Government and Politics in Pakistan*. Karachi: Pakistan Publishing House, 2nd ed., rev., 1963. A journalist's account of the leaders and major political events that shaped Pakistan's political development since independence; including a discussion of political parties and government institutions.

1003

Stephens, Ian. *Pakistan*. New York: Praeger, 1963; A survey of Pakistan's political history and major problems since 1946, written by a British journalist who served for many years as editor of *The Statesman* in India.

1004

Symonds, Richard. *The Making of Pakistan*. London: Faber & Faber, 3rd ed., 1951. A brief, sometimes uncritical account of developments leading to the creation of Pakistan and the condition of the country during its initial year of existence, when the author was performing relief work in Pakistan.

1005

Sayeed, Khalid B. *Pakistan: The Formative Phase*. Karachi: Pakistan Publishing House, 1960. Distributed by the Publications Centre, University of British Columbia, Vancouver, Canada. A survey of Pakistan's historical background, beginning with 1857, with an account of political events and constitutional developments from 1947 to 1958; though wanting in analysis, it provides information not readily available elsewhere.

1006

Wilcox, Wayne A. *Pakistan: The Consolidation of a Nation*. New York: Columbia University Press, 1963. Political factors affecting Pakistan's national unity in the initial years following independence are here explored through a study of the ten princely states that acceded to Pakistan during the 1947 partition of India.

1007

Choudhury, Golam Wahed. *Democracy in Pakistan*. Vancouver: University of British Columbia, 1964. An analysis of problems and issues besetting the establishment of democratic institutions in Pakistan; includes a review of post-independence developments that led to the founding and fall of the First Republic, and an analysis of the constitution of 1962.

1008

Jafri, A. B. S. *From the Gallery*. Lahore: Progressive Papers, 1963. A collection of articles written for the *Pakistan Times* during the first two sessions of the National Assembly of Pakistan; provides a journalist's record of political events and personalities of the day.

1009

Khan, Liaquat Ali. *Pakistan: Heart of Asia*. Cambridge: Harvard University Press, 1951. A selection from speeches delivered by the Prime Minister of Pakistan during his visit to the United States in 1950.

1010

Khan, Mohammad Ayub. *Speeches and Statements*. 3 vols. Karachi: Pakistan Publications, 1961. A collection of the public pronouncements of Field Marshal Mohammad Ayub Khan, President of Pakistan; covers the period October, 1958 to June, 1961.

1011

Callard, Keith B. *Pakistan's Foreign Policy*. New York: Institute of Pacific Relations, 2nd ed., 1959. A brief analysis of factors influencing Pakistan's foreign policy and the main trends in this policy prior to 1958.

1012

Ahmad, Mushtaq. *The United Nations and Pakistan*. New York: Institute of Pacific Relations, 1955. A presentation of Pakistan's position on major issues that have developed in the United Nations; includes an outline of U. N. efforts to settle the Kashmir dispute.

1013

Hasan, K. Sarwar. *Pakistan and the United Nations*. New York: Manhattan Publishing Co., 1960. An account of Pakistan's role in the United Nations, prepared for the Pakistan Institute of International Affairs.

1014

Chaudri, Mohammed Ashen. *Pakistan and the Regional Pacts*. New York: Institute of Pacific Relations, 1959. A short account of Pakistan's commitments in the SEATO and Baghdad pacts; includes the texts of these pacts and other agreements with the United States and Turkey.

1015

Government of Pakistan. *Ministry of Law*. The Constitution of the Islamic Republic of Pakistan. Karachi: Manager of Publications, 1956. The official text of the Constitution adopted in March of 1956, and later abrogated.

1016

Government of Pakistan. *The Constitution of the Republic of Pakistan.* Washington, D.C.: Embassy of Pakistan, 1962. The text of the constitution adopted in 1962.

1017

Gledhill, Alan. *Pakistan: The Development of its Law and Constitution.* London: Stevens, 1957. A detailed study of Pakistan's constitution, abrogated in 1958, and the legal system emanating from it that continues to remain in effect.

1018

Jennings, Sir Walter Ivor (ed.). *Constitutional Problems in Pakistan.* Cambridge: Cambridge University Press, 1957. A technical study edited by a former constitutional adviser to the Government of Pakistan; includes an appraisal of decisions rendered by the Pakistan Federal Court in several constitutional cases.

1019

Binder, Leonard. *Religion and Politics in Pakistan.* Berkeley: University of California Press, 1961. A study, completed in 1956, of the influence exerted by groups favoring an Islamic state in the political processes that accompanied the preparation of Pakistan's first constitution.

1020

Arnold, F. B. (ed.). *Pakistan: Economic and Commercial Conditions.* London: H. M. Stationery Office, 1955. A descriptive and analytical survey of Pakistan's economy; provides a guide to source materials.

1021

Andrus, J. Russell and A. F. Mohammed. *The Economy of Pakistan.* Stanford: Stanford University Press, 1958. A detailed descriptive account of the economic problems confronting Pakistan and the resources available to meet this challenge.

1022

Peach, W. Nelson, M. Uzair, and G. W. Rucker. *Basic Data of the Economy of Pakistan.* Karachi: Oxford University Press, paperbound, 1959. A useful compilation of information on Pakistan's economy, presented in the form of charts and tables.

1023

Government of Pakistan. Planning Board. *The First Five Year Plan. 1955–1960.* 2 vols. Karachi: Manager of Publications, 1956. A draft of Pakistan's comprehensive plan for economic development; this document supersedes the last two years of the Six Year Plan prepared for the years 1951-57.

1024

Government of Pakistan. Planning Commission. *The Second Five Year Plan. 1960–65.* Karachi: Manager of Publications, 1961. The text of Pakistan's plan for the integrated development of its economy; includes revised estimates of November, 1961.

1025

Qureshi, Ishtiaq H. *The Pakistani Way of Life.* New York: Praeger, 1956. A brief sketch of Pakistan's historical background written to elucidate the social, religious, and political forces at work in contemporary Pakistan.

1026

Maron, Stanley (ed.) *Pakistan: Society and Culture.* New Haven: Human Relations Area Files, 1957. A collection of brief field studies by six social scientists, whose research included rural and urban segments of Pakistan society.

1027

Linch, Orville F. *A Passage Through Pakistan.* Detroit: Wayne State University Press, 1959. An American professor's impression of life in contemporary Pakistan, gained while teaching for a year in the small arts college of a provincial town.

1028

Government of Pakistan. Commission on National Education. *Report of the Commission on National Education.* Karachi: Government of Pakistan Press for the Ministry of Education, 1961. A review and appraisal of Pakistan's educational system with detailed recommendations for improvements; prepared by a commission that investigated the subject from January to August of 1959. This report provides some interesting examples of the aspirations and frustrations of Pakistan's intellectuals.

POLITICAL PATTERNS

An authoritarian form of government, possibly a theocracy, has been postulated for the prehistoric Indus Valley civilization that came to an end about 2500 B.C. Archaeological evidence indicating the persistence of formal city planning for many centuries is the principal basis for this interpretation. Literary evidence, beginning with Rig Vedic hymns composed about 1000 B.C., indicate an early date for the concept of kingship as a major feature of Indian government. Vedic literature also contains fragmentary evidence of oligarchies and popular assemblies governing tribal states characterized by some scholars as republics. However, the earliest known Indian treatise on statecraft, Kautilya's *Arthaśastra,* describes in detail an administrative system governed by a strong king whose powers encompass all governmental functions unfettered by constitutional limitations. This monarchial ideal also appears a century or two later in the *Laws of Manu* and sections of the *Mahabharata,* works written early in the Christian era. These religious texts also assume the existence of a relatively fixed social order beyond the realm of human invention or debate. The king was expected to maintain this social order through a judicious use of punishment exercised in keeping with the advice of Brahman priests well versed in sacred lore. Little concern is to be found in this tradition with individual rights other than rights defined in terms of caste prerogatives including differential punishment for the same crime depending on the offender's caste rank. Although courts of justice existed at the municipal and higher levels of government in ancient India, the administration of justice at the local level was conducted by judicial councils (*panchayats*) composed of elders and other community leaders assembled for the particular occasion. Caste tradition and religious texts provided guidance in their deliberations.

The ideal of an absolute monarch was realized in practice throughout most of Indian history although the unit of government was generally confined to a region sharing a common language and ethnic identity. The most notable exception was the Mauryan Empire (c. 322–183 B.C.), which exercised a varying degree of suzerainty over most of the sub-continent. A comparable level of political unity was approached for a brief time during the last half of the 17th century under Mughal rule, but the most common situation was one of competing petty kingdoms whose rapid rise and fall enliven the pages of history.

Muslim conquerors, who ruled much of north and central India during the 13th to the 18th centuries, maintained monarchical rule and much of the earlier administrative system. They also introduced a system of justice based on Islamic law and some notable changes in the administrative organization of provinces and revenue collection that prevail to the present day. The most fundamental changes in Indian government occurred during modern times under British rule. Although many features of traditional administration were retained by the British, European institutions of jurisprudence and representative government were introduced during the 19th and 20th centuries, often in response to the demands of English-educated Indians. This same class of Indians provided the leadership in India's struggle for independence, realized in 1947. The commitment of these leaders to the ideal of parliamentary democracy is most evident in the constitution adopted by the Republic of India in 1950. The extent to which this national political system can be integrated with traditional local political systems remains to be seen.

REFERENCES AND SOURCES

Biographical accounts of Indian politicians and related reference works may be found above under HISTORY, 20th Century, "Indian Leaders."

1029

Wilson, Patrick. *Government and Politics of India and Pakistan, 1885–1955.* Berkeley: University of California, 1956. A bibliography of more than 5,000 works in Western languages, including books, articles, and doctoral dissertations. An author index and the arrangement of writings by periods greatly enhance the usefulness of this basic reference.

1030

India (Republic). Lok Sabha (House of the People). *Catalogue of Parliamentory Publications.* New Delhi: Lok Sabha Secretariat, Sales Section, 1960. A useful catalogue of publication for sale including official reports, abstracts of reports, and the Lok Sabha *Debates* begun in 1952, in which appear speeches presented in the most important legislative body of the Indian government.

1031

Indian Journal of Political Science. Vol. 1–. Lucknow: Indian Political Science Association, 1939–. Many useful articles on Indian government and politics by Indian and foreign scholars appear in this professional journal.

1032

Public Opinion Surveys. Vol. 1–. New Delhi: Indian Institute of Public Opinion, 1956–. A monthly publication reporting the results of surveys on a wide range of topics relating to government and politics including attitudes towards government policies, elections, and social problems.

1033

Indian Affairs Record. New Delhi: Diwan Chand Information Centre, 1955–. A monthly review of major political events based on extensive quotation from the press, political parties, and government; references are provided for important articles and documents, with an occasional reprinting of major documents in full.

GENERAL WORKS

1034

Kahin, George McT. (ed.). *Major Governments of Asia.* Ithaca: Cornell University Press, 2nd ed., rev., 1963. First published in 1958. An excellent survey of the political development and contemporary governments of China, Japan, India, Pakistan, and Indonesia.

1035

Tinker, Hugh. *India and Pakistan: A Political Analysis.* New York: F. A. Praeger, paperbound, 1962. A judicious interpretation of the background, form, and major forces of contemporary politics in these two countries.

1036

Palmer, Norman D. *The Indian Political System.* Boston: Houghton Mifflin, paperbound, 1961. A succinct description of the formal organization of the Republic of India with a survey of the politics of planning, the party system, and foreign relations. Historical background material, mainly of the modern period, is provided for the general reader.

1037

Brown, W. Norman. *The United States and India and Pakistan.* Cambridge: Harvard University Press, rev. ed., 1963. First published in 1953. A scholarly survey addressed to the general reader who seeks an objective appraisal of historical and cultural factors affecting contemporary developments (mainly political) in India and Pakistan. A brief concluding chapter treats the relations of these countries with the United States.

1038

Dodwell, Henry H. (ed.). *The Cambridge History of India.* 6 vols. Cambridge: Cambridge University Press, 1922–53. A revised edition of Volume VI, published in 1958, brings the historical coverage up to 1947. Volumes V and VI consist in the main of essays on the political and administrative activities of the British in India.

1039

Park, Richard L. and Irene Tinker (eds.). *Leadership and Political Institutions in India.* Princeton: Princeton University Press, 1959. A collection of articles treating many aspects of contemporary Indian politics ranging from the inner workings of Parliament to the basis of power in village communities.

1040

Philips, Cyril H. (ed.). *Politics and Society in India.* London: Allen & Unwin, 1963. A collection of essays, three on traditional Indian political systems and six treating various facets of modern politics and society; the contributions of P. Hardy, W. H. Morris-Jones and F. G. Bailey are especially noteworthy.

1041

Weiner, Myron. *Political Change in South Asia.* Calcutta: K. L. Mukhopadhyay, 1963. An astute appraisal of the forces affecting contemporary political developments in India; by an American political scientist with considerable research experience in India.

1042

Rose, Saul (ed.). *Politics in Southern Asia.* New York: St. Martin's Press, 1963. A collection of papers treating contemporary politics in Southern Asia; presented in a symposium held at Oxford University in 1961.

SPECIAL TOPICS

1043

Smith, Donald Eugene. *India as a Secular State.* Princeton: Princeton University Press, 1963. An analysis of political, educational, and constitutional efforts made since independence to develop the Republic of India into a secular democratic state; the influence of Indian tradition on this process is considered and prospects for the future discussed.

1044

Weiner, Myron. *The Politics of Scarcity; Public Pressure and Political Response in India.* Chicago: University of Chicago Press, 1962. A study of the emergence of organized pressure groups in the Republic of India, with an appraisal of the disruptive influence of such groups on the maintenance of public order and economic development.

1045

Harrison, Selig S. *India: The Most Dangerous Decade.* Princeton: Princeton University Press, 1960. An analysis of the divisive influence on contemporary Indian politics of such factors as caste and language differences, regionalism, and styles of party politics.

1046

Bondurant, Joan V. *Regionalism Versus Provincialism: A Study in Problems of Indian National Unity.* Berkeley: University of California Press, 1958. Monograph Series No. IV, Indian Press Digests. A study of the divisive effects of linguistic regionalism in contemporary India and government efforts to offset such threats to national unity through the creation of inter-state coordinating councils.

1047

India (Republic). States Reorganization Commission. *Report of the States Reorganization Commission.* New Delhi: Government of India Press, 1955. A carefully organized presentation of the historical background and contemporary economic, social and language factors considered in a proposed realignment of state boundaries; most of the commission's recommendations have been implemented by the Government of India.

1048

Roy, Naresh Chandra. *Federalism and Linguistic States.* Calcutta: K. L. Mukhopadhyay, 1962. A discussion of the effect on India's federal system of recent decisions to realign state boundaries according to linguistic divisions.

1049

India (Republic). Official Language Commission. *Report of the Official Language Commission, 1956.* New Delhi: Government of India Press, 1957. A detailed review and assessment of problems stemming from the linguistic diversity of India with recommendations for language policy in government, judicial, educational, and cultural affairs.

1050

India (Republic). Official Language Commission. *Report of the Official Language Commission, 1958.* New Delhi: Government of India Press, 1959. A later report on the subject described in the previous entry.

1051

Desai, Maganbhai Prabhudas. *Our Language Problem.* Ahmedabad: Navajivan Publishing House, 1956. A collection of articles from the journal *Harijan* setting forth the Gandhian position on the role of regional languages in government and education with particular attention to the problems of implementing Hindi as the official language of the Republic of India.

1052

Tinker, Hugh. *The Foundations of Local Self-Government in India, Pakistan, and Burma.* London: Athlone, 1954. An account of British efforts, begun in 1882, to establish a viable system of local government in South Asia, with an astute appraisal of the results of such measures at the time of India's Independence in 1947.

1053

Retzlaff, Ralph H. *Village Government in India, A Case Study.* New York: Asia Publishing House, 1962. A revealing study of political life in a North Indian village, including an account of the villagers' response to the new system of selecting leaders by formal elections.

1054

Dey, Surendra Kumar. *Panchayat-i-Raj. A Synthesis.* New York: Asia Publishing House, 1962. An unduly optimistic account of the Indian Government's efforts to develop responsible and effective government at the village level; written by the Minister in charge of the program.

1055

Bailey, Frederick G. *Tribe, Caste, and Nation; A Study of Political Activity and Political Change in Highland Orissa.* Manchester: Manchester University Press, 1960. An anthropological study of the effect of government administration and economic changes on the political institutions of a region including both tribal and caste systems of government and politics.

1056

Bailey, Frederick G. *Politics and Social Change: Orissa in 1959.* Berkeley: University of California Press, 1963. An extension of an analysis presented in two earlier books on contemporary life in the Kond hills of Orissa; in contrast to the author's previous concern with village and regional political institutions, this work traces the political linkage of these units to the state and national levels of politics.

LAW

1057

Kane, Pandurang Vaman. *History of Dharmaśastra.* 5 vols. in 7 tomes. Poona: Bhandarkar Oriental Research Institute, 1930–62. A monumental collection of facts, including lists of authors and works, concerning ancient and medieval Hindu religious and civil law. The Dharmaśastra literature, consisting of such works as the *Laws of Manu,* was composed by members of the Brahman class and reflects their point of view. Although grounded in Hindu sacred lore, the Dharmaśastras became almost purely legal textbooks by the Middle Ages.

1058

Sen Gupta, Nares Chandra. *Evolution of Ancient Indian Law.* London: A. Probsthain, 1953. A historical survey of the development of Indian law to Muslim times.

1059

Jolly, Julius. *Hindu Law and Custom.* Tr. by Batakrishna Ghosh. Calcutta: Greater India Society, 1928. This once authoritative work, based on an intimate knowledge of ancient Hindu legal lore, continues to be of value. First published in German in 1896.

1060

Banerji, Sures Chandra. *Dharma Sutras.* Calcutta: Punthi Pustak, 1962. A study of the origin and development of the earliest sources of Hindu law; the *sutras* are brief aphorisms. In this class of literature they are used to convey instruction in proper human conduct *(dharma).*

1061

Bühler, Georg (ed. & tr.). *The Sacred Laws of the Aryas.* 2 vols. Oxford: Clarendon Press, 1879–82. Sacred Books of the East, vols. 2 and 14; to be reprinted in paperbound form by Dover Publications of New York. A translation of the most important Dharma Sutras, prose manuals of instruction in human conduct written in the form of brief aphorisms, probably composed between the 6th and 2nd centuries B.C.; the *sutras* in this selection are traditionally attributed to the sages: Gautama, Baudhayana, Vasistha and Apastamba.

1062

The Laws of Manu. Tr. by G. Bühler. Oxford: Clarendon Press, 1886. Sacred Books of the East, volume 25; to be reprinted in paperbound form by Dover Publications of New York. A translation of the earliest *Dharma Shastras* ("Instructions in the Sacred Law") composed in verse form early in the Christian era. Manu's *Dharma Shastra,* also known as the *Manu Smriti,* treats in great detail the rules and regulations governing human conduct as viewed from an extreme Brahmanical point of view. Many niceties of proper behavior and punishment advocated by Manu were seldom if ever realized in actual practice.

1063

Jain, Mahabir P. *Outlines of Indian Legal History.* Delhi: Dhanwantra Medical & Law Book House, 1952. A survey of major developments in the administration of justice in India from Warren Hastings establishment of a court system in 1772 to the post-Independence period.

1064

Rankin, George C. *Background to Indian Law.* Cambridge: Cambridge University Press, 1946. A survey of the development of law in India during the period of British rule.

1065

Mayne, John Dawson. *Mayne's Treatise on Hindu Law and Usage.* Ed. by N. C. Aiyar. Madras: Higginbotham, 11th ed., 1950. A comprehensive survey of traditional codes of Hindu law used in litigation under the British.

1066

Derrett, J. Duncan M. *Hindu Law, Past and Present.* Calcutta: A. Mukherjee, 1957. An account of the controversy concerning the enactment of the Hindu Code by the Republic of India; includes a copy of the text of the code. This code altered or removed the legal basis for many privileges and disabilities based on caste and custom.

1067

Mulla, Dinshah F. *Principles of Hindu Law.* Ed. by S. T. Desai. Bombay: N. M. Tripathi, 12th ed., 1959. A standard work on Hindu personal law including the Hindu Marriage Act of 1955 and the Hindu Succession Act of 1956, with a general introduction and commentaries by Justice S. T. Desai.

1068

India (Republic). *Statutory Changes in Hindu Law.* Allahabad: Law Book Co., 1962. A compilation of all acts pertaining to Hindu laws from 1850 to 1961 with a Hindu law digest for the period 1951–61 and short commentaries by S. N. Bagga.

1069

Fyzee, Asaf A. A. *Outlines of Muhammadan Law.* London: Oxford University Press, 2nd ed., 1955. A detailed account of Muslim Law as practiced in India; provides case law down to 1951.

1070

Manek, Mohanlal D. *Handbook of Mohammedan Law.* Bombay: N. M. Tripathi, 6th ed., rev., 1961. A standard reference work to Muslim personal law as practiced in modern India.

1071

Verma, Babu Ram. *Mohammedan Law in India and Pakistan.* Allahabad: Law Book Co., 3rd ed., 1959. A handbook of Islamic law in South Asia regarding family relations, including matters of marriage and dowry, and Hanafi and Shia laws of inheritance; accompanied by a general historical background.

1072

Mahmud, I. *Muslim Law of Succession and Administration.* Karachi: Pakistan Law House, 1958. A lucid presentation of a major facet of Muslim law as practiced in modern India and Pakistan with a comparison of this legal tradition and the "genuine Muslim law" set forth in the Shari's texts of the Middle Ages.

1073

Ebb, Lawrence F. (ed.). *Public Law Problems in India.* Stanford: Stanford University School of Law, 1957. A collection of fifteen papers by Indian and American jurists surveying, with a view to future research, contemporary Indian legal problems in such fields as federal-state and international relations.

1074

Alexandrowicz, Charles H. *A Bibliography of Indian Law.* New York: Oxford University Press, 1958. A useful guide to the subject.

ANCIENT AND MEDIEVAL POLITICAL THOUGHT

1075

Basham, Arthur L. *The Wonder That Was India.* London: Sidgwick & Jackson, 1954. New York: Grove Press, paperbound ed., 1959. Chapter Four provides an excellent summary of political life and thought in India prior to the coming of the Muslims.

1076

Brown, Donald Mackenzie. *The White Umbrella; Indian Political Thought from Manu to Gandhi.* Berkeley: University of California, 1953. Paperbound ed., 1958. A concise survey of Hindu political ideas, ancient and modern, presented through selections from the classics and from writings of such modern leaders as Gandhi. An introductory analysis and brief introductions to each section provide the general reader with excellent guidance.

1077

Kautilya. *Arthaśastra.* Mysore: Mysore Printing and Publishing House, 7th ed., 1961. A reprint of the 3rd edition published in 1929. Available from Probsthain of London. This ancient treatise on statescraft is the major source of much that has been written on traditional Indian polity. Though attributed to a 4th century B.C. prime minister of the Mauryan ruler Chandragupta, its present form probably dates from early in the Christian era.

1078

Krishna Rao, M. V. *Studies in Kautilya.* Delhi: Munshi Ram Manohar Lal, 2nd ed., rev., 1958. First published in 1953. A discussion of political theories from the *Arthaśastra* attributed to Kautilya, with comparisons to similar ideas in Indian and Western works.

1079

The Mahabharata. 13 vols. Calcutta: Oriental Publishing Co., rev. ed., c. 1952–1962. Material relating to ancient Indian political theory and practice appears throughout this monumental epic poem. The most extensive discussion of politics appears in the *Santiparvan* section of volume eight in this edition.

1080

The Laws of Manu. Tr. by G. Bühler. Oxford: Clarendon Press, 1886. Sacred Books of the East, volume 25; to be reprinted in paperbound form by Dover Publications of New York. Traditionally attributed to Manu, the first Hindu lawgiver, this ancient work probably attained its present form early in the Christian era. This detailed exposition of rules relating to the proper ordering of man and society, including the role of the king and state administration, is generally held to reflect the ideals of the Brahman class rather than actual practices.

1081

The Sukraniti. Tr. by Benoy K. Sarkar. Allahabad: Panini Office, 1914. Sacred Books of the Hindus, volume 13. A translation of the most important work of medieval Hindu political theory, traditionally attributed to the mythical sage Sukra, also known as Usanas.

1082

Ghoshal, Upendra N. *A History of Indian Political Ideas: The Ancient Period and the Period of Transition to the Middle Ages.* Bombay: Oxford University Press, 3rd ed., 1959. A revision of *A History of Hindu Political Theories* first published in 1923 with a second revised version in 1927. This is a scholarly analysis of Hindu political theories prior to the Muslim invasion of India: a basic reference work with numerous comparisons between Indian and European political ideas.

1083

Sharma, Ram Sharan. *Aspects of Political Ideas and Institutions in Ancient India.* Delhi: Motilal Banarsidass, 1959. A collection of scholarly essays including chapters on Vedic institutions, Kushan polity, and the origins of "feudalism" in India during the period c. A.D. 400 to 650.

1084

Saletore, Bhasker Anand. *Ancient Indian Political Thought and Institutions.* New York: Asia Publishing House, 1963. A study of Indian works on polity attributed to Manu and Kautilya with comparisons to similar features of the political legacy of Hammurabi and Aristotle.

1085

Mookerji, Radha Kumud. *Local Government in Ancient India.* Delhi: Motilal Banarsidass, reprint, 1958. First published in 1919. A fairly objective presentation of the thesis that elements of democracy existed in the village and district assemblies of ancient India.

1086

Jayaswal, Kashi Prasad. *Hindu Polity; A Constitutional History of India in Hindu Times.* Bangalore: Bangalore Printing and Publishing Co., 3rd ed., enl., 1955. First published in 1918. An attempt to demonstrate the existence of republican institutions in ancient India; a thesis frequently cited by leaders of the Indian nationalist movement to prove that India possessed its own traditions of democracy and therefore was capable of self-rule along British lines.

1087

Altekar, Anant Sadashiv. *State and Government in Ancient India.* Banaras: Motilal Banarsidass, 3rd ed., rev. 1958. First published in 1949. An excellent survey of Indian political thought and practice from Vedic times to about A.D. 1000; Altekar documents the existence of a variety of governmental institutions in ancient India.

1088

Prasad, Beni. *The State in Ancient India.* Allahabad: Indian Press, 1928. A classic account of ideal and actual forms of government in ancient North India as portrayed in Hindu religious texts of the post-Vedic period.

1089

Chatterjee, Hiralal. *International Law and Inter-State Relations in Ancient India.* Calcutta: K. L. Mukhopadhyay, 1958. An application of modern categories of international law to ancient Indian works on polity, including the *Arthasastra* and *Mahabharata,* with a view to determining similar lines of thought in different cultural milieus.

1090

Drekmeier, Charles. *Kingship and Community in Early India.* Stanford: Stanford University Press, 1962. An interpretation, based in the main on social science concepts, of political life and thought from Vedic to late Gupta times with most attention given to the period 800–300 B.C. Changes in the relationship of kingship to social organization and to religious values are examined as part of the transformation of Indian society from a tribal culture to an integrated agrarian civilization.

1091

Aiyangar, Kumbakonam V. Rangasvami. *Rajadharma.* Adyar: Adyar Library, 1941. A collection of essays by a modern Indian scholar presenting the orthodox point of view on the concept of kingship and the inter-relations and canonical validity of the Arthaśastra and Dharmaśastra literature.

1092

Forster, Edward M. *The Hill of Devi.* New York: Harcourt, Brace, 1953. A personal account of life in the court of a Hindu prince early in the 20th century; conveys with literary insight some of the subtle aspects of Indian government and politics.

1093

Mahalingam, T. V. *South Indian Polity.* Madras: University of Madras, 1955. A useful account of theories and practices of political organization differing in many ways from those found in North India, especially in the distribution of political power at the local level.

1094

Krishnasvami Aiyangar, Sakkottai. *Evolution of Hindu Administrative Institutions in South India.* Madras: University of Madras, 1931. A classic study of the institutions that linked the state with South Indian social and economic life.

1095

Tripathi, Ram Prasad. *Some Aspects of Muslim Administration.* Allahabad: Central Book Depot, 1956. First published in 1936. A scholarly discussion of pre-Mughal Muslim government with an interesting account of the Turko-Mughal theory of kingship.

1096

Sharma, Sri Ram. *Mughal Government and Administration.* Bombay: Hind Kitabs, 1951. A comprehensive survey of Mughal government practices during the period 1526–1707.

1097

Sherwani, Haroon Khan. *Studies in Muslim Political Thought and Administration.* Lahore: Sh. Muhammad Ashraf, 3rd ed., rev. 1959. A collection of scholarly essays on the political thought and practice of the Muslims in India during their period of political dominance and after, including a chapter on the 19th century Muslim leader Syed Ahmad Khan.

MODERN POLITICAL THOUGHT

1098

De Bary, William T., S. Hay, R. Weiler, and A. Yarrow (compilers). *Sources of Indian Tradition.* New York: Columbia University Press, 1964. Many of the selections in this source book concern indigenous Indian political thought, including a substantial section on the modern period.

1099

Brown, Donald Mackenzie. *The Nationalist Movement; Indian Political Thought from Ranade to Bhave.* Berkeley: University of California Press, paperbound, 1961. The political ideas of nine leaders of the Indian National Congress are presented through excerpts from their writings reflecting major developments in the movement from its early years through the first decade of Independence. Background information is provided by the compiler.

1100

Shay, Theodore L. *The Legacy of the Lokamanya: The Political Philosophy of Bal Gangadhar Tilak.* London: Oxford University Press, 1956. A sympathetic appraisal of the political ideas advanced early in the 20th century by a leader of the Indian Nationalist movement who was among the first to advocate enlisting mass support and the use of violence in the struggle for independence.

1101

Gandhi, Mohandas K. *Satyagraha (Non-Violent Resistance).* Ahmedabad: Navajivan Publishing House, 1951. A detailed exposition of the philosophical basis and practical application of Gandhi's ideas concerning political action.

1102

Bondurant, Joan V. *Conquest of Violence; The Gandhian Philosophy of Conflict.* Princeton: Princeton University Press, 1958. A lucid exposition of Gandhi's ideas on peaceful means for the resolution of conflict; one of the most influential aspects of Gandhi's thought outside India.

1103

Smith, Donald Eugene. *Nehru and Democracy.* New York: Longmans, Green, 1959. A useful ordering of Nehru's ideas concerning democracy, culled from Nehru's published works spanning more than three decades. Nehru is credited with an unwarranted degree of systematic thinking on the subject, and little attention is given to the milieu in which these ideas were formed.

1104

Fisher, Margaret W. and Joan V. Bondurant. *Indian Approaches to a Socialist Society.* Berkeley: Institute of International Studies, University of California, 1956. Indian Press Digests, Monograph Series, No. 2. Most of this monograph, based in the main on information from the Indian press, concerns Gandhian "Socialism," particularly the land gift movement led by Vinoba Bhave; some attention is given the Congress Party espousal of a "Socialistic pattern of society," but other parties including the Socialists are mentioned only in passing.

1105

Chandra, Jag Parvesh. *India's Socialistic Pattern of Society.* Delhi: Metropolitan Book Co., 1956. A presentation of the Congress Party's views on the role of the state in the field of economic development and social change.

1106

Lanza del Vasto, Joseph J. *Gandhi to Vinoba; the New Pilgrimage.* London: Rider, 1956. A day-by-day record of the life and teachings of Vinoba Bhave, Gandhi's spiritual heir and founder of the Bhoodan (land-gifts) movement that seeks to solve India's rural problems by voluntary means, independent of government assistance and control; written by a follower of Vinoba's.

1107

Bhave, Vinoba. *Shanti Sena.* Tr. by Marjorie Sykes. Kashi (Banaras): Akhil Bharat Sarva Seva Sangh, 1961. A translation of writings setting forth Vinoba Bhave's views on Indian problems and their solution.

1108

Tennyson, Hallam. *India's Walking Saint: The Story of Vinoba Bhave.* Garden City, N. Y.: Doubleday, 1955. A popular uncritical account of the Bhoodan movement and its founder.

1109

Sachidanand. *Sarvodaya in a Communist State.* Bombay: Popular Book Depot, 1961. A fairly objective critique of the Gandhian program of rural development, involving community ownership of land and co-operative farming, in the state of Kerala; based on a two-month visit in 1958, when a Communist ministry governed Kerala.

1110

Mehta, Asoka. *Democratic Socialism.* Hyderabad: Prakashan, 2nd ed., 1954. A presentation of the views of a leading theoretician and major spokesman of the Praja Socialist Party.

1111

Sampurnanand. *Indian Socialism.* New York: Asia Publishing House, 1961. A brief exposition of a highly personal view of socialism, by a high-ranking Congress politician; an interesting example of the way traditional values and Western concepts are combined in contemporary Indian political thought.

1112

Roy, Manabendra Nath. *Politics, Power and Parties.* Ed. by Mrs. Ellen Roy. Calcutta: Renaissance Publishers, 1960. A collection of writings on Indian politics by a former member of the Comintern, who played an active role in the radical revolutionary side of India politics prior to World War II. Roy claims that mass ignorance and a lack of political consciousness negate the possibility of establishing an effective political party system in contemporary India.

THE REPUBLIC OF INDIA

Constitution of 1950

1113

Sharma, Sri Ram. *A Constitutional History of India.* New York: St. Martin's Press, 2nd ed., 1955. A survey of the main features of India's constitutional development during the years 1765 to 1954: more detailed accounts of this subject may be found above under the "Constitutional History" section of BRITISH RULE.

1114

Rau, Sir Benegal Narsinga. *India's Constitution in the Making.* Ed. by B. Shiva Rao. New York: Allied Publishers, 2nd ed., rev., 1963. First published in 1960. A collection of papers reflecting major phases in the drafting of India's 1950 Constitution; selected from the working papers of B. N. Rau, Constitutional Adviser to the Constituent Assembly.

1115

India (Republic). *The Constitution of India as Modified up to the 1st July, 1960.* Allahabad: Law Book Co., 1963. The text of India's Constitution as amended up to date, with appendices and index by S. N. Bagga. One of the largest documents of its kind when adopted in 1950; more than 70 articles have been added to the original 395. This document describes in detail the legal framework of the Indian government and expresses the aspirations of India's leaders.

1116

Basu, Durga Das. *Commentary on the Constitution of India.* 2 vols. Calcutta: S. C. Sarkar, 4th ed., rev., 1961-62. A scholarly work providing extensive commentary on each article of the Indian Constitution, including comparative references to foreign constitutions and related documents; addressed to the specialist.

1117

Pylee, Moclamattom V. *Constitutional Government in India.* New York: Asia Publishing House, 1959. An abridged version of this work, *India's Constitution,* was issued by the same publisher in 1962. An account of the actual workings of the Indian Constitution during its initial decade, including a review of major court decisions relating to the Constitution; a detailed bibliography is provided.

1118

Joshi, Gulabbhai N. *The Constitution of India.* New York: St. Martin's Press, 4th ed., rev., 1961. An analysis of the Indian Constitution by an Advocate of the Supreme Court of India, who formerly taught constitutional law.

1119

Alexandrowicz, Charles H. *Constitutional Development in India.* Bombay: Oxford University Press, 1957. A general discussion of constitutional government in the Republic of India.

1120

Sen, Dhirendra Kumar. *A Comparative Study of the Indian Constitution.* Bombay: Orient Longmans, 1961. A description and analysis of legal principles underlying India's Constitution, viewed in relation to constitutions of other nations and decisions of the Indian Supreme Court.

1121

Douglas, William O. *We the Judges: Studies in American and Indian Constitutional Law from Marshall to Mukherjea.* Garden City, N. Y.: Doubleday, 1956. A collection of lectures by a Justice of the United States Supreme Court, delivered at Calcutta University in 1955.

1122

Jain, Mahabir P. *Indian Constitutional Law.* Bombay: N. M. Tripathi, 1962. A detailed account of the development and workings of Indian constitutional law.

1123

Aggarwal, Om Prakash. *Cases on the Constitution of India, 1950-1957.* Delhi: Metropolitan Book Co., 1958. An annotated digest of the decisions of the Supreme Court relating to the Constitution of India. A companion volume surveying the period 1958-1959 was issued by the same publisher in 1960.

Government Organization and Administration

Related works treating developments prior to 1947 may be found above under *British Rule, British Administration* and *Constitutional History.*

1124

Morris-Jones, Wyndraeth H. *Parliament in India.* Philadelphia: University of Pennsylvania Press, 1957. One of the best accounts of the composition, organization, and procedures of India's state and central legislatures. Most attention is given to the *Lok Sabha* or lower house of the central Parliament, including an analysis of the role played by the Congress Party in this most important of India's legislative assemblies.

1125

Lal, A. B. (ed.). *The Indian Parliament*. Allahabad: Chaitanya Publishing House, 1956. A collection of fifteen essays by thirteen specialists, including members of Parliament, on the formal organization and procedures of the central Indian legislature.

1126

Indian Institute of Public Administration. *The Organisation of the Government of India*. Bombay: Asia Publishing House, 1958. A useful description of the organization and functions of the central government, including separate chapters on the various ministries whose personnel and hierarchical relations are presented in chart form.

1127

India (Republic). States Reorganization Commission. *Report of the States Reorganization Commission*. New Delhi: Government of India Press, 1955. The report of a commission appointed in 1953 by the Government of India to study demands for new state boundaries based on language differences and similar factors. The commission's recommendations were reflected a year later in the seventh amendment of the constitution, which abolished the earlier classification of states into three categories.

1128

Singh, Brigadier Rajendra. *Organization and Administration in the Indian Army*. Ambala: Army Educational Stores, 2nd ed., 1957. First published in 1952 by Hampshire Gale & Polden of Aldershot, England. A manual outlining the formal structure and administrative procedures followed in the Republic of India Army.

1129

Braibanti, Ralph & J. J. Spengler (eds.). *Administration and Development in India*. Durham: Duke University Press, 1962. A variety of opinions, some contradictory, appear in this collection of ten papers on the present state of India's bureaucracy and its ability to meet future demands.

1130

Appleby, Paul H. *Public Administration for a Welfare State*. New York: Asia Publishing House, 1961. An appraisal of the ability of India's bureaucracy to implement large-scale programs of social and economic development; based on research conducted in India by the author at the invitation of the Indian government.

1131

Sharma, Sri Ram. *Some Aspects of the Indian Administrative System*. Sholapur: Institute of Public Administration, 1957. A critique of four major reports, including Paul Appleby's 1956 report, on the state of India's government administration since Independence; includes an abridged version of the reports.

1132

Hart, Henry C. *Administrative Aspects of River Valley Development*. New York: Asia Publishing House, 1961. A general discussion of planning and coordinating problems faced by administrators of India's multi-purpose river valley projects; the author makes judicious use of his experience as a staff member of the Tennessee Valley Authority.

1133

Chanda, Asok, K. *Indian Administration*. London: G. Allen & Unwin, 1958. An excellent exposition of "financial administration" in the Republic of India, reflecting the author's interest and experience as Comptroller and Auditor-General of India. Although a brief historical survey of Indian administration is provided, little attention is given to administrative organization at the state and lower levels.

1134

Santhanam, Kasturiranga I. *Union-State Relations In India*. New York: Asia Publishing House, 1961. A brief analysis of the loss of constitutionally prescribed powers by the states in contemporary India due to the influence of central government planning; the author was a member of the Finance Commission entrusted with the distribution of central revenues to state governments.

1135

Misra, B. R. *Indian Federal Finance*. Bombay: Orient Longmans, 2nd ed., 1954. A description of the Republic of India's system of public finance at the union, state, and local level; accompanied by a historical account of public finance in India since 1855.

1136

Bhargava, Rajendra N. *The Theory and Working of Union Finance in India*. London: G. Allen & Unwin, 1956. A comprehensive study of public finance in India after World War II with particular attention to problems of taxation; includes an account of the financial relations between the central and state governments.

1137

Chanda, Asok K. *Aspects of Audit Control*. New York: Asia Publishing House, 1960. A study of an important aspect of union-state relations in India; written by the Auditor General of India for the general reader.

1138

Harvard University. International Program in Taxation. *Taxation in India*. Boston: Little, Brown, 1960. A technical work prepared by the Harvard Law School in consultation with the United Nations Secretariat.

1139

Khera, S. S. *District Administration in India*. New Delhi: Indian Institute of Public Administration, 1960. An account of a little known though crucially important level of India's administrative system.

1140

Desai, N. B. *Report on the Administrative Survey of the Surat District*. Bombay: Indian Society of Agricultural Economics, 1958. A Planning Commission sponsored study of administrative structure and procedure for development programs in rural areas. A review of Mughal and British district administration precedes this report of the weak spots in the present system.

1141

Tinker, Hugh. *The Foundations of Local Self-Government in India, Pakistan, and Burma*. London: Athlone Press, 1954. An account of efforts, begun in 1882, to establish a viable system of local government in South Asia, with an appraisal of the system in 1947.

1142

Sharma, Mahadeo Prasad. *Local Self-Government in India*. Allahabad: Kitab Mahal, 3rd ed., rev., 1960. First published in 1951: a brief standard text on the subject.

1143

Retzlaff, Ralph H. *Village Government in India, A Case Study*. New York: Asia Publishing House, 1962. A study of contemporary government in a North Indian village, based on interviews, and observations obtained by the author while residing in the village.

1144

Desai, K. S. *Problems of Administration in Two Indian Villages*. Baroda: M. S. University of Baroda, 1961. A political scientist's study of difficulties encountered in efforts to establish effective government at the village level.

1145

Malaviya, Harsh Dev. *Village Panchayats in India*. New Delhi: All India Congress Committee, 1956. A nebulous survey of village councils (*panchayats*), past and present, providing much statistical information from government sources but little interpretation or critical analysis.

Political Parties and Elections

Accounts of the Indian National Congress, other pre-independence political organizations, and Indian politicians are cited above in the *20th Century* section of *History*. Relevant entries may also be found above under *Modern Political Thought*.

1146

Weiner, Myron. *Party Politics in India. The Development of a Multi-Party System*. Princeton: Princeton University Press, 1957. An analysis of India's emerging political party system based on case histories obtained through research in India; consideration is given to minor parties and splinter groups about which little has been published. A detailed bibliography of books, articles, and pamphlets is provided.

1147

Curran, Jean A. *Militant Hinduism in Indian Politics*. New York: Institute of Pacific Relations, 1951. A study of the ideology and organization of the Rashtriya Swayam Sevak Sangh, a militant Hindu revival organization with extremist political inclinations; although this is brief and published in mimeographed form, there is little else available on the subject.

1148

Prakash, Indra. *A Review of the History and Work of the Hindu Mahasabha and the Hindu Sanghatan Movement*. New Delhi: Hindu Mahasabha, 1952. An official account of the leading Hindu communal organization from which emerged the only Hindu national political party, the *Bharatiya Jana Sangh*.

1149

Rose, Saul. *Socialism in Southern Asia*. New York: Oxford University Press, 1959. An account of men, events, organizational and ideological developments of the Socialist parties that emerged after World War II in the nations ranging from Pakistan to Indonesia: mainly based on formal statements with little analysis of actual practices.

1150

Overstreet, Gene D. and Marshall Windmiller. *Communism in India*. Berkeley: University of California Press, 1959. A detailed, well-documented account of the history, organization, and activities of the Communist Party of India.

1151

Kautsky, John H. *Moscow and the Communist Party of India*. New York: John Wiley, 1956. A study of Communist strategy and tactics in India with particular attention to policy changes in the years 1945 to 1954; based mainly on published documents and other public sources.

1152

Druhe, David N. *Soviet Russia and Indian Communism, 1917–1947*. New York: Bookman Associates, 1959. A useful though often uncritical and error-ridden account of Russian efforts to establish a viable Communist Party in India; much of this narrative concerns the role of the Indian revolutionary M. N. Roy. An epilogue extends the account through one more decade.

1153

Spratt, Philip. *Blowing Up India*. Calcutta: Prachi Prakashan, 1955. The reminiscences and reflections of a British emissary of the Comintern, who participated in early efforts to organize a Communist Party of India.

1154

Democratic Research Service. *Indian Communist Party Documents, 1930–1956*. Introduction by V. B. Karnik. Bombay: The Democratic Research Service and the Institute of Pacific Relation, 1957. Distributed by the Institute of Pacific Relations of New York. A collection of documents, mainly confidential and very likely authentic, treating in frank terms the major organizational and ideological issues within the Indian Communist Party. Much of this material consists of draft resolutions and reports submitted at the CPI Congresses held in 1953 and 1956 — information previously published by the Democratic Research Service in two volumes entitled, *Communist Conspiracy at Madurai* and *Communist Double-Talk at Palghat*.

1155

Communist Party of India. *Constitution*. New Delhi: D. P. Sinha, 1959. The text of the Constitution of the Communist Party of India, adopted at a meeting held in Amritsar in April, 1958.

1156

Democratic Research Service. *Kerala Under Communism*. Bombay: Democratic Research Service, 1959. A brief account of the duly elected Communist ministry that governed the state of Kerala from April, 1957 to July, 1959.

1157

Bhagat, K. P. *The Kerala Mid-Term Election of 1960*. Bombay: Popular Book Depot, 1962. An analysis of Communist party electoral gains in the state of Kerala.

1158

Kogekar, Sadanand V. and Richard L. Park (eds.). *Reports on the Indian General Elections, 1951–52*. Bombay: Popular Book Depot, 1957. A useful source book on the results of India's first general election. Election returns are organized by states with many valuable statistical tables not readily available elsewhere. Summary accounts of the political parties and candidates are also provided.

1159

Fisher, Margaret W. and Joan V. Bondurant. *The Indian Experience with Democratic Elections*. Berkeley: Institute of International Studies, University of California, 1956. Indian Press Digests, Monograph No. 3. An analysis, published shortly before India's second general election, of the election returns of the first general election and the by-elections and three state elections that followed: statistics and press accounts are used to convey the enormity of the task of organizing elections in India.

1160

Poplai, Sundar Lal (ed.). *National Politics and the 1957 Elections in India*. Delhi: Metropolitan Book Co., 1957. Distributed by the Institute of Pacific Relations of New York. A collection of essays on the history of the four major political parties of India between the general elections of 1951–52 and 1957, written by party spokesmen; includes the 1957 election manifestos and policy statements of the parties.

1161

Poplai, Sundar Lal (ed.). *1962 General Elections in India*. Bombay: Allied Publishers, 1962. A collection of papers on the political parties and issues involved in India's third national election.

1162

Suri, Surinder. *1962 Elections, A Political Analysis*. New Delhi: Sudha Publications, 1962. A study of Indian national politics based on an analysis of the distribution of legislative seats following the general election of 1962.

Land Reform

1163

Thorner, Daniel. *The Agrarian Prospect in India*. Delhi: Delhi University Press, 1956. A review and trenchant critique of efforts at land reform in the Republic of India, with an analysis of related features of rural politics: persuasive presentation of a view favoring more fundamental reforms in rural India.

1164

Patel, Govindlal D. *The Indian Land Problem and Legislation*. Bombay: N. M. Tripathi, 1954. An appraisal of India's land problem by an official of the Bombay land reform program; includes a topically arranged and comprehensive account of land reform legislation in India.

1165

Malaviya, Harsh Dey. *Land Reforms in India*. New Delhi: All-India Congress Committee, 1954. An official statement of Congress Party land-reform policies with an account of efforts to implement such policies by Congress state ministries.

1166

India (Republic). Planning Commission. *Reports of the Committees of the Panel on Land Reforms*. Delhi: Manager of Publications, Government of India Press, 1959. An official account of the achievements and failures of government programs of land reform in India.

1167

Neale, Walter C. *Economic Change in Rural India.* New Haven: Yale University Press, 1962. A study of the land tenure system in the state of Uttar Pradesh between 1880 and 1955, with an assessment of the consequences of land reform policies adopted by the British and post-independence governments.

1168

Singh, Baljit. *Next Step in Village India.* New York: Asia Publishing House, 1961. An appraisal of land reform programs in Uttar Pradesh during the past decade; the pre-reform structure of land ownership and patterns of cultivation are held to have changed very little.

1169

Rao, N. Prasada. *Progress of Land Reform.* New Delhi: New Age Printing Press, 1960. A brief review and critique of efforts at land reform in India; a Communist party publication.

1170

Bhave, Vinoba. *Bhoodon Yajna.* Ahmedabad: Navajivan Publishing House, reprint, 1957. First published in 1953; a collection of articles from the Gandhian journal, *Harijan,* written by the founder and current leader of the land-gift (Bhoodan) movement that seeks land reform through a voluntary redistribution of land holdings. This publication describes Bhave's aims and methods regarding Bhoodan. Other works treating Bhave's role in contemporary Indian politics appear above under "Modern Political Thought."

1171

Ramabhai, Suresh. *Vinoba and His Mission.* Kashi (Banaras): Akhil Bharata Sarva Seva Sangh, 3rd ed., rev., 1962. A detailed account of the rise and growth of the Bhoodan Yajna Movement founded by Vinoba Bhave in 1951.

1172

India (Republic). Ministry of Food & Agriculture. Directorate of Economics & Statistics. *Agricultural Legislation in India.* 6 vols. Delhi: Manager of Publications, Government of India, 1951–55. This series provides the texts of agricultural legislation with useful introductions and glossaries; collections of interest here are: Volume IV, *Land Reforms: Abolition of Intermediaries* (1953); Volume V, *Village Panchayats* (1954); and Volume VI, *Land Reforms: Reforms in Tenancy* (1955).

ECONOMIC PATTERNS

Prior to the 19th century, the Indian economy was able to meet the basic needs of the populace through the productive efforts of relatively self-sufficient village units. Village agriculturists and artisans provided most of the goods and services, other than a few items such as salt and iron, needed to sustain a standard of living that may not have differed greatly from that of pre-industrial Europe. Handicraft industries, for which India was world-famous prior to the machine age, were also based on village-derived patterns of organization. The division of labor and control of economic power were mainly determined by custom and hereditary rights perpetuated by the caste system. While the right to levy land taxes was recognized as the prerogative of those commanding political power, the concept of private property in land as developed in 18th century Europe, had few counterparts in traditional India.

British conquest of India radically altered the old structure of village life by introducing in many areas the *zamindari* system of land revenue collection. This system created a new class of landlords with proprietary rights comparable to those of Western private property, and deprived the cultivator of his ancient claims to the use of the land. A different system adopted by the British in other areas, sought to establish a direct link between the state and the individual cultivator. Known as the *ryotwari* system, it allowed for the alienation of land holdings when revenue payments were not paid, and seriously disrupted older systems of communal land holdings. The consequent impoverishment and dislocation of the Indian peasant, coupled with increasing rural indebtedness, forced the British to initiate ameliorative legislation that was greatly increased after India's independence; but to little avail. Such measures were readily offset by the increasing pressure of population, stemming from a variety of forces originating in the 19th century; especially the greater control of famines through the use of modern transport and the reduction of the death rate by modern medicine.

With the exception of the textile industry, modern manufacturing in India has not kept pace with the country's needs. The minor role of large-scale industry is reflected in the percentage of factory workers in the population, less than one per cent in 1900 and even less today, due to the slow rate of industrialization and the rapid expansion of population. This lack of industrial growth coupled with the decline of handicraft industries has increased the percentage of people dependent on agriculture for their livelihood and swelled the ranks of landless laborers.

The immensity of India's economic problems in recent times, particularly the fundamental task of feeding her own people, has dominated the literature on India's economy. Economic development is the main concern of most works in this field, whether the subject concerned is agriculture or industry. Five Year Plans, seeking to accelerate growth in all spheres of the economy, have been adopted to cope with this challenge. Another aspect of government effort in this area is the Community Development Program that seeks to infuse new ideals of local initiative and community cooperation as well as more efficient techniques of farming. Foreign aid has played a crucial part in India's efforts to promote economic growth since independence, and will remain a critical factor in the future, as self-sufficiency in even the most rudimentary sense of an adequate food supply appears unlikely within the next two or three decades.

SURVEYS AND SPECIAL STUDIES

1173

Morris, Morris D. and Burton Stein. "The Economic History of India," in *Journal of Economic History,* XXI,

(June, 1961), pp. 179–207. An excellent guide to the poorly developed field of Indian economic history with lucid appraisal and full citation of major works; coverage extends from earliest times to about 1950.

1174

Wadia, Pestonji A. and K. T. Merchant. *Our Economic Problem.* Bombay: Vora, 5th ed., rev., 1957. A general survey of most aspects of the Indian economy.

1175

Jathar, Ganesh B. and K. G. Jathar. *Indian Economics; A Comprehensive and Critical Survey.* New York: Oxford University Press, rev. ed., 1957. A standard textbook on the subject.

1176

Banerjea, Pramathanath. *A Study of Indian Economics.* Calcutta: University of Calcutta, 6th ed., 1951. One of the better introductions: a standard textbook for many years.

1177

Arokiaswami, M. and T. M. Royappa. *Modern Economic History of India.* Madras: University of Madras, 4th ed., 1955. A survey of India's resources and of the main features of their development in the 20th century.

1178

Basu, Saroj Kumar. *The Managing Agency System in Prospect and Retrospect.* Calcutta: World Press, 1958. A study of the quasi-monopolistic system of industrial finance and organization developed in India under British rule. Within this system individual mercantile houses act as the central management for a dozen or more business firms engaged in a wide variety of economic activities.

1179

Spencer, Daniel L. *India: Mixed Enterprise and Western Business.* The Hague: M. Nijhoff, 1959. An account of the post-1918 development under British rule of joint ventures in sugar, paper, and other enterprises between private business and the governments of such states as Mysore, Baroda, and Hyderabad. Two chapters treat the role of foreign capital, private and public, in Indian enterprises.

1180

Gupta, Om Prakash. *Central Banking in India, 1777–1934.* New Delhi: Hindustan Times Press, 1953. A historical account of the development of a modern banking system in India.

1181

Simha, S. L. N. *The Capital Market of India.* Bombay: Vora, 1960. By an official of the Reserve Bank of India, a useful survey of the system for financing India's private industry, with one chapter on capital in rural areas and another on legislation affecting the capital market.

1182

Chacko, Kollenparampil C. *The Monetary and Fiscal Policy of India.* Bombay: Vora, 1957. A description of the Indian money market and its components, including banks, cooperatives, and rural credit associations. The dangers of inflation are discussed with particular attention to fiscal measures adopted to finance the Five-Year Plans.

1183

Rangnekar, D. K. *Poverty and Capital Development in India.* London: Oxford University Press, 1958. A carefully prepared estimate of capital formation in the major sectors of India's economy during the four years following India's independence in 1947. The influence of social and cultural factors on capital growth are discussed and recommendations for government planning presented.

1184

Desai, Rajanikant. *Standard of Living in India and Pakistan, 1931–32 to 1940–41.* Bombay: Popular Book Depot, 1953. A useful estimate of Indian national income during the decade preceding World War II.

1185

India (Republic). Department of Economic Affairs, Ministry of Finance. *Final Report of the National Income Committee, February, 1954.* New Delhi: Manager of Publications, Government of India, 1954. An official estimate of India's national income for the years 1948–1949 through 1950–51.

1186

Rao, V. K. R. V., S. R. Sen, M. V. Divatia, and U. Datta (eds.). *Papers on National Income and Allied Topics.* 2 vols. New York: Asia Publishing House, 1960–62. The initial volumes in a continuing series of technical papers prepared by the Indian Conference on Research in National Income. Primarily of interest to the specialist, these papers of varying quality discuss statistics and methods of analysis for the study of India's national income.

1187

Chaudhry, Mahinder D. and B. F. Hoselitz. *State Income of Delhi State, 1951–52 and 1955–56.* Chicago: University of Chicago Press, 1963. Published as part II of Vol. XI, No. 3 of the *Journal of Economic Development and Cultural Change.* This monograph is probably one of the most accurate estimates of income data and its composition for an Indian urban area. Information on the working force, wages, and range of economic activity is presented in a succinct and lucid manner.

1188

Harris, Frank R. *Jamsetji Nusserwaniji Tata.* Bombay: Blackie & Son, 1958. First published in 1925 by Milford of London. An adulatory biography of one of the first members of the Indian business community to venture into heavy industry.

1189

Moraes, Francis R. *Sir Purshotamdas Thakurdas.* Bombay: Asia Publishing House, 1957. A popular biography of one of India's leading business men.

1190

Indian Economic Journal, Vol. 1–. Bombay: School of Economics and Sociology, University of Bombay, 1953–. A quarterly publication, the official organ of the Indian Economic Association.

1191

Eastern Economist. Vol. 1–. New Delhi: Eastern Economist, 1943–. A weekly journal of business and finance.

ECONOMIC DEVELOPMENT

1192

Malenbaum, Wilfred. *Prospects for Indian Development.* London: G. Allen & Unwin, 1962. A critical review of India's efforts at economic development during 1951–61, and an appraisal of the Third Five-Year Plan which will end in 1966. Private as well as public sectors of the economy are considered along with political and cultural factors: a fairly technical study, best read with a basic knowledge of formal economics.

1193

Braibanti, Ralph and J. J. Spengler (eds.). *Administration and Development in India.* Durham: Duke University Press, 1962. A collection of ten essays appraising the ability of India's bureaucracy to implement the government's many ambitious plans for economic and social development.

1194

Gadgil, Dhananjaya R. *Planning and Economic Policy in India.* New York: Asia Publishing House, 2nd ed., 1963. A valuable collection of critical essays on some of the major problems confronting those seeking rapid economic development through planning in India today.

1195

Reddaway, W. Brian. *The Development of the Indian Economy.* Homewood, Ill.: Irwin, 1962. A presentation of the author's input-output model for the Third Five-Year Plan, based on a judicious appraisal of tenuous statistics, with a lucid survey of the present state of India's economy.

1196

Venkatasubbiah, Hiranyappa. *Indian Economy Since Independence.* New York: Asia Publishing House, 2nd ed., rev., 1961. A survey of major events affecting the Indian economy in the past decade; mainly concerned with the urban sector and the implementation of government policy. The author, an economic journalist, provides informative details and insight on policies, but little systematic analysis.

1197

Vakil, Chandulal N. and P. R. Brahmananda. *Planning for an Expanding Economy.* Bombay: Vora, 1956. About half of this book is occupied with an unduly optimistic three-stage scheme, with utilization of the under-employed as a primary means of capital formation. The remainder is a review of India's First Five-Year Plan and a critique of the assumptions and goals of the Second.

1198

Deshmukh, Chintaman D. *Economic Developments in India, 1946–56.* Bombay: Asia Publishing House, 1957. Personal account of a decade of economic development by a former finance minister of the central government; originally presented in the form of lectures.

1199

Zinkin, Maurice. *Development for Free Asia.* New York: Oxford University Press, rev. ed., 1963. The social, political, and administrative aspects of economic development in India are lucidly surveyed in this account, addressed to the general reader, by a former member of the Indian Civil Service. Zinkin is a strong advocate of more private enterprise and less government control in Asia's economic development.

1200

Palekar, Sheekant A. *Problems of Wage Policy for Economic Development: With Special Reference to India.* New York: Asia Publishing House, 1962. A critique of the wage policy adopted in India's Five-Year Plan; based on comparisons with other countries and on an analysis of wages in India during the years 1950–55. Contains extensive statistics presented in comprehensible tables.

1201

Agarwal, Shriman Narayan. *Principles of Gandhian Planning.* Allahabad: Kitab Mahal, 1960. An attempt to present in an orderly manner the wide variety of views on economic and social planning expressed by Gandhi and his followers.

1202

Jha, Shiva Nand. *A Critical Study of Gandhian Economics.* Agra: Lakshmi Narain Agarwal, 1961. A non-critical compilation of Gandhi's economic ideas, drawn from a variety of sources, with little documentation or background.

1203

Commonwealth Consultative Committee on South and Southeast Asia. *The Colombo Plan for Co-operative Economic Development in South and Southeast Asia.* London: Her Majesty's Stationery Office, 1950. An account of the plan adopted in Colombo, Ceylon in 1950 to further the economic development of Commonwealth countries in Asia. India, a major recipient of this assistance, has also aided in the intra-regional training of technicians. In 1958 the United States joined England, Canada, and Australia as a donor country in the program. Annual reports of the Plan's progress are published by H. M. Stationery Office in London. A monthly newsletter is issued by The Colombo Plan Bureau, located in Colombo, Ceylon.

FIVE-YEAR PLANS

1204

India (Republic). Planning Commission. *First Five-Year Plan.* Delhi: Manager of Publications, Government of India, 1952. A statement of goals and the proposed means of their attainment, during the years 1951 to 1956. India's Five-Year Plans encompass a wide range of economic and social problems in both the argicultural and industrial sectors of the economy.

1205

India (Republic). Planning Commission. *Review of the First Five-Year Plan.* Delhi: Manager of Publications, 1957. An official appraisal of government efforts at economic and social development during the years 1951–56.

1206

The New India; Progress Through Democracy. New York: Macmillan, 1958. An uncritical, though informative, account of the aims, methods, and underlying philosophy of India's Second Five-Year Plan; prepared for foreign readers at the request of the Indian Planning Commission.

1207

India (Republic). Planning Commission. *The Second Five-Year Plan of the Indian Union.* Delhi: Manager of Publications, Government of India, 1956. A statement of more than six hundred pages of goals and methods for their attainment in the 1956–61 period.

1208

India (Republic). Planning Commission. *Third Five-Year Plan.* Delhi: Manager of Publications, Government of India Press, 1961. A document of more than seven hundred pages setting forth detailed plans for the 1961–66 period. A two-hundred page summary of the plan was also issued by the Planning Commission in 1961.

FOREIGN AID

1209

Rao, V. K. R. V. and Dharm Narain. *Foreign Aid and India's Economic Development.* New York: Asia Publishing House, 1963. A brief account of the source, amount, and use of foreign aid received by India up to 1962; a useful exposition for the general reader.

1210

Lewis, John Prior. *Quiet Crisis in India.* New York: Macmillan, 1963. A sombre account of India's problems of economic development and the implication for United States foreign policy.

1211

Bauer, Peter T. *Indian Economic Policy and Development.* New York: Praeger, 1961. A revision of the author's *United States and India,* published in 1959. A polemic critique of Indian economic planning and the part played by United States economic assistance in India's development. The author calls for a major revision of policy allowing private enterprise to cope with India's development problems.

1212

Wolf, Charles, Jr. *Foreign Aid: Theory and Practice in Southern Asia.* Princeton: Princeton University Press, 1960. An account of the United States' military and economic programs in Southern Asia during the years 1951–57, prefaced with a discussion of similar efforts elsewhere in 1945–50. This is followed by a complex model based on Indian data presented as a guide for future allocations of foreign aid.

1213

Ward, Barbara. *India and the West.* London: Hamish Hamilton, 1961. New York: W. W. Norton, paperbound, rev. ed., 1963. An account of India's efforts at economic development presented in relation to the state of contemporary world politics: a strong plea for economic aid to India.

INDUSTRY

1214

Rosen, George. *Industrial Change in India: Industrial Growth, Capital Requirements, and Technological Change, 1937–1955.* Glencoe: The Free Press, 1958. A study of capital-output and capital-labor ratios of five major Indian industries based on financial data from the companies' balance-sheets; the implications of these findings are then extended in a useful, perhaps unduly optimistic, evaluation of India's industrial prospects.

1215

Sharma, Tulsi Ram. *Location of Industries in India*. Bombay: Hind Kitabs, 3rd ed., rev., 1954. A classic work on the distribution and regional character of such industries as iron and steel, jute, and textiles, with an examination of the factors governing their location including resources, labor supply, and communications.

1216

Dhar, P. N. and H. F. Lydall. *The Role of Small Enterprises in Indian Economic Development*. New York: Asia Publishing House, 1961. A brief insightful critique of the Indian government's program for supporting business enterprises with fewer than fifty employees.

1217

Nanjundan, S., H. E. Robinson, E. Staley. *Economic Research for Small Industry Development*. London: Asia Publishing House, 1962. A description and assessment of the efforts of the Government of India to stimulate small industry through service institutes, extension centers and other organizations designed to supply business men with the findings of economic research.

1218

Singh, Baljit. *The Economics of Small-Scale Industries*. New York: Asia Publishing House, 1961. An appraisal of the problems and relative productivity of small-scale industries in the North Indian town of Moradabad. Based on a survey conducted by the Economics Department of Lucknow University.

1219

Berna, James J. *Industrial Entrepreneurship in Madras State*. New York: Asia Publishing House, 1960. A study of the origin and development of several medium-size business firms in South India with suggestions for government policy; the author concludes that economic rather than social or religious factors are the most decisive influence on business ventures of this kind.

1220

Baldwin, George B. *Industrial Growth in South India. Case Studies in Economic Development*. Glencoe: The Free Press, 1959. A collection of case histories, obtained by interviews in 1953, concerning leadership, finance, labor relations and related matters in several dozen business firms of Bangalore City.

1221

Khera, S. S. *Government in Business*. New York: Asia Publishing House, 1964. A survey of the administration of industries managed by the Government of India.

1222

Hart, Henry C. *New India's Rivers*. Calcutta: Orient Longmans, 1956. A detailed account of the history and scope of major multi-purpose river projects undertaken by the Republic of India.

LABOR

1223

Myers, Charles A. *Labor Problems in the Industrialization of India*. Cambridge: Harvard University Press, 1958. Also published in Bombay by Asia Publishing House under the title: *Industrial Relations in India*. A critical appraisal of India's contemporary labor force, viewed against its historical and cultural background, and the part played by unions, management and government in preparing labor to meet the demands of modern industry; contains a copy of the labor sections of the First and Second Five-Year Plans.

1224

Mukerjee, Radhakamal. *The Indian Working Class*. Bombay: Hind Kitabs, 3rd ed., rev., 1951. A general survey of India's industrial labor force including information

on their standards of living, conditions of employment, methods of recruitment, and trade union organization.

1225

Lambert, Richard D. *Workers, Factories, and Social Change in India*. Princeton: Princeton University Press, 1963. A study of industrial labor recruitment and commitment based on a comparison of the occupational experience and socio-economic characteristics of factory workers in Poona and of the local non-factory population. Provides interesting data on the role of caste in an industrial setting.

1226

Punekar, S. D. *Trade Unionism in India*. Bombay: New Book Co., 1948. A relatively dispassionate historical survey of the development of trade unions in India.

1227

Giri, V. V. *Labour Problems in Indian Industry*. Bombay: Asia Publishing House, 3rd ed., rev., 1959. A detailed account of employment practices, industrial relations, and related matters, with some information on current conditions.

1228

Vaid, K. N. (ed.). *Labour-Management Relations in India*. Delhi: Delhi University School of Social Work, paperbound, 1960. A brief collection of lectures by representatives of labor and management actively engaged in the framing or implementing of labor legislation and agreements.

1229

Singh, V. B. and A. K. Saran (eds.). *Industrial Labour in India*. New York: Asia Publishing House, 1960. A collection of academic essays by nineteen authors on such topics as wage policy, collective bargaining, and unemployment; mainly based on data from the British period with little reference to current labor problems. Prepared for use as a graduate text.

1230

India (Republic). Labour Bureau, Ministry of Labour. *The Indian Labour Year Book*. Delhi: Manager of Publications, Government of India Press, 1948–. An annual reference work, first published in 1948 for the year 1946–47; information on employment, labor legislation, industrial relations, standard of living, and a detailed bibliography are generally included. The same agency also issues the monthly *Indian Labour Gazette* containing similar material and the most recent findings of the Labour Investigation Committee. In 1960 the Labour Bureau began publishing the *Indian Labour Journal*.

1231

India (Republic). Labour Bureau, Ministry of Labour. *Agricultural Labour in India: Report on the Second Agricultural Labour Enquiry, 1956–1957*. Vol. 1–. Delhi: Manager of Publications, Government of India Press, 1957–. A basic source of information on India's rural labor force; includes information on wages, living conditions, and under-employment. The Labour Bureau also issued, during 1951–55, a seven-volume series of similar reports based on the Agricultural Labour Enquiry of 1950–51.

1232

Patel, Surendra J. *Agricultural Labourers in Modern India and Pakistan*. Bombay: Current Book House, 1952. A useful survey of the living and working conditions of the rural labor force; viewed in relation to its historical setting. Related works are cited below under "Agriculture."

AGRICULTURE

Related works treating the human factor in India's rural economy appear above under *Labor* and below under *Community Development*. Accounts of land reform are cited above under *Politics*.

1233

Bhattacharjee, Jyoti Prasad (ed.). *Studies in Agricultural Economics*. Bombay: Indian Society of Agricultural

Economics, 1958. A collection of essays providing useful statistics on the production of major food crops during the first five decades of this century, and on the decreasing ratio of land to people. One of the few historical studies of Indian agriculture.

1234

Mukherjee, P. K. *Economic Surveys in Under-developed Countries.* Bombay: Asia Publishing House, 1959. Review and assessment of problems encountered in the collection and analysis of Indian rural survey material; includes a useful summary of the economic features of Indian village life.

1235

Nanavati, Manilal B. and J. J. Anjaria. *The Indian Rural Problem.* Bombay: Indian Society of Agricultural Economics, 5th ed. rev., 1960. An extensively rewritten version of a standard, though cumbersome, work on Indian agriculture and agrarian relations; first published in 1945.

1236

Thorner, Daniel and Alice. *Land and Labour in India.* Bombay: Asia Publishing House, 1962. A collection of authoritative articles on such problems as agricultural production, credit, and development in India's rural economy.

1237

Mann, Harold H. *Land and Labour in a Deccan Village.* Bombay: Oxford University Press, 1917. Mann, Harold H. and N. V. Kanitkar. *Land and Labour in a Deccan Village, Study No. 2.* Bombay: Oxford University Press, 1921. These two volumes are respectively Nos. 1 and 3 in the University of Bombay Economic Series; they are the first and probably the best surveys of village economic life. The 1917 report, based on three years of intensive research in a village near Poona, includes a careful recording of soil types, rainfall and other environmental factors with direct measures of inputs and outputs by a trained staff. The second study was conducted with similar rigor in a village further removed from Poona.

1238

Diskalkar, P. D. *Resurvey of a Deccan Village: Pimple Saudagar.* Bombay: The Indian Society of Agricultural Economics, 1960. A resurvey, conducted in 1951–53, of the first village studied by H. H. Mann and his associates during the years 1913–1916.

1239

Bailey, Frederick G. *Caste and the Economic Frontier.* Manchester: Manchester University Press, 1957. An anthropological study of the influence of a century of British rule on the economy of a rural area in Orissa.

1240

Epstein, T. Scarlett. *Economic Development and Social Change in South India.* Manchester: Manchester University Press, 1962. One of the most detailed studies of village economic life in India: based on extended residence for research purposes in the communities studied.

1241

Mayer, Adrian C. *Land and Society in Malabar.* London: Oxford University Press, 1952. One of few studies based on first-hand observation of agrarian relations and economic conditions in a specific region of India.

1242

Ali, Hashim Amir, T. K. Basu, & J. Talkudar. *Then and Now.* Bombay: Asia Publishing House, 1960. A report of an economic survey conducted in five Bengal villages in 1931–34 combined with a re-survey of these villages by the same research team in 1956–57.

1243

Beidelman, Thomas O. *A Comparative Analysis of the Jajmani System.* New York: J. J. Augustin, 1959. "Monographs of the Association for Asian Studies, No. VIII." A review and analysis of accounts from various rural areas of India concerning economic relationships based on hereditary rights. Other works on this subject are cited below under "Village Communities."

1244

India (Republic). Ministry of Food & Agriculture. Directorate of Economics & Statistics. *Agricultural Legislation in India.* 6 vols. Delhi: Manager of Publications, Government of India, 1951–55. This series provides the texts of agricultural legislation passed in the early years of India's independence to further land reform and related ameiliorative measures; includes useful introductions and glossaries.

1245

Dantwala, Mohanlal L. *India's Food Problem.* New York: Asia Publishing House, 1961. A discussion of the problem posed by the inability of Indian agriculture to supply adequate food for a rapidly expanding population. Related accounts are cited below under "Population."

1246

India (Republic). Ministry of Food and Agriculture. *Report on India's Food Crisis and Steps to Meet It.* Delhi: Manager of Publications, Government of India Press, 1959. A report by an agricultural production team sponsored by the Ford Foundation presenting a dismal estimate of India's ability to feed her people in the near future.

COMMUNITY DEVELOPMENT AND COOPERATIVES

1247

Mayer, Albert in collaboration with McKim Marriott and R. L. Park. *Pilot Project, India: The Story of Rural Development at Etawah, Uttar Pradesh.* Berkeley: University of California Press, 1958. An insightful portrayal of problems encountered in translating community development plans into action. Project records, correspondence and other original source material are skillfully used to convey the subtleties of development programs led by Mayer during the years 1948–55.

1248

Dube, Shyama C. *India's Changing Villages: Human Factors in Community Development.* Ithaca: Cornell University Press, 1958. A first-hand account and evaluation by a trained social scientist of a community development block in western Uttar Pradesh; includes detailed information on the life and problems of personnel in the project's lower echelons.

1249

Nair, Kusum. *Blossoms in the Dust. The Human Factor in Indian Development.* New York: F. A. Praeger, 1962. A journalist's perceptive account of the achievements and failures of the Community Development Program in rural India. Major problems are poignantly illustrated with anecdotes and observations obtained during a year-long trip through the principal rural regions.

1250

Mukerji, B. *Community Development in India.* Bombay: Orient Longmans, 1961. An uncritical view of the Government's Community Development Program, written by an administrator whose views reflect official philosophy and doctrine.

1251

India (Republic). Planning Commission. Program Evaluation Organization. *Seventh Evaluation Report on Community Development and Some Allied Fields.* New Delhi: Government of India, Planning Commission, 1960. One of a series of candid appraisals of the Community Development Program initiated by the Government of India in 1952 to improve village education, leadership, health, and related matters as well as the economic side of rural life. This report indicates that in spite of almost a decade of effort, the villagers have not developed much enthusiasm for the program's goal of helping people to help themselves.

1252

India (Republic). Planning Commission. Program Evaluation Organization. *Report of the Team for the Study of Community Projects and National Extension Service Blocks.* 3 vols. New Delhi: Planning Commission, Committee on Plan Projects, 1957. An influential report, sometimes referred to as the Balvantray Mehta (name of the team leader) report, which strongly recommended further decentralization of government administration. A number of state governments have introduced changes in keeping with these recommendations for *Panchayati Raj* (government by locally-elected councils) in the hope that greater responsibility for community development will be fostered at the local level.

1253

India (Republic). Planning Commission. *Social Welfare in India.* New Delhi: Publications Division, Ministry of Information & Broadcasting, Government of India, 1960. A lengthy survey of India's social problems and programs for their amelioration, with a listing of welfare agencies engaged in this field.

1254

Brayne, Frank L. *Socrates in An Indian Village.* Calcutta: Oxford University Press, 5th ed., 1941. First published in 1929. An account of problems and methods of village improvement cast in the form of conversations with Indian peasants; written by a senior officer in the Indian Civil Service who initiated some of the earliest programs of rural reconstruction in India.

1255

Darling, Malcolm L. *The Punjab Peasant in Prosperity and Debt.* Bombay: Oxford University Press, 4th ed., 1947. An account of problems confronting peasants in northwestern India during the post World War I period; written by a British official involved in the organization of cooperative societies in the Punjab.

1256

Hatch, D. Spencer. *Toward Freedom from Want, from India to Mexico.* Bombay: Oxford University Press, 1949. An exposition of knowledge gained in more than a decade of community development work in rural India; written by a pioneer in the field, who later applied his principles to similar problems in a Mexican village.

1257

Singh, Tarlok. *Poverty and Social Change.* London: Longmans, Green, 1945. An early statement of the need and methods for reorganizing the economy of rural India in terms of government-sponsored cooperatives.

1258

Khusro, A. M. and A. N. Agarwal. *The Problem of Cooperative Farming in India.* New York: Asia Publishing House, 1961. A review and appraisal of various proposals to increase the economic use of land in India by enlarging the units of cultivation.

1259

Democratic Research Service. *Cooperative Farming.* Bombay: Democratic Research Service, 1959. A compilation of speeches and public statements by major Indian political figures for and against the adoption of cooperative farming as a means of offsetting India's food shortage. Includes a full range of opinions from India's political spectrum.

SOCIAL PATTERNS

Indian society is predominantly agrarian, with caste, kinship, and village organization providing the framework for social relations. Although powerful forces of change affecting the social order may be found in cities created through European contacts in modern times, most of the Indian populace resides and works in rural areas where traditional ways of life prevail. Even in the cities, most marriages are arranged by family elders, with mate selection limited to members of the same caste or sub-caste. Although forces of urbanization have influenced the size and composition of city families, the patrilineal, joint family remains as an ideal in the countryside. Under this form of family organization, land and other major economic assets are jointly owned by the family and the oldest man directs production and consumption. Ideally, a family of this kind includes a man, his sons, grandsons, their wives and children. Few adult women reside in their parental home due to sanctions imposed on parents who fail to arrange their daughter's marriage prior to late adolescence. Despite general acceptance of the joint family ideal, its realization in practice is limited to the relatively well-to-do. Most of the populace has lived in a variety of family types, and in some regions radically different systems of kinship, including some based on matrilineal descent, have existed from remote antiquity.

Indian village organization also appears in many forms, varying from the centralized village settlement and joint tenancy of land common in North India to the dispersed hamlets and individual land holdings of South India. Such diversity is accompanied by variety in community organization and the exercise of local authority. Despite variations of this kind, life in most rural communities in India is regulated to a great extent by the pervasive system known as caste.

Historical evidence relating to the origin of caste in India is fragmentary and many competing explanations appear in scholarly accounts of the subject. Orthodox Hindus find scriptural authority for caste in references to a fourfold division of society contained in Vedic literature composed three thousand years ago. These divisions are presented in later Hindu literature as parts of an immutable hierarchy with the Brahman (priest) at the top, followed by the Kshatriya (warrior), Vaishya (merchant), and Shudra (artisan). Boys of the upper three groups undergo an initiation ceremony from which they emerge as "twice born." A fifth category, considered outside the orthodox Hindu community, was created early in the Christian era. Commonly referred to as Untouchables, Scheduled Castes, or Harijans, members of this group suffer many social disabilities and do most of the degrading work.

The four main divisions of the caste system encompass more than two thousand endogamous groups known as sub-castes, or *jatis*. Sub-castes tend to be identified with a particular occupation although considerable variation exists in actual practice. Each sub-caste possesses a distinct body of social customs; failure to abide by caste traditions of this kind might result in the "outcasting" of the offender. The obligation to perform caste duties is supported by the Hindu concept of duty (*dharma*) and related religious beliefs including that of rebirth and the chain of moral causation (*karma*) which accounts for differences in caste status as the direct result of deeds performed in previous lives. Although Hinduism provides the ideological basis of caste, most of the other religious communities in India have adopted one or another feature of this system of social stratification.

The assimilative power of caste may be seen at work today among many of the tribal groups who occupy isolated enclaves in the forests and hill tracts of India. These tribes, numbering more than two hundred in recent years, appear in various stages of transition ranging from distinctive ways of life based on hunting and gathering, to sedentary farmers practicing many of the religious and social customs of their Hindu neighbors.

Although towns and cities have existed in India from ancient times, the creation of large metropolitan centers as relatively independent units with a distinct civic tradition is a result of European contacts during the past century. The emergence of a new middle class oriented to the technological and organizational needs of the modern world is a major feature of the new city environment. Changes emanating from urban centers constitute a powerful challenge to the traditional Indian social order, a challenge recently expressed in legislation affecting fundamental family relations, caste rights and disabilities, and community organization. The actual transformation of tradition, however, is more likely to occur as a result of the ongoing mass migration from rural to urban areas.

REFERENCES, PERIODICALS, COLLECTIONS OF ESSAYS

1260

Kanitkar, J. M. (Compiler). *A Bibliography of Indology*. Vol. I, Indian Anthropology. Ed. & rev. by D. L. Banerjee & A. K. Ohdedar. Calcutta: Indian National Library, rev. ed., 1960. The first in a series of volumes, "Enumerating Basic Publications on All Aspects of Indian Culture." Volume one consists of 2,067 entries, about half with annotations, of anthropological interest; it was first published in 1951 as a mimeographed list of 1,387 entries.

1261

Patterson, Maureen L. P. and R. B. Inden. *South Asia: An Introductory Bibliography*. Chicago: Syllabus Division, University of Chicago Press, 1962. The section on "Social Structure and Organization" in this work provides hundreds of references to articles and essays on all aspects of Indian society. Due to the relatively recent development of social science enquiry in South Asia, many pioneering studies in this field have not as yet appeared in book form. However, the journal articles cited in this volume provide an excellent guide to areas of current enquiry and to social scientists interested in South Asia.

1262

Fürer-Haimendorf, Elizabeth von. *An Anthropological Bibliography of South Asia*. Paris: Mouton, 1958. The basic reference work in the field; contains full references to books, articles, and monographs on all aspects of anthropological research in India, Pakistan, Nepal, Sikkim, Bhutan, and Ceylon. Limited for the most part to works in Western languages with coverage to 1954. Includes a survey of cultural and social anthropological field work conducted during the 1940–54 period. A supplementary volume for the years 1955–59 is in preparation.

1263

Beals, Alan R. and J. T. Hitchcock. *Field Guide to India*. Washington, D. C.: National Acadamy of Sciences, 1960. Includes a section on Pakistan by Mary J. Kennedy. A useful booklet providing guidance for those undertaking social science research in South Asia; contains practical advice on problems of everyday life with information on scientific institutions and suggestions for future research.

1264

Ranganathan, S. R. and G. Kumar. *Social Science Research and Libraries*. New York: Asia Publishing House, 1960. A collection of papers, including one on the organization of research collections in India, presented in a library science seminar on research in the social sciences held in Delhi in 1959.

1265

Park, Richard L. and Irene Tinker (eds.). *Leadership and Political Institutions in India*. Princeton: Princeton University Press, 1959. Several essays in this collection provide firsthand accounts of the political side of caste organization and village life, while other essays indicate the importance of kinship and family loyalties in Indian politics.

1266

Singer, Milton (ed.). *Traditional India: Structure and Change*. Philadelphia: American Folklore Society, 1959. Volume 10 in the Society's Bibliographical and Special Series. A collection of essays on various facets of Indian tradition, including urban and rural social organization, and changes in the old order brought about by science, technology and other forces of modernization.

1267

Rowe, William L. (ed.). *Contours of Culture Change in South Asia*. A special issue of "Human Organization," Vol. 22, No. 1. Ithaca, New York: The Society for Applied Anthropology, 1963. This issue consists of a dozen articles based in the main on recent anthropological field work in six different areas of South Asia. The adaptation of traditional institutions to modern ways and problems encountered in directing contemporary changes are of major concern in this collection.

1268

Dumont, Louis and David Pocock (eds.). *Contributions to Indian Sociology. No. 1–*. Paris: Mouton, 1957–. A publication appearing irregularly containing articles by the editors and others on current social science research in South Asia and related subjects, primarily of interest to the specialist.

1269

The Economic Weekly. 1949–. Published in Bombay: during the past decade this journal has served as a lively forum for the presentation and discussion of recent social science research in India, including studies of family, village, and caste.

1270

Sociological Bulletin. Vol. I–. Bombay: Indian Sociological Society, 1952–. A professional journal containing articles by Indian and Western scholars on all aspects of Indian society.

1271

Man in India. Vol. I–. Ranchi (Bihar state): Man in India Office, 1921–. An anthropological journal published quarterly; most of the articles treat Indian subject matter.

FAMILY AND KINSHIP

1272

Mandelbaum, David G. "The Family in India" in the *Southwestern Journal of Anthropology*, Vol. 4, No. 2, pp. 123-139, 1948. A concise description of the structure and interpersonal relations of the ideal Indian family, with due consideration of major variations.

1273

Bilimoria, Faili (director). *Fifty Miles From Poona.* A 20 minute black and white film. Produced by the National Film Board of Canada, 1959. An intimate portrayal of an ordinary day in the life of a Hindu family residing in a village of Maharashtra located fifty miles from the city of Poona.

1274

Karve, Irawati. *Kinship Organization in India.* Poona: Deccan College, 1953. A survey of the principal systems of kinship found in India; includes a reconstruction of the ancient Indo-Aryan system described in Hindu religious texts. Variations in modern kinship systems are examined in relation to language and geographical differences of a regional order.

1275

Ghurye, Govind Sadashiv. *Family and Kin in Indo-European Culture.* Bombay: Popular Book Depot, 2nd ed., 1962. A useful summary description of Indo-European kinship as depicted in Sanskrit, Greek, and Latin sources with an analysis of developments within each tradition in relation to ritual, inheritance, marriage practices, and related topics.

1276

Prabhu, Pandhari Nath. *Hindu Social Organization.* Bombay: Popular Book Depot, rev. ed., 1954. First published in 1939 as *Hindu Social Institutions.* An account of the philosophical and ideological basis of Hindu social thought concerning such institutions as family and caste.

1277

Kapadia, Kanailal Motilal. *Marriage and Family in India.* Bombay: Oxford University Press, 2nd ed., 1958. A survey of some major variants in marriage practices and forms of family organization found in India, including those of Hindu, Muslim, and tribal origin; based in the main on documentary sources supplemented with information from sociological surveys and anthropological studies.

1278

Dumont, Louis. *Hierarchy and Marriage Alliance in South Indian Kinship.* London: Royal Anthropological Institute, "Occasional Papers No. 12," 1957. A brief monograph utilizing Levi-Strauss' theories of kinship in an analysis of preferential cross-cousin marriage in South India and its influence on the perpetuation of status and hierarchy in a unilineal descent system. Primarily of interest to the specialist.

1279

Schneider, David M. and Kathleen Gough (eds.). *Matrilineal Kinship.* Berkeley: University of California Press, 1961. Four of the nine cases described in this study are presented by Gough from her field work among matrilineal groups in the state of Kerala, southwestern India.

1280

Majumdar, Dhirendra Nath. *Himalayan Polyandry: Structure, Functioning and Culture Change.* New York: Asia Publishing House, 1962. Primarily an ethnographic account of Hindus residing in the sub-Himalayan region of Jaunsar-Bawar in the state of Uttar Pradesh. Most attention is given to political organization and kinship, including a detailed discussion of fraternal polyandry as practiced by these people. This study is based on intermittent field work in three villages conducted between 1937–60.

1281

Ross, Aileen D. *The Hindu Family in Its Urban Setting.* Toronto: University of Toronto Press, 1961. A study of changing patterns of family life as found in a sample of urban middle class, mainly Brahman, families in a South Indian city; based on 157 intensive interviews.

1282

Kurian, George. *The Indian Family in Transition. A Case Study of Kerala Syrian Christians.* The Hague: Mouton,

1961. A brief case study of attitudes towards marriage practices and family organization in a South Indian Christian community, and of the implications of such opinions for social change.

1283

Meyer, Johann J. *Sexual Life In Ancient India.* New York: Barnes and Noble, 1953. A reprint of an earlier two-volume edition published in London in 1930. Despite the title, this work is mainly concerned with the role and status of women as described in the *Mahabharata and Ramayana*: a scholarly study,

1284

Altekar, Anant Sadashiv. *The Position of Women in Hindu Civilisation.* Banaras: Motilal Banarsidass, 2nd ed., 1956. First published in 1938. A historical survey of the range of activities open to women in Hindu society and of the institution of marriage from earliest times to the present day.

1285

Cormack, Margaret. *The Hindu Woman.* New York: Bureau of Publications, Teachers College, Columbia University, 1953. An attempt to delineate patterns of "typical" role behavior for Hindu women; based on interviews with ten Indian women students at Columbia University.

1286

Tilak, Lakshmibai. *I Follow After: An Autiobiography.* Tr. by E. Josephine Inkster. Madras: Oxford University Press, 1950. A vivid and poignant account of Hindu family life and interpersonal relations by the wife of the Maharashtrian poet, N. W. Tilak. The author's narrative includes a dramatic contrast between her childhood in a strict orthodox Brahman home and her later years as an outcaste due to her husband's conversion to Christianity.

1287

Ranade, Mrs. Ramabai. *Himself, the Autobiography of a Hindu Lady.* Translated and adapted from the Marathi by Katherine Van Akin Gates. New York: Longmans, Green, 1938. An account of life in an upper-caste family of Western India in the late nineteenth century, written by a woman married at the age of eleven, who became a leading spokesman for women's rights in the nationalist movement.

VILLAGE COMMUNITIES

1288

Baden-Powell, B. H. *The Indian Village Community.* New Haven: Human Relations Area Files, 1958. A reprint of a classic history of land tenure in India, first published in 1896. Based on official records now difficult to obtain, this survey of the variegated patterns of legal rights to land, remains of value for students of rural India where variations in inheritance systems markedly affect other features of village life.

1289

Bose, Nirmal Kumar. *Peasant Life in India.* Calcutta: The Anthropological Survey of India, Indian Museum, 1962. The first in a proposed series of distribution studies of culture traits in India, this work describes variations in village types, food, tools, and dress.

1290

Marriott, McKim (ed.). *Village India: Studies in the Little Community.* Chicago: University of Chicago Press, 1955. Also published as ("American Anthropological Association, Memoir No. 83"). A collection of eight carefully prepared papers on various aspects of village life based on recent field work in five areas of India. The problem of relating village studies to a greater social and cultural context is a major theme of this volume.

1291

Srinivas, Mysore N. (ed.). *India's Villages.* New York: Asia Publishing House, 2nd ed., rev., 1960. First published in 1955. A collection of articles, many of them preliminary analyses of recent field work, providing brief outlines of life and forces of change in a wide variety of villages from most areas of India.

1292

Hitchcock, Patricia J., J. T. Hitchcock, and M. E. Opler (directors). *North India Village.* A 40 minute color film. Produced by the Cornell University India Program, 1958. The main features of life in a village of western Uttar Pradesh are accurately portrayed in this documentary film.

1293

Beals, Alan R. *Gopalpur: A South Indian Village.* New York: Holt, Rinehart & Winston, paperbound, 1962. A brief comprehensive description of a village in Mysore state, prepared as an anthropological case study for undergradutes, particularly useful for its analysis of inter-personal relations. Gopalpur is located about one hundred miles west of the village described by Dube (cited in the next entry).

1294

Dube, Shyama C. *Indian Village.* Ithaca: Cornell University Press, 1955. One of the most comprehensive descriptions of life in an Indian village, based on anthropological research conducted in 1951–52 in a village near Hyderabad.

1295

Berreman, Gerald D. *Hindus of the Himalayas.* Berkeley: University of California Press, 1963. A detailed ethnographic account based on research in a village of the Central Pahari region, with particular attention to the distinctive caste features of the area; includes an appraisal of government programs of community development and education.

1296

Eglar, Zekiye. *A Punjabi Village in Pakistan.* New York: Columbia University Press, 1960. An anthropological study of the distaff side of village life by a Turkish woman who resided in the area for more than five years. Contains valuable, though sometimes contradictory, descriptive material.

1297

Lewis, Oscar. *Village Life in Northern India: Studies in a Delhi Village.* Urbana: University of Illinois Press, 1958. Essentially a compilation of previously published, problem-oriented articles based on reasearch conducted in 1952 in a village located fifteen miles from Delhi; includes a discussion of the nature and consequences of group alignments within the village.

1298

Wiser, William H. and Charlotte V. *Behind Mud Walls, 1930–1960.* Berkeley: University of California Press, 2nd ed., rev., 1963. Available in cloth and paper editions. A classic account by an American missionary couple of life in a North Indian village thirty years ago; Mrs. Wiser's insightful account of her return to this village after three decades provides a vivid impression of the forces of change and stability in Indian rural life.

1299

Sen, Gertrude (Emerson). *Voiceless India.* New York: John Day, 2nd ed., 1944. First published in 1930. An American woman's sensitive account of her experiences and impressions while residing in a North Indian village; one of the first accounts of its kind, addressed to the general reader.

1300

Majumdar, Dhirendra Nath. *Caste and Communication in an Indian Village.* Bombay: Asia Publishing House, 1958. Primarily a description of the main features of life in a village of Uttar Pradesh with some attention to outside contacts, and a slight concern with communications per se.

1301

Mayer, Adrian C. *Caste and Kinship in Central India.* Berkeley: University of California Press, 1960. A study based on research in a village located in the Malwa region of Central India, with particular attention to the extension of kinship and caste beyond the village.

1302

Bailey, Frederick C. *Caste and the Economic Frontier: A Village in Highland Orissa.* Manchester: Manchester University Press, 1957. An analysis of changes in the internal organization of a multi-caste peasant community stemming from the extension of economic and government influence into a relatively isolated area.

1303

Epstein, T. Scarlett. *Economic Development and Social Change in South India.* London: Oxford University Press, 1962. A study of economic, political, and social changes in two villages of the state of Mysore, with particular attention to differences related to the introduction of irrigation in one village and not the other.

1304

Mayer, Adrian C. *Land and Society in Malabar.* Bombay: Oxford University Press, 1952. An analysis of the relationship between changes in ownership and utilization of land and the social system, particularly caste structure, in a coastal region of southwestern India.

1305

Leach, Edmund R. *Pul Eliya: A Village in Ceylon.* Cambridge: Cambridge University Press, 1961. A detailed case study of land tenure and related kinship and marriage practices in a small Sinhalese village. Presents a strong argument for ecological influence on social patterns, primarily of interest to the specialist.

1306

Wiser, William H. *The Hindu Jajmani System.* Lucknow: Lucknow Publishing House, new ed., 1959. First published in 1936. The first study of a socio-economic system that exists in many rural communities of India; based on research conducted in a village of Uttar Pradesh described in the author's *Behind Mud Walls* (cited above).

1307

Beidelman, Thomas O. *A Comparative Analysis of the Jajmani System.* Locust Valley, New York: J. J. Augustin, 1959. ("Monograph VIII of the Association for Asian Studies.") A review of the literature treating an aspect of village economic relations first studied by W. H. Wiser (see preceding entry).

1308

Pickett, Jarrell W. *Christian Mass Movements in India.* New York: Abingdon Press, 1933. A study of social and economic conditions in Christian communities throughout India, with particular attention to the consequences of "mass" conversions in which homogenous groups rather than individuals became Christians. One of the first studies to employ questionnaire survey methods in the rural areas of India.

SURVEYS OF CASTES AND TRIBES

Although difficult to obtain, the works cited below provide descriptive materials of permanent value. Much of the information in these works was obtained by British officials while preparing gazetteers and census reports, sources that should also be consulted by anyone seeking material of this kind.

1309

Hodson, Thomas C. *India, Census Ethnography, 1901–1931.* Delhi: Manager of Publications, Government of India Press, 1937.

1310

Crooke, William. *Natives of Northern India.* London: A. Constable, 1907.

1311

————. *Tribes and Castes of the Northwestern Provinces and Oudh.* 4 vols. Calcutta: Superintendent of Government Printing, 1906.

1312

Rose, Horace A. *A Glossary of the Tribes and Castes of the Punjab and the North-west Frontier Province.* 3 vols. Lahore: Supt. of Government Printing, 1911–19.

1313

Ibbetson, Sir Denzil C. J. *Punjab Castes.* Lahore: Superintendent of Government Printing, 1916.

1314

Mitra, Asok (ed.). Land and Land Revenue Department. *The Tribes and Castes of West Bengal.* Alipore: West Bengal Government Press, 1953.

1315

Risley, Herbert H. *The Tribes and Castes of Bengal.* 2 vols. Calcutta: Bengal Secretariat Press, 1891–92.

1316

Russell, Robert Vane, and Hira Lal. *The Tribes and Castes of the Central Provinces of India.* 4 vols. London: Macmillan, 1916.

1317

Enthoven, Reginald E. *The Tribes and Castes of Bombay.* 3 vols. Bombay: Government Central Press, 1920–22.

1318

Thurston, Edgar. Assisted by K. Rangachari. *Castes and Tribes of Southern India.* 7 vols. Madras: Madras Government Press, 1909.

1319

Anantha Krishna Iyer, L. Krishna. *Mysore Tribes and Castes.* 4 vols. and appendix. Mysore: Mysore University, 1928–35.

1320

Anantha Krishna Iyer, L. Krishna. *The Travancore Tribes and Castes.* 3 vols. Trivandrum: Superintendent Government Press, 1937–41.

1321

Anantha Krishna Iyer, L. Krishna. *The Cochin Tribes and Castes.* 2 vols. Madras: Higginbotham for the Government of Cochin, 1909–1912.

CASTE STUDIES

1322

Zinkin, Taya. *Caste Today.* London: Oxford University Press, paperbound, 1962. A brief account addressed to the general reader; treats the origin and nature of the Indian caste system with a discussion of recent changes. Undue rigidity is here attributed to past caste practices.

1323

Hutton, John H. *Caste in India.* Bombay: Oxford University Press, 3rd ed., 1961. First published in 1946. A standard comprehensive survey of the subject; various theories about the origin of caste are discussed with an analysis of the nature and function of caste in Indian society.

1324

Ghurye, Govind Sadashiv. *Caste, Class, and Occupation.* Bombay: Popular Book Depot, rev. ed., 1962. An expanded version of a work first published in 1932 as *Caste and Race in India* and subsequently revised and retitled as *Caste and Class in India.* A review and appraisal of various views concerning the origin and nature of caste in India with some attention to similar phenomena elsewhere: provides interesting information on recent changes in India, and a detailed summary of theories about the racial origin of caste divisions.

1325

Blunt, Edward A. H. *The Caste System of Northern India.* Madras: Oxford University Press, 1931. Although based extensively on material relating to castes of present-day Uttar Pradesh, this remains one of the best descriptions and analyses of caste in India. Blunt considers occupational groupings to have played an important part in the creation and perpetuation of caste divisions.

1326

Karve, Irawati. *Hindu Society—An Interpretation.* Poona: Deccan College Postgraduate and Research Institute, 1961. An interpretation of the historical development and distinctive features of the Indian caste system, with recommendations for caste reforms that will further national unity while retaining certain ethnic traditions. Karve views the caste system as a response to the problem of integrating disparate ethnic groups into a common social system.

1327

Srinivas, Mysore N. *Caste in Modern India and Other Essays.* New York: Asia Publishing House, 1962. This collection includes an account of contemporary changes in the Indian caste system including developments that tend to strengthen and perpetuate many features of caste in spite of counter forces stemming from modernization.

1328

Mayer, Adrian C. *Caste and Kinship in Central India.* Berkeley: University of California Press, 1960. The first detailed study of all aspects of caste as practiced in a specific locality, with information on inter-caste relations, caste and village leadership, and the relation of caste to kinship.

1329

Srinivas, Mysore N. *Religion and Society Among the Coorgs of South India.* London: Oxford University Press, 1952. A functional analysis of the religious beliefs and practices of the Coorgs, a caste of high rank in a mountainous region between Mysore and Malabar. The Coorgs make little use of Brahmans, eat meat, and differ in many other respects from the way of orthodox Hindus.

1330

Bailey, Frederick G. *Caste and the Economic Frontier.* Manchester: Manchester University Press, 1957. A lucid description and analysis of economic and political life in a peasant village in the Kond hills of Orissa. Particular attention is given to the declining importance of caste-based institutions.

1331

Ryan, Bryce. *Caste in Modern Ceylon.* New Brunswick: Rutgers University Press, 1953. A study by an American sociologist who taught and conducted research in Ceylon from 1948 to 1952; includes a review of the historical background of caste in Ceylon, and regional variations, with an analysis of the role of caste in the urbanization and modernization of Ceylon.

1332

Raghavan, M. D. *The Karava of Ceylon: Society and Culture.* Colombo: K. V. G. de Silva & Sons, 1961. A useful general account of one of the largest and most important castes of Ceylon, whose members consist of Catholics, Buddhists, and some Hindus.

1333

Leach, Edmund R. (ed.). *Aspects of Caste in Southern India, Ceylon, and Northwestern Pakistan.* New York: Cambridge University Press, 1960. A collection of descriptive essays, based on recent field work, showing variations in caste organization as practiced in three areas of South Asia; includes a provocative discussion of the nature of caste by the editor.

1334

Marriott, McKim. *Caste Ranking and Community Structure in Five Regions of India and Pakistan.* Poona: Deccan College Postgraduate and Research Institute, 1960. A technical monograph comparing regional variations in the elaboration of hierarchical ranking of caste groups and the relationship of such variations to other features of social structure.

1335

Man in India. Vol. 39, No. 2. Ranchi, Bihar: Man in India Office, 1959. This issue consists of technical articles on caste ranking and related features of Indian life; based on recent field work by social scientists.

1336

Dumont, Louis and D. F. Pocock (eds.). *Contributions to Indian Sociology.* No. 2. Paris: Mouton, 1958. Most of this issue of a journal, published at irregular intervals, is devoted to a discussion of various aspects of caste; this includes translation of a selection from the work of Bouglé.

1337

Singh, Mohinder. *The Depressed Classes.* Bombay: Hind Kitabs, 1947. A general account of the social and economic conditions of the "Scheduled Castes" in the arc of northern provinces ranging from the Punjab to Bengal; based mainly on census reports and personal inquiries conducted by the author shortly before World War II. Information on the characteristic customs and features of social organization of these groups is also included.

1338

Fuchs, Stephen. *The Children of Hari.* New York: F. A. Praeger, 1951. A detailed description of an "untouchable" caste, often referred to as children of God (Hari), residing in the upper Nerbudda valley of Madhya Pradesh; based on ten years residence in the area.

1339

Hazari. (pseud. of Marcus Abraham Malik). *I Was An Outcaste.* New Delhi: The Hindustan Times, 1957. First published in 1951 by the Bannisdale Press of London under the title: *An Indian Outcaste.* A fascinating autobiography of an Indian "untouchable" who, through luck and ability, broke free from his inherited position in the lowest stratum of Indian society and ultimately moved to Paris.

1340

Carstairs, G. Morris. *The Twice-Born: A Study of a Community of High-Caste Hindus.* Bloomington: Indiana University Press, 1958. A psychoanalytic study of personality development and the formation of group character among members of the Brahman, Rajput, and Vaisha castes in a community of Rajasthan; based on life-history interviews and psychological tests administered to thirty-six men from these "twice-born" castes.

1341

Vidyarthi, L. P. *The Sacred Complex in Hindu Gaya.* New York: Asia Publishing House, 1961. A study of a north Indian place of pilgrimage with particular attention to a group of Brahmans, known as Gayawals, whose history and present condition as ritual specialists is described in detail, including several life histories that provide an intimate view of Brahman family life.

1342

O'Malley, Lewis S. S. *Indian Caste Customs.* Cambridge: Cambridge University Press, 1932. A compilation of interesting tidbits of information concerning caste customs from various areas of India.

TRIBAL STUDIES

1343

India (Republic). Department of Anthropology. *Tribal Map of India.* Calcutta: Department of Anthropology, Government of India, 1956. A map 70 x 71 cm., with a scale of eighty miles per inch, providing the name, location, and population of two hundred and fifty tribes as reported in the 1931 and 1941 census.

1344

India (Republic). *Report of the Committee on Special Multipurpose Tribal Blocks.* New Delhi: Ministry of Home Affairs, 1960. An account of the social and economic condition of the approximately thirty million tribal peoples of India with an appraisal of government programs to improve their lot; Verrier Elwin served as chairman of this committee.

1345

India (Republic). *Report of the Commissioner for Scheduled Castes and Scheduled Tribes.* Delhi: Manager of Publications, Government of India Press, 1951–. An annual report on the social and economic conditions of those groups designated by the government of India as deserving special assistance due to their "depressed" or "backward" position in society. Sometimes these reports are referred to by the Commissioner's name, L. M. Shrikant.

1346

Thakkar, Amritlal V. (compiler). *Tribes of India.* 2 vols. Delhi: Bharatiya Adimjati Sevak Sangh, 1950–51. A collection of forty-eight articles by social workers and others with experience in programs to ameliorate conditions among the tribal peoples of India. The publisher, roughly translated as: Servants of the aboriginal peoples of India, has issued a number of books describing various tribes with particular attention to contemporary problems stemming from the integration of tribes with the rest of Indian society and to programs directed at their solution. These accounts, often written by administrators, generally lack organization and interpretation although they contain many disparate bits of interesting information.

1347

Elwin, Verrier. *A Philosophy for NEFA.* Shillong: North-East Frontier Agency, 2nd ed., rev., 1959. A useful introduction to the tribal peoples residing in a part of Assam known as the North-East Frontier Agency (NEFA), with an extended discussion of the problem of formulating government policies most beneficial to an isolated people upon whom outside forces have begun to intrude. The author has served for several years as Adviser for Tribal Affairs in the NEFA.

1348

Roy, Sachin. *Aspects of Padam-Minyong Culture.* Shillong: North-East Frontier Agency, 1960. One of the more extensive publications of the NEFA on the tribal people residing in the sub-Himalayan region of Assam. Most of these publications are brief and poorly organized descriptions of tribal life, prepared for the general reader and members of the NEFA staff. This work describes two subgroups of the Abor, a group of tribes in the Siang Division of NEFA, with most attention given to their material culture.

1349

Mills, James Philip. *The Rengma Nagas.* London: Macmillan, 1937. An account of one of five major divisions of the Naga tribe residing in the hills of northeastern Assam. Mills estimates the population of the Rengmas to be much greater than the 6,329 reported in the 1931 census.

1350

Fürer-Haimendorf, Christoph von. *The Apa Tanis and Their Neighbours.* New York: The Free Press of Glencoe, 1962. A description of the Apa Tani tribe, numbering about 10,000, residing in a small valley on the Himalayan slopes of northern Assam. Based in the main on field work conducted in 1944–1945.

1351

Burling, Robbins. *Rengsanggri: Family and Kinship in a Garo Village.* Philadelphia: University of Pennsylvania Press, 1963. An ethnographic account of a Garo village in Assam with an analysis of the changing relationship between these relatively isolated tribal people and the outside world.

1352

Das, Tarak Chandra. *The Purums: An Old Kuki Tribe of Manipur.* Calcutta: Calcutta University Press, 1945. The major source of ethnographic information on a tribe of Mongoloid stock and Tibeto-Burman linguistic identity located near the Indo-Burma border. Although the tribe numbered very little more than three hundred at the time of this study, 1931–36, the analysis of their social organization has been a lively subject of anthropological debate.

1353

Roy, Jyotirmoy. *History of Manipur.* Calcutta: K. L. Mukhopadhyay, 1958. The first published history of the state of Manipur on the Indo-Burma border, covering the period from early in the eighteenth century to the present: of interest to anthropologists studying the Meitei or the Kuki-Chin peoples of the area.

1354

Majumdar, Dhirendra Nath. *The Affairs of a Tribe: A study in Tribal Dynamics.* Lucknow: The Ethnographic and Folk Culture Society, Universal Publishers Ltd., 1950. Essentially a revision of the author's 1937 publication, *A Tribe in Transition.* An ethnographic account of the Hos, a Munda-speaking tribe of the Chota Nagpur plateau; particular attention is given to changes in Ho life due to contact with the non-tribal world.

1355

Dube, Shyama C. *The Kamar.* Lucknow: The Ethnographic and Folk Culture Society, Universal Publishers Ltd., 1951. An ethnographic account of the Kamar tribal people of southwestern Madhya Pradesh with an appraisal of the forces altering their forest-based way of life.

1356

Fuchs, Stephen. *The Gond and Bhumia of Eastern Mandla.* New York: Asia Publishing House, 1960. A detailed description of representatives of two of India's largest tribal groups residing in the district of Mandla in the state of Madhya Pradesh.

1357

Nath, Y. V. S. *Bhils of Ratanmal: An Analysis of the Social Structure of a Western Indian Community.* Baroda: M. S. University of Baroda, 1960. A monograph based on research in several communities of an ethnic group located about seventy miles east of Baroda. The Bhils, though of tribal origin, are mainly agriculturalists with many characteristics of the Hindu peasant.

1358

Chapekar, Laxman N. *Thakurs of the Sahyadri.* Bombay: Oxford University Press, 1960. A descriptive study of a people, numbering about 95,000 in 1941, residing in a hill tract about one hundred miles east of Bombay City; based on intermittent field work between 1940–45. The final chapter discusses the Thakurs transition from a hunting and gathering way of life to one based on agriculture.

1359

Trivedi, Harshad R. *The Mers of Saurashtra: An Exposition of Their Social Structure and Organization.* Baroda: M. S. University of Baroda, 1961. A descriptive account, based on field work between 1951 and 1954, of an agricultural caste known as the Mers, who occupy a position of prominence in a region within the Saurashtrian peninsula of Gujarat State.

1360

Elwin, Verrier. *The Religion of an Indian Tribe.* New York: Oxford University Press, 1955. A detailed systematic description of the religion of the hill Saora of Orissa, a tribal people numbering more than 100,000 in the districts of Ganjam and Koraput where this study was intermittently conducted in the late 1940's. Background information on other aspects of Saora life is also provided.

1361

Bailey, Frederick G. *Nation, Caste, and Tribe.* Manchester: University of Manchester Press, 1960. A study of changes affecting the Kond tribal people of Orissa as a result of conflict with their Hindu peasant neighbors and the influence of modern politicians and government administrators.

1362

Ehrenfels, U. R. *The Kadar of Cochin.* Madras: University of Madras, 1952. An account of a small Tamil-speaking tribe residing in the forests of Cochin State in southwest India. In addition to a general description of Kadar life, the author discusses changes of the past fifty years that are undermining traditions.

URBAN COMMUNITIES

1363

Turner, Roy (ed.). *India's Urban Future.* Berkeley: University of California Press, 1962. A valuable collection of twenty-three essays on problems of urbanism in India and related aspects of industrialization; includes a survey of the literature on urbanism in India.

1364

Gadgil, Dhananjaya R. *Poona: A Socio-Economic Survey.* 2 vols. Poona: Gokhale Institute, 1945–52. One of the most detailed surveys of an Indian city, primarily descriptive, with information on population, industry, government, housing, occupation, and family structure.

1365

Sovani, N. V. and others. *Poona: A Resurvey.* Poona: Gokhale Institute, 1956. A study of changes in patterns of employment and earnings a decade after Gadgil's survey of Poona.

1366

Lambert, Richard D. *Workers, Factories, and Social Change in India.* Princeton: Princeton University Press, 1963. A study of the socio-economic characteristics of factory workers in Poona with comparisons to similar features of the city's general population.

1367

Bopegamage, A. *Delhi: A Study in Urban Sociology.* Bombay: University of Bombay, Sociology Series, No. 7, 1957. A descriptive account of the major areas of Delhi and the spatial distribution of various classes of activity.

1368

Sen, Saurendra Nath. *The City of Calcutta.* Calcutta: Bookland, 1960. Issued under the auspices of the Economics Department, University of Calcutta. A report of findings obtained in a socio-economic survey of Calcutta for the period 1954–55 to 1957–58.

1369

Rajagopalan, C. *The Greater Bombay.* Bombay: Popular Book Depot, 1962. A study of suburban expansion in the Bombay metropolitan area with an analysis of the social and economic implications of such development.

1370

Lakdawala, Dansukhalal T. and others. *Work, Wages and Well-Being in an Indian Metropolis.* Bombay: University of Bombay, 1963. A report of an economic survey of Bombay city; published as No. 11 in the "University of Bombay Series in Economics."

1371

Mukerjee, Radhakamal and Baljit Singh. *Social Profiles of a Metropolis. Social and Economic Structure of Lucknow, Capital of Uttar Pradesh, 1954–56.* New York: Asia Publishing House, 1961. Though wanting in analysis and the organization of statistics, this work provides useful information on employment, housing, family composition, immigration, and other factors relating to urbanization.

1372

Majumdar, Dhirendra N., N. S. Reddy and S. Bahadur. *Social Contours of an Industrial City.* New York: Asia Publishing House, 1960. A presentation of socio-economic information obtained by survey methods in the city of Kanpur (Cawnpore), Uttar Pradesh during 1954–56.

1373

Misra, Babu Ram. *Report on a Socio-Economic Survey of Jamshedpur City.* Patna: Patna University, 1959. A description of the main features of a city in Bihar, developed around a major iron and steel producing center.

OVERSEAS COMMUNITIES

1374

Kondapi, C. *Indians Overseas, 1838–1949.* Bombay: Oxford University Press, 1951. A detailed study of the economic, social, and political conditions of Indians residing outside India.

1375

Mahajani, Usha. *The Role of Indian Minorities in Burma and Malaya.* Bombay: Vora, 1960. A study of the areas of activity, particularly in economic matters, of Indians residing in Burma and Malaya.

1376

Mayer, Adrian C. *Peasants in the Pacific: A Study of Fiji Indian Rural Society.* Berkeley: University of California Press, 1961. A study, based on research conducted in 1950–1951, of three settlements on the island of Fiji composed of Indians from different religious and regional backgrounds. Particular attention is given to emerging patterns of social organization.

1377

Benedict, Burton. *Indians in a Plural Society.* London: H. M. Stationery Office, 1961. Colonial Research Studies, No. 34, Colonial Office. A report on the role of Indian migrants in the life of Mauritius, an island in the Indian Ocean, where more than 50 per cent of the population is of Indian origin including Hindus, Muslims, and representatives of five linguistic regions of India.

1378

Kuper, Hilda. *Indian People in Natal.* Natal, South Africa: University Press, 1960. An account of the history and present subculture of Indian immigrants to the Natal part of the Union of South Africa with particular attention to their adaptation to the Natal environment.

1379

Klass, Morton. *East Indians in Trinidad: A Study of Cultural Persistence.* New York: Columbia University Press, 1961. An account of life in a Trinidad village of immigrants from India and their descendants, with particular attention to the retention of Indian culture in the sphere of marriage and the family, community organization, and religion. Little attention is given to the larger Indian community which constitutes about half of Trinidad's total population.

1380

Niehoff, Arthur and Juanita. *East Indians in the West Indies.* Milwaukee, Wisconsin: Milwaukee Public Museum, 1960. A description of a relatively isolated East Indian rural community in Trinidad with an emphasis on those features of Indian culture retained in the West Indian setting.

POPULATION

1381

Davis, Kingsley. *The Population of India and Pakistan.* Princeton: Princeton University Press, 1951. The only substantial historical demography of South Asia, this volume provides a synthesis of census reports for the period 1872 to 1931 supplemented with 1941 census information and a variety of other sources on factors affecting population growth; includes an estimate of India's population between 1600 and 1870. The author's broad conception and treatment of his subject, including history, geography, and social structures, makes this a useful introduction to India.

1382

Coale, Ansley J. and E. M. Hoover. *Population Growth and Economic Development in Low-Income Countries: A Case Study of India's Prospects.* Princeton: Princeton University Press, 1958. A projection of three alternative rates of population growth in India to 1981, with a judicious discussion of the consequences for economic development and the implications for government birth control policies.

1383

Chandrasekhar, Sripati. *Population and Planned Parenthood in India.* New York: Macmillan, 2nd ed., rev., 1961. A brief pessimistic appraisal of problems posed by India's rapidly expanding population, with an assessment of various birth control methods.

1384

Mamoria, C. B. *Population and Family Planning in India.* Allahabad: Kitab Mahal, 2nd ed., 1963. A review and assessment of recent efforts to reduce India's population growth.

1385

Agarwala, Shriman N. (ed.). *India's Population.* New York: Asia Publishing House, 1960. A collection of fourteen scholarly papers on India's population problems and the implications for government planning; edited by the Chief of the Demographic Research Centre whose contribution includes projections of population growth based on the 1951 census.

1386

Driver, Edwin D. *Differential Fertility in Central India.* Princeton: Princeton University Press, 1963. A study of the relationship between fertility and the social and economic factors of caste, income, and occupation, as found in three thousand households of Central India. Based on interviews which also explored attitudes towards government economic development plans and birth control.

1387

Belshaw, Horace. *Population Growth and Levels of Consumption.* New York: Institute of Pacific Relation, 1956. A forceful summary of the awesome problem faced by overpopulated and underdeveloped nations, with considerable attention given to India.

RELIGION AND PHILOSOPHY

Creativity in the realm of speculative thought, including the inception of two major religions and a wide variety of metaphysical systems, figure among the great achievements of Indic civilization. The earliest literary evidence of such endeavors is the Rig Veda, set down in its present form around 1000 B.C. These hymns, composed by Aryans who entered India during the 2nd millennium B.C., are one of four collections (*Samhitas*) of metrical works compiled over a period of several centuries. Appended to these "hymnals" are ritual texts (*Brahmanas*) followed by philosophical treatises (*Upanishads*) composed towards the middle of the first millennium B.C. These works, known collectively as the Veda, provide fragmentary evidence of a highly developed Aryan cult often referred to as Vedism. Contained in the last phase of this literature, the Upanishads, are ideas and insights of Aryan and indigenous origin that dominated the religious and philosophical thought of India for more than two thousand years.

Key concepts of the Upanishadic literature include the belief in rebirth (*samsara*), governed by the workings of a cosmic law of moral causality (*karma*), and the corollary goal of release from rebirth. These concepts, and a tendency towards spiritual monism, later served as the doctrinal base of Buddhism, Jainism, and Hinduism, and contributed to a world view favoring withdrawal from mundane affairs in marked contrast to the worldly concerns of the Vedic cult. In addition to this common core of beliefs, these religions and their myriad sects developed a variety of views regarding the nature of liberation from rebirth and the means for its attainment. Extreme asceticism, a reluctance to destroy life in any form, theism, pantheism, a fervent commitment to ritualism, and contrary views, also appear in this religious heritage.

Although an integral part of the Veda, the Upanishads contain protests against the emphasis on ritualism and the importance attributed to the Brahman priestly class in the earlier Vedic literature. Similar objections gave rise to reform movements in the 6th century B.C., of which only Buddhism and Jainism survive to the present day. In response to these and other forces, the orthodox tradition underwent many fundamental changes during the latter part of the first millennium B.C. While retaining a belief in the Veda as revealed truth, the orthodox replaced the Vedic gods with other deities, relinquished much of Vedic ritual, and adopted new beliefs including the attribution of sacred status to the cow. This markedly different religion, emerging early in the Christian era, came to be known as Hinduism.

Creativity in religious thought during the last half of the first millennium B.C. was paralleled by similar developments in philosophy. Doctrines formulated during this period provided the basis for lines of enquiry later systematized in the written works of Buddhist, Jain, and Hindu schools of formal philosophy. Speculations by atheists, materialists and others of similar persuasion also appear at this time, although little evidence remains of their ideas. The intellectual ferment of this period stimulated an outburst of philosophical enquiry and system building that eventually dwindled to a relatively sterile tradition of commentaries upon commentaries in medieval times.

Foreign religions played a minor role in Indian life prior to the Muslim invasions of the 13th century, although Christians, Jews, and Zorastrians had settled on the West coast of India many centuries earlier. Historical evidence indicates the existence of Syrian Christians on the Malabar coast by the fifth century, while native tradition traces the founding of this church to St. Thomas, the apostle. Active proselytizing by Catholic missionaries in the 16th and 17th centuries resulted in conversions, mainly in coastal areas under Portuguese control. Only in modern times, through the efforts of Protestant missionaries, has Christianity reached throughout the land, and this movement met with limited success. Today approximately seven million Christians reside in India, mainly in the southern coastal region. Judaism can also be traced back to the great commercial centers of fifth century Malabar. Though numbering less than thirty thousand today, the Jews maintain a community in the Malabar area and a few reside in the larger cities. After the Arab conquest of Persia in the 7th century, many Zorastrian refugees fled to India where they became known as Parsis (Persians). Initially settling in Gujarat, they later spread to other centers of trade and commerce.

Today, more than 100,000 Parsis reside in India, mainly in the major cities, where they often play a prominent role in commerce and industry.

Accounts of the numerous tribal religions of India may be found above under *Social Patterns*.

GENERAL

Histories and Surveys

1388
Farquhar, John N. *An Outline of the Religious Literature of India*. London: Oxford University Press, 2nd ed., rev., 1920. A useful guide through the maze of indigenous religious texts and the writings that stem from the influence of Islam in India. The period surveyed extends from earliest times to the early 18th century, the literature of each major period is organized according to religion and sects.

1389
Basham, Arthur L. *The Wonder That Was India*. London: Sidgwick and Jackson, 1954. Grove Press of New York published a paperbound edition in 1959. Chapter VII provides a concise, authoritative account of India's indigenous religions with a brief reference to religions introduced from other lands.

1390
Renou, Louis. *Religions of Ancient India*. New York: DeGraff, 1953. A concise authoritative review and assessment of present knowledge about Vedism, Hinduism, and Jainism; Buddhism is not included in this survey of the principal problems confronting scholars in the religious branch of Indic studies.

1391
Eliot, Sir Charles N. C. *Hinduism and Buddhism; an Historical Sketch*. 3 vols. New York: Barnes & Noble, reprint, 1954. Although considerable research has been conducted since this work was first published in 1921, it remains one of the best and most extensive introductions to Hinduism and Buddhism.

1392
Barth, Auguste. *Religions of India*. Tr. by J. Wood. Varansi: Chowkhamba Sanskrit Studies, Vol. XXV, 1963. Reprint of a 1921 ed. Though written in the late 19th century, this scholarly survey of India's indigenous religions remains a standard work.

1393
Majumdar, Ramesh C. (ed.) *The History and Culture of the Indian People*. Bombay: Bharatiya Vidya Bhavan, 1951–. A proposed ten-volume work. India's religious and philosophical heritage is described and discussed throughout this series, especially in the first three volumes.

1394
Bhattacharyya, Haridas and others (eds.). *The Cultural Heritage of India*. 4 vols. Calcutta: The Ramakrishna Mission, Institute of Culture, rev. ed., 1953-61. This ongoing series includes essays by various hands on Indian religion and philosophy; though often uncritical, these writings convey some contemporary Hindus' view of their religious tradition.

1395
Winternitz, Maurice. *History of Indian Literature*. 2 vols. Tr. by Mrs. S. Ketkar & H. Kohn. Calcutta: University of Calcutta Press, 1927–33. A translation of a revised work first published in German in 1908–22; provides detailed information on the historical setting and content of many Indian religious texts. Volume one treats Vedic and Hindu works, volume two, Buddhist and Jain.

1396
Dasgupta, Surendra Nath. *A History of Indian Philosophy*. 5 vols. Cambridge: Cambridge University Press, 1922–55. A detailed technical description of the indigenous

philosophical systems of India, including those of Hindu, Buddhist, and Jain origin.

1397

Radhakrishnan, Sarvepalli. *Indian Philosophy*. 2 vols. London: Allen & Unwin, rev. ed., 1958. A lucid exposition of the Indian philosophical tradition by one of India's foremost contemporary scholars, somewhat biased by the author's efforts to reconcile differences between Indian and Western ideas.

1398

Sinha, Jadunath. *A History of Indian Philosophy*. 2 vols. Calcutta: Central Book Agency, 1952–56. A detailed survey of the development of Hindu religious and philosophical thought, with less extensive consideration of the Jain and early Buddhist formal systems of philosophy.

1399

Zimmer, Heinrich R. *Philosophies of India*. Ed. by J. Campbell, New York: Meridian, paperbound, 1956. The ready availability of this panoramic, insightful, and readable survey might prompt its use as an introductory text. However, many of Zimmer's interpretations are very controversial and should be viewed in the light of other scholarly work.

1400

Sharma, Chandradhar. *Indian Philosophy: A Critical Survey*. London: Rider, 1960. New York: Barnes & Noble, paperbound ed., 1962. A concise readable introduction to the major concepts and thinkers of the indigenous philosophical systems; includes a useful glossary of Sanskrit terms.

1401

Chatterjee, Satischandra and D. M. Datta. *An Introduction to Indian Philosophy*. Calcutta: University of Calcutta, 5th ed., 1954. A standard introductory text, well-written and concise.

1402

Hiriyanna, Mysore. *Outlines of Indian Philosophy*. London: Allen & Unwin, 1932. A detailed survey of the ancient and classical Indian philosophies.

1403

Hiriyanna, Mysore. *The Essentials of Indian Philosophy*. London: Allen & Unwin, 1949. A reworking and condensation of the work cited above. Though prepared as a college text, it is so brief and assumes so much prior knowledge that use as an introductory text requires considerable supplementary material.

1404

Potter, Karl H. *Presuppositions of India's Philosophies*. Englewood Cliffs, New Jersey: Prentice-Hall, 1963. A Western philosopher here examines some of the basic assumptions of Indian speculative thought and presents a novel classification of the Hindu, Buddhist, and Jain schools of philosophy.

1405

Radhakrishnan, Sarvepalli and J. N. Muirhead (eds.). *Contemporary Indian Philosophy*. London: Allen & Unwin, 2nd ed., 1952. A collection of essays by several outstanding contemporary Indian philosophers.

1406

Hiriyanna, Mysore. *Indian Philosophical Studies*. Mysore: Kavyalaya Publishers, 1957. A collection of essays on traditional Indian philosophy by one of the most eminent of contemporary Indian philosophers.

Special Topics

1407

Brown, W. Norman. "Mythology of India" in *Mythologies of the Ancient World* edited by S. N. Kramer. Garden City, New York: Doubleday, paperbound, 1961. A succint and lucid discussion of some "symbolizing ideas" of Buddhist, Jain, and Hindu mythology.

1408

Thomas, Paul. *Epics, Myths and Legends of India*. Bombay: D. B. Taraporevala, 12th ed., 1961. This popular survey of Hindu, Buddhist, and Jain sacred lore provides illustrations of various deities and tidbits of information, some of it unreliable, but much of it not readily available elsewhere.

1409

Zimmer, Heinrich R. *Myths and Symbols in Indian Art and Civilization*. Ed. by J. Campbell. New York: Pantheon Books, 1946. Harper and Row of New York published in 1962 a paperbound edition of this book, a sprightly account of the basic tenets of Hinduism, Buddhism, and Jainism, with emphasis on those features which provide the inspiration and principal themes of Indian religious art.

1410

Bosch, F. D. K. *The Golden Germ. Introduction to Indian Symbolism*. The Hague: Mouton, 1960. An analysis of the form and religious-philosophical significance of symbols appearing in Buddhist and Jain decorative art.

1411

Tucci, Giuseppe. *The Theory and Practice of Mandalas*. Tr. by A. H. Brodrick. London: Rider, 1959. A brief, intriguing account of the doctrinal basis and symbolism of mystical ritual designs used in Hinduism and Tibetan Buddhism.

1412

Dasgupta, Surendra Nath. *Hindu Mysticism*. New York: F. Ungar, paperbound ed., 1959. First published in 1927; an introductory account, addressed to the Western reader, of the development of Indian mysticism. Five types of mysticism ranging from Vedic times to medieval bhakti cults are described and inter-related; Buddhist as well as Hindu mysticism is treated here.

1413

Sen, Kshitimohan. *Medieval Mysticism of India*. Tr. by Manomohan Ghosh. London: Luzac, 1936. An account of the part played by mysticism during a period noted for its proliferation of syncretic sects and widespread devotional movements.

1414

Rudolf, Otto. *Mysticism East and West*. Tr. by B. L. Bracey and R. C. Payne. New York: Macmillan, 1932. Paperbound edition published by Meridian Books of New York in 1957 with several subsequent reprints. An analysis of the parallels and dissimilarities between the views of mysticism held by such Western mystics as Meister Eckhart and those developed in the Indian tradition, especially the school of Shankara.

1415

Ghurye, Govind S. *Indian Sadhus*. Bombay: Popular Book Depot, 1953. A survey of the origins, development, and present organization of the wandering mendicants and ascetics who have played an important role in the religions of India.

1416

Hopkins, E. Washburn. *Ethics of India*. New Haven: Yale University Press, 1924. One of the few works on the subject; based on Vedic, Buddhist, and Hindu sources.

1417

Schweitzer, Albert. *Indian Thought and Its Development*. Tr. by Mrs. C. E. B. Russell. Boston: Beacon Press, paperbound ed., 1957. Previously published by Henry Holt of New York in 1936. A critique of Indian religious values which the author holds to be "life negating" in contrast to the "life affirming" world view of Christianity.

1418

Radhakrishnan, Sarvepalli. *Eastern Religions and Western Thought*. New York: Oxford University Press, 1959. A reprint of the second edition published in London in 1940. This work contains a description of the leading religious and philosophical ideas of India with an account of probable Indian influence on Greek and Christian thought. Indian ideals are also defended against such attacks as those ventured by Schweitzer in the preceding entry.

1419

Chatterjee, Satis Chandra. *The Problems of Philosophy.* Calcutta: Das Gupta, 1949. A comparative study of the philosophical views of eminent Indian and Western thinkers.

1420

Weber, Max. *The Religion of India, the Sociology of Hinduism and Buddhism.* Tr. and ed. by H. H. Gerth and D. Martindale. Glencoe, Ill.: Free Press, 1958. First published in German in 1921; though outdated and based upon an uncritical use of sources, this is one of the few attempts to analyze Indian religions in relation to a general sociological problem, namely, Weber's concern with the origins of capitalism. Weber considers the Indian "spirit" to be antithetical to the development of economic institutions characteristic of the West.

1421

Dasgupta, Surendra Nath. *Indian Idealism.* Cambridge: Cambridge University Press, reprint, 1962. First published in 1933; this useful survey traces out some of the most important developments of Indian idealism as expressed in Buddhist and Hindu classic texts.

1422

Raju, Poola Tirupati. *Idealistic Thought of India.* London: G. Allen & Unwin, 1953. This work differs from the preceding entry in that it gives greater attention to the metaphysical aspects of Buddhist and Hindu idealism, treating them as a common core of interrelated ideas viewed apart from their historical and religious context.

1423

Devandan, Paul D. *The Concept of Maya.* London: Butterworth Press, 1950. A historical survey of Hindu ideas concerning the nature of reality; ranges from Vedic times to the present with special reference to the Advaita tenets of the Vedanta school.

1424

Chattopadhyaya, Debiprasad. *Lokayata. Ancient Indian Materialism.* Delhi: People's Publishing House, 1959. A Marxist interpretation of those aspects of ancient Indian writings in which the Lokayata or materialist point of view is discussed.

1425

Riepe, Dale. *The Naturalistic Tradition in Indian Thought.* Seattle: University of Washington Press, 1960. A survey of protoscientific elements appearing in Indian philosophical writings from about 500 B.C. to A.D. 500; contributions from Buddhist, Jain, and Hindu works are included.

1426

Basham, Arthur L. *History and Doctrines of the Ajivikas.* London: Luzac, 1951. An account of a little-known heretical sect that developed at about the same time as the Buddhists and Jains. The Ajivikas practiced severe asceticism and rejected the idea of free will.

Series of Translations

1427

Müller, F. Max (ed.) *The Sacred Books of the East.* 51 vols. Oxford: Oxford University Press, 1879–1910. Many of the major religious and philosophical texts of ancient and classical India are included in this series of scholarly translations; specific works are cited below. A complete unabridged reprint of the series in paperbound form has recently been undertaken by Dover Publications of New York.

1428

Ingalls, Daniel H. H. (ed.). *Harvard Oriental Series.* Vol. 1– . Cambridge: Harvard University Press, 1891– . Previously under the general editorship of Charles R. Lanman. Scholarly translations of many important

Indian texts appear in this series; specific works are cited below.

1429

London Oriental Series. Vol. 1– . London: Oxford University Press, 1953– . A series containing scholarly translations of South Asian religious and philosophical texts; published under the auspices of the London School of Oriental and African Studies.

1430

Cranmer-Byng, J. L. and S. A. Kapadia (eds.). *Wisdom of the East Series.* London: J. Murray, 1921– . A popular series addressed to the general reader; contains translations of Indian religious texts.

Collections of Translated Texts

1431

Emeneau, Murray B. *A Union List of Printed Indic Texts and Translations in American Libraries.* New Haven: American Oriental Society, 1935.

1432

De Bary, William T., et al. (compilers). *Sources of Indian Tradition.* New York: Columbia University Press, 1958. Lucid and informative introductions are provided for each major section of this collection of texts prepared as a college introductory source book. It represents the major facets of Indian thought from ancient to modern times, including a substantial section on Islam in India.

1433

Radhakrishnan, Sarvepalli and C. A. Moore. *A Source Book in Indian Philosophy.* Princeton: Princeton University Press, 1957. A selection of translations by various hands from indigenous philosophical works of the ancient and classical period, with excerpts from two modern Indian philosophers: Sri Aurobindo and Sarvepalli Radhakrishnan. Brief introductory notes are provided for the general reader; contains an excellent bibliography.

1434

Lin Yutang (ed.). *The Wisdom of China and India.* New York: Modern Library, 1942. A readily available anthology; includes a few selections from Hindu and Buddhist sacred writings translated by various hands.

1435

Nivedita, Sister (Margaret E. Noble) and A. K. Coomaraswamy. *Myths of the Hindus and Buddhists.* London: G. G. Harrap, 1913. Includes a popular retelling in summary form of the Hindu epics, several Puranic episodes, and selections from the Buddhist *Jataka.*

VEDISM

References and Studies

1436

Renou, Louis. *Bibliographie Vedique.* Paris: Adrien Maisonneuve, 1931. A compilation of more than 6,000 entries in various languages; provides a comprehensive listing of published Vedic texts and related studies appearing prior to 1930.

1437

Dandekar, Ramchandra N. *Vedic Bibliography.* Bombay: Karnatak Publishing House, 1946. A continuation of Renou's work cited above; covers the period 1930–42. References to book reviews are given for some entries.

1438

Macdonell, Arthur A. and A. B. Keith. *Vedic Index of Names and Subjects.* 2 vols. Delhi: Motilal Banarasidass, reprint, 1958. First published in 1912 by J. Murray of London. A standard reference work in the field of Vedic studies, especially useful for the Samhitas and Brahmanas.

1439

Macdonell, Arthur A. *Vedic Mythology.* Strassburg: Trübner, 1897. Description of the Vedic pantheon, cosmology, and related subjects: a basic reference work.

1440

Macdonnell, Arthur A. *A History of Sanskrit Literature.* London: W. Heinemann, 2nd ed., 1905. Much of this valuable work discusses the historical development and content of Vedic religious and philosophical texts.

1441

Renou, Louis. *Religions of Ancient India.* London: Athlone Press, 1953. The Vedic section of this work provides an authoritative and readable overview of the subject and of the present state of research in this field.

1442

Keith, Arthur B. *The Religion and Philosophy of the Vedic and Upanishads.* 2 vols. Cambridge: Harvard University Press, 1925. Volumes 31 and 32 of the Harvard Oriental Series. A detailed scholarly survey of the Vedic tradition with a discussion of its relation to other Indo-European cultures and non-Vedic Indian religions.

1443

Bloomfield, Maurice. *The Religion of the Veda, the Ancient Religion of India (from Rig-Veda to Upanishads).* New York: G. P. Putnam's, 1908. The main features of the earliest known phase of India's religious tradition are lucidly and authoritatively described in this classic work.

1444

Müller, F. Max. *The Vedas.* Calcutta: Susil Gupta, 1956. Abridged selections from essays on the history and significance of the Vedas and problems of interpretations, written in the 19th century by the editor of the "Sacred Books of the East" series.

1445

Ghose, Aurobindo. *On the Veda.* Pondicherry: Sri Aurobindo Ashram, 1958. An example of native exegesis by a modern Indian religious leader.

1446

Kaegi, Adolf. *The Rigveda: The Oldest Literature of the Indians.* Tr. by R. Arrowsmith. Boston: Ginn, 1902. Though first published in 1878, this work retains much of value for the general reader as a scholarly survey of society and religion in the early Vedic period.

1447

Bloomfield, Maurice. *The Atharvaveda.* Strassburg: Trubner, 1899. A classic monograph on the subject. No comparable work exists for the other three Samhitas.

1448

Shende, N. J. *The Religion and Philosophy of Atharvaveda.* Poona: Bhandarkar Oriental Research Institute, 1952. A study of unorthodox tendencies in the *Atharva Veda* and their influence on later Upanishadic thought.

1449

Heesterman, Johannes C. *The Ancient Indian Royal Consecration.* The Hague: Mouton, 1957. A scholarly description and interpretation of a major Vedic ceremony, the Rajasuya, based on a comparative study of several Brahmanas.

1450

Stall, J. F. *Nambudiri Veda Recitation.* The Hague: Mouton, 1961. The recitation of the Veda by contemporary Brahmans of Kerala is here examined as an example of the tradition of oral transmission by which the Vedas have been preserved through the centuries.

Samhitas and Brahmanas—Texts in Translation

1451

Vedic Hymns. 2 vols. Tr. by F. M. Müller and H. Oldenberg. Oxford: Clarendon Press, 1891–97. Sacred Books of the East, volumes 32 and 46. To be reprinted in paperbound form by Dover Publications of New York. A scholarly translation of major portions of the most ancient of the Vedic Samhitas, the Rigveda. Traditional Indian exegesis is represented in the commentary by translations from the 14th century writings of Sayana.

1452

Macdonell, Arthur A. *A Vedic Reader for Students.* London: Oxford University Press, 5th impression, 1960. First published in 1917; a selection of thirty hymns from the Rigveda presented in the original texts with transliteration and translation. Detailed explanatory notes and a brief introduction are provided.

1453

Hymns From the Rigveda. Tr. by A. A. Macdonell. London: Oxford University Press, 1922. A selection of forty hymns accompanied by a brief introduction and descriptive notes.

1454

Hymns of the Rigveda; Translated with a Popular Commentary. 2 vols. Tr. by R. T. H. Griffith. Benares: E. J. Lazarus, 3rd ed., 1920–26. This is the only complete translation of the Rigveda available in English; it contains many inaccuracies.

1455

Rigveda Sanhita. 6 vols. Tr. by H. H. Wilson. Bangalore: Bangalore Printing & Publishing Co., 2nd ed., 1946. A reprint of the first English translation of the Rigveda first published in 1850; much outdated.

1456

Rigveda Brahmanas, the Aitareya and the Kausitaki Brahmanas. Tr. by A. B. Keith. Cambridge: Harvard University Press, 1920. Harvard Oriental series, volume 25. These texts consist of mystical speculations on the minute details of Vedic rituals in which hymns from the Rigveda Samhita were recited.

1457

The Veda of the Black Yajus School, Entitled Taittiriya Sanhita. 2 vols. Tr. by A. B. Keith. Cambridge: Harvard University Press, 1914. Harvard Oriental series, volumes 18 and 19. The *Yajur Veda,* compiled a century or two later than the Rigveda, served as a guide for the priests who performed the manual part of the Vedic sacrifice. The *Taittiriya Sanhita* is one of four recensions of the *YajurVeda* belonging to the "Black" type in which sacrificial formulae appear with rubricated instructions.

1458

The Texts of the White Yajur Veda; Translated with a Popular Commentary. Tr. by R. T. H. Griffith. Benares: E. J. Lazarus, 1899. The texts of the "White" *Yajur-Veda* are held to be less ancient than the "Black" type and differ from the earlier recensions in that instructions in prose appear as an appendix to the main work.

1459

The Satapatha-Brahmana. 5 vols. Tr. by J. Eggeling. Oxford: Clarendon Press, 1882–1900. Sacred Books of the East, volumes 12, 26, 51, 53, 54. To be reprinted in paperbound form by Dover Publications of New York. A translation of the Madhayandian recension of a Brahmana associated with the *Yajur Veda.* This text provides considerable information about Vedic society in the origin stories used to elucidate ritual practices.

1460

Hymns of the Atharva-Veda. Tr. by Maurice Bloomfield. Oxford: Clarendon Press, 1897. Sacred Books of the East, volume 42. To be reprinted in paperbound form by Dover Publications of New York. A scholarly translation of selections from the latest of the four *Samhitas,* noted for inclusion of charms and magical incantations of probable folk origin, in contrast to other Vedic literature which is generally attributed to the priests.

1461

Atharva Veda Samhita. 2 vols. Tr. by W. D. Whitney and C. R. Lanman. Cambridge: Harvard University Press, 1905. Harvard Oriental series, volumes 7 and 8. A scholarly translation with a critical and exegetical commentary. This work was reprinted in Delhi in 1962.

Upanishads—Studies and Texts in Translation

1462

The Thirteen Principal Upanishads. Tr. by R. E. Hume. London: Oxford University Press, 2nd ed., rev., 1962. This scholarly work ranks among the most readable translations of Vedic material. It includes an introductory essay on Upanishadic philosophy and an annotated bibliography of related works.

1463

The Upanishads. 4 vols. Tr. by Swami Nikhilananda. New York: Harper & Row, 1949–59. Part of a proposed six volume translation prepared with commentary and detailed notation for a Western audience.

1464

The Upanishads. Tr. by Swami Nikhilananda. London: G. Allen & Unwin, 1963. New York: Harper Torchbook, paperbound ed., 1964. A one-volume abridgment of the previous entry.

1465

The Principal Upanishads. Tr. by S. Radhkrishnan. New York: Harper, 1953. Eighteen of the major Upanishads in translation. The extensive introduction is based on a revision of the translator's interpretation of the Upanishads contained in the two volume work, *Indian Philosophy* (entry 1397).

1466

Upanishads. 2 vols. Tr. by F. Max Müller. Oxford: Clarendon Press, reprint, 1926. Sacred Books of the East, volumes 1 and 15, first published 1879–84. New York: Dover Publications, paperbound ed., 2 vols., 1962. Eleven of the most important Upanishads are here translated with a view to scholarly accuracy rather than readability; the problems of dating and evaluating Sanskrit sources are discussed in the introduction.

1467

The Upanishads. Tr. by Swami Prabhavananda and F. Manchester. New York: New American Library, Mentor paperbound ed., 1957. First published in hardcover form by the Vedanta Society of Southern California. This abridged translation of twelve principal Upanishads is highly condensed, freely rendered, and emphasizes those features most compatible with Western values.

1468

Saiva Upanishads. Tr. by T. R. Srinivasa Ayyangar, ed. by G. S. Murti. Adyar, Madras: Theosophical Society, Adyar Library Series, No. 85, 1953. A translation of selections from the Upanishads bearing on Shaivism. It includes passages from some of the minor Upanishads.

1469

Deussen, Paul. *The Philosophy of the Upanishads.* Tr. by A. S. Geden. Edinburgh: T. & T. Clark 1906. A comprehensive survey of the subject as seen by a Western scholar.

JAINISM

Although relatively few in number throughout their history, the Jains have existed in India as a viable religious community from the 6th century B.C. At that time the Jains formed an order of ascetics that repudiated the authority of the Brahman priests and the sacred literature known as the Veda. However, Jainism retained the concepts of reincarnation and *karma* first articulated in the Upanishads, and in later times members of the Jain community often called upon Brahman priests to perform various domestic ceremonies. A distinctive Jain doctrine, *ahimsa,* prohibiting injury to any living creature, has in turn influenced Hinduism in some areas of India. This prohibition, which applies to microscopic forms of life, accounts for such Jain practices as the wearing of gauze covering over the nose and mouth to avoid inhaling minute creatures floating in the air. Although the Jains do not believe in a universal god, they recognize many minor deities viewed as bound to the same system of rebirth affecting humans. The Jain conception of this process and the nature of liberation from rebirth, differs from similar ideas of other Indian religions. The Jains conceive of *karma* as a material substance that accumulates in sheaths about the pure soul, due to both good and evil acts. The removal of *karma* necessitates rigorous ascetic practices and the cessation of all activity best realized by starvation unto death. By such means, the soul of an occasional, spiritually advanced person is freed of the bonds of *karma* and ascends to the summit of the universe, where it enjoys perfect bliss. Approximately one and a half million Jains reside in India today.

Studies and Texts in Translation

1470

Jain, Chhote Lal. *Jaina Bibliography.* Calcutta: Bharati Jaina Parisat, 1945. Prepared as a supplement to a French work by A. Guerinot published in 1906; this volume surveys the literature on Jainism from 1906 to 1925, a second volume covering the period 1925–44 is said to have been prepared.

1471

Stevenson, Mrs. Margaret Sinclair. *The Heart of Jainism.* London: Oxford University Press, 1915. Probably the best introduction to the history, beliefs, and practices of the Jains.

1472

Renou, Louis. *Religions of Ancient India.* London: Athlone Press, 1953. Chapter six provides a brief, authoritative survey of the main features of Jainism.

1473

Jaini, Jagmandar Lal. *Outlines of Jainism.* Cambridge: Cambridge University Press, 1940. A lucidly descriptive summary of Jain religion and philosophy accompanied by translated selections from Jain texts, first published in 1916.

1474

Schubring, Walther. *The Doctrine of the Jainas.* Tr. by W. Beurlen. Delhi: Motilal Banarsidass, 1962. A translation from the revised edition of a scholarly work in German based on the study of ancient Jain texts.

1475

Mookerjee, Satkari. *The Jaina Philosophy of Non-Absolutism.* Calcutta: Bharati Mahavidyalaya Publications, 1944. Jaina Series No. 2. A study of the Jaina metaphysical doctrine of *anekantavada,* which holds that reality expresses itself in so many forms that no absolute affirmation or negation is possible.

1476

Tatia, Nathmal. *Studies in Jaina Philosophy.* Banaras: Jain Cultural Research Society, 1951. A noteworthy essay in this collection is chapter IV, "The Jaina Doctrine of Karman."

1477

Chakravarti Nayanar, Appasvami. *The Religion of Ahimsa.* Bombay: R. Hirachand, 1957. A popular exposition of the Jain concept of non-violence and its implications for Jain philosophy and ethics.

1478

Williams, R. *Jaina Yoga. A Survey of the Mediaeval Sravakacaras.* London: Oxford University Press, 1963. A study of Jain treatises, dating from the 5th to the 13th centuries, concerning the proper way of life for Jain laymen.

1479

Saletore, Bhasker A. *Medieval Jainism, With Special Reference to the Vijayanagara Empire.* Bombay: Karnatak Publishing House, 1938. A historical account of medieval Jain teachers, leaders, and writers in Western and Southern India and their influence upon the political life of their time.

1480

Sheth, Chimanlal B. *Jainism in Gujarat.* Poona: Deccan College, 1953. A historical study of the Jain community in a region of western India which was a principal center of Jainism during the years A.D. 1100–1600.

1481

Sangave, Vilas A. *Jaina Community: A Social Survey.* Bombay: Popular Book Depot, 1959. Problems confronting Jains in modern India are discussed in relation to the history of the Jain community and the basic features of their religion and philosophy.

1482

Gaina Sutras. 2 vols. Tr. by H. G. Jacobi. Oxford: Clarendon Press, 1884–95. Sacred Books of the East, volumes 22 & 45. To be reprinted in paperbound form by Dover Publications of New York. A translation of ancient Jain texts containing the fundamental tenets of Jain religious belief and practice; including an account of the life and teaching of the historic Jain founder, Mahavira, and his legendary predecessors.

1483

Hemacandra. *A critique of Organ of Knowledge.* Tr. by S. Mookerjee and N. Tatia. Calcutta: S. C. Seal, 1946. A translation of the 12th century work, *Pramana-mimamsa* by the Jain scholar Hemacandra; a major Jain text on logic and epistomology.

1484

Ghoshal, Sarat C. (ed.). *The Sacred Books of the Jainas.* 11 vols. Arrah and Lucknow: Central Jaina Publishing House, 1917–37. This series of translations by various scholars includes many basic works of Jain religion and philosophy.

BUDDHISM

Other works treating Buddhism as a part of India's religious heritage may be found above, under *Religion* and *Philosophy;* many facets of Buddhism also appear below, under *Art.*

General Works

1485

Bibliographie Bhouddique. Paris: P. Guenther, 1928–. The most comprehensive bibliography on Buddhism, issued serially in annual volumes. Several volumes are often published simultaneously at irregular intervals; volumes 24–27, covering the period 1950–54, appeared in 1958. Coverage for the years prior to 1928 appears in the following entry.

1486

Hanayama Shinsho. *Bibliography on Buddhism.* Ed. by the Commemoration Committee for Professor Shinsho Hanayama's Sixty-first Birthday. Tokyo: Hokuseido Press, 1961. A comprehensive bibliography of materials on Buddhism published in European languages prior to 1928; complements the series cited above, begun in 1928.

1487

Humphreys, Christmas. *A Popular Dictionary of Buddhism.* London: Arco Publications, 1962. A useful reference for those seeking guidance through the maze of Buddhist terminology.

1488

Conze, Edward. *Buddhism: Its Essence and Development.* Oxford: Cassirer, 1951. Paperbound edition published by Harper of New York in 1959. A comprehensive readable introduction to world Buddhism.

1489

Morgan, Kenneth W. (ed.). *The Path of the Buddha: Buddhism Interpreted by Buddhists.* New York: Ronald Press, 1956. A collection of essays by contemporary scholars providing a survey of the tenets and practices of Buddhism in the major Buddhist areas of the world.

1490

Bapat, Purushottam V. (ed.). *2500 Years of Buddhism.* Delhi: Publications Division, Ministry of Information and Broadcasting, Government of India, 1956. A collection of essays by Indian scholars describing the major facets of Buddhism, including art, literature, beliefs and practices, and historical developments outside India.

1491

Eliot, Charles N. E. *Hinduism and Buddhism: An Historical Sketch.* 3 vols. New York: Barnes & Noble, reprint, 1954. First published in 1921 by E. Arnold of London. A standard history of Buddhism from its origin to modern times.

1492

Humphreys, Christmas. *Buddhism.* Harmondsworth, England: Penguin, paperbound ed., rev. 1955. A general survey of the history, teachings, and present status of world Buddhism, by the founder of the Buddhist Society of London; a spirited though sometimes uncritical presentation.

1493

Pratt, James B. *The Pilgrimage of Buddhism and a Buddhist Pilgrimage.* New York: Macmillan, 1928. A detailed summary of the history of Buddhism, enlivened by the author's observations of contemporary Buddhism while traveling in Asia.

Special Studies

1494

Thomas, Edward J. *The Life of the Buddha as Legend and History.* New York: Barnes & Noble, 3rd ed. rev., 1952. First published in 1927 by K. Paul, Trench, and Trubner of London. A lucid presentation and judicious appraisal of a subject shrouded in conjecture and conflicting testimony.

1495

Foucher, A. *The Life of the Buddha.* Tr. by S. B. Boas. Middletown: Wesleyan Univ. Press, 1963. An abridged edition of *La Vie du Bouddha,* published by Editions Payot in 1949. An attempt to reconstruct the life and historical setting of the Indian prince of the 6th century B.C. who founded Buddhism; based on ancient texts and those events from the Buddha's life depicted on monuments.

1496

Dutt, Sukumar. *Early Buddhist Monachism.* New York: Asia Publishing House, 1960. A historical account of the origin and development of monastic orders in Theravada Buddhism with a detailed description of rules governing life in the monastic community.

1497

Giles, Herbert A. (trans.). *The Travels of Fa-Hsien.* London: Routledge Kegan Paul, 1956. An account of India in the 5th century by a Chinese Buddhist pilgrim-scholar, who resided in northern India from A.D. 405–411.

1498

Watters, Thomas (trans.). *On Yuan Chwang's Travels in India.* 2 vols. London: Royal Asiatic Society, 1904–05. A first-hand account of Buddhism in India during the 7th century, by a Chinese Buddhist pilgrim-scholar.

1499

Conze, Edward. *Buddhist Thought in India*. London: G. Allen and Unwin, 1962. An account of the development of Buddhism in its land of origin.

1500

Grimm, George. *The Doctrine of the Buddha*. Berlin: Akademie-Verlag, 2nd ed., rev., 1958. A detailed introduction to the development of Buddhist doctrine in India.

1501

Thomas, Edward J. *History of Buddhist Thought*. London: Kegan Paul, 2nd ed., 1951. First published in 1933 by Kegan Paul; a standard work, addressed to the specialist rather than to the general reader; surveys the development of Buddhist philosophy including sectarian developments outside India.

1502

Keith, Arthur B. *Buddhist Philosophy in India and Ceylon*. Oxford: Clarendon, 1923. A succinct survey of the subject. Though wanting in interpretation and analysis, the detailed citation of original sources provides a useful guide for the general reader.

1503

Stcherbatsky, Th. *Buddhist Logic*. 2 vols. New York: Dover, paper ed. 1962. First published in 1932 in Leningrad by the Academy of Sciences of the U.S.S.R. A classic work on Buddhist logic of the Mahayana school of Dignaga. Brief biographical sketches of major Buddhist thinkers are provided with an introductory exposition of Buddhist philosophy and the relation of logic to it. Volume two consists in the main of a translation of Dharmakirti's *Nyayabindu*.

1504

Murti, T. R. V. *The Central Philosophy of Buddhism: A Study of the Madhyamika System*. London: G. Allen & Unwin, 1955. A study of a major philosophical school of Mahayana Buddhism. The Madhyamika (intermediate) position of qualified realism stands midway between the idealism of the Yogacara school and extreme realism of the Sarvastidins. Also known as the Sunyavada (Doctrine of the Void), this system flourished in the first three centuries of the Christian era.

1505

Guenther, Herbert V. *Philosophy and Psychology in the Abhidharma*. Lucknow; Buddha Vihara, 1957. An exposition of psychological views contained in Abhidharma texts, presented in modern philosophical terms. Guenther's interpretation of Buddhist epistemology is markedly different from that advanced by Murti in the preceding entry.

1506

Banerjee, Ankul Chandra. *Sarvastivada Literature*. Calcutta: D. Banerjee, 1957. An account of the Sanskrit canon, known today solely through Tibetan and Chinese sources, of a sect of Theravada (Hinayana) Buddhism that existed in northern India early in the Christian era. This sect held that the constituents of phenomena exist forever in latent form.

1507

Dayal, Har. *The Bodhisattva Doctrine in Buddhist Sanskrit Literature*. London: K. Paul, Trench, Trübner, 1932. A scholarly survey of the Bodhisattva, or Buddha-to-be, concept initially formulated in relation to Gautama Buddha, later elaborated into a major tenet of Mahayana Buddhism. Bodhisattva's are enlightened ones who perform acts of kindness and mercy during their final series of transmigrations.

1508

The Perfection of Wisdom; the Career of the Predestined Buddhas. Tr. by E. J. Thomas. London: J. Murray, 1952. A selection of Mahayana scriptures, translated from Sanskrit, that treat the nature of Bodhisattvas or enlightened beings destined to be future Buddhas.

1509

Buddhist Meditation. Tr. by E. Conze. London: Allen & Unwin, 1956. An anthology of Buddhist texts treating the principles and practices of meditation; accompanied by an instructive introduction and a brief discussion of the relationship of Buddhist meditation to Western psychotherapy.

1510

Dasgupta, Sashi Bhusan. *An Introduction to Tantric Buddhism*. Calcutta: University of Calcutta, 2nd ed., 1958. An account of a movement, common to Hinduism and Buddhism, in which worship of the feminine aspect of the divine is combined with a magical mysticism; this tradition attained great popularity in Tibet.

1511

Waddell, Laurence A. *The Buddhism of Tibet*. Cambridge: Heffer, reprint, 1958. First published in 1895; an account of Lamaism, a Tibetan form of Buddhism which incorporated elements of the Tantric tradition with native forms of shamanism.

1512

Snellgrove, D. L. *The Hevajra Tantra. A Critical Study*. 2 vols. London: Oxford University Press, 1959. A scholarly translation from Sanskrit and Tibetan of one of the most important texts of Tantric Buddhism; accompanied with an analysis of the teachings of this ancient, though undated work and its relationship to other Buddhist and Hindu traditions.

1513

Bhattacharyya, Benoytosh. *The Indian Buddhist Iconography*. Calcutta: K. L. Mukhopadhyay, 2nd ed., rev., 1958. First published by Oxford University Press in 1924; a classic study based on extensive use of literary sources; illustrated for reference rather than aesthetic purposes.

1514

Mookerjee, Satkari (ed.). *Nava-Nalanda-Mahavihara Research Publication*. Vol. I.–Patna: Nalanda Institute of Research, 1957. The first in a proposed series of technical monographs, mainly of interest to the specialist, published by the Buddhist and Pali study center established in the ancient Buddhist center of Nalanda by the government of Bihar state in 1951.

Texts in Translation

1515

Sacred Books of the Buddhists. Oxford: Oxford University Press, 1899–. A series of scholarly translations by various hands of Buddhist texts; initially edited by C. A. F. Rhys Davids, the current editor is I. B. Horner.

1516

Pali Text Society Translation Series. London: Pali Text Society, 1909–. London: Oxford University Press for the Pali Text Society, 1909–. This series of scholarly translations by various hands was initially edited by T. W. Rhys Davids, the present editor is I. B. Horner.

1517

Conze, Edward, I. B. Horner, D. Snellgrove, A. Waley (eds.). *Buddhist Texts Through the Ages*. Oxford: B. Cassirer, 1954. New York: Harper Torchbook, paperbound ed. An anthology of translations from Pali, Sanskrit, Chinese, Tibetan, Japanese, and Apabhramsa sources. Guidance is provided for those seeking more extensive translations.

1518

Buddhism in Translations. Tr. by H. C. Warren. Cambridge: Harvard University Press, reprint, 1953. First published in 1896 as volume three of the Harvard Oriental Series. An excellent translation of selected passages from the Pali texts.

1519

Buddhist Scriptures. Tr. by E. Conze. Baltimore: Penguin, 1959. An anthology of texts illustrating the principal concepts of Buddhism and the doctrinal issues that gave rise to the Mahayana and Hinayana traditions.

1520

Burtt, Edwin A. (ed.). *The Teachings of the Compassionate Buddha.* New York: New American Library, paperbound ed., 1955. A sourcebook of readings drawn from published translations of basic Buddhist texts, with introductory statements on the history and practices of Buddhism.

1521

Hamilton, Clarence H. (ed.). *Buddhism, a Religion of Infinite Compassion.* New York: Liberal Arts Press, paperbound ed., 1952. An anthology of Buddhist texts accompanied by introductory background material.

1522

Buddha's Teachings. Tr. by Lord Chalmers. Cambridge: Harvard University Press, 1932. Harvard Oriental Series, volume 37. A translation from Pali of one of the oldest texts of Buddhism, known as the *Sutta Nipata* (discourse collection). Part of this work is included in the Theravada (Hinayana) canon.

1523

Vinayapitaka. 3 vols. Tr. by T. W. Rhys Davids and H. Oldenberg. Oxford: Clarendon, 1881–85. Sacred Books of the East, volumes 13, 17, and 20; to be reprinted in paperbound form by Dover Publications of New York. A translation from Pali of one of the three main sections, called *pitaka* (baskets), of Theravada (Hinayana) canonical literature. The *Vinaya Pitaka* contains various rules of conduct for monks attributed to the Buddha.

1524

Some Sayings of the Buddha. Tr. by F. L. Woodward. London: Oxford University Press, 1939. Selections from the *Sutta Pitaka,* the largest and most important section of the Pali canon of Theravada Buddhism; consists of sermons (*suttas*) and sayings attributed to the Buddha.

1525

Buddhist Suttas. Tr. by T. W. Rhys Davids. Oxford: Clarendon, 1881. Sacred Books of the East, volume 11; to be published in paperbound form by Dover Publications of New York. A translation of seven major sermons from the *Sutta Pitaka* collection of Theravada texts written in Pali.

1526

Dialogues of the Buddha. 3 vols. Tr. by T. W. Rhys Davids. London: Luzac, 1956. A translation of Theravada canonical texts, from one of the five "Groups" (*nikaya*) of the *Sutta Pitaka.* This collection consists of long (*digha*) sermons attributed to the Buddha and accounts of the circumstances in which they were preached.

1527

The Dhammapada; The Sayings of Buddha, Tr. by Narada Thera. New York: Grove, paperbound ed., 1954. A free rendering by a devout Buddhist of a moral and ethical classic; includes an introductory essay by E. J. Thomas and explanatory notes. This brief work forms part of the *Khuddaka* (minor) *Nikaya* of the *Sutta Pitaka.*

1528

The Dhammapada. Tr. by F. Max Müller. Oxford: Clarendon, 1881. Sacred Books of the East, volume 10; to be reprinted in paperbound form by Dover Publications of New York. A scholarly version of a Pali text that ranks among the most important works of Theravada Buddhism; accompanied by an introduction and extensive notation. A translation by V. Fausböll of the *Sutta Nipata* also appears in this volume.

1529

Cowell, Edward B. (ed.). *The Jataka; or Stories of the Buddha's Former Births.* 6 vols. in 3. London: Luzac, reprint, 1957. First published in six volumes by Cambridge University Press in 1895–1907. A collection of over five hundred brief tales, translated by various hands, attributed to the Buddha as recollections of his previous births as a Bodhisattva. Although most of these tales are secular in content and spirit, they are considered part of the *Khuddaka Nikaya.*

1530

Beswick, Ethel. *Jataka Tales.* London: J. Murray, 1956. A brief popular retelling of thirty-three tales of the Buddha's former births; based on the translations cited in the previous entry.

1531

The Questions of King Milinda. 2 vols. Tr. by T. W. Rhys Davids. Oxford: Clarendon, 1890–94. Volumes 35 & 36 of the Sacred Books of the East series, to be reprinted in paperbound form by Dover Publications of New York. A translation from Pali of a basic Theravada text, the *Milinda-pañha,* a semi-canonical account of philosophical discussions between a Greco-Bactrian King, Milinda (Menander), and the Buddhist monk Nagasena.

1532

Buddhist Mahayana Texts. Tr. by E. B. Cowell, F. M. Müller, and J. Takakusu. Oxford: Clarendon, 1894. Sacred Books of the East, volume 49; to be published in paperbound form by Dover Publications of New York. A collection of major Mahayana texts including Asvaghosa's life of Buddha (*Buddhacarita*), the earliest extant work of classical Sanskrit poetry, dating from about the first century A.D., and *The Diamond Sutra,* a famous metaphysical work written about 350 A.D.

1533

The Saddharma-Pundarika. Tr. by H. Kern. New York: Dover, paperbound ed., 1963. First published in 1884 as volume twenty-one of the Sacred Books of the East series issued at Oxford by Clarendon. A translation from the Sanskrit of "The Lotus of the Good Law," the basic text of Mahayana Buddhism.

1534

Santideva. *The Path of Light.* Tr. by L. D. Barnett. New York: Grove, paperbound ed., 1947. First published in 1909; an abridged translation of the *Bodhicharyavatara,* a Mahayana manual concerning the nature and attainment of enlightenment; probably composed in the 7th century.

1535

Selected Sayings from the Perfection of Wisdom. Tr. by E. Conze. London: Buddhist Society, 1955. An anthology of selections from the Prajñaparamita books of Mahayana Buddhism that discuss the nature of perfect wisdom. The Mahayana school considers these texts to be *Sutras* or sayings attributed to the Buddha.

1536

The Lankavatara Sutra. Tr. by D. T. Suzuki. London: Routledge, 1932. A translation from Sanskrit of a major Mahayana philosophical text; accompanied by a helpful introduction.

HINDU PHILOSOPHICAL SYSTEMS

General histories and surveys of the Hindu systems appear as part of comprehensive works on Indian philosophy cited above under *Religion* and *Philosophy — General.*

General Works

1537

Madhava. *Sarvadarsanasamgraha.* Tr. by E. B. Cowell and A. E. Gough. London: K. Paul, 1914. A translation of a classic 14th-century treatise which summarizes the six main schools of Hindu philosophy and places them within a common framework of orthodoxy that belies their diverse origins and conceptual differences.

1538

Bernard, Theos. *Hindu Philosophy.* New York: Philosophical Library, 1947. An outline of the "six systems" of Hindu philosophy addressed to the general reader; contains a glossary of Sanskrit terms.

1539

Müller, F. Max. *The Six Systems of Indian Philosophy.* London: Longmans, Green, 1919. A description and analysis of the "six systems" by a pioneer in the field of Indic studies.

Samkhya

1540

Keith, Arthur B. *The Samkhya System.* Calcutta: Y.M.C.A. Publishing House, 2nd ed., 1949. First published in 1918. A brief historical survey of the oldest school of Hindu philosophy; original sources are described and the relation of Samkhya to other traditions, including Buddhism and Greek philosophy, are discussed.

1541

Johnston, Edward H. *Early Samkhya.* London: Royal Asiatic Society, 1937. A brief monograph treating the sources, historical development, and basic concepts of the first systematic effort to reconcile the disparate philosophical elements of the Veda. Early Samkhya postulates a dualism of soul and matter and was essentially atheistic; in medieval times, monism and theism were introduced into the system.

1542

Kapila. *The Samkhya Philosophy of Kapila.* Tr. by Jag Mohan Lawl. Edinburgh: Orpheus Publishing House, 1921. A translation and exposition of the *Samkhya-pravacana-sutra,* traditionally attributed to a legendary sage of the sixth century B.C., known as Kapila.

1543

Iśvara Krishna. *The Sankhya-karika of Iśvara Krishna.* Tr. by S. S. Suryanarayana Sastri. Madras: University of Madras, 1948. A translation of the oldest extant text containing a systematic exposition of Samkhya; generally held to have been written in the third century. This manual serves as a Samkhya textbook today.

1544

Gaudapada. *Karika.* Tr. by R. D. Karmarkar. Poona: Bhandarkar Oriental Research Institute, 1953. A scholarly translation of a classic commentary on the *Samkhya-karika* of Iśvara Krishna; Gaudapada lived in the 8th century. A useful introduction summarizes what is known of Gaudapada and identifies him as a "traditional Vedantist."

1545

Vacaspati Misra. *The Tattva-kaumudi.* Tr. by Ganganatha Jha. Poona: Oriental Book Agency, 2nd ed., rev., 1957. First published in Bombay in 1896. A major commentary on the *Samkhya-karika* of Isvara Krishna; written in the ninth century by Vacaspati Misra, a member of the Advaita school of Vedanta.

1546

Sinha, Nandalal. *The Samkhya Philosophy.* Allahabad: The Panini Office, 1915. Sacred Books of the Hindus, vol. 11. This work includes translated excerpts from the writings of later Samkyha philosophers, ranging from the 14th through the 18th century.

1547

Phukan, Radhanath. *The Samkhya Karika of Iśvara Krishna.* Calcutta: K. L. Mukhopadhyay, 1960. A discussion of Samkhya philosophy in which Advaita dialectics and views of "modern science" are used to advance a new interpretation; includes a translation of the *Samkhya-karika.*

1548

Majumdar, Abhay Kumar. *The Samkhya Conception of Personality.* Calcutta: Calcutta University Press, 1930. A modern interpretation of Samkhya concepts relating to the determinants of personality.

Yoga

1549

Eliade, Mircea. *Yoga: Immortality and Freedom.* Tr. from the French by W. R. Trask. New York: Pantheon, 1958. Bollingen Series, No. 56. This translation is based on a 1954 revised edition of a monograph published in 1936. A comprehensive scholarly survey of the history, theory and practice of Yoga from earliest times to the present; includes a consideration of Yoga in Buddhist and aboriginal Indian traditions. This work contains many original, often controversial, interpretations and an extensive bibliography.

1550

Wood, Ernest. *Great Systems of Yoga.* New York: Philosophical Library, 1954. One of the best non-technical summaries of the practices and philosophy of the various developments within the Yoga school which seeks to attain "liberation" through psychic training.

1551

Dasgupta, Surendra Nath. *Yoga Philosophy in Relation to Other Systems of Indian Thought.* Calcutta: University of Calcutta, 1930. A scholarly account of the school in which psychic training is stressed as a means of attaining "liberation," and its link to other systems where Yoga in the broader sense of religious exercises is to be found. Common metaphysical tenets, such as those existing between Yoga and Samkhya are also discussed.

1552

The Yoga System of Patañjali. Tr. by J. H. Woods. Cambridge: Harvard University Press, 2nd ed., 1927. Harvard Oriental Series, vol. 17. A scholarly translation of the three texts described in the following entry; includes an introduction and a concordance of Sanskrit terms.

1553

The Yoga Sutras of Patañjali with the Commentary of Vyasa and the Gloss of Vacaspati Misra. Tr. by Rama Prasada. Allahabad: The Panini Office, 3rd ed., 1924. Sacred Books of the Hindus, vol. 4. Patañjali's *Sutras,* the basic text of the Yoga system, were probably written in the second century B.C. Patañjali's highly condensed exposition is elucidated by Vyasa's Bhasya, an important commentary of the fourth century. Vacaspati Misra's glossary on Vyasa's *Bhasya* is called the *Tattvavaisaradi.* It was written in the 9th century.

1554

Radhakrishnan, Sarvepalli and C. A. Moore (eds.). *A Source Book in Indian Philosophy.* Princeton: Princeton University Press, 1957. Rama Prasada's translation of Patañjali's *Yoga Sutras,* cited in the previous entry, is reprinted with a few modifications on pages 454-485 of this source book; selections from the commentaries translated by Prasada are also included.

1555

The Yoga Sutra of Patañjali, Tr. by J. R. Ballantyne and S. Deva. Calcutta: Susil Gupta, 1960. Originally published in the *Pandit* of Banaras; this translation is accompanied by the Sanskrit text and a medieval commentary by Bhoja.

1556

The Yoga Sutras of Patañjali. Tr. by C. Johnston. London: J. M. Watkins, reprint, 1952. First published in 1912. A readable translation with a brief commentary from the translator, addressed to the general reader.

1557

Vishnudevananda, Swami. *The Complete Illustrated Book of Yoga.* New York: Julian Press, 1960. A pictorial presentation of various postures employed in Hatha Yoga, a disciplining of the body often used for non-ascetic purposes.

1558

Coster, Frances G. H. *Yoga and Western Psychology.* London: Oxford University Press, 2nd ed., 1945. A somewhat outdated comparison of two views of human psychology; first published in 1935.

1559

Behanan, Kovoor T. *Yoga, a Scientific Evaluation.* New York: Macmillan, 1937. Published in paperbound form by Dover Publications of New York in 1959. An appraisal of the philosophical and physiological concepts of Yoga as seen from a "scientific" point of view.

1560

Bagchi, B. K. and M. A. Wenger. *"Electrophysiological Correlates of Some Yogi Exercises,"* in *Proceedings of the First International Congress of Neurological Sciences Held at Brussells in 1957.* London: Pergamon Press, 1958. One of the few scientific studies of the control of body functions by practitioners of Yoga.

Nyaya and Vaisesika

1561

Keith, Arthur B. *Indian Logic and Atomism.* Oxford: Clarendon Press, 1921. A survey of the literature and basic concepts of two systems of Indian philosophy. Nyaya, primarily concerned with logic and epistemology, and Vaisesika, which assumes the universe to be composed of atoms and strives to explain the world of experience by rational means; though of different origins these two systems merged in medieval times.

1562

Bhaduri, Sadananda. *Studies in Nyaya-Vaisesika Metaphysics.* Poona: Bhandarkar Oriental Research Institute, 1947. An exposition and analysis of solutions offered by Indian realists to account for problems relating to the physical order, including questions concerning time, space, and causality.

1563

Mishra, Umesha. *Conception of Matter According to Nyaya-Vaisesika.* Allahabad: M. N. Pandey, 1936. A study of the atomistic conception of nature held by these Indian schools of philosophy.

1564

Sinha, Jadunath. *Indian Realism.* London: Kegan Paul, Trench, Trubner, 1938. A study of the Vaisesika system in which reality is held to consist of substances possessed of qualities that can be perceived or logically inferred.

1565

Chatterjee, Satis Chandra. *The Nyaya Theory of Knowledge.* Calcutta: University of Calcutta, 2nd ed., 1950. A standard exposition of the Hindu "science of reasoning" in which canons of logical proof are used for an analytical investigation of the basis of knowledge.

1566

Bagchi, Sitansusekhar. *Inductive Reasoning.* Calcutta: Calcutta Oriental Press, 1953. A useful description of the main line of development in the Nyaya tradition: includes a detailed account of *tarka,* a mode of reasoning used to demonstrate the fallacies in an opponent's argument. The author's assessment of Nyaya ideas is often based on out-moded Western concepts of logic.

1567

Vidyabhusana, Satis Chandra. *A History of Indian Logic.* Calcutta: University of Calcutta, 1921. A survey of the Nyaya tradition in Indian philosophy including the ancient, medieval, and "modern" schools. Gangesa, a 12th century philosopher, is considered to be the founder of the modern school.

1568

Randle, Herbert N. *Indian Logic in the Early Schools.* London: Oxford University Press, 1930. A description and analysis of the early commentaries on the *Nyaya Sutra,* notably the work of Vatsyayana, who is believed to have lived in mid-fifth century.

1569

Gautama. *Gautama's Nyayasutras with Vatsayana's Bhasya.* Tr. by Ganganatha Jha. Poona: Oriental Book Agency, 1939. A translation of the earliest known Indian treatise on logic, probably written early in the Christian era, though traditionally attributed to a sage of earlier date known as Guatama (Gotama) or Aksapada. Vatsayana's classic commentary (*Bhasya*) on the *Nyaya Sutra* is a work of the fifth century.

1570

Kanada. *The Vaisesika Sutra.* Tr. by Nandalal Sinha. Allahabad: The Panini Office, 2nd ed., 1923. Sacred Books of the Hindus, vol. 6. A translation of the earliest systematic account of the Vaisesika system; traditionally attributed to Kanada, believed to have lived in the 3rd century B.C.

1571

Prasastapada. *The Padarthadharmasamgraha of Prasastapada with the Nyayakandali of Sridhara.* Tr. by Ganganatha Jha. Allahabad: E. J. Lazarus, 1916. The *Padarthadharmasamgraha* is a classic Vaisesika treatise of the 4th century; presented as a commentary on the *Vaisesika Sutra* of Kanada, it is actually an independent work of the first order. Sridhara's *Nyayakandali* is a 10th century work of the same school.

1572

Ingalls, Daniel H. H. *Materials for the Study of Navya-nyaya Logic.* Cambridge: Harvard University Press, 1951. Harvard Oriental series, volume 40. A small collection of translated texts representing an Indian system of formal logic, dating from the 13th century. Biographical information on the main contributors to this system is provided and occasional comparisons are made with Western concepts of symbolic logic.

1573

Raghunatha Siromani. *Padarthatattvanirupanam.* Tr. by K. H. Potter. Cambridge: Harvard University Press, 1957. Harvard-Yenching Institute Studies, No. 17. A useful introduction provides the historical background of this 16th century text on logic which attacks the categorical framework of the older Vaisesika system; a work of the Navya-nyaya syncretic school that developed in North India from the 13th to the 17th century.

Purva Mimamsa

1574

Thadani, Nanikram V. *The Mimamsa: the Sect of the Sacred Doctrines of the Hindus.* Delhi: The Bharati Research Institute, 1952. A study of the system which sought to demonstrate that the Vedas are eternal and self-existent, this school provides detailed rules for interpreting Vedic texts employed in Hindu rites and ceremonies. The Mimamsa school also strongly influenced the formulation of Hindu law.

1575

Jha, Ganganatha. *Purva Mimamsa in Its Sources.* Banaras: Banaras Hindu University, 1942. An account of the principal texts of a system noted for its concern with *dharma,* right action or duty. Purva Mimamsa emphasizes the ethical rather than the speculative side of Hindu philosophy.

1576

Keith, Arthur B. *The Karma Mimamsa.* London: Oxford University Press, 1921. An introduction to Purva Mimamsa, also known as Karma Mimamsa due to its concern with Vedic injunctions relating to *karma.* Another division of this system, known as Jñana Mimamsa, Uttara Mimamsa, or Vedanta, is primarily concerned with interpreting knowledge contained in the Veda relating to the attainment of ultimate release.

1577

Shastri, Pashupatinath. *Introduction to the Purva Mimamsa.* Calcutta: A. N. Bhattacharya, 1923. A survey of a system based on the premise that right action is essention for the attainment of "liberation" conceived as life in heaven, rather than the state of ultimate release set forth in other Hindu systems.

1578

The Mimamsa Sutras of Jaimini. 2 vols. Tr. by M. L. Sandal. Allahabad: The Panini Office, 1923–25. Sacred

Books of the Hindus, vols. 27 and 28. This most ancient of Mimamsa texts, traditionally attributed to Jaimini, are thought to have been written during the last half of the first millenium B.C. The *sutra* style of brief, highly condensed statements requires recourse to later commentaries for their elucidation.

1579

Jaimini. *Mimamsa Sutra, with the Commentary of Sabara.* 3 vols. Tr. by Ganganatha Jha. Baroda: Oriental Institute, 1933, 1934, 1936. Gaekwad's Oriental Series, vols. 66, 70, 73. Jaimini's *Sutra* is here translated with a major commentary by Sabara, who probably lived in the 1st century B.C. or the early centuries of the Christian era. Sabara's work, known simply as *Bhasya*, serves as the basis for most of the later commentaries.

1580

Jha, Ganganatha. *The Prabhakara School of Purva Mimamsa.* Benares: Benares Hindu University, 1918. Prabhakara's 7th century commentary on the *Bhasya* of Sabara reflects major changes in the Mimamsa system.

1581

Bhatt, Govardhan P. *Epistemology of the Bhatta School of Purva Mimamsa.* Varanasi (Banaras); Chowkhamba Sanskrit Series, vol. 17, 1962. A study of methods and concepts developed in the 8th century by Kumarila Bhatta and his followers in their works on the limits and validity of knowledge.

1582

Kumarila Bhatta. *Slokavarttika.* Tr. by Ganganatha Jha. Calcutta: Asiatic Society of Bengal, Bibliotheca Indica series, 1906. An important commentary on the first part of Jaimini's *Sutra,* written in the early 8th century by Kumarila Bhatta, founder of a distinct school within the Mimamsa system.

1583

Kumarila Bhatta. *Tantravarttika.* Tr. by Ganganatha Jha. Calcutta: Asiatic Society of Bengal, Bibliotheca Indica series, 1903. The second part of Kumarila's commentary on Jaimini's *Sutra.*

1584

The Mimamsa Nyaya Prakasa of Apadevi. Tr. by F. Edgerton. New Haven: Yale University Press, 1929. A translation of an elementary Mimamsa manual or textbook written in the 17th century.

Vedanta

GENERAL

1585

Badarayana. *The Brahma Sutra.* Tr. by S. Radhakrishnan. London: G. Allen & Unwin, 1960. This recondite text, also known as the *Vedanta Sutra,* was written around the beginning of the Christian era. It served as a point of departure for later commentators whose views on the highly condensed *sutras* often lead to the development of independent systems or separate schools subsumed under the common heading of Vedanta. Radhakrishnan's extensive introduction provides an account of the main ideas and principal works of the major commentators. His annotation to the text includes the interpretations of earlier commentators as well as his own and occasional references to similar ideas of Western philosophy.

1586

Badarayana. *The Vedanta-Sutras.* 3 vols. Tr. by G. Thibaut. Oxford: Clarendon Press, 1890–1904. Sacred Books of the East, vols. 34, 38, and 48. Reprinted in a two-volume paperbound edition by Dover Publications of New York in 1962. The *Vedanta-Sutras,* also called *Brahma Sutras,* are here translated with an introduction explaining their background and purpose. Two of the major commentaries on this basic text are also included: the non-dualistic (monistic) interpretation of the 8th century philosopher, Shankara, and the commentary by Ramanuja (1017–1127) whose qualified non-dualistic views strongly influenced the development of *bhakti* (devotional theism) in Hinduism.

1587

Badarayana's Brahma-Sutras With Shankaracharya's Commentary. Tr. by V. M. Apte. Bombay: Popular Book Depot, 1960. A close translation of the basic text of Vedanta philosophy.

1588

Guénon, René. *Man and His Becoming, According to the Vedanta.* Tr. from the French by R. C. Nicholson. New York: Noonday, paperbound ed., 1958. First published in 1925. A provocative exposition of those aspects of Vedanta relating to the nature and constitution of human beings; by a Western advocate of Vedanta metaphysics.

1589

Deussen, Paul. *The System of the Vedanta.* Tr. from the French by C. Johnston. Chicago: Open Court, 1912. The Vedanta or Uttara Mimamsa school of Hindu philosophy attempts to reconcile in one system the mystical speculations of the Upanishads. Deussen's scholarly work treats at length the basic text of this school, Badarayana's *Brahma Sutras,* and its classic commentary by Shankara. Also included is a brief survey of Vedanta's development to modern times where it is the dominant school of intellectual Hinduism.

1590

Nikhilananda, Swami. *Essence of Hinduism.* Boston: Beacon Press, 1948. An introduction to Vedanta originally prepared as lectures for an American audience.

ADVAITA

1591

Mahadevan, T. M. P. *Gaudapada. A study in Early Advaita.* Madras: University of Madras, 2nd ed., 1954. A scholarly study of the teachings of an 8th century philosopher, who occupies an important position among the pre-Shankara Vedantins; based on a study of Gaudapada's *Mandukya Karika.*

1592

Gaudapada. *The Agamasastra of Gaudapada.* Tr. by V. Bhattacharya. Calcutta: University of Calcutta, 1943. A translation of the earliest extant treatise, also known as the *Mandukya Karika* or *Gaudapada Karika,* on Advaita Vedanta. Tradition holds that one of Gaudapada's pupils was the teacher of the famous 8th century philosopher Shankara. The translator's contention that this work pre-dates the *Mandukya Upanishad* is not generally accepted.

1593

Menon, Y. Keshava and R. F. Allen. *The Pure Principle.* East Lansing: Michigan State University Press, 1960. An introduction to the philosophy of Shankara, an 8th century non-dualist (monist) of the Vedanta, whose brilliant dialectic continues to influence intellectual Hinduism and has earned Shankara a position of eminence among Indian philosophers.

1594

Shankaracharya. *Self-Knowledge.* Tr. by Swami Nikhilananda. New York. Ramakrishna-Vivekananda Center, 1946. A translation of the *Atmabodha* believed to have been written by Shankara, the 8th century Advaitin. An extensive introduction, based on the 15th century *Vedantasara* of Sadananda, provides a lucid exposition of Shankara's teachings.

1595

Vacaspati Mishra. *The Bhamati of Vacaspati.* Tr. by S. S. Suryanarayana Sastri and C. K. Raja. Adyar, Madras: Theosophical Publishing House, 1933. A partial translation of a 9th century commentary, by the Advaitin philosopher Vacaspati Mishra, on Shankara's *Brahmasutra-bhasya* of the eighth century.

1596

Hasurkar, S. S. *Vacaspati Misra on Advaita Vedanta.* Darbhanga: Mithila Institute, 1958. A study of the writings of an eminent ninth-century philosopher of the Advaita school.

1597

Vidyaranya. *Panchadasi*. Tr. by H. P. Shastri. London: Shanti Sadan, 2nd impression, 1956. A fourteenth-century treatise on Advaita metaphysics.

1598

Mahadevan, T. M. P. *The Philosophy of Advaita*. Madras: Ganesh, rev. ed., 1957. A survey of Advaita dialectics with particular reference to the works of Bharatitirtha, a 14th-century South Indian philosopher.

1599

Dharmaraja Adhvarin. *Vedantaparibhasa*. Tr. by S. S. Suryanarayana Sastri. Adyar, Madras: The Adyar Library, 1942. A classic treatise on Advaita epistemology and ontology, probably written in the 17th century.

1600

Datta, Dhirendra Mohan. *Six Ways of Knowing*. Calcutta: University of Calcutta, 2nd ed., rev., 1960. First published in 1932; an analysis of some basic epistemological theories of the Advaita Vedanta school, formulated in terms of Western philosophy.

1601

Malkani, Ghanshamdas R. *Vedantic Epistemology*. Amalner: Indian Institute of Philosophy, 1951. The work of a modern champion of the Advaita school of Vedanta; orthodox doctrines are here presented in a systematic manner in contrast to the traditional form of commentaries.

1602

Chennakesavan, Saraswati. *The Concept of Mind in Indian Philosophy*. Bombay: Asia Publishing House, 1960. A study of the nature and discipline of the mind and the process of perception as treated in the Advaita, or non-dualist, literature of the Vedanta.

1603

Murthy, Satchidananda K. *Revelation and Reason in Advaita Vedanta*. Waltair: Andhra University, 1959. To be reprinted by Asia Publishing House of New York. A description and analysis of the non-dualist (monist) view of scriptural testimony, with a comparison of this Advaita position and that of the other five classical systems of Hindu philosophy; biased by the author's theism.

1604

Devandan, Paul D. *The Concept of Maya*. London: Butterworth Press, 1950. A historical survey of Hindu ideas concerning the nature of reality; ranges from Vedic times to the present with special reference to the Advaita tenets of the Vedanta school.

1605

Chaudhuri, Anil K. R. *The Doctrine of Maya*. Calcutta: Das Gupta, 2nd ed., 1950. A study of a major concept of the Advaita school of Vedanta which holds that the phenomenal universe as viewed by man is illusion.

OTHER SCHOOLS

1606

Srinivasachari, P. N. *The Philosophy of Bhedabheda*. Adyar, Madras: Adyar Library, rev. ed., 1950. A study of the teachings of Bhaskara and Yadava, whose little known systems stand logically and chronologically between the developments of Vedanta associated with Shankara and Ramanuja.

1607

Mishra, Umesha. *The Nimbarka School of Vedanta*. Allahabad: University of Allahabad, 1940. An interpretation of the doctrine of *bhedabhedavāda* as expounded by a South Indian Brahmin of the 12th or 13th century, Nimbarka, in his commentary on the *Brahma Sutras*.

1608

Srinivasachari, P. N. *Advaita and Visistadvaita*. New York: Asia Publishing House, 1961. A lucid exposition of the Visistadvaita school of Vedanta, most notably expounded by Ramanuja of the 12th century, and its critique of the philosophic monism of the Advaita school.

1609

Ramanuja. *Vedantasara of Bhagavad Ramanuja*. Ed. by V. Krishnamacharya and tr. by M. B. Nara Sinha Ayyangar. Adyar, Madras: Adyar Library, 1953. An annotated translation of Ramanuja's commentary on the *Brahma Sutra* of Badarayana. Ramanuja, a South Indian Brahmin said to have lived from 1017 to 1127, rejected Shankara's doctrine of an impersonal World Soul and an illusory universe in favor of a personal God and the inalienable individuality of selves.

1610

Ramanuja. *Vedarthasamgraha*. Tr. by J. A. B. van Buitenen. Poona: Deccan College, 1957. A critical edition and translation of a Sanskrit text written in the 12th century as an introduction to the Visistadvaita school of Vedanta.

1611

Sharma, B. N. K. *A History of the Dvaita School of Vedanta and its Literature*. 2 vols. Bombay: Booksellers' Publishing Co., 1960–61. A detailed survey of the Dvaita (unqualified dualism) school founded by Madhva (c. 1199–1278), who vigorously attacked the monist views of Shankara. Madhva taught that God, souls, and matter exist as three eternally separate entities.

1612

Vedanta-sutras with the Commentary of Sri Madhwacharya. Tr. by S. Subba Rao. Tirupati: Sri Vyasa Press, 2nd ed. rev., 1936. A translation of the *Vedanta Sutras* with the *Brahma-sutra-bhasya* (commentary) of Madhva, a thirteenth century advocate of Dvaita (unqualified dualism) whose views appear to have been strongly influenced by Christianity.

1613

Madhva. *Srimad Visnu Tattva Vinirnaya*. Tr. by S. S. Raghavachar. Mangalore: Sri Ramakrishna Ashrama, 1959. A major work by the thirteenth century champion of the Dvaita (unqualified dualism) school. Madhva (c. 1199–1278) taught that souls are distinct from and dependent upon God (Vishnu); salvation occurs through grace granted to those who lead virtuous lives. The many similarities between Madhva's theology and that of Christianity are generally attributed to influence from the Syrian Christians of Malabar near whom Madhva resided.

1614

Bhattacharya, K. C. (1875–1949). *Studies in Philosophy*. Calcutta: Progressive Publishers, 1956. This is the first of a two-volume collection of the works of a Vedantin considered by many to be one of the greatest philosophers of modern India.

1615

Prem, Sri Krishna. *The Yoga of the Kathopanishad*. London: J. M. Watkins, 2nd ed., rev., 1955 An interpretation of the symbolism contained in a major Upanishad, written by a modern Vedantin opposed to the "sterility" of Western academic views on the subject.

HINDUISM

The mainstream of India's indigenous religious tradition is often referred to as Hinduism, in contrast to such heterodoxies as Buddhism and Jainism, religions of foreign origin, and the Vedic cult whose literature provides the earliest historical evidence of religion in India. During the first millennium of the Christian era, elements of Vedism, the heterodoxies, regional cults, and internal developments in the orthodox tradition gave rise to what is known as classical Hinduism. The disparate features subsumed under this rubric are sometimes grouped into two categories; Brahmanism, applied to the more "refined" or "higher" forms cultivated and preserved by Brahman priests from Vedic times to the present, and Popular Hinduism, the "vulgar" and less systematized beliefs and practices rooted in local cults of the common folk. The many qualifications and exceptions required of this distinction have lead to its general abandonment in recent years.

Viewed from a theological perspective, Hinduism in not one, but many religions ranging from simple forms of animism through polytheism, monotheism, to a rigorous philosophical monism. Hinduism encompasses a corresponding range of religious practices from the worship of local fertility goddesses to techniques of meditation leading to the comprehension of an abstract impersonal reality. The absence of a formal creed, and standardized cult practices, is accompanied by the minor role of ecclesiastical organization in Hinduism. Despite such disparities, Hindus maintain a strong sense of group identity through their acceptance of a common body of religious literature and the caste system.

All Hindus accept the Veda, religious texts composed early in the first millenium B.C., as revealed truth. Knowledge of the Veda, however, is confined to a relatively few Brahmans whose command of the archaic language is essential for their priestly functions. Most Hindus turn to the two epics, *Mahabharata* and *Ramayana,* for religious guidance. Composed in Sanskrit early in the Christian era, the epics were later rendered in Hindi and other vernacular languages. A similar, though less sacred, body of literature known as the *Puranas* was composed several centuries after the epics. The *Puranas* contain numerous myths, legends and theories of cosmogony and cosmology that are accepted in varying degrees by most Hindus. Religious law appears in systematic form in the *Shastras* composed between the second to the seventh centuries A.D. by Brahmans, whose writings reflect their class interest.

In addition to the ancient religious classics, there exists a vast body of religious literature in Sanskrit and the vernaculars. Much of this literature consists of devotional poetry and hymns addressed to one or another aspect of the two major Hindu deities, Shiva and Vishnu, who displaced the Vedic gods early in the Christian era. The proliferation of cults associated with Shiva and Vishnu, particularly those of Krishna and Ram (*avatars* or manifestations of Vishnu), occurred on a grand scale in medieval times. Numerous *bhakti* (devotional theism) movements appeared in this period and many continue as viable sects to the present day. Variations in cult practices also gave rise to a substantial literature. A major development of this kind is known as Tantrism (named after its texts called *tantras*), or Shaktism.

The Shakta cults worship the female principle or power called Shakti, conceived as a goddess representing the creative forces of the universe.

Although Hinduism has no formal creed, a few basic concepts provide a common world view. One key concept is that of *dharma,* the law of moral order underlying the universe; another is belief in the rebirth (*sansara*) of every living creature. The form of each rebirth is determined by the deeds (karma) of each creature in previous lives. These beliefs provide the justification for the caste system that has sustained the Hindu way of life. Each caste has a place in the divine order of *dharma,* and the degree to which an individual adheres to this moral law determines, through the workings of *karma,* his position in the caste order. Opposition to the social, economic, and political inequalities sanctioned by Hinduism appeared in a number of reform movements, notably the Sikh and Kabir Panthi sects that originated in the 15th century and continue to the present day. Reform movements stimulated by European contact also developed in modern times. The acceptance of these movements and of their predecessors were confined, however, to particular regions and a relatively small segment of the population.

General Works

Studies and texts cited above under *Vedism* contain much that is relevant to Hinduism. Some of the best introductions to Hinduism appear above under *Religion* and *Philosophy — Histories* and *Surveys.*

1616
Dowson, John. *A Classical Dictionary of Hindu Mythology and Religion.* London: Routledge Kegan Paul, 10th ed., 1961. A useful reference for names and terms encountered in Western works on Hindu mythology and religion; includes short descriptions of major Sanskrit texts.

1617
Daniélou, Alain. *Religious Music of India.* Ethnic Folkways Library P 431. New York: Folkways Records, 1952. A phonograph recording of Hindu ritual and devotional music recorded in India by Alain Daniélou, who also prepared the written introduction, transliteration, translation, and scores that accompany the record.

1618
Morgan, Kenneth. *Hinduism.* A collection of more than one hundred colored photographic slides depicting Hindu temples, shrines, holy men, and religious activities. A catalog identifying each slide, with comments about its content, accompanies the collection. This set of slides is distributed by: Visual Education Service, 409 Prospect St., New Haven 11, Conn.

1619
Morgan, Kenneth (ed.). *The Religion of the Hindus.* New York: Ronald Press, 1953. An excellent collection of essays by modern Hindu scholars surveying the history, beliefs, and practices of Hinduism; selections from Hindu sacred writings appear as a separate section.

1620
Monier-Williams, Sir Monier. *Brahmanism and Hinduism.* London: J. Murray, 4th ed., 1891. A detailed scholarly survey of the Hindu tradition, including the early Vedic period, based mainly on sacred texts. Attention is given to sectarian developments and the beliefs and practices

known as "popular" Hinduism. Although some of the author's theories are antiquated, this remains a standard work.

1621

Farquhar, John N. *Primer of Hinduism*. London: Oxford University Press, 2nd ed., rev., 1912. Although slightly colored by Christian zeal, this early work provides a useful historical sketch of the main features of Hinduism from pre-historic to modern times; a ready reference for identifying major religious works and personages.

1622

Bhattacharyya, Haridas (ed.). *The Cultural Heritage of India*. 4 vols. Calcutta: Ramakrishna Mission, Institute of Culture, rev. ed., 1953–62. Many of the essays in this series treat Indian philosophy and religion from the perspective of a devout Hindu.

1623

Zaehner, R. C. *Hinduism*. London: Oxford University Press, 1962. A concise description and history of Hindu religious beliefs with an analysis of major concepts and an appraisal of the changes occurring within Hinduism in modern times.

1624

Mahadevan, T. M. P. *Outlines of Hinduism*. Bombay: Chetana, 2nd ed., rev., 1960. A brief account of Hindu beliefs, rituals, sacred literature, cults, and philosophies with a section on Hinduism as it is practiced today.

1625

Sen, Kshiti Mohan. *Hinduism*. Baltimore: Penguin Books, paperbound, 1961. A brief account of the main features of Hindu religious belief and practice and their historical development; includes a few extracts from Hindu scriptures.

1626

Radhakrishnan, Sarvepalli. *The Hindu View of Life*. London: Allen & Unwin, 10th imp., 1957. First published in 1927; a brief, popular introduction to Hinduism addressed to the Western reader, by a contemporary Indian philosopher now serving as President of India.

1627

Chatterjee, Satis Chandra. *The Fundamentals of Hinduism*. Calcutta: Das Gupta, 1950. A brief philosophical study of Hinduism addressed to the general reader.

1628

Thomas, Paul. *Hindu Religion, Customs and Manners*. Bombay: D. B. Taraporevala, 4th ed., rev., 1960. A popular compilation of interesting, though sometimes inaccurate, tidbits of information about Hindu influence on Indian art and customs.

Special Topics Including "Popular" Hinduism

Other works on "Popular" Hinduism may be found above in *Village and Tribal Studies* sections of *Social Patterns*.

1629

Singer, Milton (ed.). *Traditional India: Structure and Change*. Philadelphia: American Folklore Society, 1959. Volume X of the American Folklore Society Bibliographical and Special Series. A collection of recent studies by academicians of diverse disciplines; methods of religious instruction and the transmission of religious tradition are among the many topics relevant to religion included in this work.

1630

Dumont, Louis and D. Pocock (eds.). *Contributions to Indian Sociology. No. 3*. Paris: Mouton, 1959. Most of this issue is devoted to an appraisal of recent research on that aspect of contemporary Indian religion known as Popular Hinduism; addressed to the specialist.

1631

O'Malley, Lewis S. S. *Popular Hinduism, the Religion of the Masses*. New York: Macmillan, 1935. An account of deities, beliefs, and rites considered by some scholars to be a distinct "level" of Hinduism; often regional in character, these traditions are perpetuated in many instances without recourse to the Brahman priesthood or sacred texts. Though the author's contempt for many of these practices mars his interpretations, this work contains useful descriptive material not readily available elsewhere.

1632

Crooke, William. *Religion and Folklore of Northern India*. 2 vols. London: Oxford University Press, 1926. This valuable work contains much information about "Popular Hinduism" in Northern India obtained through interviews and observation by the author and other British officials.

1633

Whitehead, Henry. *The Village Gods of South India*. London: Oxford University Press, 2nd ed., rev., 1921. A valuable descriptive account based mainly on the author's observation and inquiry; his interpretations reflect his views as a Christian missionary.

1634

Dubois, Jean A. *Hindu Manners, Customs and Ceremonies*. Tr. by H. K. Beauchamp. Oxford: Clarendon Press, 3rd ed., 1928. A classic account by a French missionary who resided in South India during the early 19th century. One of the most detailed early accounts of Hinduism.

1635

Srinivas, M. N. *Religion and Society Among the Coorgs*. London: Oxford University Press, 1952. One of the first studies of Indian religious life viewed in its societal context by a trained anthropologist; noted for Srinivas' efforts to conceptualize the transition of the South Indian Coorgs from tribal beliefs and practices to those of the Sanskrit-borne Brahmanical tradition.

1636

Jacobs, Hans. *Western Psychotherapy and Hindu Sadhana*. London: International Universities Press, 1961. A comparative study of concepts and methods employed by Freud, Jung, and the Hindu tradition of religious exercises; well written and highly subjective.

1637

Banerjea, Jitendra Nath. *The Development of Hindu Iconography*. Calcutta: University of Calcutta, 2nd ed., 1956. An encyclopedic study of ancient Indian religious art forms and their meaning, including works of Buddhist and Jain origin, with a review of developments in icon types in later Hindu devotional art. Emphasis is placed on the relation of art forms to religious concepts expressed in texts.

1638

Devandan, Paul D. *The Concept of Maya*. London: Butterworth Press, 1950. A historical survey of Hindu ideas concerning the nature of reality, ranges from Vedic times to the present. Related works are cited above under the Advaita school of VEDANTA in which the concept of *maya* occupies a position of major importance.

Anthologies and Translation Series

1639

Renou, Louis (ed.). *Hinduism*. New York: G. Braziller, 1961. An anthology of translations by various hands of Sanskrit and vernacular sources that convey the principal ideas, beliefs and practices of Hinduism from Vedic to modern times; includes a brief insightful introduction.

1640

Macnicol, Nicol (ed.). *Hindu Scriptures*. New York: Dutton, 1938. An excellent anthology of translations by Western scholars including R. Griffith's version of thirty Rigvedic hymns, M. Müller's translation of five Upanishads, and L. Barnett's rendition of the Bhagavad Gita.

1641

Raghavan, V. *The Indian Heritage*. Bangalore: Indian Institute of Culture, 2nd ed., rev., 1958. An anthology of Hindu religious texts selected and translated by V. Raghavan; includes selections from the Veda, law books, epics, and Puranas. An overview of Indian literature, religion, and philosophy prefaces this brief collection.

1642

Basu, B. D. (ed.). *The Sacred Books of the Hindus*. Allahabad: The Panini Office, Bhuvaneswari Asrama, 1909–1929. Basic Hindu texts not readily available elsewhere appear in this series of translations by Indian and European scholars.

Epics and Puranas—Translations and Studies

1643

The Ramayana and The Mahabharata. Tr. by R. C. Dutt. London: J. M. Dent, reprint, 1953. First published in 1910; a condensed metrical version of the famous Indian epics composed in their present form several centuries before the Christian era. The *Ramayana*, traditionally attributed to the sage Valmiki, appears to be the work of a single author. The *Mahabharata* is held to be the work of various hands. These works are probably the most popular religious writings of the Hindus, especially in northern India.

1644

Valmiki. *The Ramayana of Valmiki*. 3 vols. Tr. by H. P. Shastri. London: Shanti Sadan, 1952–59. A prose translation of the *Ramayana*. This version of the famous Hindu epic, attributed to the sage Valmiki, was probably composed by the second century B.C. The secular origin of this religious epic in the martial legends of earlier times is more evident in the Valmiki version than in later reworking of the same theme.

1645

Valmiki. *The Ramayana of Valmiki*. Tr. by R. T. H. Griffith. Benares: E. J. Lazarus, 1895. An excellent translation in verse form; difficult to obtain.

1646

Tulasidasa. *The Holy Lake of the Acts of Rama*. Tr. by W. D. P. Hill. London: Oxford University Press, 1952. A prose translation of a 16th century version of the *Ramayana* written in Hindi. Known as the *Ramacaritamanasa,* this poem differs markedly in content and spirit from Valmiki's Sanskrit version of ancient times. Tulasi Das's use of the vernacular and his concern with doctrinal matters may account for the great popularity and esteem accorded this religious work in northern India.

1647

Kamban. *The Ayodhya Canto of the Ramayana*. Tr. by C. Rajagopalachari. London: G. Allen & Unwin, 1961. A translation of selections from a 9th-century version of the *Ramayana* written in Tamil. Kamban's epic portrays Rama, the North Indian hero, as being rather ineffectual in contrast to the villain of South Indian origin.

1648

Sarma, D. S. *The Prince of Ayodhya*. Mylapore, Madras: Sri Ramakrishna Math, 1946. A popular retelling of the *Ramayana* in a narrative style.

1649

Lin Yutang (ed.). *The Wisdom of China and India*. New York: Modern Library, 1942. A condensed version of the *Ramayana,* translated in poetic form, appears in this readily available anthology.

1650

The Mahabharata of Krishna-Dwaipayana Vyasa. 13 vols. Calcutta: Oriental Publishing Co., 2nd ed., rev., (c. 1952–62). This prose translation, mainly the work of K. M. Ganguly, was published in Calcutta at the Bharata Press by Pratap Chandra Roy (sometimes cited as Protap Chundra Ray), who is often cited as the sole translator.

The first edition was published in one hundred parts during the years 1883–96. The second edition was revised by Hiralal Haldar. The monumental size of this epic and the range of materials from diverse sources incorporated in its text has led many to call it an "encyclopedia" of Hinduism. Although traditionally attributed to the sage Vyasa, it is a work by numerous hands living at different times.

1651

A Prose English Translation of the Mahabharata. 18 vols. Tr. by Manmatha N. Dutt. Calcutta: H. C. Dass, 1895–1905. A heroic attempt at a literal translation that was never completed.

1652

Rajagopalachari, C. (ed.). *Mahabharata*. Bombay: Bhavan Book University, 4th ed., 1955. A popular retelling of the main features of the famous Hindu epic.

1653

Sukthankar, Vishnu S. *On the Meaning of the Mahabharata*. Bombay: Asiatic Society of Bombay, 1957. A review and assessment of various views held by Western scholars concerning the date, composition, and meaning of the *Mahabharata*.

1654

Bhagavad Gita. 2 vols. Tr. by F. Edgerton. Cambridge: Harvard University Press, 1944. Third printing, 1952. Volume I contains a close scholarly translation with a transliteration of the original Sanskrit. Volume II includes an interpretation of the Gita's historical setting and its influence on Indian literature and thought as seen by Western scholars; Sir Edwin Arnold's free translation of the *Gita* also appears in this volume.

1655

Bhagavad Gita. Tr. by F. Edgerton. New York: Harper Torchbook, paperbound ed., 1964. A one-volume edition of the entry cited above; the preface and notations are revised and the Sanskrit text omitted.

1656

The Bhagavad Gita. Tr. by Swami Nikhilananda. New York: Ramakrishna-Vivekananda Center, 1944. Third printing, 1952. A prose translation with extensive notes and explanations based in many instances on the classic commentary of Shankara. A synopsis of the *Mahabharata* enhances the value of this excellent introduction directed to the general reader of the Western world.

1657

The Bhagavad Gita. Tr. by S. Radhakrishnan. New York: Harper, 1948. A useful introduction and explanatory notes accompany this translation which is reprinted without the supplementary information in *A Source Book in Indian Philosophy* (entry 1433) edited by S. Radhakrishnan and C. A. Moore.

1658

The Song of God: Bhagavad-Gita. Tr. by Swami Prabhavananda and C. Isherwood. New York: New American Library, paperbound ed., 1954. A free translation in prose and verse, addressed to Western readers seeking spiritual enlightenment.

1659

Ghose, Aurobindo. *Essays on the Gita*. New York: Sri Aurobindo Library, 1950. A provocative interpretation of the religious and philosophical significance of the *Bhagavad Gita* by a religious leader of modern India.

1660

Dikshitár, V. R. Ramachandra. *The Purana Index,* 3 vols. Madras: University of Madras, 1951–55. A guide to names and subjects appearing in the Puranas, post-epic collections of legends and religious lore of indeterminate date used to convey religious instruction to the masses. Eighteen major Puranas are distinguished within the amorphous body of Puranic literature, the remainder, known as Upapuranas, number in the hundreds and tend to be sectarian works.

1661

The Vishnu Purana. Tr. by H. H. Wilson. Calcutta: Punthi Pustak, reprint, 1961. A one-volume edition of a translation first published in 5 vols. in London in 1840. The *Vishnu Purana,* one of the most important of the eighteen major Puranas, includes accounts of the creation and destruction of the universe, the genealogy of gods, and the legends associated with ancient rulers. An extensive preface and detailed notes accompanying the text relate this Purana to other Puranas and the vast body of Hindu literature.

1662

The Srimad-Bhagabatam of Krishna-Dwaipayana Vyasa. 5 vols. Tr. by J. M. Sanyal. Calcutta: Oriental Publishing Co., 1952–54. A translation of the *Bhagavata Purana,* previously published in Calcutta in 1930–34. This Purana relates episodes in the life of Krishna, a human manifestation of the god Vishnu.

1663

Archer, William G. *The Loves of Krishna.* London: G. Allen & Unwin. 1957. A paperbound edition has been published by Grove Press of New York. Chapters three and four provide a lucid narration of the *Bhagavata Purana* with an analysis of the development of Krishna from a minor to a major deity in the Hindu pantheon.

1664

Mukerjee, Radhakamal. *Lord of the Autumn Moons.* Bombay: Asia Publishing House, 1957. Approximately half of this work consists of translated selections from the *Bhagavata Purana,* mainly erotic episodes in the life of Lord Krishna; the balance of the book treats the religious and philosophical implications of Krishna's amours as viewed by a devout Hindu.

1665

Hazra, R. C. *Studies in the Upapuranas.* Calcutta: Sanskrit College, 1958. The first of four projected volumes that seek to stimulate interest in Puranic works other than the eighteen major Puranas. Primarily of interest to the specialist, most of this work concerns the identification of manuscript materials; includes an extensive bibliography of Puranic texts and translations.

Deities and Religious Lore

1666

Dowson, John. *A Classical Dictionary of Hindu Mythology and Religion.* London: Routledge and Kegan Paul, 10th ed., 1961. A useful reference containing the names and characteristics of Hindu deities, mythical beings, and places mentioned in Sanskrit texts; derived entirely from the publications of European scholars.

1667

Daniélou, Alain. *Hindu Polytheism.* New York: Pantheon Books, 1962. An attempt to explain the Hindus' view of their major gods; a separatum containing Sanskrit texts of all quotations used in this study may be obtained on request.

1668

Hopkins, E. Washburn. *Epic Mythology.* Strassburg: Trubner, 1915. A scholarly description of gods, heroes, and the multitude of supernatural beings appearing in the *Ramayana* and *Mahabharata;* well-indexed for ready reference.

1669

Barnett, Lionel D. *Hindu Gods and Heroes.* London: J. Murray, 1922. A scholarly account of Hindu gods and heroes appearing in Sanskrit literature.

1670

Wilkins, William J. *Hindu Mythology, Vedic and Puranic.* Calcutta: Thacker, Spink, 1882. A guide to the myths and legends of Hinduism with an index of deities and descriptive summaries of their attributes, in some instances accompanied by illustrations.

1671

Getty, Alice. *Ganesa.* Oxford: Clarendon Press, 1936. A monograph on a famous minor deity of the Hindu pantheon; Ganesha, distinguished by an elephant head on a human body, is a prime example of the elevation of a regional cult figure to pan-Indian status.

1672

Vogel, Jean P. *Indian Serpent-lore or the Nagas in Hindu Legend.* London: A. Probsthain, 1926. A study of the role and supernatural power attributed to serpents in Hindu legends.

1673

Kumarappa, Bharatan. *The Hindu Conception of the Deity.* London: Luzac, 1934. A survey of Hindu views on the conception of a deity from Upanishadic times to the 11th century; attempts to offset the common impression that Hinduism is primarily monistic. About half of this work concerns Ramanuja's exposition of Visistadvaita (qualified non-dualism) doctrines which supported devotional theism.

1674

Macnicol, Nicol. *Indian Theism from the Vedic to the Mohammedan Period.* London: Oxford University Press, 1915. A useful historical survey of the subject.

1675

Campbell, Joseph. *The Masks of God: Oriental Mythology.* New York: Viking Press, 1962. A substantial portion of this work concerns the origin and development of Indian mythology; though interesting and provocative, many of the interpretations are based on tenuous evidence and are highly conjectural.

1676

Brown, W. Norman. "Mythology of India" in *Mythologies of the Ancient World* edited by S. N. Kramer. Garden City, New York: Doubleday, paper, 1961. A succinct and lucid discussion of some "symbolizing ideas" of Buddhist, Jain, and Hindu mythology.

Rites, Ceremonies, and Sacred Places

1677

Underhill, Muriel M. *The Hindu Religious Year.* London: Oxford University Press, 1921. A description of festivals and religious customs associated with the Hindu calendrical cycle including information on religious fairs, auspicious and inauspicious seasons, and places of pilgrimage.

1678

The Grihya-Sutras; Rules of Domestic Vedic Ceremonies. 2 vols. Tr. by H. Oldenberg. Oxford: Clarendon Press, Sacred Books of the East, volumes 29 & 30, 1886–92. A paperbound edition will be issued in the near future by Dover Publications. The *Grihya-Sutras* contain directions for domestic rites generally performed by householders rather than priests. Though part of the Vedic traditions followed by Hindus today, these texts are classed as *smirti* (memorized tradition) as opposed to the Veda proper or *sruti* (direct revelation) literature.

1679

Apte, V. M. *Social and Religious Life in the Grihya Sutras.* Bombay: Popular Book Depot, 1954. An account based on Vedic domestic ritual manuals.

1680

Manavagrhyasutra. Tr. by M. J. Dresden. Groningen: J. B. Wolters, 1941. A translation, accompanied by lucid commentary, of a Vedic manual used in the performance of Hindu weddings and other domestic rites.

1681

Pandey, Raj Bali. *Hindu Samskaras, A Socio-Religious Study of the Hindu Sacraments.* Banaras: Vikrama Publications, 1949. A study of beliefs and practices associated with Hindu birth, marriage, and death rites.

1682

Stevenson, Margaret (Sinclair) *Rites of the Twice-Born.* London: Oxford University Press, 1920. An account, prepared in collaboration with three Hindu priests, of life cycle and calendrical rites performed for members of the three upper groups in the four-fold Hindu caste system. Although filled with errors and mainly concerned with customs of Gujarat, this work provides information not readily available elsewhere.

1683

Lewis, Oscar. *The Festival Cycle in a North Indian Jat Village.* Philadelphia: Proceedings of the American Philosophical Society, vol. 100, no. 3, 1956. A description of festivals observed during the course of a year in a village near Delhi; based on anthopological enquiry and a study of earlier accounts of rites practiced in the region. Much of this information appears in the author's *Village Life in Northern India* published in 1958 by the University of Illinois Press.

1684

Diehl, Carl G. *Instrument and Purpose.* Lund: C. W. K. Gleerup, 1956. A scholarly study of South Indian rites and rituals.

1685

Jagadisa Ayyar, P. V. *South-Indian Festivities.* Madras: Higginbothams, 1921. A descriptive account of calendrical rites and other religious festivals observed in South India.

1686

Mukerji, Abhay Charan. *Ancient Indian Fasts and Feasts.* London: Macmillan, rev. ed., 1932. A brief descriptive account of the principal Hindu calendrical rites; based in the main on traditions learned and practiced by the author.

1687

Roy, Dilip Kumar. *Kumbha, India's Ageless Festival.* Bombay: Bharatiya Vaidya Bhavan, 1955. An account of a major Hindu festival held on the banks of the Ganges; often attended by more than a million pilgrims.

1688

Hastings, James (ed.). *Encyclopedia of Religion and Ethics.* 13 vols. New York: Scribner's, 1908–26. This standard work contains numerous articles on various facets of Hinduism including descriptive accounts of Hindu shrines and pilgrimage centers not readily available elsewhere.

1689

Lal, Kanwar. *Holy Cities of India.* Delhi: Asia Press, 1961. A descriptive account of major shrines and pilgrimage centers.

1690

Vidyarthi, Lalita P. *The Sacred Complex in Hindu Gaya.* Bombay: Asia Publishing House, 1961. An anthropological study of a pilgrimage center in Bihar state; includes a detailed analysis of the present role and prospects of Gaya religious specialists.

1691

Havell, Ernest B. *Benares, the Sacred City.* London: Blackie & Son, 1905. A popular account of the temples, shrines, and religious practices that may be seen in this major Hindu religious center.

1692

Krishnasvami Aiyangar, Sakkotai. *A History of Tirupati.* 2 vols. Madras: C. S. Pantulu, 1940-41. A detailed historical account of the Sri Venkatesa shrine located in the South India pilgrimage center of Tirupati.

1693

Pillai, K. K. *The Sucindram Temple.* Adyar: Kalakshetra Publications, 1953. A history of a famous South Indian religious center.

1694

Kramrisch, Stella. *The Hindu Temple,* 2 vols. Calcutta: University of Calcutta, 1946. A well illustrated study of Hindu temple architecture with provocative interpretations of the religious significance of structural features.

Ethics

Translations and studies of the *Bhagavad Gita,* a major statement of Hindu ethics, are cited above under *Epics.* Related works appear above under *Political Patterns — Law.*

1695

Banerji, Sures Chandra. *Dharma Sutras.* Calcutta: Punthi Pustak, 1962. A study of the origin and development of Hindu law as expounded in manuals concerning human conduct (*dharma*) composed in the form of brief aphorisms (*sutras*) during the last half of the first millenium B.C.

1696

The Sacred Laws of the Aryas. 2 vols. Tr. by G. Bühler. Oxford: Clarendon Press, 1879–82. Sacred Books of the East, volumes 2 and 14; to be reprinted in paperbound form by Dover Publications of New York. A translation of *Dharma Sutras* attributed to Gautama, Baudhayana, Vasistha and Apastamba; probably composed between the sixth and second centuries B.C.

1697

Kane, Pandurang V. *History of Dharma Shastra.* 5 vols. Poona: Bhandarkar Oriental Research Institute, 1930–62. A monumental survey of ancient and medieval religious and civil law in India.

1698

The Laws of Manu. Tr. by G. Bühler. Oxford: Clarendon Press, 1886. Sacred Books of the East, volume 25; to be reprinted in paperbound form by Dover Publications of New York. A translation of the earliest *Dharma Shastra* ("Instructions in the Sacred Law"), composed in verse form early in the Christian era. Manu's *Dharma Shastra,* also known as the *Manu Smrti,* treats in great detail the rules and regulations governing human conduct as viewed from an extreme Brahmanical point of view. Many niceties of proper behavior and punishment advocated by Manu were seldom if ever realized in actual practice.

1699

Hopkins, Edward W. *Ethics of India.* New Haven: Yale University Press, 1924. A standard work based on the traditional literature.

1700

Vora, Dhairyabala P. *Evolution of Morals in the Epics.* Bombay: Popular Book Depot, 1959. Examples from literary sources, mainly the *Mahabharata,* are here used to reconstruct some of the major values of ancient India, especially those values governing inter-personal relations. Although the analysis is seldom profound and often in error, the groupings of illustrative material may interest the general reader.

1701

Scott, Roland W. *Social Ethics in Modern Hinduism.* Calcutta: Y.M.C.A. Publishing House, 1953. An examination of the nature and development of Hindu ethical thought from the early 19th century to about 1947, including religious reforms and the introduction of democratic standards.

1702

Gandhi, Mohandas K. *The Gita According to Gandhi.* Tr. by M. H. Desai. Ahmedabad: Navajivan Publishing House, 3rd ed., 1951. A translation of Gandhi's Gujarati version of the *Bhagavad Gita,* prepared for a mass audience. Gandhi's role as a major spokesman for modern India and the value which he placed on the *Gita* as an ethical guide, enhance the importance of his views on this classic Hindu work. More scholarly translations of the *Gita* are cited above under *EPICS.*

Sects and Cults

An earlier section entitled *Vedanta* should be consulted for accounts of various religious teachers whose lives and teachings inspired numerous medieval and modern sects and cults.

1703

Wilson, Horace H. *Religious Sects of the Hindus.* Ed. by E. R. Rost. Calcutta: Susil Gupta, 2nd ed., 1958. A history and description of popular Hindu sects, mainly of North India, investigated by the author in the early 19th century.

1704

Chattopadhyaya, Sudhakar. *The Evolution of Theistic Sects in Ancient India.* Calcutta: Progressive Publishers, 1962. An account of the origin and development of the Vaishnava, Shaiva, and minor sects from earliest times to about the 8th century; much of this study concerns the incorporation of foreign elements into the Brahmanical tradition.

1705

Bhandarkar, Ramkrishna G. *Vaishnavism, Shaivism and Minor Religious Systems.* Strassburg: K. J. Trübner, 1913. A reprint of this work was published in Poona, India in 1928. A still valuable study that helps fill the gap between accounts of contemporary Hinduism and ancient Vedic traditions.

1706

Sen, Kshitimohan. *Medieval Mysticism of India.* Tr. by Manomohan Ghosh. London: Luzac, 1936. An account of famous mystics whose lifes and teachings served to inspire the development of various medieval sects.

1707

Carpenter, Joseph E. *Theism in Medieval India.* London: Williams & Norgate, 1921. A detailed study of the widespread popularity of devotional theism in medieval times and the development of numerous sects organized to worship particular deities.

SHAIVISM

1708

Shivapadasundaram, S. *The Saiva School of Hinduism.* London: G. Allen & Unwin, 1934. An account of the history and basic tenents of sects which consider Shiva to be the highest or only God. Emerging early in the Christian era, Shaivite sects and those devoted to Vishnu came to be the major divisions within Hinduism; however, sectarian differences seldom lead to conflict.

1709

Hymns of the Tamil Saivite Saints. Tr. & ed. by Francis Kingsbury and G. E. Philips. London: Oxford University Press, 1921. A translation of hymns composed in Tamil between the 7th and 10th centuries by the Nayanars, or teachers of a South Indian Shaivite sect.

1710

Mahadevan, T. M. P. *The Idea of God in Saiva-Siddhanta.* Annamalainagar: Annamalai University, 1955. The Saiva-Siddhanta system of philosophy, built upon the devotional teachings of Tamil hymnodists, developed one of the most monotheistic theologies of any Hindu sect.

1711

Pooniah, V. *The Saiva-Siddhanta Theory of Knowledge.* Annamalainagar: Annamalai University, 1952. A study of concepts contained in the philosophical system developed by devotees of Shaiva in the Tamil area of South India prior to the 14th century.

1712

Meykanda Devar. *Sivañana Bodham of Meykanda.* Tr. by G. Matthews. Oxford: Oxford University Press, 1948. A translation of a 13th century manual of Shaiva religious doctrine, written by a leader of the Saiva-Siddhanta school.

1713

Hunashal, S. M. *The Lingayat Movement; A Social Revolution in Karnatak.* Dharwar: Karnatak Sahitya Mandira, 1947. A study of a South Indian Shaivite sect, also known as Virashaivism, founded in the 12th century.

Noted for their doctrines of social equality and rejection of Brahmanical authority, the Lingayats consider the linga of Shiva to be the only sacred symbol.

1714

Nandimath, S. C. *A Handbook of Virasaivism.* Dharwar, South India: Lingayat Education Association, 2nd ed., 1953. A scholarly account of the origin, beliefs, and practices of the Virasaiva or Lingayat sect that is one of the largest contemporary bhakti groups in India.

VAISHNAVISM

1715

Archer, William G. *The Loves of Krishna.* London: G. Allen & Unwin, 1957. Available in paperbound form from Grove Press of New York. A lucid, succinct survey of the emergence of Krishna as a major deity in the Vaishnavite literature of the medieval period. Krishna, viewed as a manifestation of Vishnu, became the central figure in various sects based on devotional theism.

1716

Gonda, Jan. *Aspects of Early Vishnuism.* Utrecht: V. A. Oosthoek's, 1954. A scholarly study of the emergence of Vishnu as a major deity in the Hindu pantheon and the consequent displacement of earlier Vedic gods.

1717

Raychaudhuri, Hemchandra. *Materials for the Study of the Early History of the Vaishnava Sect.* Calcutta: University of Calcutta, rev. ed., 1936. A scholarly compilation and appraisal of historical materials relating to the emergence of sects devoted to the worship of Vishnu.

1718

De, Sushil Kumar. *Early History of the Vaishnava Faith and Movement in Bengal.* Calcutta: K. L. Mukhopadhyay, 2nd ed., 1961. A detailed study, based on Sanskrit and Bengali sources, of a major center of Vaishnavism prior to the 17th century. Most attention is given to the development of ideas and beliefs stemming from the teachings of Chaitanya (1485–1533), rather than to organizational aspects of the movement.

1719

Kennedy, Melville T. *The Chaitanya Movement. A Study of the Vaishnavism of Bengal.* Calcutta: Y.M.C.A. Press, 1925. Contemporary activities of this sect, devoted to the worship of Vishnu, are discussed in relation to Christianity and the history and teachings of this major movement founded by the medieval mystic Chaitanya.

1720

Krishnadasa. *Chaitanya's Life and Teachings From His Contemporary Bengali Biography.* Tr. by Jadunath Sarkar. Calcutta: M. C. Sarkar, 1922. A translation of the *Chaitanya-charit-amrita* written in the 16th century. Chaitanya (1485–1533) was a leader in the bhakti (devotional theism) movement that swept Bengal and Orissa in the 16th century with its advocacy of personal devotion to god as incarnate in Krishna.

1721

Mukhopadhyay, Prabhat. *The History of Medieval Vaishnavism in Orissa.* Calcutta: R. Chatterjee, 1940. A historical account of the religious fervour that developed in Orissa around the worship of Krishna as an incarnation of Vishnu during the 16th century.

1722

Thoothi, N. A. *The Vaishnavas of Gujarat.* London: Longmans, 1935. A detailed study of devotional theism in a region of western India, viewed as a methodological exercise in the investigation of social phenomena.

1723

Hymns of the Alvars. Tr. by J. S. M. Hooper. Calcutta: Association (Y.M.C.A.) Press, 1929. A brief collection of devotional poetry composed in Tamil from approximately the 7th to the 10th centuries; attributed to the Alvars or saints of a South Indian Vaishnavite sect.

TANTRISM

1724

Bose, Dhirendra N. and H. Haldar. *Tantras: Their Philosophy and Occult Secrets.* Calcutta: Oriental Publishing Co., 3rd ed., rev., 1956. An inadequate introduction to an ancient though little known Indian religious tradition, whose beliefs and practices appear in various Hindu and Buddhist cults. Tantric cults, so named for the texts or *Tantras* they employ, make use of secret formulae and mystic symbols to obtain magic powers for the attainment of spiritual goals. They are also known as Shakti cults, due to their worship of the female or Shakti counterpart of a god, or Shakta. Tantric rites, especially in medieval times, sometimes include illicit sexual intercourse, meat eating, and other violations of orthodox beliefs and practices.

1725

Bhattacharya, Shiva C. V. *Principles of Tantra.* Ed. by J. G. Woodroffe. Madras; Ganesh, 2nd ed., 1952. First published in two volumes by Luzac of London, 1914–16. A detailed study, supported by citations from Tantric texts, of the principles and practices of the Tantric tradition.

1726

Woodroffe, Sir John G. *Introduction to Tantra Sastra.* Madras: Ganesh, 3rd ed., 1956. First published in 1913; a brief account of the beliefs and practices to be found in Tantric literature and the difference between the Vedic and Tantric traditions.

1727

Woodroffe, Sir John G. *Shakti and Shakta.* Madras: Ganesh, 5th ed., rev., 1959. A collection of essays addressed to the general reader on the doctrines and practices of Tantric cults in which the gods, Shaktas, are thought of as inactive and transcendent males best approached through their wives or Shaktis, the active, personified expression of divine power. The author, whose publications often appear under the pseudonym Arthur Avalon, is primarily responsible for what little is known in the West of the Tantric tradition. Woodroffe translates more than a dozen Tantric texts now available in various editions from Ganesh & Co. of Madras.

1728

Das, Sudhendu Kumar. *Sakti or Divine Power.* Calcutta: University of Calcutta, 1934. A historical study based on Sanskrit texts of the origin and development of the concept of Shakti from the Vedic mother goddesses to the Tantric sects of medieval and modern times.

1729

Bagchi, Prabodh C. *Studies in the Tantras.* Calcutta: University of Calcutta, 1939. A collection of scholarly essays on various facets of Tantric belief and practice.

1730

Woodroffe, Sir John G. *The World as Power.* Madras: Ganesh, 2nd ed., 1957. This volume consists of the first five books of a series written to explain the philosophical principles expressed in the Tantras or sacred writings of the Shakta school of Advaita Vedanta.

1731

Woodroffe, Sir John G. *Garland of Letters.* Madras: Ganesh, 3rd ed., 1955. A collection of essays on the *Mantra-Shastra,* a Tantric text treating the power, meaning and use of *mantras,* a verse or phrase believed to have magical or religious efficiency.

1732

Woodroffe, Sir John G. *Serpent Power.* Madras: Ganesh, 6th ed., rev., 1958. A discussion of theories and practices of Yoga, particularly those aspects treated in two Tantric texts whose translations are included in this work.

1733

Pandit, M. P. *Kundalini-Yoga.* Madras: Ganesh, 1959. A brief study of Sir John Woodroffe's views on Yoga presented in the entry cited above.

1734

Brown, W. Norman (ed. & tr.). *The Saundaryalahari: or, Flood of Beauty.* Traditionally ascribed to Sankaracarya. Cambridge: Harvard University Press, 1958. Harvard Oriental Series, vol. 43. A translation of a Sanskrit poem belonging to Tantric Shaktism: one of the most widely used devotional texts of modern Hinduism. An introduction systematizes the philosophical and religious teachings of the text. Beautifully illustrated with reproductions of sixteenth century paintings that embellish the original manuscripts of the text.

Movements of Medieval Origin

KABIR PANTH AND MINOR SECTS

1735

Ramananda to Ram Tirath: Lives of the Saints of Northern India. Madras: G. A. Natesan, 2nd ed., 1947. A collection of twelve brief biographical sketches, by various hands, of medieval religious leaders whose lives and teachings inspired the founding of various sects and ascetic orders in northern India. Ramananda, a native of South India, migrated to North India in the early 15th century. He preached in the vernacular, admitted all castes into his sect, and taught that there is one personal God full of love and pity for his worshippers. These features, particularly the idea of bhakti or devotional theism, was common to most medieval sects.

1736

Wescott, George H. *Kabir and the Kabir Panth.* Calcutta: Susil Gupta, 2nd ed., 1953. First published in 1907; an account of the life and teachings of a North Indian mystic, Kabir (1440–1518). Kabir was a Banaras weaver who became a disciple of Ramananda. The sect that he inspired, known as the Kabir Panth, is basically Hinduistic though influenced by Islam. Although Kabir used the name Rama for God, he rejected the Hindu doctrine of reincarnation, and condemned the worship of idols and the caste system.

1737

Keay, Frank E. *Kabir and His Followers.* London: Oxford University Press, 1931. A study of the history, literature, beliefs, and practices of the Kabir Panth sect and related groups. Though relatively small, this sect remains active in India today.

1738

Kabir. *One Hundred Poems of Kabir.* Tr. by R. Tagore. New York: Macmillan, 1961. A translation from Hindi of poems composed by Kabir in the 15th century and preserved by oral tradition. First published by Macmillan in 1916 under the title *Songs of Kabir.*

1739

Orr, William G. *A Sixteenth-Century Indian Mystic.* London: Lutterworth Press, 1947. An excellent account of the life and teachings of Dadu, founder of the Dadu Panthis, with a history of the sect and its literature to modern times. Dadu was most active in the kingdom of Jaipur; his theology was derived mainly from the deistic teachings of Kabir.

1740

Deleury, G. A. *The Cult of Vithoba.* Poona: Poona University and Deccan College Publication in Archaeology and History of Maharashtra, 1960. A historical study of the origin and development of one of the most important cults in Maharashtra, devoted to the god Vithoba or Viththala. A good illustration of the importance of pilgrimages in Indian religious life.

1741

Tukaram. *An Indian Peasant Mystic.* Tr. by J. S. Hoyland. London: Allenson, 1932. A translation of hymns, by the Maharashtrian poet, Tukaram (1608–1649), whose compositions rank high in the bhakti tradition of devotional theism still prevailing among the common folk. Tukaram was a devotee of the god Vithoba.

1742

Bahirat, B. P. *The Philosophy of Jñanadeva.* Pandhapur, Maharashtra: Pandharpur Research Society, 1956. An account of the life and teachings of a 13th century religious leader whose devotional theism influenced the development of bhakti cults in Maharashtra.

1743

Deming, Wilbur S. *Ramdas and the Ramdasis.* Calcutta: Association Press (Y.M.C.A.), 1928. An account of the life and teachings of a 17th century poet-saint of Western India, who combined Advaita Vedanta philosophy with the worship of the god Rama. His followers remain active today in the region of Maharashtra.

1744

Briggs, George W. *Gorakhnath and Kanphata Yogis.* Calcutta: Y.M.C.A. Publishing House, 1938. An account of the history and tenets of a medieval North Indian sect, also known as Natha Yogis, that followed the Hatha-Yoga tradition in which acrobatic exercises and difficult postures are used to attain mystical experience.

THE SIKHS
1745

Singh, Khuswant. *The Sikhs.* London: G. Allen & Unwin, 1953. A survey of the history, doctrine, and practices of a sect founded in the 15th century by Guru Nanak, a disciple of Kabir. The Sikhs, though rejecting idol worship and caste distinctions, share many beliefs and practices with the Hindus.

1746

Macauliffe, Max A. *Sikh Religion.* 6 vols, in 3. Oxford: Clarendon Press, 1909. A detailed account of the life and teachings of the Sikh Gurus, or religious leaders, accompanied by extensive translations of their writings now held to be sacred.

1747

Selections From the Sacred Writings of the Sikhs. Tr. by T. Singh and others. London: G. Allen & Unwin, 1960. A translation of portions of the *Adi Granth* or Original Book, compiled by Guru Arjun in 1601. The Sikh scriptures contain, in addition to the writings of their Gurus, hymns and sayings composed by other famous medieval religious teachers of North India.

1748

Singh, Jogendra. *Sikh Ceremonies.* Bombay: International Book House, 1941. A brief description of major life-cycle rites, with translations of those portions of the Sikh sacred writing recited on such occasions.

1749

Archer, John C. *The Sikhs in Relation to Hindus, Moslems, Christians, and Ahmadiyyas.* Princeton: Princeton University Press, 1946. A study in comparative religion with considerable attention given to the history of the Sikhs. The Ahmadiya movement, a heretical Islamic sect, arose in the Punjab in 1879.

1750

Macauliffe, Max A. and others. *Sikh Religion; A symposium.* Calcutta: Susil Gupta, 1958. A collection of brief essays by five authors; written between 1810 and 1925, they include information on Sikh doctrine, civil and religious institutions, and the Sikh's militant tradition.

Modern Movements
1751

Farquhar, John N. *Modern Religious Movements in India.* New York: Macmillan, 1915. A historical survey of major religious movements in 19th-century India and their relation to efforts at social reform and nascent nationalism; written in outline form with an extensive bibliography.

1752

Sarma, Dittakavi S. *The Renaissance of Hinduism.* Banaras: Banaras University Press, 1944. A collection of biographical studies of major Hindu leaders of the nineteenth and early twentieth centuries.

1753

Leonard, G. S. *A History of the Brahmo Samaj.* Calcutta: Adi Brahmo Samaj Press, 2nd ed., 1934. An account of a reform movement centered in Bengal, from its inception by Ram Mohun Roy (1772–1833) to 1878. The Brahmo Samaj strongly opposed many Hindu practices including *sati,* idol worship, and caste.

1754

Rammohun Roy, Raja. *The English Works of Raja Rammohun Roy.* 3 vols. Ed. by K. Nag and D. Burman. Calcutta: Sadharan Brahmo Samaj, 1945–51. A collection of writings by the founder of the Brahmo Samaj. Rammohun Roy played a major role in the Hindu reform movements of early 19th century Bengal.

1755

Sen, Keshub Chunder. *Life and Works of Brahmananda Keshav.* Compiled by P. S. Basu. Calcutta: Navavidhan Publication Committee, 1940. A collection of the writings of K. C. Sen (1838–1884), under whose leadership the Brahmo Samaj was strongly influenced by Christianity.

1756

Lajpat Rai, Lala. *The Arya Samaj.* London: Longmans, Green, 1915. An account of the history and doctrines of a militant movement founded by Dayananda Sarasvati in 1875. The Arya Samaj acknowledges only the Vedas as sacred scriptures and rejects many of the social customs and ritual practices of Hinduism. The author was a major leader in this movement.

1757

Ramakrishna. *The Gospel of Sri Ramakrishna.* Tr. by Swami Nikhilananda. New York: Ramakrishna-Vivekananda Center, 1942. An abridged version of this work was published by Harper of New York in 1948 under the title: *Ramakrishna: Prophet of New India.* This record of Sri Ramakrishana's (1836–1886) teachings, conveys through use of dialogue form some understanding of the mode of instruction characteristic of Hinduism. Ramakrishna was considered a saint in his time, and though lacking extensive formal education, his mystical experiences and experiments with all aspects of Hinduism and other religions provide his discourses with great authority in the eyes of many modern Hindus.

1758

Saradananda, Swami. *Sri Ramakrishna, the Great Master.* Tr. by Swami Jagadananda. Hollywood: Vedanta Society of Southern California, 2nd ed., 1952. A translation of a five volume Bengali work; provides a detailed account of the life and teachings of Ramakrishna.

1759

Müller, F. Max. *Ramakrishna: His Life and Sayings.* Mayavati, Almora: Advaita Ashrama, 1951. An earlier edition was published by C. Scribner's Sons of New York in 1899. Newspaper accounts and other contemporary sources provide the basis for this biographical sketch and collection of sayings that reflect Ramakrishna's great wit and common sense; Ramakrishna never committed his thoughts to writing.

1760

Gambhirananda, Swami. *History of the Ramakrishna Math and Mission.* Calcutta: Advaita Ashrama, 1957. An account of the organization founded by Vivekananda (1863–1902), a disciple of Ramakrishna, whose members perform social service and relief work as part of their religious life; many branches of this organization exist outside India.

1761

Vivekananda, Swami. *Vivekananda; the Yogas and Other Works.* New York: Ramakrishna-Vivekananda Center, rev. ed., 1953. An extensive biographical sketch of Vivekananda (1863–1902), founder of the Ramakrishna Mission and a major spokesman for modern Hinduism, prefaces this collection of his lectures and writings addressed mainly to a non-Indian audience.

1762

Vivekananda, Swami. *The Complete Works of Swami Vivekananda.* 7 vols. Mayavati, Almora: Advaita Ashrama, 1924–32. A comprehensive collection of Vivekananda's English writings with translations of his work in Bengali and Sanskrit; includes an index.

1763

Ghose, Aurobindo. *The Life Divine.* New York: E. P. Dutton, rev. ed., 1951. Pondicherry: Sri Aurobindo Ashram, reprint, 1960. A major work by Sri Aurobindo (1872–1950), who reinterpreted classic Hindu concepts to form a new type of "integral yoga" addressed to the problems of modern times. First published as a series of journal articles during the years 1914–1919.

1764

Donnelly, Motwenna. *Founding the Life Divine.* New York: Hawthorn Books, 1956. A popular introduction to Sri Aurobindo's principles of integral yoga; written by one of his followers.

1765

Chaudhuri, Haridas and F. Spiegelberg (eds.). *The Integral Philosophy of Sri Aurobindo.* London: G. Allen & Unwin, 1960. A collection of papers on the life and teachings of Aurobindo Ghose, prepared for a commemorative symposium.

1766

Ramana Maharshi. *Collected Works.* Ed. by A. Osborne. London: Rider, 1959. A collection of the writings of a contemporary Hindu religious leader, considered by many to be a saint. Annotations by the editor provide background information.

1767

Osborne, Arthur. *Ramana Maharshi and the Path of Self-Knowledge.* London: Rider, 1954. An account of the life and teachings of a modern Hindu saint.

1768

Krishnamurti, Jiddu. *Commentaries on Living.* 2 vols. Ed. by D. Rajagopal. New York: Harper, 1956–58. Selections from essays recounting the ideas and experiences of a modern Hindu religious leader.

1769

Gandhi, Mohandas K. *Hindu Dharma.* Ed. by B. Kumarappa. Ahmedabad: Navajivan Publishing House, 1950. A collection of writings relating to religion by the famous Indian nationalist leader, commonly known as "Mahatma" Gandhi (1869–1948). Numerous other works of a religious nature by Gandhi are maintained in print by the Navajivan Publishing House.

1770

Tennyson, Hallam. *India's Walking Saint; the Story of Vinoba Bhave.* Garden City, New York: Doubleday, 1955. An account of the life, ideas, and activities of Gandhi's spiritual heir. Vinoba Bhave has for many years lead a program of land reform and rural improvement based on Gandhian ideals.

CHRISTIANITY AND JUDAISM

Information concerning the efforts of early Jesuit missionaries may be found under *History — Mughal Empire.*

1771

Thomas, Paul. *Christians and Christianity in India and Pakistan.* London: G. Allen & Unwin, 1954. A historical survey ranging from the time of St. Thomas, reputed founder of the Christian church in India, to modern times; contains little information on contemporary events. The author, an Indian Christian, is fairly objective except when discussing the influence of Christianity on Hinduism.

1772

Tisserant, Cardinal Eugene. *Eastern Christianity in India.* Bombay: Orient Longmans, 1957. A translated, revised version of a French work published in 1941. A general review of major events in the history of the Syrian Christian Church in Malabar from earliest times to the present; includes an extensive bibliography.

1773

Brown, Leslie W. *The Indian Christians of St. Thomas.* Cambridge: Cambridge University Press, 1956. An account of the Syrian church in Malabar, on the southwestern coast of India, from the 16th century to modern times.

1774

Plattner, Felix A. *Christian India.* New York: Vanguard Press, 1957. A brief, primarily pictorial, account of ancient sites and contemporary activities of Roman Catholic missions in India.

1775

Pickett, Jarrell W. *Christian Mass Movements in India.* New York: Abingdon Press, 1933. An analysis, based on social and economic data gathered through systematic research, of Christian communities in the major regions of India; particular attention is given to the consequences of "mass" conversions in which homogeneous groups rather than individuals became Christians.

1776

Bayne, Stephen F. (ed.). *Ceylon, North India, Pakistan; a Study in Ecumenical Decision.* London: S. P. C. K., 1960. A collection of papers treating contemporary efforts to unite the various Christian churches in India.

1777

McKenzie, John. *Two Religions.* Boston: Beacon Press, 1952. A comparative study of some distinctive ideas and ideals in Hinduism and Christianity; an able presentation of the Christian missionary point of view.

1778

Gandhi, Mohandas K. *Christian Missions.* Ahmedabad: Navajivan Press, 1941. A presentation of the views of "Mahatma" Gandhi, famous political leader and spokesman for modern Hinduism, on the place of Christian missions in India.

1779

Kehimkar, Haeem, S. *The History of the Bene-Israel of India.* London: G. Salby, 1937. An account of the Jewish community residing in the Bombay region of India, by a member of the community who believes the Jews reached India about 175 B.C.

1780

Fischel, Walter Joseph. *The Jews in India.* Jerusalem: Ben-Zvi Institute, Hebrew University, 1960. An account, in Hebrew, of the small Jewish community in India and the part Jews have played in the political and economic life of South Asia.

ISLAM

Historical accounts of Islam in India and Muslim works containing religious material are cited above under *History — Muslim Period.*

1781

Gibb, H. A. R. *Mohammedanism; an Historical Survey.* New York: Mentor, paperbound ed., 1958. One of the best brief surveys of the history and main tenets of Islam. It includes an account of the penetration and influence of Islam in India.

1782

Morgan, Kenneth W. (ed.). *Islam: The Straight Path.* New York: Ronald Press, 1958. A collection of essays by Muslim scholars on the beliefs and practices of Islam and its historical development including changes that occurred in India.

1783

Kramers, J. H., H. A. R. Gibb, and E. Lévi-Provencal (eds.). *The Encyclopedia of Islam.* 5 vols. London: Luzac, rev. ed., 1956. The basic Western language reference on the subject.

1784

Titus, Murray T. *Islam in India and Pakistan.* Calcutta: Y.M.C.A. Publishing House, rev. ed., 1959. An earlier edition was published by Oxford University Press in 1930 under the title: *Indian Islam.* Probably the best single account of the religious history of Islam in South Asia; provides an excellent analysis of the changes in Islam affected by the Indian environment.

1785

Smith, Wilfred C. *Modern Islam in India; A Social Analysis.* London: V. Gollancz, rev. ed., 1946. A study of ideological issues and political movements that developed within the Muslim community of India during the past seventy-five years.

1786

Dar, Bashir Ahmad. *Religious Thought of Sayyid Ahmad Khan.* Lahore: Institute of Islamic Culture, 1957. An account of the religious views of a 19th-century leader of the Indian Muslim community, who was instrumental in establishing Muslim institutions of higher learning that incorporated knowledge from the West.

1787

Iqbal, Sir Muhammad. *Islam as an Ethical and Political Ideal.* Ed. by S. Y. Hashimy. Lahore: Orientalia, 1955. An introduction and extensive annotation accompanies this version of a major speech delivered in 1908 by an Indian Muslim poet and philosopher whose ideas helped inspire the creation of Pakistan.

1788

Iqbal, Sir Muhammad. *The Secrets of the Self.* Lahore: S. M. Ashraf, rev. ed., 1944. First published by Macmillan of New York in 1920. A translation of the *Asr'ar-i-khud'i,* a philosophical poem written in Persian by Iqbal, whose life and work are discussed at length in the introduction.

1789

Walters, Howard A. *The Ahmadiya Movement.* Calcutta: Association Press, (Y.M.C.A.), 1918. A popular account of a modern sect within Islam that arose in the Punjab in 1879. The use of Western rationalistic methods in their interpretation of Islam and various doctrinal differences set them off from the orthodox.

1790

Hollister, John N. *The Shia of India.* London: Luzac, 1953. An account of the history and contemporary role of Shiism in India with particular attention to the Ismaili sects.

1791

Ivanov, Vladimar A. *Brief Survey of the Evolution of Ismailism.* Leiden: E. J. Brill, 1952. Ismaili Society Publication Series B. No. 7. A useful introduction to the history and literature of the Ismaili sect from its origin to modern times.

1792

Greenwall, Harry J. *His Highness the Aga Khan, Imam of the Ismailis.* London: Cresset Press, 1952. An account of the hereditary leader of an Islamic sect with an active following in western India.

1793

Arberry, Arthur J. *Sufism, an Account of the Mystics of Islam.* London: G. Allen & Unwin, 1950. A brief though comprehensive survey of a tradition of mysticism within Islam that won many converts to Islam in India.

1794

Chand, Tara. *Influence of Islam on Indian Culture.* Allahabad: Indian Press, 1954. A superficial survey containing many provocative and often unsubstantiated interpretations of the influence of Islam on indigenous Indian social, political, and religious traditions.

1795

Jafar Sharif. *Islam in India.* Tr. by G. A. Herklots. London: Oxford University Press, rev. ed., 1921. A new edition, revised by W. Crooke, of the *Qanun-Islam,* first published in 1832. A description compiled under the direction of G. A. Herklots, of Islamic manners and customs as practiced in early 19th-century India.

1796

Koran. *The Koran Interpreted* by Arthur J. Arberry. 2 vols. New York: Macmillan, 1955. An authoritative translation of the basic religious text of Islam.

ZOROASTRIANISM

1797

Jackson, A. V. Williams. *Zoroastrian Studies.* New York: Columbia University Press, 1928. Probably the best introduction to a religion brought to India around the 8th century by refugees fleeing the Arab conquest of Persia; followers of this religion are generally known in India as Parsis (Parsees), approximately 125,000 of whom now reside in India, mainly in Bombay.

1798

Duchesne-Guillemin, Jacques. *The Western Response to Zoroaster.* Oxford: Clarendon, 1958. A brief summation and appraisal of the present state of knowledge about the Zoroastrian religion.

1799

Haug, Martin. *Essays on the Sacred Language, Writings and Religion of the Parsis.* London: Trubner, 4th ed., enl. 1907. First published in the late 19th century, this is a collection of scholarly essays on the history, beliefs, and practices of the Zoroastrian community in India.

1800

Modi, Sir Jivanji J. *Religious Ceremonies and Customs of the Parsees.* Bombay: J. B. Karani's Sons, 2nd ed., 1937. A description of various life-cycle and liturgical ceremonies and related customs of the Parsees, with a little information on their origin and meaning.

1801

Avesta. Gatha. *The Divine Songs of Zarathustra.* Ed. by I. J. S. Taraporewala. Bombay: D. B. Taraporewala, 1951. A fairly complete edition of the sacred hymns of the Parsis.

INTELLECTUAL AND AESTHETIC PATTERNS

Religion and philosophy emerge early in Indian history as the major stimuli for intellectual and aesthetic creativity, and archaeological evidence indicates similar influence in the art and architecture of the prehistoric Indus Valley Civilization. Changes in the popularity or royal patronage of the major religions are reflected in the content of Indian art and provide the main referent in the periodization of more than a millennium of artistic creativity. Despite variations in subject matter, the development of numerous regional styles and foreign influence, a distinct view of art and its place in life may be traced throughout India's history.

Beginning with Buddhist-inspired works of the 2nd century B.C., the primary expression of Indian architecture may be seen in religious monuments and temples. The role of sculpture, as an ancilliary feature of architecture, also appears at this early date with the casual mingling of naturalism and symbolism that remains a characteristic of Indian sculpture throughout its development. The assimilation of Iranian and Greek influence in a distinct tradition of sculpture early in the Christian era, indicates the existence of an earlier indigenous tradition, although no evidence of such work has been found. A major achievement of this assimilative process appears in the development of the Buddha image that later spread through Central Asia to China and Japan.

The few extant works of ancient Indian painting indicate religion also provided the main impetus for this mode of aesthetic expression. However, scenes depicted in such painting as the Ajanta cave murals of the 5th century are often secular in nature. While seeking to narrate events in the life of the Buddha, the artists of Ajanta painted scenes of court life and everyday activities of their time. Similar use of contemporary scenes appear in miniature paintings of late medieval times, in which episodes from the life of the Hindu god Krishna are presented in the costumes and court life of the day.

Music appears as an integral part of Vedic rites early in the first millennium B.C. and the use of song as a mode of religious expressions continues to play an important role in Hinduism today. Dancing also appears in certain Vedic ceremonies, and Hindu temple dancers in medieval times served to perpetuate a highly refined dance tradition that approached spoken language in the range and variety of ideas and moods conveyed by gesture. Dance poses with specific meanings appear in many works of sculpture and paintings, most notably, the portrayal of the god Shiva. The integration of music, dance, and drama in the classical Indian theater continues to the present day in folk "opera" and the modern cinema.

Classic Indian drama also draws heavily on religious themes, and efforts to inculcate piety or virtue appear in many plays. The classic theater rarely sought to hold a mirror to life, rather, the aesthetic goal was to evoke a particular mood or *rasa*. The development of plot and character were of minor importance, and prose passages served mainly as a frame for a series of lyrics treating the beauties of nature or the subtleties of an emotion.

Sanskrit is the language of the most ancient and important literary tradition of India; most vernacular literatures, excepting the venerable Tamil and other Dravidian literatures, are derived from this common source. Works of literary as well as religious interests, date from around the beginning of the Christian era, when two epics, the *Mahbharata* and the *Ramayana,* were composed in their present form. These poems encompass martial legends of great antiquity,

the popularization of philosophical and religious teachings, and much extraneous material. The most noted example of a self contained work within these epics is the famous religio-ethical treatise known as the *Bhagavad Gita,* which appears as a section of the *Mahabharata.* The varied content of the Epics, and to a lesser extent later prose works in a similar vein known as the *Puranas,* provide an endless store of subject matter for all forms of artistic expression down to the present day.

The political dominance of large areas of northern India by Muslim rulers during the 13th to the 18th centuries was accompanied by the introduction of alien art traditions. Under the Mughals, Persian architects came to India to design religious structures, tombs, and civic buildings. However, their dependance on Hindu artisans and the influence of the Indian setting led to the incorporation of Hindu and Jain architectural features with Muslim abstractionism. The synthesis of these traditions gave rise to a distinct Indo-Muslim style. Muslim courts also provided patronage for poets writing in Urdu, a language combining indigenous and foreign elements, and for similar efforts in the fields of painting and music.

Western influence on India's aesthetic tradition is most evident in literature, notably the introduction of the novel and a concern with social problems and human affairs for which few precedents can be found in the traditional literature.

GENERAL WORKS

1802

Basham, Arthur L. *The Wonder That Was India.* London: Sidgwick & Jackson, 1954. New York. Grove Press, paperbound ed., 1959. Descriptive materials and astute interpretation relating to intellectual and aesthetic patterns appear throughout Basham's account of Indic Civilization to about A.D. 1000. Chapter VIII on the arts, and chapter IX on language and literature are particularly useful. Brief summaries of ancient Indian scientific thought appear as appendices.

1803

Rawlinson, Hugh G. *India: A Short Cultural History.* New York: F. A. Praeger, rev. ed., 1952. First published in 1937. A scholarly survey intended for the general reader; Indian history up to modern times is examined primarily in terms of aesthetic and intellectual achievements, including developments during the Islamic period.

1804

DeBary, William T., et al. *Sources of Indian Tradition.* New York: Columbia University Press, 1958. The same publisher issued a paperbound edition in 1964. Economic, social, political, and religious facets of India's intellectual tradition from ancient to modern times may be found in this collection of translations prefaced with lucid introductions for the undergraduate student.

1805

Majumdar, Ramesh C. (ed.). *The History and Culture of the Indian People.* Bombay: Bharatiya Vidya Bhavan, 1951–. To date 6 volumes have been published of this proposed ten-volume work surveying in detail India's history from earliest times to the present; chapters of uneven quality on art, literature, and science appear throughout.

1806

Garratt, Geoffrey T. (ed.). *The Legacy of India*. London: Oxford University Press, reprint, 1962. A collection of scholarly articles addressed to the general reader on major aspects of India's intellectual and aesthetic tradition including science, religion, literature, and the arts.

1807

Macdonell, Arthur A. *India's Past*. Varanasi (Banaras): Motilal Banarsidass, reprint, 1956. First published by the Clarendon Press of Oxford in 1927. A historical survey of Indian thought including mathematics, medicine, and grammar, with a chapter on the vernacular languages and literature.

1808

Bharata. *Natyasastra*. Tr. by Manomohan Ghosh. Calcutta: Royal Asiatic Society of Bengal, 1950. A Sanskrit treatise, probably composed in the sixth century A.D. though attributed to the ancient sage Bharata. It is the earliest textbook extant on Indian drama, music, and dancing. The detailed classifications of gestures and stage conventions provide an interesting glimpse of the highly stylized and complex art tradition of the day.

SCIENCE IN ANCIENT AND MEDIEVAL TIMES

Summary accounts of ancient Indian medicine, astronomy, chemistry, mathematics and related subjects may be found in many of the histories of Sanskrit literature cited below.

1809

Riepe, Dale. *The Naturalistic Tradition in Indian Thought*. Seattle: University of Washington Press, 1961. An appraisal of the extent to which naturalistic and scientific thought may be found in Hindu, Jain, and Buddhist writings prior to the sixth century A.D.

1810

Zimmer, Heinrich R. *Hindu Medicine*. Baltimore: Johns Hopkins Press, 1948. An account of Indian ideas about the body, medicine, and the role of the physician as described in Vedic and classical Hindu texts.

1811

Filliozat, Jean. *The Classical Doctrine of Indian Medicine*. Delhi: Munshi Ram Manohar Lal, 1964. First published in French in 1949. A study of the origins of traditional Indian medicine and parallel concepts found in Greek texts predating the time of Alexander the Great.

1812

Jolly, Julius. *Indian Medicine*. Tr. with notes by C. G. Kashikar. Poona: C. G. Kashikar, 1951. First published in German in 1901. A detailed description of ancient Indian medicine based on an analysis of ancient texts.

1813

Ray, Priyadaranjan (ed.). *History of Chemistry in Ancient and Medieval India*. Calcutta: Indian Chemical Society, 1956. A detailed survey ranging from earliest times to the 19th century; incorporates a classic work on the subject by A. P. Chandra Ray.

1814

Datta, Bibhuti Bhusan and A. N. Singh. *History of Hindu Mathematics*. New York: Asia Publishing House, 1962. First published in Lahore in 1935 as a two-volume work. A detailed account of the achievements of Hindu scholars whose knowledge of mathematics in the fourth to the seventh centuries transcended that of any other known people of antiquity.

1815

Aryabhata. *Aryabhatiya, an Ancient Indian Work on Mathematics and Astronomy*. Tr. by W. E. Clark. Chicago:

University of Chicago Press, 1930. This brief text, written in A.D. 449, indicates the advanced state of Indian astronomy of the day including speculations about the earth's rotation on its axis.

ART AND ARCHITECTURE

Related works, particularly those treating the Indus Valley Civilization and early Buddhist sites, may be found above under *Prehistory* and *Archaeology*.

General Works and References

1816

Kern Institute. *Annual Bibliography of Indian Archaeology*. Leyden: E. J. Brill, 1926–. References to works on art and architecture of the historic and prehistoric periods appear in this annotated bibliography.

1817

Desai, Madhuri. *India: Architectural and Sculptural Monuments. A Map*. New Delhi: Director-General of Archaeology, Government of India, 2nd ed., n.d. First published by the Legation of India in Berne, Switzerland. Many of India's greatest artistic achievements are dramatically portrayed through photographic reproduction imposed on this handsome map, two by three feet in size.

1818

Morgan, Kenneth. *Hinduism*. A collection of more than one hundred colored photographic slides depicting Hindu temples, shrines, icons, and related objects often richly embellished with decorative details. A catalog identifying each slide with comments as to its content accompanies this set of slides distributed by the Visual Education Service, 409 Prospect St., New Haven 11, Conn.

1819

Zimmer, Heinrich. *The Art of India Asia*. 2 vols. Completed and ed. by Joseph Campbell. New York: Pantheon Books, 1955. Bollingen Series No. 39. Volume two is one of the finest collections of black and white photographs of sculpture and monuments in the Indian art tradition including works from Southeast Asia and Tibet. Volume one is a pastiche of Zimmer's views on myths and symbols in Indian art and a catalogue of the works reproduced in the companion volume.

1820

Rowland, Benjamin (ed.). *Early Indian and Indonesian Art*. Newton, Mass.: University Prints, 1938. An inexpensive unbound collection of eighty-five small plates depicting representative works of Indian art and architecture; useful as a teaching aid.

1821

Goetz, Herman. *India: Five Thousand Years of Indian Art*. New York: Crown Publishers, 1959. An introductory historical survey of Indian art, including architecture, painting, sculpture, and handicrafts, from the late stone age to modern times; well illustrated with a glossary and a detailed bibliography.

1822

Rowland, Benjamin. *The Art and Architecture of India*. Baltimore: Penguin, 2nd ed., 1956. Pelican History of Art Z 2. First published in 1933. A well illustrated descriptive survey of Buddhist, Hindu, and Jain works and the influence of Indian art in Southeast Asia.

1823

Winstedt, Sir Richard O. (ed.). *Indian Art*. New York: Philosophical Library, 1948. A collection of four lucid essays on sculpture, painting, the minor arts including textiles and ornaments, and the historical background of Indian art; intended as a general introduction.

1824

Smith, Vincent Arthur. *A History of Fine Art in India and Ceylon. Revised by K. Khandalavala.* Bombay: D. B. Taraporevala, 3rd ed., rev. 1962. First published in 1911. A detailed account of the main developments in Indian art and architecture in ancient and medieval times, including a chapter on such decorative and minor arts as the embellishments of coins and seals; consideration is also given to the influence of Indian art in Java, Tibet, and Central Asia.

1825

Coomaraswamy, Ananda K. *History of Indian and Indonesian Art.* New York: E. Weyhe, 1927. A well-illustrated survey of major styles and periods in indigenous Indian art and architecture from pre-Mauryan times through developments in Hindu sculpture and Rajput painting in the medieval period. Muslim works are not considered. The art of Southeast Asia including that of Java, Champa, and Cambodia is discussed in relation to Indian influence in the area.

1826

Kramrisch, Stella. *The Art of India Through the Ages.* New York: Phaidon Press, 1954. An interpretive survey of Indian art to the 18th century with particular attention to sculpture and architecture of the classic period; provides an erudite, though often recondite view of the relationship between Indian art, religion, and philosophy. Contains 180 illustrations with notes on each plate.

1827

Anand, Mulk Raj. *The Hindu View of Art.* New York: Asia Publishing House, 1957. First published in London in 1933. A popular account of the religious, philosophical, and aesthetic concepts underlying Hindu art.

1828

Brown, Percy. *Indian Architecture.* 2 vols. Bombay: D. B. Taraporevala, 3rd ed., rev., 1956. A historical and descriptive survey of Indian architecture; volume one treats the Buddhist and Hindu periods, volume two is one of the most comprehensive surveys of Muslim monuments in India.

1829

Fabri, Charles. *An Introduction to Indian Architecture.* New York: Asia Publishing House, 1962. A brief survey of stylistic change and foreign influence affecting a few characteristic features of Indian architecture from early Buddhist structures through buildings of the Mughal period.

1830

Rambach, Pierre and Vitold de Golish. *The Golden Age of Indian Art, V-XIII Century.* New York: Studio Publications in association with Crowell, 1955. Provides excellent photographs of Hindu sculpture and temples.

1831

Ashton, Sir Leigh and others. *The Art of India and Pakistan.* A Commemorative Catalogue of the Exhibition held at the Royal Academy of Arts, London 1947–48. London: Faber & Faber, 1950. Essentially a catalog with one hundred and sixty plates illustrating sculpture, painting, bronzes, textiles, and minor arts; brief historical and descriptive introductions preface each section.

Special Studies

1832

Zimmer, Heinrich R. *Myths and Symbols in Indian Art and Civilization.* Ed. by J. Campbell. New York: Pantheon, Bollingen Series 6, 1946. A paperbound edition was published by Harper & Row of New York in 1964. A most readable account of Hindu, Buddhist, and Jain myths and symbols and their expression in Indian art.

1833

Bosch, Frederik D. K. *The Golden Germ; An Introduction to Indian Symbolism.* The Hague: Mouton, 1960. An analysis of the form and religious-philosophical significance of symbols appearing in Buddhist and Jain decorative art.

1834

Bhattacharyya, Benoytosh. *Indian Buddhist Iconography.* Calcutta: K. L. Mukhopadhyay, rev. ed., 1958. First published by Oxford University Press of London in 1924. A detailed illustrated survey of the form and meaning of Buddhist icons based mainly on literary sources including the *Sadhanamala* and other cognate Tantric texts.

1835

Banerjea, Jitendra Nath. *The Development of Hindu Iconography.* Calcutta: University of Calcutta, 2nd ed., rev., 1956. First published in 1941. An encyclopedic study of ancient Indian religious art forms and their meaning, including works of Buddhist and Jain origin, with a review of developments in icon types in later Hindu devotional art. Emphasis is placed on the relation of art forms to religious concepts expressed in texts.

1836

Jouveau-Dubreuil, Gabriel. *Iconography of Southern India.* Tr. by A. C. Martin. Paris: P. Geuthner, 1937. A classic account of icons in an area where the bronze casting of Hindu icons reached its apex in India.

1837

Thapar, D. R. *Icons in Bronze.* New York: Asia Publishing House, 1961. An illustrated introduction to the symbols and special characteristics of Indian images with an account of the chronological sequence of extant works.

1838

Tucci, Giuseppe, *The Theory and Practice of Mandalas.* Tr. by A. H. Brodrick. London: Rider, 1959. A brief, intriguing account of the doctrinal basis and symbolism of mystical ritual designs used in Hinduism and Tibetan Buddhism; accompanied by an annotated reproduction of a *mandala.*

1839

Kramrisch, Stella. *The Hindu Temple.* 2 vols. Calcutta: University of Calcutta, 1946. A well illustrated study of Hindu temple architecture with an interpretation of the religious significance of structural features.

1840

Monod-Bruhl, Odette. *Indian Temples.* Tr. by R. Hawkins. London: Oxford University Press, reprint, 1955. First English edition published in 1937. A pictorial survey, accompanied by brief descriptive notes, providing 135 illustrations of temple structures and sculptures from earliest times to the present day; includes examples from Nepal.

MAJOR SITE REPORTS AND REGIONAL SURVEYS

1841

Wheeler, Sir Mortimer. *Early India and Pakistan.* New York: F. A. Praeger, 1959. A summary and interpretation of what is known about Indian prehistory up to the third century, B.C., with most attention given to the Indus Valley Civilization; includes illustrations of art and architecture.

1842

Marshall, Sir John H. *The Buddhist Art of Gandhara.* Cambridge: Cambridge University Press, 1960. Published for the Pakistan Department of Archaeology. A well illustrated survey of a school of Buddhist art that flourished in the Indus valley region early in the Christian era; some of the first representations of the Buddha in human form were created in this style which fused indigenous and Greco-Roman traditions of art.

1843

Gandhara Sculpture From Pakistan Museums. New York: The Asia Society, 1960. An extensive and most illuminating introduction by Benjamin Rowland accompanies the excellent photographs of this exhibition of Buddhist sculpture dating from the 2nd to the 5th centuries A.D.

1844

Ingholt, Harald and Islay Lyons. *Gandharan Art in Pakistan.* New York: Pantheon Books, 1957. A collection of approximately six hundred illustrations of sculpture from the Gandhara region of northwestern India. Includes detailed notes for each illustration and a brief introduction.

1845

Marshall, Sir John. *Taxila*. 3 vols. Cambridge University Press, 1951. A well illustrated report of twenty-two years of archaeological research at a site located in the Gandhara region. Taxila was a major center of trade and cultural exchange between India and Central and Western Asia from about 500 B.C. to A.D. 500.

1846

Marshall, Sir John H. *Monuments of Sanchi*. 3 vols. London: Probsthain, 1940. A comprehensive account of the sculpture and architecture of a major Buddhist religious center that flourished in central India during the two centuries preceding the Christian era.

1847

Marshall, Sir John H. *A Guide to Sanchi*. Delhi: Manager of Publications, Government of India, 1955. An abridged version of the previous work.

1848

Rao, P. R. Ramachandra. *The Art of Nagarjunikonda*. Madras: Rachana, 1956. A monograph with fifty-six plates on Buddhist sculpture at the site of Nagarjunikonda near the Krishna river in modern Andhra state. The art forms of this area were a major influence in the overseas diffusion of Indian art early in the Christian era.

1849

Yazdani, Ghulam. *Ajanta*. 4 vols. London: Oxford University Press, 1930–55. A comprehensive account of the Ajanta caves of central India. These caves served as a monastic center and shrine for several centuries and are most noted for murals painted in them during the fifth century when the Gupta style of painting is generally held to have attained its peak of development.

1850

Goswami, A. & O. C. Gangoly. *The Art of the Rashtrakutas*. Calcutta: Orient Longmans, 1958. Mainly a collection of annotated reproductions of the famous monuments of Elura and Elphanta in Western India, left near the modern city of Bombay by the Rashtrakuta dynasty that ruled the area from 753 to 974.

1851

Zannas, Eliky. *Khajuraho*. The Hague: Mouton, 1960. A well illustrated account of the Hindu temples built between 954 and 1002 at Khajuraho in north central India, a few hundred miles southwest of the modern city of Allahabad; these temples are noted for the erotic scenes depicted in relief on their facade.

1852

Arts Council of Ceylon. *Art and Architecture of Ceylon. Polonnaruva Period*. Introduction by Senerat Paranavitana. Bombay: Printed at the Times of India Press for the Arts Council of Ceylon, 1954. The first in a proposed series on the art of Ceylon for the general reader. This carefully prepared publication provides a brief survey of extant monuments, sculpture, and painting from Polonnaruva, a major center of art in the eleventh and twelfth centuries. Seventy-six illustrations are provided.

SCULPTURE

1853

Boner, Alice. *Principles of Composition in Hindu Sculpture; Cave Temple Period*. Leiden: E. J. Brill, 1962. A description and analysis of twenty-one sculptures of the 6th to the 9th century, from the Hindu cave temples of Elura, Mahabalipuram, and Badamai. These images are discussed in relation to Indian metaphysics and to the author's interpretation of geometric patterning.

1854

Fouchet, Max Pol. *The Erotic Sculpture of India*. London: Allen & Unwin, 1959. A study of sculptures depicting sexual relations that appear in relief on various medieval Hindu temples, notably those at the site of Khajuraho.

1855

Saraswati, Sarasi Kumar. *A Survey of Indian Sculpture*. Calcutta: K. L. Mukhopadhyay, 1957. A well illustrated general account of the main lines of development in Indian sculpture.

PAINTING

1856

Vishnudharmottara. Tr. by Stella Kramrisch. Calcutta: University of Calcutta, 1924. A translation of the oldest and most complete treatise codifying the techniques and conventions of painting. This technical literature, the composition of which began about the seventh century, was often rigid and stultifying.

1857

Archer, William G. *Indian Miniatures*. Greenwich, Conn.: New York Graphic Society, 1960. Volume 9 of the series, Great Masters of the Past. A survey of Indian miniature painting ranging in time from the early twelfth century to the late eighteenth; one hundred plates provide representative reproductions, half of them in color, of the various schools. Background information is provided in a brief introduction, each plate is accompanied by a short historic and stylistic sketch.

1858

Singh, Madanjeet. *India: Paintings from Ajanta Caves*. Greenwich, Conn.: New York Graphic Society, 1954. UNESCO World Art Series, No. 1. A collection of thirty-two photographic reproductions in color of murals painted during the Gupta era of the 4th to 6th centuries. Though inspired by religious themes, these paintings depict scenes from court life in sensuous color and detail.

1859

Archer, William G. *The Loves of Krishna*. London: G. Allen & Unwin, 1957. A paperbound edition has been published by Grove Press of New York. Much of this work consists of a retelling of the religious literature describing the life of Krishna, a major Hindu deity whose amorous exploits were a favorite theme in the schools of miniature painting that flourished in medieval India; accompanied by illustrations of representative paintings.

1860

Brown, W. Norman (ed. & tr.). *The Saundaryalahari: or, Flood of Beauty*. Cambridge: Harvard University Press, 1958. Harvard Oriental Series, vol. 43. A translation of a Sanskrit poem of the Tantric school, one of the most popular devotional texts of modern Hinduism; beautifully illustrated with reproductions of sixteenth-century paintings that embellish the original manuscripts of the text.

1861

Wilkinson, J. V. Stewart. *Mughal Painting*. London: Faber, 1948. A selection of representative paintings from the Mughal period, 16th–18th centuries; mainly a collection of excellent plates with a brief account of foreign and indigenous features of these paintings.

1862

Reiff, Robert (ed.). *Indian Miniatures: The Rajput Painters*. Rutland, Vermont: C. E. Tuttle, 1959. A collection of twelve reproductions of miniature paintings from a school that flourished in northern and central India during the 17th to the 19th centuries under the patronage of provincial rulers of the Rajput caste.

1863

Khandelavala, Karl. *Pahari Miniature Painting*. Bombay: New Book Co., 1958. A detailed study of the schools of painting that flourished in the sub-Himalayan regions, such as Kangra and Garhwal, of northern India during the 17th–19th centuries.

1864

Randhawa, Mohindar Singh. *Kangra Valley Painting*. Delhi: Publications Division, Ministry of Information and

Broadcasting, Government of India, 1954. A collection of forty colored reproductions of paintings from the Kangra school that emerged in mid-18th century as a fusion of Rajput and Mughal styles and flourished for a century in the hill states of northern India. Many of these paintings are previously unpublished works from family collections in the Kangra valley.

1865

Rao, P. R. Ramachandra. *Modern Indian Painting*. Madras: Rachana, 1953. A survey of trends, movements, and individual painters in India during the past century, includes 204 black and white illustrations and 22 color plates; a sequel treating sculpture and graphic arts as well as painting will soon be issued by the same publisher under the title, *Contemporary Indian Art*.

1866

Archer, William G. *India and Modern Art*. London: G. Allen & Unwin, 1959. A brief competent survey of an uninspiring subject.

MINOR ARTS: TEXTILES, ORNAMENTS, CLOTHING

1867

Wheeler, Monroe, P. Jayakar and J. Irwin. *Textiles and Ornaments of India: A Selection of Designs*. New York: Museum of Modern Art, 1956. A beautifully illustrated survey of the two most famous handicrafts of India with essays on the history and regional distribution of these crafts. Includes more than a hundred plates and a bibliography.

1868

Bhushan, Jamila Brij. *Costumes and Textiles of India*. Bombay: D. B. Taraporevala, 1958. Mainly a collection of plates illustrating the variety of clothing and material to be found in India today and in the past.

1869

Bhushan, Jamila Brij. *Indian Jewelery*. Bombay: D. B. Taraporevala, 1954. An illustrated survey of the major varieties of Indian jewelery, past and present.

1870

Ghurye, Govind S. *Indian Costume*. Bombay: Popular Book Depot, 1951. A detailed historical account of the creation and use of clothing and ornament in India, mainly based on descriptive passages in ancient texts.

1871

Fabri, Charles A. *A History of Indian Dress*. Calcutta: Orient Longmanns, 1961. A brief survey of the subject.

1872

Mehta, Rustam J. *The Handicrafts and Industrial Arts of India*. Bombay: D. B. Taraporevala, 1960. A pictorial and descriptive survey of representative works.

1873

Mookerjee, Ajitcoomar (ed.). *5,000 Indian Designs and Motifs*. Calcutta: Indian Institute of Art in Industry, 1958. Provides two hundred pages of illustrations of designs and motifs used in Indian commercial art.

1874

Aryan, K. C. *Rekha*. Delhi: Rekha Prakashan, 1952. A brief guide prepared for the Indian commercial artist; much of this illustrated booklet discusses the calligraphy of the Devanagari script used in writing Sanskrit and related languages. A few pages illustrate and identify typical objects of everyday use in India, including hair styles, musical instruments, weapons, shoes, and turbans.

MUSIC AND DANCE

1875

Quarterly Newsletter of the Society For Asian Music. New York: Society For Asian Music. The Society for Asian Music was formed in 1959 to encourage the appreciation, dissemination, and performance of Asian music in the United States and Canada. The headquarters of this organization is: 112 East 64 Street, New York 31, New York.

1876

Joshi, Baburao. *Understanding Indian Music*. New York: Asia Publishing House, 1963. A brief introduction to Indian music prepared for the uninitiated person seeking to enhance his ability to listen to the subtleties of Indian music.

1877

Rao, Tirupasoor V. Subba. *Studies in Indian Music*. New York: Asia Publishing House, 1963. South Indian music is discussed in considerable detail in this collection of studies that also includes an account of the 15th century musician Tyagaraja.

1878

Daniélou, Alain. *A Catalogue of Recorded Classical and Traditional Indian Music*. Paris: UNESCO, 1952. This is volume one in "Series B, Oriental Music," of UNESCO's archives of recorded music. An introduction to Indian musical theory and instruments is included in this more than two hundred-page reference.

1879

Popley, Herbert A. *The Music of India*. Calcutta: Y.M.C.A. Publishing House, 2nd ed., 1950. First published in 1921. A brief introduction to the history and theory of Indian music.

1880

Prajnananda. *The Historical Development of Indian Music*. Calcutta: K. L. Mukhopadhyaya, 1960. A detailed survey of Indian music from earliest times to the present; includes illustrations.

1881

Daniélou, Alain. *Northern Indian Music*. 2 vols. London: C. Johnson, vol. I, 1949; Halcyon Press, Vol. II, 1954. Volume I treats the theory and technique of music in northern India. Volume II discusses the main *Ragas* and provides a discography of Indian music. Questions of chronology and statements concerning historical background should be compared with other authorities as the author mainly relies on traditional Indian dates.

1882

Boatwright, Howard. *A Handbook on Staff Notation for Indian Music*. Bombay: B. H. Bhavan, 1960. A fifty-six page handbook with exercises for practice, and notated examples of traditional Hindustani pieces.

1883

Lentz, Donald A. *Tones and Intervals of Hindu Classical Music*. Lincoln: University of Nebraska, 1961. A brief technical discussion of the basic tones and intervals of Hindu classical music with a comparison to those of Western music.

1884

Banerji, Projesh. *Dance of India*. Allahabad: Kitabistan, 1947. A detailed survey of the origins and techniques of Indian classical dance with an account of regional folk dance traditions.

1885

Bowers, Faubion. *The Dance in India*. New York: Columbia University Press, 1953. An excellent introduction to the history, traditions, and modes of performance of Indian classical and folk dance. Illustrations are included.

1886

Ram Gopal and Serozh Dadachanji. *Indian Dancing*. London: Phoenix House, 1951. A brief illustrated account of the history and major forms of Indian dance, including the language of gestures and the present state of the art. Ram Gopal is one of the greatest living exponents of this tradition.

1887

Ambrose, Kay and Ram Gopal. *Classical Dances and Costumes of India*. New York: Macmillan, 1951. A brief descriptive account with many photographs illustrating the basic movements of Indian classical dance.

1888

Zoete, Beryl de. *The Other Mind*. London: Gollancz, 1953. A study of South Indian dance traditions.

1889

Hughes, Russell M. *The Gesture Language of the Hindu Dance*. By La Meri (pseud.). New York: Columbia University Press, 1941. A well illustrated presentation of the form and meaning of the highly stylized gestures employed in the Hindu dance.

Phonograph Records

1890

Daniélou, Alain. *Religious Music of India*. Ethnic Folkways Library P 431. New York: Folkways Records, 1952. A phonograph recording of Hindu ritual and devotional music recorded in India, accompanied by a written introduction, transliteration and translation of the songs, and the scores of the music.

1891

Classical Music of India. Ethnic Folkways Album FP 66. Folkways Records and Service Corp., 117 West 46th Street, New York 36, N. Y. A recorded explanation and demonstration of Indian classical music by Nazir Ali Jairazbhoy with a brief written introduction to the technical features of Indian music.

1892

Ravi Shankar. *The Sounds of India*. Columbia WL 119. Columbia Records, Division of C.B.S., 799 Seventh Ave., New York, N. Y. An introduction to Indian music by Ravi Shankar, one of India's foremost musicians, who plays three *ragas* and a tune in the Thumri style on his *sitar*.

1893

Music of India. Album 2. Three Ragas. Angel 35468. Angel Records, 319 West 44th Street, New York, N. Y. Ravi Shankar's rendition of a North Indian *raga* on this record provides an excellent example of the range of sound encompassed by a *sitar* and the leisurely style of development characteristic of this music. He is accompanied by Chatur Lal on the *tabla* and Pradyot Sen on the *tamboura*.

1894

Music of India. Angel 35283. Angel Records, 319 West 44th Street, New York, N. Y. Ustad Ali Akbar Khan plays a morning and evening *raga* on the *sarod* with an accompaniment on the *tabla* by Chatur Lal and an introduction by Yehudi Menuhin.

1895

India's Master Musician Ravi Shankar. World Pacific WP 1248. World Pacific Records, Division of Pacific Enterprises, Hollywood, California. This record provides an example of North and South Indian styles of classical music played on the *sitar* by Ravi Shankar with the accompaniment of Chatur Lal on the *tabla*.

1896

Indian Folk Music. Volume XIII of the Columbia World Library of Folk and Primitive Music. Columbia Records KL 215. Columbia Records, Division of C.B.S., 799 Seventh Ave., New York, N. Y. Most of the major regions of India are represented in this recording of folk music, Alain Daniélou provides notes, photographs, and a translation of the songs in a written account attached to the album cover.

1897

Music of India: Folk, Traditional & Classical. Ethnic Folkways Album Nos. P 409 and P 422. Folkways Records and Service Corp., 117 West 46th Street, New York 36, N. Y. A brief written account of Indian musical instruments and terms accompanies this recording of short selections from a wide variety of Indian vocal and instrumental music.

FOLK ART AND FOLKLORE

1898

Thompson, Smith, and Jonas Balys. *The Oral Tales of India*. Bloomington: Indiana University Press, 1958.

Indiana University Publications, Folklore Series no. 10. Thousands of stories, derived from 259 sources, are covered in this classification of motifs that rest upon the system developed in Stith Thompson's six volume work, *Motif-Index of Folk-Literature*. A listing of sources by region provides excellent guidance for those seeking English language sources of Indian folklore.

1899

Indian Folklore. Vol. 1–. Calcutta: Indian Folklore Society, 1956–. The official journal of the Indian Folklore Society.

1900

Archer, William G. *The Blue Grove: The Poetry of the Uraons*. New York: Grove Press, reprint, 1953. Much of this work consists of translated songs and poems collected in 1934–37 from the Uraons, a tribe of central India; the social and ritual context of this poetry, mainly activities associated with marriage, is ably portrayed.

1901

Archer, William G. *The Dove and the Leopard; More Uraon Poetry*. Bombay: Orient Longmans, 1948. A sequel to the work cited above.

1902

Elwin, Verrier. *Myths of Middle India*. Bombay: Oxford University Press, 1949. A substantial collection of myths recorded by an anthropologist with many years experience in the area. Several volumes of folk songs recorded by Elwin in the same region have also been published by the Oxford University Press.

1903

Gover, Charles E. *The Folk-Songs of Southern India*. Tirunelveli, Madras: South India Saiva Siddhanta Works Publishing Society, 2nd ed., 1959. A substantial collection of folk songs from South India recorded in the 19th century.

1904

Goswami, Praphulladatta. *Ballads and Tales of Assam*. Gauhati: University of Gauhati, 1960. A study of Assamese folklore issued as publication number three of the University of Gauhati, Department of Tribal Culture and Folklore Research.

1905

Archer, William George. *The Vertical Man*. London: G. Allen & Unwin, 1947. A study in primitive Indian sculpture.

1906

Elwin, Verrier. *The Tribal Art of Middle India*. Bombay: Oxford University Press, 1951. A well illustrated account of art forms encountered during twenty years of ethnographic research among tribal peoples of Madhya Pradesh, Orissa, and Bihar; includes information on the social and cultural setting in which these objects are made and used.

1907

Elwin, Verrier. *The Art of the Northeast Frontier of India*. Shillong: North-East Frontier Agency, 1959. A descriptive account of the distinctive art traditions of tribal people residing in the sub-Himalayan region of Assam.

1908

Banerji, Projesh. *Folk Dance of India*. Allahabad: Kitabistan, 2nd ed., rev., 1959. A brief illustrated survey of the major folk dance traditions of India.

1909

Agarkar, A. J. *Folk-Dance of Maharashtra*. Bombay: Rajabhu Joshi, 1950. A description of regional dance traditions in Western India; including peasant dances of the Konkan coastal area and those of hill tribes.

1910

Spreen, Hildegard L. *Folk-Dances of South India*. Bombay: Oxford University Press, 2nd ed., 1948. A brief survey of the major folk dance traditions of South India accompanied by translations of a few Tamil folk songs.

LITERATURE

Sanskrit Literature

GENERAL WORKS

1911

Winternitz, Maurice. *History of Indian Literature*. 2 vols. Tr. by Mrs. S. Ketkar and H. Kohn. Calcutta: University of Calcutta Press, 1927–33. A translation of an earlier German work, extensively revised by the author for this English version. A detailed account of the historical setting of the major works of Indian literature with substantial excerpts and summaries.

1912

Keith, Arthur B. *A History of Sanskrit Literature*. London: Oxford University Press. Reprint, 1953, This volume and Keith's *Sanskrit Drama* (cited below) provide a comprehensive survey of Indian "classical" literature, as opposed to earlier Vedic works, and the Epics and Puranas. Most of this volume treats belles-lettres and poetics and gives less attention to didactic fables, romances and scientific literature.

1913

Chaitanya, Krishna. *A New History of Sanskrit Literature*. New York: Asia Publishing House, 1962. A survey of Sanskrit literature from the Vedas through the classical period encompassing a wide variety of forms including literary aspects of the Upanishads. Much of this work consists of descriptions of the content of the epics and dramas. Critical evaluation and analysis are generally excellent though unduly short. Sanskrit treatises on medicine, astronomy, and mathematics are also discussed.

1914

Macdonell, Arthur A. *A History of Sanskrit Literature*. Delhi: Motilal Banarsidass, reprint, 1962. Although first published in 1900, this work remains of value as a compact survey of the historical setting and content of ancient and classical Sanskrit literature including the Vedas, epics, lyric poetry, drama, and fairy tales. A brief account of the technical literature on law, science, and art is provided in an appendix.

1915

Dasgupta, Surendra Nath and S. K. De. *A History of Sanskrit Literature. Classical Period*. Vol. I. Calcutta: University of Calcutta, 2nd ed., 1962. First published in 1947. A detailed account of the historical and aesthetic development of post-Vedic Sanskrit literature that reached its peak early in the Christian era and after several centuries of creativity declined into a state of relative sterility about A.D. 1000.

1916

Shastri, Gaurinath B. *A Concise History of Classical Sanskrit Literature*. Calcutta: Oxford University Press, 2nd ed., 1960. First published in 1943. A useful introduction to Sanskrit literature of the classical period that came to an end about A.D. 1000.

1917

De, Sushil Kumar. *Aspects of Sanskrit Literature*. Calcutta: K. L. Mukhopadhyay, 2nd ed., 1959. A collection of studies written between 1925 and 1955 by one of India's most prominent scholars in the field of Sanskrit literature.

1918

Brown, W. Norman. "Mythology of India" in *Mythologies of the Ancient World* edited by S. N. Kramer. Garden City, New York: Doubleday, paperbound, 1961. A brief discussion of some "symbolizing ideas" of Buddhist, Jain, and Hindu mythology; addressed to the general reader.

1919

Dowson, John. *A Classical Dictionary of Hindu Mythology and Religion*. London: Routledge Kegan Paul, 10th ed., 1961. A useful reference for names and terms encountered in Western works on Hindu mythology; includes short descriptions of major Sanskrit works.

1920

Thomas, Paul. *Epics, Myths and Legends of India*. Bombay: D. B. Taraporevala, 12th ed., 1961. This popular survey of Hindu, Buddhist, and Jain sacred lore provides illustrations of various deities and tidbits of information, some of it unreliable, but generally entertaining and not readily available elsewhere.

1921

Emeneau, Murray B. *A Union List of Printed Indic Tests and Translations in American Libraries*. New Haven: American Oriental Society, 1935. Provides more than four thousand references to works in Sanskrit, Pali, Prakrit, and Apabhramsa with a listing of serial publications of texts.

1922

Raghavan, V. *Love in the Poems and Plays of Kalidasa*. Bangalore: Indian Institute of Culture, 1954. One of a number of brief authoritative studies on Sanskrit literature by one of India's foremost Sanskrit scholars.

SPECIAL STUDIES IN DRAMA AND POETRY

1923

Keith, Arthur B. *The Sanskrit Drama*. Oxford: Clarendon, 1924. A scholarly account of the origin, development, theory and practice of drama in India from Vedic to early Medieval times.

1924

Wells, Henry W. *The Classical Drama of India*. New York: Asia Publishing House, 1963. A collection of essays including a discussion of "spiritual equilibrium" as the goal of Sanskrit drama, and an appraisal of theatrical techniques and poetic styles used in this tradition. Includes comparisons with Western drama.

1925

Gargi, Balwant. *Theatre in India*. New York: Theatre Arts Books, 1962. An introductory survey that includes classical Sanskrit drama, contemporary theater, folk "operas" and plays, puppet shows, and traditional dance-dramas.

1926

Shekhar, Indu. *Sanskrit Drama: Its Origin and Decline*. Leiden: E. J. Brill, 1960. A study of Sanskrit drama with particular attention to the "non-Aryan" elements that may have influenced its development and an attempt to explain its decline as due in part to the evils of class distinctions.

1927

Bharata. *Natyasastra*. Tr. by Manomohan Ghosh. Calcutta: Royal Asiatic Society of Bengal, 1950. The earliest extant textbook on Indian drama, it provides a detailed account of stage conventions and theatrical techniques. Although attributed to the ancient sage Bharata, it is the work of an anonymous writer who probably lived in the sixth century A.D.

1928

Sagaranandin. *The Natakalaksanaratnakosa of Sagaranandin*. Tr. by Myles Dillon. Philadelphia: American Philosophical Society, 1960. A Sanskrit treatise on the Hindu theater, probably written in the thirteenth century. The author's quotation of excerpts from otherwise unknown Sanskrit plays and his citations of various authorities indicates the existence of a much greater body of dramatic literature and critical theory than has survived to the present day.

1929

Bowers, Faubion. *Theatre in the East*. New York: Grove Press, 1956. Paperbound edition, 1960. The initial hundred pages of this survey provide a brief introduction to the dance and drama of India and Ceylon with particular attention to contemporary developments.

1930

De, Sushil Kumar. *History of Sanskrit Poetics*. 2 vols. in 1. Calcutta: K. L. Mukhopadhyay, 2nd ed., rev., 1960. A comprehensive survey of the subject first published in London, 1923–25, under the title: *Studies in the History of Sanskrit Poetics*.

1931

De, Sushil Kumar. *Sanskrit Poetics as a Study of Aesthetics*. Berkeley: University of California Press, 1963. A summation and evaluation of the various schools of Sanskrit poetic theory with comparisons to Western literary aesthetics. An authoritative review addressed to the reader with some prior knowledge of the subject.

TEXTS IN TRANSLATION

Additional works of literary interest, including other versions and translations of the epics, may be found above under *Religion*.

1932

Raghavan, V. *The Indian Heritage*. Bangalore: Indian Institute of Culture, 2nd ed., rev., 1958. An anthology of excerpts translated by V. Raghavan from the Sanskrit literature of Hinduism, prefaced with a brief discussion of Indian literature, religion, and philosophy.

1933

Brough, John (comp.). *Selections from Classical Sanskrit Literature*. Tr. and notes by J. Brough. London: Luzac, 1952. Selections from the works of major classical writers and an excerpt from the *Mahabharata* are included in this compilation prepared for students of Sanskrit; a transliteration of the texts accompanies the translations.

1934

Hymns From the Rigveda. Tr. by Arthur A. Macdonell. London: Oxford University Press, 1922. A selection of forty hymns from the most ancient Indian texts, of literary as well as religious interest.

1935

Macdonell, Arthur A. *A Vedic Reader for Students*. London: Oxford University Press, 5th impression, 1960. First published in 1917; a selection of thirty hymns from the Rigveda presented in the original texts with transliteration and translation. Detailed explanatory notes and a brief introduction are provided.

1936

Cowell, Edward B. (ed.). *The Jataka; or Stories of the Buddha's Former Births*. 6 vols. in 3. London: Luzac, reprint, 1957. First published in six volumes by Cambridge University Press, 1895–1907. A collection of more than five hundred brief tales translated by various hands. Although attributed to the Buddha as recollections of his previous births as a Bodhisattva, most of these tales are secular in content and spirit.

1937

Aśvaghosa. "Buddhacarita" (Life of the Buddha) in *Buddhist Mahayana Texts*. Tr. by E. B. Cowell, F. Max Müller, and J. Takakusu. Oxford: Clarendon Press, 1894. Sacred Books of the East, vol. 49; to be reprinted in paperbound form by Dover Publications of New York. Aśvaghosa's metrical life of the Buddha, generally held to have been written late in the first century A.D., is the earliest surviving example of Sanskrit poetry in the classical style.

1938

Wells, Henry W. (ed.). *Sanskrit Plays in English Translation*. New York: Asia Publishing House, 1963. A collection of translations by various hands. Representative selections from the works of Bhasa, Sudraka, Kalidasa, Bhavabhuti, and Harsha; addressed to the general reader.

1939

Kalidasa. *Shakuntala, and Other Works*. Tr. by Arthur W. Ryder. New York: E. P. Dutton, 1928. Paperbound edition, 1959. A translation of *Shakuntala*, one of the finest works of classical Sanskrit, with summaries of two other dramas by Kalidasa and abridged versions of four of his major poems; prefaced with an excellent introduction.

1940

Kalidasa. *Meghaduta: The Cloud Messenger*. Tr. by Sushil Kùmar De. New Delhi: Sahitya Akademi, 1957. A translation of one of Kalidasa's most famous Sanskrit poems.

1941

Sudraka. *Mrcchakatika, the Little Clay Cart*. Tr. by R. P. Oliver. Urbana: University of Illinois, 1938. A scholarly translation from Sanskrit of a drama attributed to King Shudraka; noted for its portrayal of urban life and many departures from the conventions of classical Sanskrit drama.

1942

Buitenen, J. A. B. van (tr.). *Tales of Ancient India*. New York: Bantam, paperbound, 1961. One of the most readable scholarly anthologies of Indian narrative literature, drawn mainly from the Sanskrit works of Somadeva and Budhasvamin with a few short stories from Buddhist collections written in Pali. These tales provide an entertaining and enlightening view of the secular side of Indian life during the Gupta era which reached its zenith in the fourth and fifth centuries.

1943

Dandin. *Dasha Kumara Charita; The Ten Princes*. Tr. by Arthur W. Ryder. Chicago: University of Chicago Press, 1927. Paperbound edition, 1960. A translation of Sanskrit tales of romance and adventure in India of the seventh century.

1944

The Panchatañtra. Tr. by Arthur W. Ryder. Chicago: University of Chicago Press, 1962. From a Sanskrit text of the late twelfth century, a translation of fables that present lessons in statecraft and the art of human relations in an entertaining manner.

1945

The Ramayana and The Mahabharata. Tr. by R. C. Dutt. London: J. M. Dent, reprint, 1935. First published in 1910. A condensed metrical version of the famous Indian epics composed in their present form several centuries before the Christian era. Episodes and characters from these two poems have provided subject matter for all of India's creative arts including dance and drama, sculpture and painting, and the modern cinema.

1946

Valmiki. *The Ramayana of Valmiki*. 3 vols. Tr. by H. P. Shastri. London: Shanti Sadan, 1952–59. A prose translation of the earliest known version, probably composed in the 4th century B.C. The secular origin of this religious epic in the martial legends of earlier times is more evident in the Valmiki version than in later reworking of the same theme. Vernacular versions are cited below under Hindi and Tamil.

1947

The Mahabharata. Tr. by Chakravarthi V. Narasimhan. New York: Columbia University Press, 1964. A new translation of the main narrative based on selected verses from the authoritative Sanskrit edition recently completed in Poona after years of scholarly comparisons of various recensions.

1948

Sukthankar, Vishnu S. *On the Meaning of the Mahabharata*. Bombay: Asiatic Society of Bombay, 1957. A review and assessment of various views held by Western scholars concerning the date, composition, and meaning of the *Mahabharata*.

1949

Gaer, Joseph. *The Fables of India*. Boston: Little, Brown, 1955. A popular retelling of fables from the Panchatañtra, Hitopadesa and the Jatakas, prefaced with a brief introduction.

Regional Literature: Histories, Studies, Translations

TAMIL

1950

Balakrishna Mudaliyar, Nalladai R. (tr.). *The Golden Anthology of Ancient Tamil Literature*. 3 vols. Tirunelveli, Madras: South India Saiva Siddhanta Works Publishing Society, 1959–60. A collection of translations from the

Tamil language of South India; one of India's most venerable literary traditions, whose origins can be traced back to the beginning of the Christian era.

1951

Vaiyapuri Pillai, S. *History of Tamil Language and Literature.* Madras: New Century Book House, 1956. A historical survey of a literary tradition that has contributed religious and secular works to the culture of South India for approximately two thousand years.

1952

Tiruvalluvar. *Tirukkural.* Tr. from Tamil by A. Chakravarti. Vepery, Madras: Printed at the Diocesan Press, 1953. An extensive collection of brief metrical proverbs on various aspects of life and religion; traditionally attributed to Tiruvalluvar, these moral aphorisms were probably composed in the 4th or 5th centuries A.D.

1953

Hymns of the Alvars. Tr. by J. S. M. Hooper. Calcutta: Association (Y.M.C.A.) Press, 1929. A brief collection of devotional poetry composed in Tamil from approximately the 7th to the 10th centuries; attributed to the Alvars or saints of a South Indian Vaishnavite sect.

1954

Hymns of the Tamil Saivite Saints. Tr. and ed. by Francis Kingsbury and G. E. Philips. London: Oxford University Press, 1921. A translation of hymns composed in Tamil between the 7th and 10th centuries by the Nayanars, or teachers of a South Indian Shaivite sect, whose works rank high in the ancient tradition of Tamil literature.

1955

Kamban. *The Ayodhya Canto of the Ramayana.* Tr. by C. Rajagopalachari. London: G. Allen & Unwin, 1961. A translation of selections from a ninth-century version of the *Ramayana* written in Tamil. A major work in South Indian literature. The hero is portrayed in a less favorable light than as seen by Valmiki and Tulsidasa.

BENGALI

1956

Sen, Sukumar. *History of Bengali Literature.* New Delhi: Sahitya Akademi, 1960. A descriptive study of a literary tradition of great vitality and variety that has flourished for almost a thousand years in the Bengal region of eastern India.

1957

Sen, Dinesh Chandra. *History of Bengali Language and Literature.* Calcutta: University of Calcutta, 2nd ed., 1954. A detailed survey of the subject, first delivered as a series of lectures.

1958

De, Sushil Kumar. *Bengali Literature in the 19th Century (1757–1857).* Calcutta: K. L. Mukhopadhyay, 2nd ed., rev., 1962. First published in 1919. A heavily documented historical review and appraisal of Bengali literature during a period when the British conquest of Bengal gave rise to new forms and vigor in Bengali literature.

1959

Haq, Muhammad Enamul. *Muslim Bengali Literature.* Karachi: Pakistani Publications, 1957. A translation from Bengali of a survey of Muslim authors writing in the literary medium of Bengal, a region with one of the greatest concentrations of Muslims in South Asia.

1960

Dimock, Edward C. (ed. and tr.). *The Thief of Love; Bengali Tales from Court and Village.* Chicago: University of Chicago Press, 1963. A selection from the extensive literature composed in Bengali between the thirteenth and eighteenth centuries. These tales of love and adventure are translated in an accurate and readable manner for the general reader.

1961

Vidyapati. *Love Songs of Vidyapati.* Tr. from Bengali by D. Bhattacharya. Edited by W. G. Archer. London: Allen

& Unwin, 1963. Selections from the mystical, erotic verses of a famous Bengali poet of the 15th century.

1962

Chatterji, Bankim Chandra. *Krishnakanta's Will.* Tr. from Bengali by J. C. Ghosh. New York: New Directions, paperbound, 1962. One of the first attempts by an Indian author to employ the novel as a literary form; written in the late 19th century. The passions and conflicts of life in a wealthy family of rural Bengal serve as the central theme of this story.

1963

Bannerjee, Manik. *Boatman of the Padma.* Tr. from Bengali by Hirendranath Mukerjee. Bombay: Kutub, 1948. A well written novel of life in a community of Bengal fishermen.

1964

Basu, Subodh. *The City of New Moghuls.* Tr. from Bengali by the author. Calcutta: S. C. Bose, 1947. A translation of the Bengali work *Rajdhani,* a novel recounting the experiences of a Bengali student attending a fashionable school for girls in New Delhi.

1965

Ray, Lila (ed.). *Broken Bread.* Tr. from Bengali by Lila Ray. Calcutta: M. C. Sarkar, 1957. A collection of twenty-one modern short stories written by some of the most famous authors of Bengal.

1966

Radhakrishnan, Sarvepalli (genl. ed.). *Rabindranath Tagore.* New Delhi: Sahitya Akademi, 1961. A centenary volume prepared by the Indian National Academy of Letters to honor Bengal's most famous author. Several dozen essays by scholars, poets, and those who knew Tagore, provide an appraisal of his life and work. A chronicle of Tagore's life and a bibliography of his publications in Bengali and English are also included.

1967

Tagore, Rabindranath. *A Tagore Reader.* Ed. by Amiya Chakravarty. New York: Macmillan, 1961. A selection of Tagore's poems, plays, and short stories that provides a fair sampling of his literary output. Letters and articles reflecting Tagore's interests as an educator and humanitarian are also included.

1968

Kripalani, Krishna R. *Tagore.* New York: Grove Press, 1962. A popular biography of the famous Bengali poet, Rabindranath Tagore, who received the Nobel Prize for Literature in 1913.

HINDI

1969

Jindal, K. B. *A History of Hindi Literature.* Allahabad: Kitab Mahal, 1955. A detailed historical survey of literature written in a major language of northern India that some have attempted to establish as the national language of India. Though wanting in a literary tradition such as that of Tamil and Bengali, many of the most influential and best-loved religious works of northern India were written in this medium, notably Tulasi Das's sixteenth century version of the *Ramayana.* Modern writers have also begun to express themselves in Hindi.

1970

Keay, Frank E. *A History of Hindi Literature.* Calcutta: Y.M.C.A. Publishing House, 3rd ed., 1960. A brief introductory survey of the subject.

1971

Kabir. *One Hundred Poems of Kabir.* Tr. by Rabindranath Tagore. New York: Macmillan, 1961. A brief collection of poems written in Hindi by the fifteenth century mystic, Kabir.

1972

Tulasidasa. *The Holy Lake of the Acts of Rama.* Tr. by W. D. P. Hill. London: Oxford University Press, 1952. A prose translation of a sixteenth century version of the

Ramayana written in Hindi; this poem differs markedly in content and spirit from Valmiki's Sanskrit version of ancient times.

1973

Rahbar, Hans Raj. *Prem Chand, His Life and Work*. Delhi: Atma Ram, 1957. An account of a pioneer in the use of Hindi as a medium for modern short-story writing; includes a copy of a speech given by Prem Chand in 1936, "How Do I Write My Stories."

1974

Prem Chand. (Pseud. of Dhanpat Rai Srivastava). *Godan; A Novel of Peasant India*. Tr. from Hindi by Jai Ratan and P. Lal. Bombay: Jaico Publishing House, 2nd ed., 1958. Although peasants in a village of Uttar Pradesh are the main characters in this novel, moneylenders and middle class residents of Lucknow also figure in the story. Prem Chand's concern with social justice and the opressed lot of the Indian peasant is readily apparent in this work.

1975

Prem Chand. (Pseud. of Dhanpat Rai Srivastava). *A Handful of Wheat and Other Stories*. Tr. from Hindi by P. C. Gupta. New Delhi: People's Publishing House, 1955. A selection of Prem Chand's short stories primarily concerned with life in the rural communities of Uttar Pradesh.

1976

Vaid, Krishna Baldev. *Steps in Darkness*. Trans. from Hindi by the author. New York: The Orion Press, 1962. A novelette concerning the domestic problems of a Hindu village family.

URDU

1977

Saksena, Ram Babu. *A History of Urdu Literature*. Allahabad: Ram Narain Lal, 1940. A detailed survey of a literary form of Hindustani, the lingua franca of North India, that is closely identified with Muslim culture. Urdu literature is written in the Perso-Arabic script and contains many words of Persian and Arabic origin in contrast to the Sanskrit derived vocabulary and script of Hindi literature, the other literary form of Hindustani. Urdu literature attained considerable refinement in the Muslim courts of Hyderabad and Delhi and continues to serve as a literary medium, particularly in Pakistan.

1978

Suhrawardy, Shaista A. B. *A Critical Study of the Development of the Urdu Novel and Short Story*. New York: Longmans, 1945. An extensive appraisal of the adaptation of Western literary forms in a tradition most noted for its poetry prior to modern times. Urdu became a popular medium for prose works of social protest in the 20th century.

1979

Jha, Amaranatha. *Urdu Poets and Poetry*. Allahabad: Leader Press, 1956. An exposition of an aspect of Urdu literature that remains popular to the present day; the text includes transliterated Urdu verses that are reprinted in Devanagari script at the end of the book.

1980

Gorekar, N. S. *Glimpses of Urdu Literature*. Bombay: Jaico Publishing House, 1961. A selection of representative examples of Urdu literature prepared for the general reader.

1981

Vahid, Syed Abdul. *Iqbal: His Art and Thought*. London: J. Murray, 1959. An account of the work of Sir Muhammad Iqbal, poet and philosopher, whose writings in Persian and Urdu gave expression to the aspirations of the Muslims in 20th century India.

1982

Iqbal, Muhammad. *Poems From Iqbal*. Tr. by E. V. G. Kiernan. London: J. Murray, 1955. A brief selection of poems written in Persian and Urdu by the most famous of India's modern Muslim poets. The Government of Pakistan has established an academy to promote the study and appreciation of Iqbal's work.

MARATHI

1983

Tukarama. *Village Songs of Western India*. Tr. from Marathi by John S. Hoyland. London: Allenson, 1934. A brief collection of poems by Tukaram, a Maharashtrian poet-saint of the early 17th century, whose devotional hymns are still sung by peasants of the region.

1984

Madgulkar, Vyankatesh. *The Village Had No Walls*. Tr. from Marathi by Ram Deshmukh. Bombay: Asia Publishing House, 1958. A semi-fictional account that captures the harsh realities of Indian peasant life; based on the author's experience as a school teacher in a Maharashtrian village.

1985

Phadke, Narayan Sitaram. *The Whirlwind (Jhanjavat)*. Bombay: Jaico Publishing House, 1956. Originally written in Marathi; this novel takes place in Maharashtra during the Quit India Movement of 1942.

1986

Gokhale, Aravind. *The Unmarried Widow and Other Stories*. Tr. from Marathi by S. Pradhan. Bombay: Jaico Publishing House, 1957. A collection of twelve short stories depicting a variety of women from various strata of Indian society.

OTHER

1987

Munshi, Kanaiyalal M. *Gujarat and Its Literature*. Bombay: Bharatiya Vidya Bhavan, 2nd ed., 1954. A survey of the historical development of Hindu thought and literature in a region of western India from early times to 1852; a second volume extending coverage to modern times is in preparation.

1988

Kakati, Banikanta (ed.). *Aspects of Early Assamese Literature*. Gauhati, Assam: Gauhati University, 1953. A collection of essays on the literary tradition of Assam, an area of northeastern India that developed aesthetic traditions quite different from the mainstream of Sanskrit-borne culture.

1989

Rice, Edward P. *A History of Kanarese Literature*. Calcutta: Association (Y.M.C.A.) Press, 1921. A brief survey of literature written in Kanarese, also known as Kannada, that developed in the southwestern region of India.

1990

Godakambura, C. E. *Sinhalese Literature*. Colombo: Colombo Apothecaries, 1955. A detailed historical survey of the principal literary tradition of Ceylon.

1991

Raju, Poolla Tirupati. *Telugu Literature*. Bombay: International Book House, 1944. A brief survey of the history and main works of the Telugu, also known as Andhra, literary tradition that developed in the eastern part of the Indian peninsula.

1992

Suryanarayana, Peri (tr.). *Gems of Andhra Literature*. Rajahmundry: Srinivas Publishing House, 1958. A translation of selections from Telegu poetry composed between 1000 A.D. to 1350.

1993

Ahluwalia, Jasbir S. *Tradition and Experiment in Modern Panjabi Poetry*. Ferozerpor: Bawa Publishing House, 1960. A brief discussion of the literature and philosophy of a small band of poets writing in Panjabi.

Modern Indian Literature

1994

Kesavan, B. S. and V. Y. Kulkarni (Genl. eds.). *The National Bibliography of Indian Literature, 1901–1953*. New Delhi: Sahitya Akademi, 1962. The first in a proposed four volume bibliography of Indian works of literary merit published in English and the major languages of India during the period 1901–1953. This volume surveys: Assamese, Bengali, English and Gujarati. The bibliography is in Roman script with annotations in English. Books on philosophy, religion, history and related subjects are included in those instances where they meet the editors canons of literary value.

1995

Sahitya Akademi. *Who's Who of Indian Writers.* New Delhi: Sahitya Akademi, 1961. A useful collection of biographical sketches of contemporary Indian authors in the field of literature; prepared by India's national academy of letters.

1996

Chatterji, Suniti Kumar. *Languages and Literatures of Modern India.* Calcutta: Bengal Publishers, 1963. A scholarly survey of the major languages and regional literary traditions to be found in India today.

1997

Sahitya Akademi. *Contemporary Indian Literature.* New Delhi: Sahitya Akademi, 1959. A collection of papers by Indian academicians and authors presented in a symposium sponsored by the Sahitya Akademi, India's national academy of letters.

1998

Milton, Daniel L. and W. Clifford (eds.). *A Treasury of Modern Asian Stories.* New York: New American Library, paperbound, 1961. This anthology contains stories written in English by Indian authors as well as modern stories translated from Bengali, Hindi, Marathi, Tamil, and Urdu.

1999

Indian Literature. Ed. by K. R. Kripalani. Address: Indian Literature; Rabindra Bhavan; New Delhi 1, India. A semiannual publication of the Sahitya Akademi, India's national academy of letters. This literary magazine consists in the main of translated contemporary poems, stories, and reviews from India's major languages, with an annual survey of the vernacular literatures.

2000

Mahfil. A Quarterly Magazine of South Asian Literature. 1963–. Address: Box 39, Foster Hall, University of Chicago, Chicago, Illinois. A mimeographed publication providing translations and reviews of contemporary South Asian literature.

JOURNALISM AND THE PRESS

2001

India (Republic). Press Commission. *Report of the Press Commission.* 3 vols. Delhi: Manager of Publications, 1954. A detailed report of the findings and recommendations of a commission appointed in 1952 to inquire into the state of the press in India. Volume one describes such aspects of the press as competition, journalistic standards, and government controls. Volume two is a history of Indian journalism, also cited in the following entry. Volume three provides the questionnaire used by the Commission, the statements of witnesses, and statistics about Indian publications.

2002

Natarajan, S. *A History of the Press in India.* New York: Asia Publishing House, 1963. A privately published edition of volume two of the Government of India Press Commission Report cited above. The author, editor of the Ambala *Tribune,* describes the Indian press from the days of the East India Company to the present.

2003

Wolseley, Roland E. (ed). *Journalism in Modern India.* Bombay: Asia Publishing House, 1953. A collection of essays appraising the role of the press in India today by men actively engaged in journalism.

CINEMA

2004

Barnouw, Erik and S. Krishnaswamy. *Indian Film.* New York: Columbia University Press, 1963. A detailed history of the Indian film industry that now ranks among the largest in the world.

2005

Holmes, Winifred. *Orient: A Survey of Films Produced in Countries of Arab and Asian Culture.* London: British Film Institute, 1959. Includes information on films produced in India, Pakistan, and Ceylon.

2006

Asia Society. *Films on Asia.* New York: The Asia Society, 1959. Approximately one dozen films on India appear in this select list of recommended films and film sources; includes a brief summary of each film with information on rentals, purchase costs, and the address of distributors. This excellent guide and periodic supplements may be obtained from The Asia Society, 18 East 50th Street, New York 22, N. Y.

EDUCATION

Prior to the 19th century, formal education was confined to a small segment of Indian society composed of government administrators, religious specialists, and men of commerce. Hindu or Muslim divines were the main instructors and their religious views strongly influenced the content of what they taught. Religion, philosophy, and law were the major subjects of study with other fields of learning confined to the mastery of medieval texts.

Western education was first introduced in India late in the 18th century under the private auspices of Protestant missionaries whose schools remain among the best in India today. Bengal, particularly the city of Calcutta, was an active center of innovation in education by such Indian reformers as Ram Mohun Roy (1772–1833), who sought to transform Indian society in the light of Western learning and institutions. In 1835, a major step towards the modernization of India was taken when the government inaugurated a system of education in which English was the medium of instruction and Western learning the subject of study. This system, designed to supply personnel for the lower echelons of government administration, gave rise to a tradition of education that many consider a major handicap today. Despite the limitations of this system of education, social and political ideas introduced through Western learning served as a catalyst for changes discussed in works cited above in the *Transformation of Social and Intellectual Tradition* section of *History — British Rule.* Accounts of ancient Indian education may be found under *Intellectual and Aesthetic Patterns, Religion* and *Philosophy,* and the *Ancient India* section of *History.*

2007

Mookerji, Radha Kumud. *Ancient Indian Education.* London: Macmillan, 2nd ed., 1951. A scholarly account of

Brahmanical and Buddhist educational theories and practices from Vedic times to about A.D. 1000.

2008

Altekar, Anant Sadashiv. *Education in Ancient India.* Benares: Nand Kishore, 4th ed., rev., 1951. A less technical version of the initial edition; an introductory work addressed to those interested in comparative studies.

2009

Keay, Frank E. *A History of Education in India and Pakistan.* London: Oxford University Press, 3rd ed., 1959. First published in 1918 as: Indian Education in Ancient and Later Times. A history of India's indigenous educational systems from ancient times up to the introduction of Western education.

2010

Nurullah, Syed & J. P. Naik. *A History of Education in India During the British Period.* Bombay: Macmillan, 2nd ed., rev., 1951. A detailed account of the development of education at all levels under British rule including private institutions; provides an appraisal of legislation relating to education in India.

2011

Zellner, Aubrey A. *Education in India; a Survey of the Lower Ganges Valley in Modern Times.* New York: Bookman Associates, 1951. A descriptive history of education under British rule with particular attention to Bengal where many innovations in education originated in response to Western influence.

2012

India (Republic). Ministry of Education. *Review of Education in India (1947–1961).* Delhi: Ministry of Education, 1961. A summary account of India's educational system since independence. One of many publications issued by the Ministry of Education on a wide variety of subjects, including statements of official policy, statistical surveys, and appraisals of problems in the field of contemporary education in India.

2013

India (Republic). Ministry of Education. *Directory of Institutions for Higher Education in India.* Delhi: Ministry of Education, 1961. A listing of all the institutions of higher education in India with information on courses offered and the teaching staff.

2014

Gandhi, Mohandas K. *Basic Education.* Ahmedabad: Navajivan Publishing House, 1951. A brief essay setting forth "Mahatma" Gandhi's views on the problems of education in India.

2015

Mukherjee, Himangshu B. *Education for Fulness.* New York: Asia Publishing House, 1963. A detailed summary of Rabindranath Tagore's educational ideals and experiments including an account of the schools founded by Tagore at Santiniketan early in the 20th Century.

2016

Saiyidain, Khwajah G. *Education, Culture and the Social Order.* Bombay: Asia Publishing House, rev. ed., 1958. A critique of contemporary Indian education with some suggestions for an integrated program adapted to the needs of the day.

2017

Mukerji, Shridar Nath. *Education in India, Today and Tomorrow.* Baroda: Acharya Book Depot, 3rd ed., 1957. An examination of India's present educational system in relation to its historical background and modern needs; the author advocates a fundamental reordering of Indian education.

2018

Cormack, Margaret L. *She Who Rides a Peacock.* New York: F. A. Praeger, 1962. An appraisal of the Indian academic milieu and the attitude and behavior of Indian students viewed in relation to the needs of India today.

2019

Suri, Surinder. *Problems of Student Discipline.* New Delhi: Diwan Chand Indian Information Centre, 1960. A study of the beliefs and attitudes of Indian university officials viewed in relation to student riots and demonstrations that forced several major universities to close for considerable periods of time during the previous decade.

2020

Useem, John and Ruth H. *The Western-Educated Man in India: A Study of His Social Roles and Influence.* New York: Dryden Press, 1955. An account of changes in attitudes and values of Indians who studied in Britain and the United States, and their role in Indian society as innovators of technical and social changes; based on a year's study of 110 men and women residing in Bombay State.

2021

Singh, Amar Kumar. *Indian Students in Britain.* London: Asia Publishing House, 1963. A study of the social and economic background of Indian students attending British institutions of higher learning in recent years and of the problems and adjustments stemming from this experience.

2022

Coelho, George V. *Changing Images of America: A study of Indian Students' Perceptions.* Glencoe: The Free Press, 1958. A study of changes in the perception of America and India by sixty Indian students whose residence in the United States ranged from less than a week to seven years; based on essays written by the students and on interviews seeking to elicit attitudes toward the two countries.

2023

Lambert, Richard D. and Marvin Bressler. *Indian Students on An American Campus.* Minneapolis: University of Minnesota Press, 1956. A study by two sociologists of the reactions of nineteen South Asian students at the University of Pennsylvania to their experiences in the United States.

INDEX

Entries cited in more than one place in the text are indicated by the use of parentheses after their initial citation in the index.

The text of the India bibliography was set and composed by Morneau Typographers in Linotype Times Roman. Arizona Lithographers printed the book on Garamond text stock by Champion. The design on the cover was silk-screened by Robert Spray of Tucson. It was adapted from a detail in a contemporary silk pattern, block-printed in Assam, woven in Bombay State, and reproduced in the volume, TEXTILES AND ORNAMENTS OF INDIA, *published by the Museum of Modern Art.*